A Buddhist Critique of the Christian Concept of God

A critique of the concept of God in contemporary Christian theology and philosophy of religion from the point of view of Early Buddhism

A Buddhist Critique of the Christian Concept of God

Gunapala Dharmasiri

Golden Leaves , U.S.A

Library of Congress
Cataloging in Publication Data:

Dharmasiri, Gunapala.
A Buddhist Critique of the Christian Concept of God.

Bibliography: p.
Includes index.
1. Christianity and other religions—Buddhism.
2. Buddhism—Relations—Christianity. 3. God.
I. Title.
BR128.B8D46 1988 231 87-11989
ISBN O-942353-01-3
ISBN 0-942353-00-5 (pbk.)

Published in the United States of America by
GOLDEN LEAVES PUBLISHING COMPANY
2190 WILBUR AVENUE
ANTIOCH, CALIFORNIA 94509

Typeset in the United States of America by
Golden Leaves Publishing Company

Manufactured in the United States of America

To Venerable
Bellanwila Dhammaratana Maha Thera
of Singapore

Contents

Foreword

Dr. Dharmasiri has written a book for which rare qualifications are required in the author: an accurate and thorough knowledge of Buddhist Pali texts, a mastery of the principles of philosophy of religion, and an acutely analytical mind, able to see clearly through the misty confusion which too often surrounds the discussion of theological issues. All these qualifications Dr. Dharmasiri clearly possesses, and has made good use of writing the present book. The original work, as a thesis for the degree of Doctor of Philosophy of Lancaster University, was deservedly, given high praise by the examiners, of whom I had the honour to be one.

His book breaks new ground in the sense that no comparable study of Christian theological ideas from a scholarly Buddhist, philosophical stance has been published in English, although such a work was long overdue. The deficiency has now been splendidly remedied, and should become and remain a standard work on the subject.

Trevor Ling
Professor of Comparative Religion

Department of Comparative Religion
The University of Manchester, England

Preface

Since I published the first edition of this book, I have come to see a different set of problems concerning the concept of God that are actually more existentially important and significant than the more theoretical problems that I was discussing before. Stated briefly, I see that though the notion of God contains sublime moral strands, it also has certain implications that are extremely dangerous to the humans as well as to the other beings on this planet.

One major threat to humanity is the blindfold called 'authority', imposed on humans by the concept of God. All theistic religions consider authority as ultimate and sacred. It was this danger that the Buddha was pointing at in the Kalama Sutta, as I have explained in the 8th Chapter. At the moment, human individuality and freedom are seriously threatened by various forms of authorities. Buddhism is concerned about the 'individual', not about a particular authority, a person or a tradition. It is this 'individual' that is in danger. From Christianity to Marxism, various 'authorities' have been trying to make "you" a follower. On top of all our 'traditional' authorities, a new form of authority has emerged in the name of 'science'. And lately, the mushrooming new religions and the menace of the Gurus (as typified by Jim Jones), have become live threats to individual human freedom and dignity. If capitalism exploits human labor, these various authorities have been exploiting the very essence of the human being: the brain. All these authorities have been interested only in confirming and proving the utter impotency and incompetence of the individual turning her/him into a "slave", a mere follower. The Buddha's eternal plea is for you to become a Buddha, and he showed, in a clearly rational way, that each and every one of us has the perfect potentiality and capacity to attain that ideal.

The profound question that humans should ask themselves is why they are naturally bent towards, or are addicted to being mere 'followers'. Do we love to be slaves? Or, do people actually manufacture Gurus or authorities so that they can simplify matters for themselves by simply following the Gurus? In this paradoxical situation, the very people who crusade against authority, themselves end up as revered Gurus. For example, though Marxism started as an anti-traditional and anti-authoritarian movement, it soon settled down to be one of the strongest authoritarian systems today, clamping down on human free thinking; to take a mild, but a decisive example, though Krishnamurti was anti-organizations, he soon found himself to be the leading authority (a negative authority!) behind the International Krishnamurti Organization. The crucial question is, can any authority be either right or wrong? This is a question that you can never decide until "you" yourself wake up to the Truth.

This is so important today because there are, in the contemporary chaotic world-context, many people who are genuinely engaged in the quest for the Ultimate Truth, if there is an Ultimate Truth. For them, the situation is complicated by the fact that there are an innumerable number of religions and cults, headed by so many authorities, each promising to teach them the Truth. Once you agree even to try out some authorities, as many modern cults will illustrate, it might mean that you are thrown into a prison, incarcerated both spiritually as well as physically. Once you enter a cult-group, they will be just too quick to imprison you within their cult. Very soon you will be reduced to a mindless zombie, following some person as an authority. In this sense, many religions and "isms" can be really dangerous institutions that are waiting to capture and murder the psyches of innocent human beings. Therefore, religions have become the most threatening danger to humanity today. It is the "blind faith" that opens the door to this danger. Once you repose faith in an authority, you will not even remember to challenge or even question it, because the authorities have brainwashed you so completely that "you" will no longer exist, i.e. lost your freedom and individuality so completely. The point they make is, if you don't agree with the cult-group, something is clearly wrong with you. The harrowing details of cult life has been penetratingly analyzed in *"Crazy for God", the Nighmare of Cult Life*, by Ex-Moon Disciple Christopher Edwards (Prentice-Hall, 1979). It is significant to note that in many religions the main technique of keeping the group intact and going is through fear and guilt.

Edwards explains the methods of conversion used in the cult group: "I knew that they [the new members] would be terrorized, scared out of their socks, overwhelmed by theory, badgered, manipulated, loved and tested. Those innocent heavenly children had no idea what they were in for, but wasn't that the price one had to pay for learning the Truth?" (p.123). The frightening aspect is the way they kill the thinking capacity. If anybody doubts, the cult-leaders advise that person in the following manner: "You are going to be a great brother. Now, first thing, you have to learn the rules. Just obey. Do whatever I say. Follow whatever I do. And don't ask questions. A questioning mind is Satan's mind. You wouldn't doubt God's word, would you?" (p. 146). They are commanded to engage in any immorality in the name of their cult goals and such immoralities are conveniently termed "Heavenly Deceptions" (p. 151). This again is the explicit corollary from their basic premise that religion is superior to morality.

The scene among the Authorities or Gurus themselves is equally bizarre. As reported in Hinduism Today (Hawaii, U.S.A. Vol. 8, No. 3, May, 1986), in a religious group headed by two celebrated Gurus (sister and brother), one Guru forces the other Guru to abdicate, and then brainwashes, humiliates and beats him, to become the new, sole Guru. Some Gurus are doing nothing more than having a great time at the expense of their devotees: the commonest and the notorious pastime of the male Gurus is seducing their female devotees, [30 or more recorded in the case of one Guru (p. 11).] With all that, the particular cult group is still flourishing and continuing with its 300,000 devotees under the new Guru. Thus their 'saintly' behavior seems to be suspect even by standards of decent normal human behavior, let alone to speak of them being divine. But, in Hinduism, Guru means God Incarnate on this earth. How can 300,000 devotees of that cult still believe that their new Guru can deliver the goods? Or, not believe that the new Guru will not turn out to be another villian? Or, still, can they even consider whether the new Guru is already a villian because it was this new Guru who is supposed to have ferociously persecuted the other Guru, to capture the throne?

One of the seduced devotees confesses how it all happened. "I felt, 'well, he is the Guru, and the disciple is supposed to surrender.' In retrospect I can only see that understanding is blind faith . . ." Of course, in the context of faith, any immoral act of the Guru becomes a sacramental act by definition because, here, religion is superior to morality. Here we can clearly see the real danger of faith and authority. The suicidal nature of this type of movements is evidently seen in the ironical double-bind that exists within them; the pathetic dependence of the devotees on the Gurus or Authorities, makes, in turn, the Gurus pathologically dependent on the devotees, thus creating the humorous, but vicious, circle of devotees following the Guru, and the Guru following the devotees. What can you expect from a pathological double-bind? What all this shows is the human mind's frightening fragility, which lies deeply buried from view.

The biggest wonder is how these cult leaders so easily get around the so-called "intelligent" people? This raises the question of how rational we are. Or, are we rational at all? As I have explained at the end of the 7th Chapter, is rationality only an institutional phenomenon, and hardly an individual phenomenon? Or, do we love to be followers and slaves? It is here that the problem of faith vs. reason becomes a very significant existential problem, on which we seem to be risking our life and death.

How do we know that our traditional religions are also not doing the same thing that modern cults do, in one way or another in varying degrees? How can we be sure that they are not doing that? In the quest for an answer to this question, the most important thing is to be completely 'open'. Do our traditional and non-traditional thought systems put any clamps on our individual independent thinking? Is it possible to arrive at any Ultimate Truth, without first having this individual independence? As I have explained in the Postscript, all Western and Eastern God-oriented religions have preached that animals or even human beings could be killed in the name of religion, and that religion is superior to morality. In the West, the peoples' attitude toward animals, as food or fun, has been so much colored by their Judaic religion, that they have been made eternally blindfolded by their religion and they cannot see the simple truth of the intrinsic value and the Holy nature of Life. Their vision of nature has been completely perverted by the ethnocentric attitude these religions inculcate into their believing, credulous minds. This is typified by the Western attitude toward nature as a non-living object gifted by God to be used, exploited and raped as humans wish. Do they ever want even to look at this blindfold? Or, their blindfolding being so deep, can they?

When there are so many competing claims put forward by zillions of cults, traditional and modern, if one wants to choose between them what criteria should we use? All these competing teachings cannot be true at the same time, because the Truth is one. I think there are two profound criteria we can use: we must see (i), whether they generate Wisdom, by opening our minds rather than clamping them down by restricting thinking ability, thereby not letting ourselves be used by others as part of their trip, as part of their egomania or group-mania; (ii), whether they generate Compassion by being perfectly consistently moral, as I have explained in detail in my recent book "*The Fundamentals of Buddhist Ethics*" (Golden Leaves: U.S.A., 1988). It is the cultivation of the true wisdom and compassion that is going to be the ultimate refuge and salvation of our beleaguered humanity.

Acknowledgements

I am extremely grateful to my teacher, the late Professor K.N. Jayatilleke, who suggested this topic for research and gave me encouragement in many ways. I am very much indebted to him for my initial training under him, and for his excellent scholarship which produced the classic study of early Buddhist epistemology *Early Buddhist Theory of Knowledge*, that laid the foundations in showing the relationships between the Buddha's teachings and contemporary philosophical thinking. I have found his material very helpful particularly in my eighth chapter.

I feel very fortunate to have been able to do this research under the supervision of Professor Ninian Smart and I was much benefited by his admirable depth of scholarship in both Christianity and Buddhism. It is with the utmost respect for his scholarship that I disagree with some of his theories in the present work. From a Buddhist point of view, I found his ideas to be the strongest Christian position a Buddhist has to face because Professor Smart has been admirably sensitive to the possible Buddhist criticisms of the Christian position. I found grappling with his ideas extremely illuminating.

I am grateful to Rev. Robert Morgan, Michael Pye, Adrian Cunningham, Walter Hartt, Heward Wilkinson, David Naylor, Ivan Strenski and David Black for the very valuable and instructive discussions I had with them. I must also take this opportunity to express my gratitude to Mrs. Christianne Mullord, Mrs. Anne Naylor, David Naylor and Brian Rainey who looked after me very carefully during my work in England. Their great kindness was a constant moral encouragement to me.

Finally, I would like to thank Golden Leaves Publishing Company for putting so much time, effort and care into producing this fine American Edition.

Parts of chapter six were read at the Hamilton Fund Public Lecture at Amherst College, Massachusetts. Parts from other chapters were read at Smith College, Mount Holyoke College, University of Massachusetts and at Connecticut College, U.S.A. during April-May, 1971.

Introduction

The Buddha did not accept the existence of God. He also rejected the idea of a soul though he advocated the possibility of salvation. The present work is an attempt to elucidate the reasons that led the Buddha to such conclusions.

Here, the Buddha's arguments against theism are used for a critical evaluation of the concept of God in contemporary Christian theology and philosophy of religion. The early Buddhist teachings are used in two ways: I. When direct arguments against theism are found in early Buddhist works, they are directly applied to the present context. II. Elsewhere, the early Buddhist ideas have been used as bases to develop arguments critical of theistic ideas. In most cases, I have quoted from the early Buddhist Pali Canon itself and from other early Buddhist writings.

Though this is a critique of the Christian concept of God, my intention is not to disparage Christianity. In fact, the Buddha himself, on many occasions, has advised that one should not disparage other religions and faiths or flatter one's own religion by condemning another. He said that a good person, "because of his success in moral habit, does not exalt himself and does not disparage others".[1] He advised his disciples: "Our mode of living

1. *So tāya sīlasampadāya attamano . . . na attān'ukkaṃseti, na paraṃ vambheti. M.,* I, p. 196.

must be perfectly pure, clear, open, and without defects controlled. But not on account of this perfectly pure mode of living will we exalt ourselves or disparage others."[2] This does not mean that one cannot make criticisms of another religion if the concepts involved in that religion are unsatisfactory. The Buddha did so on many occasions, as this work illustrates.

Still, the criticism of one religion in terms of another may not be welcomed. It is the fashion today to see the similarities and parallels in religions, thus making 'positive' comparisons rather than 'negative' criticisms. From a humanitarian point of view such comparisons seem more justifiable, because it is always a nice thing to say that humanity agrees on fundamental things rather than differs. Criticisms, very often, breed only ill-feelings. But this attitude is wrong for some very important reasons. To make comparisons between religions is an easy task. To quote parallel passages from the texts of different religions is equally easy. But intellectually this a very immoral exercise, since when we quote such apparently similar passages we quote them out of their proper contexts. It is the context that gives religious statements their meaning. Therefore, religions should be compared and contrasted in terms of their whole doctrinal and cultural contexts. It is only then that comparisons or contrasts between religions can be made. What is attempted in this work is a comparison or a contrast of that type.

This type of analysis of other religions is important for many reasons. It is always a matter of concern to be clear about the validity of the claims made by various religions. It is absolutely important for us to know whether religious claims can be true or not. If they can be, then we are bound to decide which religious claims are, in fact, true. Or, at least, try to decide which religious claims are meaningful enough to make an inquiry into their truth or falsity worth-while. As Professor Ninian Smart said: "The truth or falsity of the Christian religion, and of other religions, is a serious matter . . .".[3] Further, it is instructive for Christians to see what the other religionists have to say about Christianity. Professor Smart clari-

2. *Parisuddho no ājīvo bhavissati uttāno vivaṭo na ca chiddavā saṃvuto ca, tāya ca pana parisuddhājīvatāya n'ev'attān'ukkaṃsissāma na paraṃ vambhissāmāti evaṃ hi vo bhikkhave sikkhitabbaṃ. M.*, I, p. 272.

3. Ninian Smart, 'Religion as a Discipline?' in *Universities Quarterly*, Vol. 17, 1963, p. 50.

Department of Religion, theology is liable to be subjected to the cold winds of criticism and to the need to respond to the challenge of humanism, Marxism and the like, that serious theology gets done''.[4] Any religion can be benefited in the light of such criticisms by enabling religionists to look at their own religions from new perspectives or to rephrase them in ways that would avoid the defects and pitfalls. If the Buddhist's criticisms are unsound, the Christian can always point it out and show why they are unsound and this might at least, help the Buddhist to correct his own wrong perspectives. And by these means, a real understanding among religions may be brought about.

Superficial comparisons can lead to superficially happy confrontations. But that only worsens the situation by leaving the real problems lying dormant underneath. One cannot exorcise real differences simply by emphasizing superficial similarities. Therefore, the first indispensable step to take is to show and clarify the areas of disagreement. Only then can we understand where we stand. We may thereafter attempt to map out the possible ways of making or finding comparisons.

Buddhism does not reject theism outright. While the Buddha was critical of theistic religions, he accepted that they had a limited value: he referred to them as 'unsatisfactory religions' (*anassāsika*) rather than as 'unreligious religions' (*abrahmacariyavāsa*) such as Materialism. The Buddha, very often, showed great respect to leaders and followers of other religions and strongly recommended his followers to show respect to other faiths.

In this work I have been concerned with the following main topics: problems of natural theology, speculative evaluations of the world with the help of the concept of God, religious experience, philosophical problems of the concept of God, phenomenological or experiential relevance of the idea of God, the nature of theological thinking and the place of revelation and *a priori* reason in the context of religion.

The disconcerting problems of the Christian doctrinal structure are traced to the fundamental irrationality and the anti-

4. loc. cit.

rationality of the Christian faith. Therefore, the final chapter ends with the Buddha's appeal to use rigorous rational techniques in the field of religion, too, as in other branches of knowledge.

Abbreviations

A.	*Aṅguttara Nikāya*
A.A.	*Aṅguttara Nikāya Aṭṭhakathā, i.e., Manorathapūraṇī*
Bṛh.	*Bṛhadāraṇyaka Upaniṣad*
Comy.	Commentary
D.	*Dīgha Nikāya*
D.A.	*Dīgha Nikāya Aṭṭhakathā, i.e., Sumaṅgalavilāsinī*
Dhp.	*Dhammapada*
E.B.T.K.	Early Buddhist Theory of Knowledge
G.S.	The Book of Gradual Sayings (*Aṅguttara Nikāya*)
It.	*Itivuttaka*
J.	*Jātaka*
JPTS	Journal of the Pali Text Society
K.S.	The Book of the Kindred Sayings (*Saṃyutta Nikāya*)
Kvu.	*Kathāvatthu*
Kvu. A.	*Kathāvatthuppakaraṇa Aṭṭhakathā*
M.	*Majjhima Nikāya*
M.A.	*Majjhima Nikāya Aṭṭhakathā, i.e., Papañcasūdanī*
M.L.S.	Middle Length Sayings (*Majjhima Nikāya*)
Netti.	*Nettippakaraṇa*
Nd.I.	*Mahāniddesa*
PP.	The Path of Purification
P.T.S.	Pali Text Society
S.	*Saṃyutta Nikāya*
S.A.	*Saṃyutta Nikāya Aṭṭhakathā,* i.e., *Sāratthappakāsinī*
SBB.	Sacred Books of the Buddhists
Sn.	*Sutta Nipāta*
Th.	*Thera Gāthā*
U.	*Udāna*
U.A.	*Udāna Aṭṭhakathā,* i.e., *Paramatthadīpanī*
Vsm.	*Visuddhimagga*

Chapter One

GOD AND THE SOUL

1.1 The idea of self or soul is very closely related to the idea of God. According to contemporary Christian theologians, this relationship takes various forms. One form is to treat the soul as an analogy of God. Thus Reinhold Niebuhr emphasizes the significance of the concept of *imago dei*.[1] James Richmond speaks of a clue to understanding God. "The clue, that is to say, consists of the fact that the only conceivable *analogy* which would enable the cartographer to speak intelligibly and significantly of God . . . is a certain type of human discourse or explanation referring to the human soul or self as some unobservable, non-spatio-temporal, enduring principle or entity, 'involved in' the world certainly, yet somehow (and mysteriously) referrable to as 'beyond' or 'outside' what is empirically perceptible."[2] Therefore an understanding of the soul contributes much to the understanding of God. About the degree of analogy some (e.g. Karl Barth) would significantly differ. Others (e.g. Paul Tillich) may go much further and speak of a closer and more intimate relationship of the soul with God. According to their theses, the understanding of the soul may more or less amount to an understanding of God and this is made obvious when they make their typical equations: ground of being = God; existence = God. This way of approach to the Reality or the source of salvation which is God, according to them, may be interestingly compared with the Buddha's ideas that were extremely critical of the concept of soul. In other words, the Christian and the Buddhist systems try to give two completely contrasting ways of approaching a similar problem. The Buddha's criticisms become relevant in this context because he was mainly criticizing the then prevalent Upanisadic and other theories of soul which are extremely similar to the traditional or contemporary Christian theories of soul.

1.2 Many contemporary theologians accept the traditional ideas concerning the existence and the nature of the soul. Some discuss it again (e.g. Maritain). But some try to contradict the traditional doctrine or claim to do so (e.g. Barth) while still others do in fact contradict it (e.g. Bishop Robinson). Maritain accepts the traditional doctrine of the soul as an immaterial, spiritual substance, intrinsically independent of the body. The Buddha's verificatory attitude would strongly reject such an idea because it goes beyond any possibility of knowing the soul's existence. Maritain states, ". . . concerning *what is* our soul, concerning its essence, or its quiddity, this experience tells us nothing."[3] But Maritain puts forward a non-empirical form of verification. "My (soul or my substance) cannot be experienced by myself in its essence; a quidditative experience of the soul is possible only for a separated soul . . ."[4]

1.3 This is, on the one hand, to accept the empirical meaninglessness of the soul in its essence. On the other hand, it is an attempt to make the idea of soul meaningful in a non-empirical manner. For that, Maritain proposes an eschatological form of verification. But such a method of verification would make sense only if the concept to be verified is a meaningful one. Let us see whether it can be a meaningful concept.

1.4 In traditional Christianity, the reality of soul is somehow dependent on God, in terms of the Spirit. It is in this sense that Maritain speaks of the soul as a permanent principle in man. "The person is a substance whose substanial form is a spiritual soul . . .".[5] "A soul which is spiritual in itself, intrinsically independent of matter in its nature and existence, cannot cease existing."[6] It is here when they talk of the soul as a permanent principle within the personality that it becomes really vulnerable to empirical verification. Here, it is important to notice, one of the central Christian dogmas becomes exposed to empirical investigation.

1.5 The soul as a permanent principle was a favorite idea of the Upanisads too, and the Buddha was therefore very familiar with this conception. The Buddhist critique starts by inquiring into the possibility of finding such a permanent soul in man's personality. The Buddha takes the basic constituents of personality and looks into them, viz., (i) body, (ii) feelings, (iii) sensations, (iv) dispositions, (v) consciousness. The Buddha questions his disciples:

> "Is body (consciousness, etc.) permanent or impermanent?"
>
> "Impermanent, revered sir."
>
> "But is what is impermanent non-satisfying or is it satisfying?"
>
> "Non-satisfying, revered sir."
>
> "And is it right to regard that which is impermanent, non-satisfying, liable to change, as 'This is mine, this am I, this is my self'?"
>
> "No, revered sir."[7]

The Buddha emphasizes that the selflessness of the body, consciousness, etc., are seen when they are seen as they really are (*yathābhūta*).[8] If one cannot see any such soul, the burden of proof falls on the soul-theorist.

1.6 Maritain thinks that the best proof of the existence of the soul is the working of the intellect. He maintains that intellectual activity is immaterial. It is true that sense knowledge is at least partly material, but, he states, not abstract intellectual knowledge.[9] Barth also thinks that when one says 'I think' it has soul-connotations.[10] In fact, the consciousness of mind has been the stronghold of the soul theorists from very ancient times. Upanisads refer to the soul as the *Vignātāram*.[11] The Buddha was extremely critical of this view on the ground that one could clearly see the quickness of the change of mind. "Monks, I know not of any other single thing so quick to change as the mind: insomuch that is no easy thing to illustrate how quick to change it is."[12] Therefore, the Buddha states that the soul theorists who hold that the mind is the soul end up in a paradoxical situation. "[If someone says] . . . 'mind is the self' . . . ['mental states are self' . . . 'mental consciousness is self' . . .] that is not fitting. For the arising of mind [etc.] is to be seen and its decaying. Since its arising and decaying are to be seen, one would thus be brought to the stage of saying: 'Self arises in me and passes away'."[13] Once the Buddha makes this cryptic remark: "It were better, bhikkhus, if the untaught manyfold approached this body, made up of the four great elements, as the soul rather than the mind. What is the reason for that? It is seen, bhikkhus, how this body, made up of the four great elements, persists for a year . . . persists for a hundred years and even longer. But this, bhikkhus, that we call thought, that we call mind, that we call consciousness, that arises as one thing, ceases as another, whether by night or by day"[14]

1.7 What Maritain is maintaining is that the abstract intellect is immaterial. But by saying that the abstract mental states are not-material it does not mean that the mind is an immaterial substance. Sariputta Thera defines the mind: "Feeling, perception, volition, sensory impingement, reflectiveness, this . . . is called mind. . . . There are six classes of consciousness: visual consciousness, auditory, olfactory, gustatory, bodily and mental consciousness."[15] All these types of consciousness are conditioned. "Apart from conditions, there is no origination of consciousness."[16] If the conditions are not there the consciousness would not arise. Owing to mind and mind-states, mind-consciousness arise. If these conditions were to cease, there would be no mind-consciousness.[17] Maritain apparently thinks that the abstract intellect is a special exclusive part of the spiritual soul. But a Buddhist would object to it on the grounds that there is no such exclusive function of the mind, as all the functions of the mind are fundamentally dependent on, or conditioned by, the factors derived from experience. Maritain's position could be strengthened if the possibility of innate ideas were to be proved, which is yet to be done. According to the Buddhist's standpoint, even the factors of abstract intellection are always derived *a posteriori*. For example, one cannot manipulate mathematical numbers without first learning the numbers from experience. In sum, 'thinking' and 'intellection' are extremely vague terms that denote groups of collections of various factors and activities. Even the term 'mind', according to the Buddha, did not refer to 'a thing' but only referred to a collection of activities that were called 'mental'. The Buddha has been more interested in analyzing these terms than in taking them in their gross forms.

1.8 It is interesting to note that some contemporary theologians like Barth have come to understand these difficulties in conceiving an independent soul. For example, Barth rejects the traditional Christian conception of soul. "We necessarily contradict the abstractly dualistic conception which so far we have summarily called Greek, but which unfortunately must also be described as the traditional Christian view."[18] Barth advocates a much more intimate relationship between the body and soul. "I may be identical with my soul, but my soul is not for itself, but is the besouling of my body. To this extent I am identical as soul with my body, and my movement, activity and development are never merely soulful, but as such are also bodily."[19] And therefore "I" refers to both soul and body.[20] Even one's self-knowledge, one's corporeal senses are of great importance. "In the delimitation and determination of myself as an object of my knowledge, which is decisive for the fulfillment of my self-consciousness and which is necessarily presupposed in my self-knowledge as a subject, I thus have great need even of my corporeal senses."[21] Barth is much more radical than Maritain: ". . . even thinking can take place only when it is accompanied by the functions of the whole body."[22] In fact, when Barth says that "The one (soul or body) never is without the other"[23], he goes to such an extreme that he comes very close to the Puggalavadins, a later Buddhist sect that believed in a pseudo-soul which existed essentially in relation to the body. If Barth takes his position seriously, it leads to a rejection of the Christian idea of soul. If he wants to hold on to a soul in this sense it will be only hanging on to the word 'soul' which does not mean anything precise in the context. (Nevertheless, it is important to notice that Barth, interestingly enough reaches a point very close to, if not identical with, the same traditional Christian doctrines he had so strongly rejected when he maintains, "It is thus the Spirit that unifies him and holds him together as soul and body".[24] So the traditional dichotomy persists. The introduction of the third factor, i.e. Spirit, emphasizes this dichotomy because Barth accepts the "significance of Spirit for the grounding, constituting and maintaining of man as soul of his body").[25]

1.9 The Theravadins criticized this idea of a pseudo-soul from various standpoints. It is important to note two of them. "Theravadin: Is the person (or soul) known in the sense of a real and ultimate fact? Puggalavadin: Yes. Theravadin: Is material quality (body) one thing and the person (soul) another? Puggalavadin: Nay, that cannot truly be said. Theravadin: Acknowledge the refutation: If the person (soul) and material quality (body) be each known in the sense of real and ultimate facts, then indeed, good sir, you should also have admitted that they are distinct things. You are wrong to admit the former proposition and not the latter. If the latter cannot be admitted, neither should the former be affirmed. To say that the person (soul) and material quality (body) are both known in the sense of real and ultimate facts, but that they are not mutually distinct things, is false."[26] This argument shows the dilemma the Puggalavadins and Barth have to face. What the Theravadin says is that if the soul and body are taken as *ultimate* then these two are necessarily bound to be mutually distinct and this argument pushes Barth back to the traditional Christian conception of the soul thus reducing his theory to an inconsistency. To corner the Puggalavadin to a paradox, the Theravadin puts forward another argument. He says that if the soul and body were intimately connected to each other as the Puggalavadin believed, then the soul would be necessarily conditioned like the body,[27] a conclusion that would contradict the fundamentals of the soul theory. This argument would check Barth escaping from the other side. If he says that the soul is not ultimate and related to body intimately then such a relationship would lead to a conditioning of the soul by the body and such a conclusion militates against the primacy of the soul as besouling the body, and of the soul as being immortal.

1.10 Maritain thinks that there are other reasons that strengthen the case for the existence of a soul. Conscience, the feeling of responsibility, possibility of spiritual depth, and the feeling of independence, unity and identity[28] are, he says, strongly suggestive of an immaterial self.[29] But if the term 'soul' cannot be given any proper meaning, these further reasons cannot strengthen its possibility. On the other hand, it is possible to account for the facts of responsibility, etc., as real possibilities without seeking the help of a 'soul', as we shall see later. In fact, the Buddha once explained how these very ideas can lead to the false notion of the existence of a soul. "In these ways he is not wisely attending: if he thinks, 'Now, was I in a past period? Now, was I not in a past period? Now, what was I in a past period? Now, how was I in a past period? Now, having been what, what did I become in a past period? Now, will I come to be in a future period? Now, will I not come to be in a future period? Now, what will I come to be in a future period? Now, how will I come to be in a future period? Having become what, what will I come to be in a future period?' Or, if he is now subjectively doubtful about the present period, and thinks: 'Now, am I? Now, am I not? Now, what am I? Now, how am I? 'Now, whence has this being come?' 'Whencegoing will it come to be?' To one who does not pay wise attention in these ways, one of six (wrong) views arises: 'There is for me a self'—the view arises to him as though it were true, as though it were real . . . Or a wrong view occurs to him thus: 'Whatever in this self for me that speaks, that experiences and knows, that experiences now here, now there, the fruition of deeds that are lovely and that are depraved, it is this self for me that is permanent, stable, eternal, not subject to change, that will stand firm like unto the eternal.' This, monks, is called going to wrong views, holding wrong views, the wilds of wrong views . . .''[30] In this regard it is interesting to see the Buddha's complete agreement with some contemporary philosophers of religion. C.B. Martin states the same principle that the Buddha was formulating when Martin says, "The master tautology which lies as the foundation of the chain of identity is 'I am the same person that I was and I will be the same as I am'. This sentence could be used in such a way that it would be necessarily false. That is, by growing older we change and are now not what we were, if only that we are older. It could also be used to be just false. Some people never change, are always the same, but most of us do. It can also be used so that the use of 'I' and 'same person' makes it self-contradictory to deny. Then it is a tautology and has a wonderful, but barren, security."[31]

1.11 If there is no reason to believe in a soul theory, why do some people have such a view? The Buddha maintained that if a rational explanation cannot be given to a belief, then its origin should be traced to an emotional bias. Therefore he called the ideas about 'I' and 'self' to be the "thoughts haunted by craving concerning the inner self".[32] For example, the desire for an immortal life (*Bhavataṇhā*) might prompt one to believe and find security in the idea of an eternal soul. Also, the Buddha points out that there is another form of desire at work here. It is the desire and attachment for the consciousness and its types. ". . . whatever is desire, whatever is attachment, whatever is delight, whatever is craving, for all types of consciousness as eye-consciousness and for the mind, mental states, mental consciousness with mental states cognizable through mental consciousness. . . (These are called to be) dogmas, emotional biases, tendencies . . .".[33] Therefore the idea of the soul is essentially an emotional bias. The Buddha addresses Kaccayana Thera: "Grasping after systems, imprisoned by dogmas is this world, Kaccayana, for the most part. And the man who does not go after that system-grasping, that mental standpoint that dogmatic bias, who does not grasp at it, does not take up his stand upon it, (does not think)—,It is my soul.'"[34]

1.12 The Buddhist, of course, has to clear up certain problems before he formulates the no-soul theory. A soul theorist can point out that without accepting the existence of a soul there would be no way of explaining the facts of personal identity and moral responsibility. The Buddhist can give two answers. One is to show the defective nature of the soul theorist's contention. He is presupposing the meaningfulness of the concept of soul in advancing his argument. But we have tried to show how the concept of soul becomes absolutely meaningless when it is subjected to a proper and detailed analysis. Therefore, the soul theorist, before he advances his argument, has to show that the idea of soul is a meaningful concept. Thus his contention becomes meaningless because his essential presupposition is meaningless.

1.13 The fact that the Buddha rejected the idea of the soul does not mean that he did away with the concept of a person or a being. According to him, the person is, as we saw above, a conglomeration of psychic and material factors. The standard example to illustrate this was that of the chariot. "Just as the word 'chariot' is used when the parts are put together, just so when the (psycho-physical) factors are present arises the convention of 'a being'."[35] For the Buddha the question was not how to account for a person if all we see in him are only groups of ever changing factors. Therefore, one cannot speak of "*dukkha* as done by oneself (*sayaṃkataṃ*) or by another (*parakataṃ*)" because there is no substantial entity persisting through actions and their fruitions. Also, one cannot say that *dukkha* is not done by oneself (*asayaṃkāraṃ*) because one is responsible for actions done by oneself. Why? It is because, the Buddha states, one has achieved "the right view of cause and the causal origin of things."[36]

1.14 However, there is the problem of explaining moral responsibility in terms of the no-soul theory. This was raised as a problem during the time of the Buddha himself. It is said, "The following doubt arose in the mind of a certain monk: If body feel-- ings, ideas, dispositions, and consciousness are without self, then what self can be affected by deeds not done by a self?"[37] To explain this further, one can do no better than quote Buddhaghosa who tried to give a lucid and perceptive solution to this problem: ". . . whose is the fruit since there is no experiencer? . . . Here is the reply . . . When a fruit arises in a single continuity, it is neither another's nor from other (*kamma*) because absolute identity and absolute otherness are excluded there. The formative processes of seeds establish the meaning of this. For once the formative processes of a mango seed, etc., have been set afoot, when the particular fruit arises in the continuity of the seed's (growth), later on owing to the obtaining of conditions, it does so neither as the fruit of other seeds nor from other formative processes as condition; and those seeds or formative processes do not themselves place where the fruit is. This is the analogy here. And the meaning can also be understood from the fact that the arts, crafts, medicine, etc., learned in youth give their fruit later on in maturity. Now it was also asked, 'Whose is the fruit, since there is no experiencer?' Herein, 'Experiencer' is a convention for mere arising of the fruit; they say, 'It fruits' as a convention when on a tree appears its fruit. Just as it is simply owing to the arising of tree fruits, which are one part of the phenomena called a tree, that it is said, 'The tree fruits' or 'the tree has fruited', so it is simply owing to the arising of the fruit consisting of the pleasure and pain called experience, which is one of the aggregates called 'deities' and 'human beings', that it is said 'a deity or a human being experiences or feels pleasure or pain.' There is therefore no need at all here for a superfluous experiencer."[38] Thus the problems of moral responsibility can be explained in terms of the memory and the causal continuity of the processes involved.

1.15 Moral responsibility, in turn, amounts to an explanation of the problem of personal identity. The latter assumes a significant position in the context of rebirth. Buddhaghosa explains personal identity with special reference to rebirth. Referring to the starting, co-originating consciousness of a new birth, he says, "here let the illustration of this consciousness be such things as echo, a light, a seal impression, a looking-glass image, for the fact of its not coming here from the previous becoming (birth) and for the fact that it arises owing to causes that are included in past becomings. For just such an echo, a light, a seal impression, and a shadow, have respectively sound, etc., as their cause and come into being without going elsewhere, so also this consciousness.

> And with a stream of continuity there is neither identity nor otherness. For if there were absolute identity in a stream of continuity, there would be no forming of curd from milk. And yet if there were absolute otherness, the curd would not be derived from milk. And so too with all causally arisen things. And if that were so there would be an end to all worldly usage, which is hardly desirable. So neither absolute identity nor absolute otherness should be assumed here.[39]

1.16 A 'person' is not only a series of momentary events but also a causal continuum and therefore an identity is preserved in terms of the causal continuum. That is why, "He who does the deed and he who experiences are the same" or different, are said to be two wrong extremes.[40] This does not mean that one can speak of the mind or consciousness as the persisting principle of identity. The Buddha states that one cannot speak of consciousness as running on or faring on because consciousness itself is generated by conditions.[41] A 'person' (a group of psycho-physical factors) in the present moment inherits qualities of preceding causal continuum of which the present moment is only a conditioned result. In a similar sense 'he' is responsible for 'his' future. Here one's continuity is felt through one's memory. It is important to remember that the Buddha attached a great significance to the unconscious part of the mind (*asampajāna mano saṁkhāra*).[42] This was how the Buddha accounted for the nature of a person or a being.

1.17 It should be emphasized that the Buddha's concept of mind strikingly differs from a Rylean type of reductionism.[43] He accepts the fact of mind the existence of mental states. To do away with the existence of mental states, according to him, was an obvious fallacy. However much Ryle attempted to effect a reduction and avoid talking about 'para-mechanical dramatizations' even he could not help talking about what goes on "in our heads".[44] It is even theoretically impossible to avoid talking about thoughts or about what goes on in our heads. So, very often one finds Ryle making statements that would look highly paradoxical from his own standpoint: "Saying something in this specific frame of mind, whether aloud or in one's head, *is* thinking the thought. . . . And when called on to give such an exposition, he will at particular moments be actually in the process of deploying these expressions, in his mind, or viva voce, or on his typewriter, and he may and should be doing this with his mind on his job, i.e. purposefully, with method, carefully, seriously, and on the qui vive."[45] If this analysis goes back to neural identity theory then it has its own problems. However, here one cannot do better than refer to the scholarly criticisms of Rylean reductionism done by various thinkers like C.A. Campbell and A.C. Ewing.[46]

1.18 The Buddha, however, would strongly disagree with the conclusions of the contemporary philosophers of religion who have put forward decisive objections against Rylean reductionism. Campbell and Ewing think that proof of the existence of mental states suggest the existence of a soul. H.D. Lewis argues that, contra-Ryle, one has to talk of mental states.[47] But elsewhere he comes to an invalid conclusion: "I should also wish to add that my real self is my mind, and that it is only in a derivative and secondary sense that my body is said to be myself at all."[48] In their arguments all they have proved is the existence of mental states. Once Lewis puts forward a Platonic cliche when he talks about ". . . my having 'a concept of myself' in terms of some inherent feature of consciousness itself."[49] Elsewhere Lewis goes on to elaborate this idea. He maintains that from the fact that we have an idea of being a unique being one can know the existence of a self. He says, "The elusive self: Let me first indicate how I understand these terms. For those who posit, as I do, a self that is more than its passing states, and which may not be reduced at all to observable phenomena, the problem arises at once of how such a self is to be described and identified. It cannot be identified in terms of any pattern of experience or of any relation to a physically identifiable body. How then can it be known at all? It is known, I maintain, solely in the way each one, in the first instance, knows himself to be the unique being he is."[50] It is evident that Lewis has not any criteria for positing the self except the fact that one feels the existence of such a self: "The self is not 'a thing apart' but it is all the same more than its experiences and uniquely known in each case by each person."[51]

This is of course an attempt to formulate an argument from a naivety. Some people, at times, have very vivid experiences of seeing and talking to ghosts etc., and it is the closer examination that shows them that they were, in fact, having hallucinations. The Buddha would wholeheartedly agree with Lewis's contention that we have the idea of possessing a unique self. But what was important for the Buddha was not the fact of having this mere idea but a critical attempt to examine the idea to see whether it was true or not. Instead, Lewis goes on to posit the real existence of the self from a mere idea of it. He says, "I have certainly no intention of denying that the self is real in itself". And he goes on to make his argument still more naive when he tries to say that the existence of the self is proved by the fact of our very existence. If this argument is correct then it becomes really invincible because it is an incontrovertible fact that we do exist. As Lewis says, "I simply hold that it is *sui generis* and known by each person in being himself and having the experience without which he would not exist".[52] But it is not only us that happen to exist but also many other things like chariots and animals. The fact that a chariot exists does not prove that there is a chariot ghost in it that vouchsafes its existence. As the Buddha maintained, the duty of a critical and rational mind consists not in taking gross and crude ideas as ultimate facts to build arguments upon them but in analyzing and examining them to see whether such ideas do really signify what they seem to signify.

1.19 Campbell tries to argue from self-consciousness, self-identity, and personal identity to the existence of a substantival self.[53] He goes on to say, "I as a self-conscious subject cannot doubt that I who now hear the clock strike a second time am the same being who a moment ago also heard the clock strike even though I must have become different in some respects in the interval".[54] Richmond emphasizes the same.[55] Here the soul theorists forget that memory can account for the fact of self-identity. A Buddhist would account for memory in terms of inheritance of the factors of the causally preceding mental states by the succeeding ones. As Buddhaghosa maintained, the mind is a causally conditioned unbroken succession of mental states. Thus memory and the unconscious mind are fully sufficient to account for the 'feeling' of personal identity. In fact, the Buddha maintained that this feeling of identity is a result of an epistemological confusion one makes with regard to one's existence in the past, present and future. Citta, the householder, clarifies this in answering a question put to him by the Buddha. "Well, that past personality that you had, is that real to you; and the future personality, and the present unreal? The future personality that you will have, is that real to you; and the past personality, and the present, unreal? The personality you have now, in the present, is that real to you; and the past personality, and the future, unreal?—How would you answer?" "I should say that the past personality that I had was real to me at the time when I had it; and others unreal. And so also in the other two cases." The Buddha confirms Citta: ". . . For these, Citta, are merely names, expressions, turns of speech, designations in common use in the world. And of these a Tathagata makes use indeed, but is not led astray by them."[56] Thus the Buddha maintained that some of the problems about personal identity were generated by the confusions inherent in our syntax.

1.20 Ian Crombie refers to another type of feeling. "Our willingness to entertain the notion of a being outside space and time (of what I shall call a 'spirit') is perhaps most fundamentally based on our inability to accept with complete contentment the idea that we are ourselves normal spatio-temporal objects."[57] However, though we can conceive mathematical numbers, that does not suggest we are ultimately only mere abstract entities. The willingness to conceive the notion of contradiction does not suggest we are ultimately contradictions. These things only suggest that man has got some capacity for abstract thinking. Peter Geach thinks that, "It is a savage supposition to suppose that a man consists of two pieces, body and soul, which come apart at death; the supposition is not mended but rather aggravated by conceptual confusion, if the soul-piece is supposed to be immaterial".[58] But he openly contradicts himself when he goes on to talk about disembodied existence. First he illustrates his argument with an example of thoughts or a mind affecting a roulette wheel. Here he says (very mysteriously) that "thoughts would be embodied in the numbers" and therefore the possibility of psycho-kinesis is ruled out. "This and the like examples can show the possibility of disembodied thought; thought unconnected with any living organism. And some continuing disembodied thought might have such connexion with the thoughts I have as a living man as to constitute my survival as a 'separated soul'."[59] Here he tries to find an analogy with the existence of God. But would not that analogy be 'savage'? Geach's ideas about the soul come very close to Barth's when he interprets the soul in an Aristotelian sense as the form of the body.[60] The inherent difficulties of this type of situation have forced thinkers to attempt to find new solutions. Ninian Smart thinks that "taken merely metaphysically the pure soul is a useless and superfluous entity, and in no way explains personal continuity".[61] He finds it impossible to talk of purely disembodied minds, ". . .the disembodied minds would themselves take on the characteristics of bodies, though made of a different 'stuff' from usual. . .".[62]

1.21 C.B. Daly, arguing against Hume and Ayer's arguments against Descarte's proof of the soul from *cogito*, speaks of "an 'I' *involved in* doubting, understanding" etc.[63] However, it does not make sense to speak of an 'I' apart from 'doubting' and interestingly enough Daly, quite inconsistently with his earlier position, sometimes uses the correct way of speaking about the subject when he maintains that the self "is *in* knowledge", "the self is knowing, not a thing known", and the self is "experiencing, not a datum of experience."[64]

1.22 Much of the discussions of the soul theorists center round the non-spatial and non-temporal nature of the soul.[65] Geach maintains, "If thinking is a basic activity—materialism is false—that thinking is not the activity of the brain or of any bodily organ. For the basic activities of any bodily part must be clockable in physical time in a way that thinking is not."[66] And he goes on to say that since thoughts are not clockable "there is a logically open possibility that thought should occur independently, not as the activity of a living organism".[67] It really does not make any sense to talk of mind as non-temporal. It is true that thinking cannot be temporally measured. The Buddha traced this difficulty to the great speed at which the mind changes and maintained that he had never seen anything else so quick changing as the mind. With the added factor of the 'complexity' of thoughts it is only a practical difficulty that the thoughts cannot be reckoned in temporal terms.

1.23 Here in fact we come across the biggest problem the soul theorist has to face. If the soul is a thinking principle it should change, but because it is a substantival principle it cannot change. The Buddha succinctly states this paradox of the soul theorist: ". . . still some ideas, some states of consciousness, would arise to the man, and others would pass away. On this account also, Potthapada, you can see how consciousness must be one thing, and soul another."[68] If states of consciousness are distinct from the soul, then the soul cannot be the thinker and cognizer, etc., and that would make the soul completely barren of any empirical significance, leaving it to be a pure soul, merely metaphysical, useless and a superfluous entity.

1.24 According to the Buddha, it was an arbitrary abstraction to talk of soul as cognizer and thinker, etc., because these functions involved various factors like sense organs and the body. Thinking or thoughts were essentially conditioned by these factors so that it was structurally impossible to trace thoughts to a pure principle like soul. What happened with the soul theorists who argued against Ryle was that their devotion to analysis that started with criticizing Ryle suddenly stopped after coming to the stage of proving the existence of mind and mental states. It is here that the Buddhist parts company with them in carrying the analysis further. If one is not interested in further analysis, there is no reason why one should not have stopped with Ryle rather than with the soul theory. The Buddha analyzes the mind into further factors and finds them all dynamic and essentially changing. Even the mind was not 'a thing' but only another group of activities. It was necessarily dependent on body but not in an epiphenomenalistic sense and therefore the Buddha accepted interactionism (*viññāṇapaccayā nāmarūpaṃ nāmarūpapaccayā viññāṇaṁ*). Though it was dependent on the body, the mind was regarded as a strong causal factor because it had paranormal capacities and powers like telepathy and psychokinesis. Here the Buddha would be at his strongest against any form of reductionism. The rejection of reductionist positions does not make the Buddhist position dualistic. The concept of 'person' is only a conventional one that referred to a composite of five factors. Therefore a Buddhist would agree with Strawson when the latter says, "that one's states of consciousness, one's thoughts and sensations, are ascribed *to the very same thing* to which these physical characteristics, this physical situation, is ascribed".[69] In this sense, as in Strawson, 'person' is a primitive concept[70] in Buddhism. The knowledge of the existence of other minds is not a problem for the Buddhist because he accepts telepathy as a means of knowledge. Therefore, Wisdom's[71] and Plantinga's[72] arguments from the rational mystery of other minds to an analogical rational mystery with regard to God's existence, do not make much sense in the Buddhist context.

1.25 The Buddha's empirical theory of mind can be a fruitful alternative to the extremes of reductionism and soul theories. It should be emphasized that the Buddha did not preach the doctrine of the no-soul *as a theory*. Once he clarified that if he upheld the theory of no-soul it would presuppose the meaningfulness of the concept of 'soul'. As he could not give any meaning to the concept of soul he at last rejected the theory of soul as well as the theory of no-soul. The Buddha keeps silent when Vacchagotta asks him whether there is a self or is not. The Elder Anada later questions the Buddha, " 'How is it, lord, that the Exalted One gave no answer to the question of the Wanderer Vacchagotta?' '. . . Ananda, when asked by Vacchagotta, the Wanderer: 'Is there not a self?' had I replied that there is not, it would have been more bewilderment for the bewildered Vacchagotta. For he would have said: 'Formerly indeed I had a self, but now I have not one any more.' "[73]

1.26 Therefore, to a Buddhist, the conception of God either as analogous to or as identical with, the soul would not be able to make any sense. From the point of view of salvation, such a conception would be regarded as positively harmful.

1.27 It is interesting to see how Bishop Robinson comes very close to the Buddhist standpoint when he rejects altogether the idea of the soul and advocates a theory of personality. " 'The soul' can no longer be thought of (as in the period of ontology) as an individual, non-material, substance implanted in the body to which it in no real sense belongs. Rather, if we are to go on using the word, it must be related to the whole form of the personal in its spiritual aspect. Similarly, 'immortality' cannot be seen . . . in terms of something in man which is not dissolved by physical death and which 'goes on.' Rather, it is a dimension to the whole life as personal, represented more adequately by the New Testament phrase 'eternal life'. It is better described as 'the life beyond myself' than merely 'life beyond death''.[74] Though Robinson abandons the soul theory, he indirectly approaches a similar theory as we shall see shortly. In fact, he attempts a much more radical type of theistic reductionism. This distinguishes him from theologians like Tillich who attempted to avoid the reductionist extreme by positively speaking of the existence of a transcendental 'personal' entity though they, at times, verged on existentialist reductionism. Robinson is radical to the extreme. "For the word 'God' denotes the ultimate depth of all our being, the creative ground and meaning of all our existence."[75] He rejects the idea of God as a person. ". . .to say the 'God is personal' is to say that 'reality' at its deepest level is personal', that personality is of *ultimate* significance in the constitution of the universe, that in personal relationships we touch the final meaning of existence as nowhere else."[76] He interprets 'reality' to mean the depth of personal relationships. "To believe in God as love means to believe that in pure personal relationship we encounter, not merely what ought to be, but what is, the deepest veriest truth about the structure of reality."[77] Here depth means 'love'. ". . . theological statements are not a description of 'the highest Being' but an analysis of the depths of *all* experience 'interpreted by love'."[78] Robinson gives his methodological principle when he says that, following Feuerbach, true religion consists in acknowledging the divinity of the attributes of God.[79] One can make a complete identification with this God or love in the sense of the Upanisadic saying: *Tat tvam asi.*[80]

1.28 The Buddhist views this as a version of the soul theory in a different aspect. Robinson tries to find substantiality in feelings but, as have been seeing, the Buddha was arguing against the search for substitutes in the realm of feelings. One of the Buddha's disciples explains, "As a result of this or that condition, revered sir, these or those feelings arise. From the stopping of this or that condition these or those feelings are stopped."[81] Therefore Robinson's God would be essentially relational. In fact, he is happy that it is so. And he maintains that the central conviction of theism should be the "apprehension of a relational reality",[82] because it is the nature of the 'reality': ". . .God-language does not describe a Thing-in-Itself or even a Person-in-Himself. And yet it does more than register our commitments. It points to an ultimate relatedness in the very structure of our being from which we cannot get away."[83] If the reality is thus relational and conditioned how far can it be a reality as such? The Buddha was strongly against any idea of taking emotions as a guide to any form of enlightenment because they could be positively harmful. Robinson sees much value in the realm of emotions. "Integral to any God-statement, at any rate in the Judaeo-Christian tradition, is the consciousness of being encountered, seized, held by a prevenient reality.''[84] As emotions are not susceptible to any proofs so neither are the God-statements. ''God-statements are statements about the veracity of this relationship. They cannot finally be proved or disproved, any more than human trust or love can finally be proved or disproved.''[85] The Buddha would see this as an essentially wrong way of approaching salvation. This would be grasping at emotions which are notoriously erratic and ultimately comfortless. They are comfortless in the sense that they do not give any sustaining and persisting sense of satisfaction. 'Love', in a humanistic sense, can be an exhilarating and sustaining experience, but only at times. Does it give any enlightenment or a deeper understanding of things or a sustaining satisfaction in the way of salvation? A Buddhist would say that Robinson in his search for ultimate reality has not gone beyond the realm of conditionality which is the basis of phenomenality.

1.29 It is instructive to note that some philosophers of religion do not accept the existence of soul. John Hick is willing to be satisfied with talking only about a ''finite, mortal, psychological life''[86] rejecting the idea of a ''non-physical soul''. John Macquarrie rejects the idea of a soul. For him, ''True selfhood is not something that is ours by nature; it is something to be gained, or perhaps lost. . .''[87] In a Heideggerian sense, he speaks of a temporal evolution to authentic selfhood. ''The resultant existential unity (the attainment of which will, of course, be only a matter of degree) is not the unity of a persisting self-identical substance, of which one can say 'A is A', but a unity of form.''[88] Therefore, to him, ''Timelessness would be annihilation of selfhood''.[89] Immortality etc., is to be understood in a typically existentially reductionist sense . . .''immortality, or perhaps better, eternal life or resurrection life is, as in the Fourth Gospel, the achievement of selfhood here in this world.''[90] But the interesting thing to note is that Macquarrie believes that, even in his existentialist sense, the idea of 'true selfhood' forms an analogy with the existence of God. ''Can we suppose, then, that Being or God, in a way which must go beyond anything that we can understand, though we may find a dim analogy in authentic selfhood, gathers up all time in a vaster unity?''[91] However, this analysis poses enormous problems to the Christian idea of God when he is considered to be an essentially temporal and evolving entity. Also the idea of a 'vaster unity of time' makes hardly any sense. The analogy he tries to make is not justified because the existence of developing or evolving psychophysical entities cannot suggest either an idea of a possibility or the existence of a divine person.

1.30 Macquarrie's ideas here suggest two important points. One is that the idea of the soul is not very relevant to the idea of God. God may exist even though there be no soul. The other point is that his conclusion emphasizes the significance and importance of the person as an analogy in speaking about and understanding God. If the lesson he teaches in his conclusion is correct then the idea of the soul is much more important than Macquarrie himself thinks.

1.31 There are some Christian theologians who come very close to the Buddhist position outlined before. Charles Hartshorne and John B. Cobb illustrate this new situation very well. Hartshorne states, ". . . as the subtlest Buddhists, for deep spiritual reasons, insisted—there is no simply identical self reaping rewards and punishments. Each momentary agent and sufferer is numerically new; from which it follows that I which now acts never can receive either reward or punishment, beyond the intrinsic reward or punishment of acting and experiencing as it now does. The account is immediately closed. Anything one demands for the future is demanded for another, even though this other is termed 'one's self'."[92] "The model of 'influence' which we all know in ourselves is the following: our past thoughts and feelings readily influence us simply because we are aware of them and because they are our sort of thoughts and feelings."[93] Cobb spells out these ideas much more clearly: "If we identified the soul with such an individual, there would be millions of souls during the lifetime of a single man. But when we speak in Platonic or Christian terms, we think of a single soul for a single man. If we hold fast to this usage, and Whitehead basically does so, then we must think of the soul as that society composed of all the momentary occasions of experience, that make up the life history of the man. The soul is not an underlying substance undergoing accidental adventures. It is nothing but the sequence of the experiences that constitute it.

"In contrast to some Christian views of the soul, it should also be noted at the outset that Whitehead's understanding of the soul applies to the higher animals as well as to man. Wherever it is reasonable to posit a single centre of experience playing a decisive role in the functioning of the organism as a whole, there it is reasonable to posit a soul. . .The soul is in every sense a part of nature, subject to the same conditions as all other natural entities."[94]

1.32 However, the problem with Hartshorne and Cobb is that they do not follow their thinking to its consistent conclusions. Instead, Cobb goes on to make remarks that are alarmingly inconsistent with the above statements. ". . .he (Whitehead) himself ordinarily identifies the man with the soul. It is the soul that is truly personal, the true subject. The body is the immediate environment of the person. Hence, the continued existence of the soul or the living person would genuinely be the continued existence of the life of the man. That there is a soul or living person, ontologically distinct from the body, is the first condition of the possibility of life after death."[95] This shows the fundamental dilemma of Christian theologians with regard to the soul. On the one hand they see that there is nothing above and beyond experiences that can be called soul. On the other hand, the Christian teachings force them to posit an ontologically distinct soul which is a completely superfluous and redundant entity in the context of the rest of their main doctrines.

1.33 Though their theory of momentary occasions shows certain similarities with the Buddhist doctrines, the presuppositions which the process theologians make take them far away from the Buddhist standpoint. Can their theory of soul be similar to the Buddhist theory of mind? For the Buddhists the mind is essentially a conditioned conglomeration of dynamic factors. But for every Christian theologian, even for the process theologians, the soul always means something more than that. For them, the soul is an ontologically distinct entity. Thus for the process theologians there is always an ontologically distinct soul that they want to be superimposed over the dynamic process of the mind. It is this unnecessary superimposition of entities that take the process theologians away from the Buddhist standpoint. The Buddha simply asserted that the causal sequence of momentary events could explain the happenings in the world. As Buddhaghosa states, "In all kinds of becoming, generation, destiny, station and abode there appears only mentality-materiality, which occurs by means of linking of cause with fruit. He sees no doer over and above the doing, no experiencer of the result over and above the occurrence of the result. But he sees clearly with right understanding that the wise say 'doer' when there is doing and 'experiencer' when there is experiencing simply as a mode of common usage. Hence the ancients said, 'There is no doer of a deed, or one who reaps the deed's fruit. Phenomena alone flow on and no other view than this is right. . . . The kamma is void of its fruit and no fruit exists in the kamma. And still the fruit is born from it wholly depending on the kamma. For here there is no God or Brahma, Creator of the round of births. Phenomena alone flow on cause and component being their condition'."[96] The process theologians also see this point and succeed in giving satisfactory explanations in terms of the causal process of occasions. But because of their attachment to Christian teachings they again try to posit superfluous entities like God over and above the causal mechanism of the process. That is why both Hartshorne[97] and Cobb[98] maintain that to understand the human soul one must presuppose the working of God or as Cobb says, "God must be conceived as being the reason that entities occur at all as well as determining the limits within which they can achieve their own forms".[99] Thus the superfluity of the jump from the empirical entities to God is clear and the process theologians have not been able to find a justification for that move. Therefore the process theologians have not been able to make any improvements over other natural theologians in reducing the gulf between the empirical world and God.

1.34 As far as the theory of soul is concerned they, irrespective of their critical treatment of the empirical world, go on to posit dogmatically the traditional concept of soul as an ontologically distinct entity. One can argue here that what they mean by ontologically distinct is that the mind is a different category from the body or the mind is just different from the body. But their ontological distinctness must definitely mean more than that because it is essentially related to the ontological distinctness of God and therefore should be understood as an analogy. This again shows the difficulty of making the Christian doctrines meaningful in terms of empirical data and vice versa.

1.35 It is instructive to see the Buddhist and Christian attitudes to the pragmatic value of the idea of the soul. The Christian believes that the idea of the soul is spiritually and morally satisfying and is positively conducive to moral and spiritual progress. The Buddhist reaction follows partly from the epistemological and ontological arguments discussed earlier, e.g., a fiction cannot lead to any real and enlightening moral and spiritual progress. But the Buddha opposed the idea of soul on moral and spiritual grounds too. Answering the Buddhist, Tillich maintains that a perfect society is possible only on the idea of everyone possessing a substantial self. "...the Buddhist says, 'Your two answers are incompatible; if every person has a substance, no community is possible'. To which the Christian replies, '*Only* if each person has a substance of his own is community possible, for community presupposes separation. You, Buddhist friends, have identity, but not community'."[100] However, the issue is to be decided on the relative merits of the two alternatives. The Buddha strongly maintained that the idea of a personal self is a harmful concept communally as well as individually. Referring to the fundamentals, the notion of the self gives rise to the feelings and ideas that center round the self. This is a form of conceit. " 'I am'—that is a conceit (*maññitaṃ*). 'This am I'—that is a conceit. 'I shall be'—that is a conceit. . . . A conceit is, brethren, a lust . . . an imposthume, a barb."[101] This leads to an egoism (*asmimāna*).[102] This conceit is generated in the following manner: "Owing to the existence, dependent on, by adhering to the eye . . . tongue . . . body . . . mind . . . comes the notion of 'better am I', or 'equal am I' or 'inferior am I' ".[103] A Buddhist would agree that a community needs separation but he would maintain that separation does not presuppose the existence of substances and usually it never does. On the other hand, the existence of substances might lead to the possibility of an absolute separatedness which will make community impossible. The Buddha was repeatedly clarifying how hatred, jealousy, the ideas of possessiveness etc., do always depend on the wrong idea of self and therefore how such a notion can be socially harmful. To achieve the ideals of selflessness, disinterestedness and renunciation the idea of no-soul (*anatta*) is logically more conducive than the idea of soul. "When he regards this body as impermanent, suffering, as a disease, an imposthume, a dart, a misfortune, an affliction, as other, as decay, empty, not-self, whatever is regard to body, is desire for body, affection for body, subordination to body, this is got rid of."[104]

1.36 Maritain believes that the possibility of spiritual depth necessitates the existence of a soul.[105] Also, according to Maritain, understanding myself involves understanding my 'self' which is noble, etc.[106] Barth is anxious to emphasize the intrinsic value of the soul as it is constituted by the Spirit which is identical with God.[107] On the contrary, the Buddha sees the soul as an essentially evil idea that leads to spiritually harmful results. One cannot gain any spiritual satisfaction by seeking a soul in the mind and clinging to it because the mind is liable to changes. ". . . the uninstructed average person regards consciousness (body, feelings etc.) as self or self as having consciousness or consciousness as in self or self as in consciousness. His consciousness alters and becomes otherwise; with the alteration and otherwiseness in his consciousness, his consciousness is occupied with the alteration in his consciousness; mental objects, arising, persist in obsessing his thought; because of this obsession of his thought he is afraid and annoyed and full of longing and he is disturbed by grasping. This, your reverences, is what is being disturbed by grasping."[108] By identifying oneself with a changing entity like mind one cannot be happy because it is ". . . of little strength, fading away and comfortless. . .".[109] The identification of soul with God or the noumenal reality (Upanisadic) can also lead to harmful results. "Here one is of this view: My soul is great. He having thought that the whole world is the space for his soul thinks that my soul is in everything. This is his view. (Therefore) to his very soul he gets attached and because of that he starts to feel conceited. This should be known as greed and conceit."[110]

1.37 A person who has achieved enlightenment does not think "I have achieved it". "And inasmuch as this venerable one beholds, 'Tranquil am I, without grasping am I,' this too is known as grasping on the part of that worthy recluse or Brahman."[111] In fact, the Buddha did positively inquire into the possibility of finding salvation by believing in the existence of a soul and found it was impossible. "Could you, monks, grasp that grasping of the theory of self, so that by grasping that theory of self there would not arise grief, suffering, anguish, lamentation, despair? No, revered sir."[112]

1.38 Thus a Buddhist would not find soul a morally and spiritually edifying concept. Therefore, in that sense, he would maintain that the soul cannot be a good analogy to a morally and spiritually perfect God either.

Chapter Two

GOD AS THE CREATOR AND THE DESIGNER

2.1 'Creator' is an indispensable attribute of God because the whole doctrinal edifice of Christianity rests on the assumption that God created the world and man. In Christianity, God is able to offer salvation to man because it was he who created man. However, the ideas of salvation and creation are not necessarily bound together as is seen in the later theistic Samkhya philosophy, where God can offer salvation though he is not a creator. But in Christianity the two are inseparable particularly because God is conceived as omnipotent and unique.

2.2 The Cosmological Argument which tried to prove the existence of a creator is still regarded as a strong proof by some thinkers. F.T. Geach speaks of Aquinas' Five Ways as, without qualification, "proving the existence of God"; and he later speaks of Aquinas as "having thus established the existence of a God who is the cause of the world and of the processes in it.".[1] D.J.B. Hawkins tries to maintain a more modest version of it. ". . . we make no profession of providing proofs which no one can decline to accept; we merely claim to offer reasoning which is in itself logically demonstrative, that should be enough."[2] And he goes on to say, "Our treatment is offered frankly as a natural theology on the medieval model, proceeding on grounds of objective logic and metaphysics and asserting the existence of God as a hard fact to be acknowledged by reason without reference to emotions, aspirations or any support other than honest and accurate thinking."[3] But in contemporary theology and philosophy of religion, the idea of creator is a very ambiguous term. Many thinkers do not tend to recognize the idea of creating the world at a particular point of time very meaningful. The main reason for this is that it is logically consistent to think of causes running backwards to infinity. Only if this idea were incoherent or impossible, would the idea of a literal or strict creation make any sense. Ninian Smart maintains that "the Cosmological Argument, if valid, is quite compatible with the eternity of the cosmos."[4] The other reason stems from the attempts to demythologize Christianity. As Bultmann states, the knowledge of creation "does not mean to speak of God as the first cause of all beings. . ."[5] and "this kind of faith in creation is not a theory about some past occurrence such as might be depicted in mythological tales or cosmological speculation and natural scientific research. . ."[6]

2.3 Thus the idea of creator is to be made meaningful in a different sense, or as Smart says, "To appreciate the [Cosmological] Argument rightly, we must take a new view of it, and see it as posing a problem, namely that the cosmos is contingent."[7] (Though these thinkers try to avoid the strict sense of the word 'creation', there should be an examination of how far they are permitted to do so , and how far they are consistent in this attempt.)

2.4 The starting point of the argument for a creator is the idea of contingency, or 'existence' as another for contingency. The assumption behind the argument is that existence cannot be explained by itself. Smart clarifies, ". . . in attempting to argue ourselves beyond the cosmos we seem to be going beyond the observable, and outside space and time. This provides us with another lesson—namely that any attempted explanation of the cosmos is non-scientific."[8] This permits one to speak of God as the Cosmos-Explaining-Being: "We can argue that somehow 'beyond' or 'behind' the cosmos there exists a Being which explains the existence of the cosmos."[9]

2.5 It is here that the Buddha would strongly disagree with the theist. He was conversant with the view of creation and said that some "believed as their traditional doctrine that the beginning of things was the work of God or Brahma''.[10] But he did not think that such a view could explain anything about the world. Buddhism does not call the world contingent but only impermanent. Its central thesis emphasizes that everything is subject to an unceasing flow of change (*vipariṇāmadhamma*). One of his disciples once questioned the Buddha: " 'The world! The world!' is the saying, lord. How far, lord, does this saying go? It crumbles away, brethren. Therefore it is called 'the world'. What crumbles away? The eye . . . objects . . . eye-consciousness . . . tongue . . . body . . . mind etc. It crumbles away, brethren. Therefore it is called 'the world'.''[11] What distinguishes the Buddha from the theist is that the former strongly believed the world to be explainable in its own terms. To him the world was not a 'thing' but only a vast series of evanescent changes. The law of causation (*idappaccayatā*) as affecting the physical and mental realms was regarded to be fully sufficient to explain this cosmic series of changes. But the question as to what is the cause of this causal series still remains. Buddhaghosa thinks that when the idea of a creator God is rejected this question remains yet to be answered. But he maintains that empirical causation and causal regularities, in turn, can explain the causal series. ''To begin with, he considers thus: 'Firstly this mentality-materiality is not causeless, because if that were so, it would follow that (having no causes to differentiate it), it would be identical everywhere always and for all. It has no Overlord [God] etc., because of the non-existence of any Overlord, etc., over and above mentality-materiality. And because, if people then argue that mentality-materiality itself is its Overlord etc., then it follows that their mentality-materiality, which they call the Overlord, etc., would itself be causeless. Consequently there must be a cause and a condition for it. What are they?

''Having thus directed his attention to mentality-materiality's cause and condition, he first discerns the cause and condition for the material body in this way . . . When it is born thus, its causes (root-causes) are the four things namely, ignorance, craving, clinging, and Kamma: since it is they that bring about its birth; and nutriment is its condition, since it is that that consolidates it. So five things constitute its cause and condition.''[12] In the same way, as we shall see later, Buddhism maintains that one can give a self-sufficient casual account in empirical terms of the physical and mental aspects of the world.

2.6 Here the theist can object that it is not an explanation at all, and would maintain that only by going beyond the world and postulating a Cosmos-Explaining-Being can one explain the existence of the world. Therefore we should see whether the theist really does explain the 'contingent' world. The simplest argument against the Cosmological Argument has been that it is a contradiction to speak of a non-caused cause. This argument has been uneasily silenced by pointing to the 'perfection' of God which is intended to make the argument look rather childish. The Kantian objection has been another argument against the Cosmological Proof that the latter in fact goes back to the Ontological Argument by making existence part of the definition of God. But Smart thinks that it can be stated in a way to avoid the Kantian objection.[13] He states that the Argument is not a deductive one and thinks that the idea of God can be arrived at by some form of rational consideration. But, at the same time, this rational consideration involves an imaginative leap. "To appreciate the Argument rightly, we must take a new view of it, and see it as posing a problem, namely that the cosmos is contingent. This problem can only be solved illuminatingly by making an imaginative leap, and proffering an explanation which is much richer than that of a bare CEB [i.e. Cosmos-Explaining-Being]."[14] The richer conception he finds in the act of creation (or creativity), or it is one of the ways of making the conception richer. "We sketched out an account of creative novelty in human actions which does not fit completely into the pattern of regular causes and effects. Now, admittedly, this creative novelty exists in the setting of a network of causes. But could we not boldly conceive of an act of will or discovery which has no such context?—pure creativity, as it were?"[15] This, he believes, gives a rough analogy to the idea of creation out of nothing. "It is not surprising that the word 'creativity' is used here: for it would be misleading to think of the artist as having built something up out of what was already given. In an important sense, he has made something from nothing."[16] "In any event, the idea that the world is created by an act of will—almost arbitrarily, we feel—chimes in with that sense of radical contingency which afflicts us when we contemplate the possibility that there might indeed have been no world."[17] So this idea is supposed to be capable of accounting for the contingent world. It is very important to note that Smart is, here, speaking about the strict creation (literal creation of the world out of nothing). This cannot be referring to the continuous creation, which Smart speaks of later on, for one important reason. The fact that "the world is created by an act of will" refers to an event, a particular 'unique' event, and also the context suggests that it has this meaning. The argument has value only if it refers to an event of this type. If so, if this is the way Smart tries to make the Cosmological Argument meaningful, then here he contradicts his former assertion that the Argument is quite compatible with the eternity of the cosmos.

2.7 Hawkins tries to make an uneasy reconciliation between strict creation and the everlastingness of the world. "Following St. Thomas we saw, in discussing the causal argument, no metaphysical necessity demanded a beginning of the created world. The divine creative act is eternal, and the natures of things are capable of realization at any time; hence it was absolutely possible the *God should have created a world with no beginning of its existence*. But, if the things which make up the world are genuinely to have a history, and development and a fulfillment, it seems altogether appropriate that they should have had a beginning and should eventually reach a final and lasting state. Hence, while there is no metaphysical demonstration that the world had a beginning, there is at least a strong argument for the appropriateness of this to the creative intelligence."[18] The 'appropriateness' of a way of speech does not suggest any factual conclusions. However, the attempts of these thinkers illustrate how significant and necessary is the idea of strict creation in the Christian tradition. It makes the creator concept clearly vulnerable to the argument derived from the everlastingness of the cosmos which cuts at the root of this version of the Cosmological Argument.

2.8 Another argument closely related to the creator idea is the argument from design. As Smart clarifies, there are two forms of the Teleological Argument, and according to him, ". . . Evolutionary Theory cuts at the root of the special, but not of the general form of the Teleological Argument".[19] But he tries to explain the idea of continuous creation by an indirect appeal to the special form of the Teleological Argument. ". . . God chooses just this cosmos, knowing in advance (so to speak, for he knows all at once) that creativity will in fact emerge amid the necessary regular patterns of cause and effect: or, to put the matter another way, he is the Continuous Creator."[20] However, if the evolutionary theory can account for the evolution there is no point in speaking of continuous creation withing the evolutionary process. It does not add anything to the theory. But one may say that certain aspects of evolution, e.g., the emergence of mind, life or, as Smart suggested, creativity, cannot be accounted for exclusively in terms of an unconscious evolutionary process. If this objection is valid then to say that the evolutionary theory cuts at the root of the special form of the Teleological Argument would be wrong. Also, if this objection is valid then it would be an unnecessary duplication of the evolutionary theory because it is exactly that type of emergents, like mind and rationality that leads to creativity, that the evolutionary theory tries to account for. Here, particularly, the accidental (mutational etc.) nature of the evolutionary process that led to the extinction of many forms of life etc., precludes the possibility of a conscious guidance of the evolutionary process. Therefore, the duplication of the evolutionary theory, even if it is correct, does not suggest any conscious planning. But, it may still be objected, the manifestation of complex order and scientifically unaccountable facts like man's creativity points to a conscious guidance of the evolutionary process or to a continuous creator. Notwithstanding the fact that these can be accounted for by the evolutionary theory this argument is open to much graver objections. It is open to questioning how much order is man-made or found by man or interpreted by man to suit his purposes. Order is more a relative concept than an objective one. In many cases the amount of complex order man sees depends mostly on man's creative ability. Creativity proceeds from man's rationality and the evolutionary theory accounts for the emergence of rationality, via chimpanzees and the complexities of the brain structure etc. If one calls creativity a non-scientific fact and tries to account for it by continuous creation it will have decisive effects on man's freewill. If it does not lead to a denial of man's freewill, the amount of divine intervention here cannot be decided without first deciding the amount of creativity that is due to man's rationality and freewill, a question which is even theoretically difficult to handle.

2.9 If Smart maintains that he means only the bare fact that God sets up this particular pattern of regularities ensuring that creativity will emerge amid them, then he is here putting forward an argument from the existence of values, i.e., from the fact that a good and a valuable thing, namely, creativity, emerged from this pattern. But this is only a one-sided value-argument. When one looks at the other side of the picture and sees the enormous amounts of evil that resulted from the same regularities this argument loses its value. It may be answered that the emergence of the good implies the emergence or existence of evil as well. (This point will be discussed in detail later on.) All that needs to be said here is that the existence of evil counterbalances the emergence of good and therefore the argument from the latter is not a privileged one and hence does not suggest any regularities provided by divine intentions. If, on the other hand, it is said that what is meant by the argument from continuous creation is that 'there is no happening outside divine creativity', then, as explained above, this raises insoluble problems about man's freewill and the existence of evil.

2.10 One can correctly object that it is the existence of some kind of order that facilitates creation etc. It is here that the general form of the Teleological Argument comes into focus. Here also, there can be two versions of the Argument. One is from the special form of the general order that is found in the world. Smart asks, "We may ask: 'Why this highly organized cosmos, rather than another sort?' The answer cannot be given . . . in scientific terms."[21] But the problem is whether this question can be asked at all. A. Flew clarifies why this is a wrong question. "It is put that it must be immeasurably improbable that there could be so much order without design. . . . No one could acquire an experience of universes to give him the necessary basis for this sort of judgment of probability or improbability; for the decisive reason that there could not be universes to have experiences of."[22]

2.11 The other version of the general form of the Teleological Argument is from the fact of general order. What is important here, as Hawkins maintains, is not the amount of order, but that there is order at all.[23] Smart states, "True disorderliness—absolute disorderliness—would be utter chaos; but here we could no longer speak of this, that or the next thing. In effect there would be no cosmos. Nothingness and absolute chaos would be indistinguishable."[24] Therefore the opposite of this type of order would be nothingness. So, after a long circuitous path we are back where we started: the problem of contingency. The contemporary version of the Teleological Argument is, at last, only a version of the Cosmological Argument.

2.12 Now, our central problem is the idea of contingency. The concept of God as the creator is meant to explain and solve this problem. If the solution is meaningful and correct it is meant to serve two purposes. One is that is can account for the origin of the universe or the existence of the universe. The second is that if the first task is successful it would, in turn, prove the plausibility of the existence of God. For the Buddhist this problem would be of special interest because the starting point of Buddhism is the fact of impermanence and change in the world. What would be the Buddhist attitude towards the Christian solution?

2.13 The concept of creator, as we saw, tries to account for the contingent world in two ways. First by strict and literal creation. Second by positing a necessary being. The Buddhist would regard the first solution as irrelevant. As we shall see later (*v.* 5.12), the Buddha believed in an everlasting and oscillating theory of the universe (though not strictly *as a theory* but more as a possibility [*v.* 5.13]). This, of course, does not logically rule out creation because the oscillating universe could have been created a long time ago by God. But in the absence of any evidence to the contrary it makes it logically conceivable that this oscillating universe goes back to an infinite past. In fact, the Buddhist can believe in an everlasting universe. If the universe is everlasting then the problem of creation becomes completely redundant. The idea of continuous creation cannot be introduced here because it leads to problems we have already raised.

2.14 Though Smart says that the eternity of the universe is compatible with the Five Ways and therefore with the existence of God, it poses a big problem for the theist because it affects God's uniqueness and perfections. This happens in two ways. Firstly, there is at least one thing that is not under God's power of strict, literal creation. This contradicts the Christian idea of God as Creator which Barth clarifies: ". . . creation does also denote a relationship between God and the world, i.e., the relationship of absolute superiority and lordship on the one hand and of absolute dependence on the other. Creation does not signify, however, only a mythological or speculative intensification of the concept of this relationship, but its presupposition and decisive meaning. That is, creation speaks primarily of a basis which is beyond this relationship and makes it possible; of a unique, free creation of heaven and earth by the will and act of God".[25] Though Barth states the typical belief about the Christian Creator God one can still insist that it is not the only possible version of the Christian idea of the Creator God. But an eternal world still limits God in several important ways. God ceases to be the absolute creator but only a relative creator. He does not create the world from nothing but from the existing matter. God cannot destroy the world because the world is eternal. Even if he could destroy the world the fact remains that there has been a world from eternity outside his absolute, strict and literal creative power. One can still say that this type of limitation would not make a significant limitation upon God's omnipotence etc. But one has to accept necessarily that an eternal world is, at least to a certain extent, a limitation upon an absolutely unique and all perfect God. If one says that God need not be that unique then one already accepts the fact of, at least, certain limitations. In either case it raises the grave and uneasy question about the degree of limitations one wants to attribute to God. Within the Christian tradition it is not an easy problem to solve. The second way in which the eternity of the cosmos affects an all-perfect and unique God is that if the cosmos is eternal, then there is at least one thing that shares a divine perfection, i.e., eternity. Here one can make a distinction and say that this type of limitation affects only the abstract definition of God but not the working or practical definition of God, i.e., God can carry on his divine activities quite unhindered by the presence of an eternal world. But in Christianity, the practical definition gains its power and validity on the authority of the abstraction definition, and so the change in the abstract definition has decisive repercussions on the practical definition. Further, the attempt to give a practical definition would make the concept of God subject to the charges of unfalsifiability. A Buddhist would see the possibility of an everlasting world as not only making the idea of a creator God superfluous but also as contradicting the conception of a unique and omnipotent God.

2.15 The second way of accounting for the contingent world is by positing a necessary Being. This second way seems to be the more fundamental argument because the first way still leaves God within the realm of contingency and makes it possible to ask the 'why' of God. One has necessarily to end up in a necessary existence. According to the Christian standpoint, even though the world is eternal the problem of contingency remains. Hawkins emphasizes the necessity of the idea of a necessary Being. "Being is either dependent on other being or not. All being cannot be dependent on other being, for thus there would be no being upon which it could depend. Therefore there is some being which is independent of other being and necessary of itself."[26] But the attempt to speak of the existence of a necessary being has been open to grave logical objections. One of the stock arguments against it is, as J.J.C. Smart states, that "No existential proposition can be logically necessary . . ."[27] and he maintains, " 'Logically necessary being' is a self-contradictory expression like 'round square'".[28] J.N. Findlay thinks that Anselm exposed the unfortunate predicament of the idea of a necessary being when the latter formulated his Argument. "It was indeed an ill day for Anselm when he hit upon his famous proof. For on that day he not only laid bare something that is of the essence of an adequate religious object, but also something that entails its necessary non-existence."[29]

2.16 For a Buddhist, who also looks at the world as subject to change and impermanence, the argument from contingency may look fascinating. Though he would speak of the world as changing and impermanent, the concept of contingency is completely unfamiliar to him. This raises the question whether 'contingency' is 'a fact'. The word 'contingency' is a term that functions meaningfully within the realm of logic and mathematics. It is a relative term and always denotes a relation. 'Contingency' and 'necessity' derive their meaning and significance from each other and you call a proposition contingent only because you already have the conception of a necessary proposition. Because the idea of necessity functions only within the realm of *a priori* thinking and propositions, the idea of contingency too limits itself to that realm and therefore no existential fact can be contingent. Also, the idea of contingent existence or fact cannot have any meaning because one cannot make the idea of necessary existence meaningful, because one cannot talk of a necessary existence or a fact (also *v*. 7.23). This argument does not, of course, apply to 'change' and 'impermanence' because the Buddha was making those two terms meaningful in terms of the empirical context, e.g., by illustrating 'impermanence' by appealing to experience or contrasting it with apparent 'permanence' etc. Therefore while 'impermanence' can be empirically and factually meaningful, 'contingency' cannot be so. If so, what does the Christian mean when he speaks of the world as contingent? What he is doing is expressing an attitude towards the world using the logical term 'contingence' because he is already familiar with the illegitimate idea of a necessary Being.

2.17 It may happen the other way round too. Ian Crombie clarifies it this way: "'Finite' and 'infinite', 'contingent' and 'necessary', 'derivative' and 'non-derivative': all these are pairs. When we use either member of any of them in the theological context we cannot anatomize the meaning to be attached to it. When we speak of the world as finite we do not mean that it can be counted, or travelled across; when we speak of it as derivative, we do not think of it as extracted from its origin by any normal kind of derivation. But the meaning to be attached to the second member of each pair is to be got at by seeing what kind of judgment about the world is intended by the use of the first. The kind of judgment intended by the use of such expressions . . . is an intellectual dissatisfaction with the notion of this universe as a complete system, with, as corollary, the notion of a being with which one could not be thus dissatisfied."[30] Thus, if he starts from 'contingency' then he is trying to give a logical explanation or definition of the factual world. By using that term one is only begging the question in terms of a necessary being. A purely abstract logical relationship cannot explain or give an intellectually satisfying account of an existing factual world.

2.18 But, the theist can still object that the Buddhist's treatment still leaves two questions unanswered: (i) What is the cause of all this? (ii) Why does anything exist at all? We shall take the first question first. The Buddha believed that an empirical theory of causation and the regularity of laws of nature etc., within the world could fully account for causation. It was the nature of the world. The Buddha explains: "What is causation? On account of birth arises death. Whether Tathagatas arise or not, this order exists namely the fixed nature of phenomena, the regular pattern of phenomena or conditionality. This the Tathagata discovers and comprehends; having discovered and comprehended it, he points it out, teaches it, lays it down, establishes, reveals, analyzes, clarifies it and says 'look'."[31] K.N. Jayatilleke illustrates and analyzes how the Buddha applied this theory of causation to explain both physical and mental phenomena in the world.[32] The Buddha's central theory of causality was the regularity theory of causation but he accepted the possibility of other forms of empirical causation like relative causation (e.g. mind and body are caused by consciousness and vice versa; good exists because of bad and vice versa). We saw above, as Buddhaghosa explained, how the Buddhist thinker thought this was a sufficient explanation. But the theist may still insist on seeking the cause that originates or sustains this causal series. One might allow him to proceed further if he could give a satisfying and conclusive explanation of causation. Hawkins maintains, "The divine causality is . . . the source of all other causality and combines all that is positive in other modes of causation".[33] But the fallacy here is that the argument from causation abruptly stops at God. Even an enriched form of the Cosmos-Explaining-Being still raises the question of its causation. To silence the problem of causation after coming to the idea of God is a fundamentally wrong attitude towards causation or as Schopenhauer puts it, "we cannot use the causal law as if it were a sort of cab, to be dismissed when we have reached our destination".[34]

2.19 Here a theist, following St. Augustine, can object that we are misconceiving the idea of time in the context of creation. He would say that one cannot ask about what existed prior to creation because the idea of 'prior' cannot be meaningful before creation began. 'Prior' is a temporal concept and time starts only with creation. Actually this argument does make some sense to a certain extent. The idea of time is essentially related to matter or some form of existent. Time is derivative from the processes of change in matter or existents. Every time we try to conceive of any form of time, prior to creation etc., we do it always in terms of some form of existent. Therefore, in essence, it is true that time does not exist prior to any form of existent. Thus the theist can say that it is meaningless to ask about what existed prior to creation because the 'prior' is meaningless as time is created along with the existents or is a creation relative to the existents.

2.20 Two answers can be given to this argument. One is that the theist's argument is double-edged but he uses only one edge to the exclusion of the other. If the creation of existents creates time then it creates time retrospectively as well. Then it becomes meaningful to talk about the time prior to creation. Secondly, even if the theist's contention were correct, he cannot talk about the non-existence of any existent prior to creation because God himself is so existent. The theist's obvious reply would be that God is timeless etc. But it is not a logically satisfactory or valid answer because God exists in some form, transcendent or otherwise, prior to creation and so the idea of 'prior to creation' becomes a meaningful concept. Therefore the idea of creator validly raises the question of the creator of the creator and so on *regressus ad infinitum*.

2.21 The Buddha emphasized that one has to stop at the fundamental laws of nature and regularities of causation. To go beyond that would be both unnecessary and wrong. Buddhaghosa states, ". . . knowledge of (causal) origin forestalls wrong theories of cause that occur as finding a reason where there is none, such as 'The world occurs owing to an Overlord . . .' etc".[35] Here we can ask three questions: (i) Is it necessary to go beyond this point of explanation? (ii) Is it meaningful to go beyond this point? (iii) Is it correct to go beyond this point? Flew thinks that it is not necessary to go beyond this point of explanation because it is not a deficiency to stop at some fundamentals when one is giving an explanation. "In each and every case we must necessarily find at the end of every explanatory road some ultimates which have simply to be accepted as the fundamental truths about the way things are. And this itself is a contention, not about the lamentable contingent facts of the human condition, but about what follows necessarily from the nature of explanation."[36] Is it meaningful to go beyond this point? If the theist goes beyond this point he will have to stop at some other ultimate which seems arbitrary, enigmatic and abrupt. For example, to stop at a necessary God is an arbitrary conclusion. Even before proceeding to that point he has to accept or stop at more enigmatic and uneasy ultimates. C.B. Martin points out one such ultimate: "This is one law of nature or one way of the world that would be beyond the power of God, namely, that the world should in fact go according to the will of God. God cannot ordain or will that his ordinations and will are effective. That, God's will is effective is just a fact (though a basic one) about how things happen. To ask why God's will is effective is to invite the answer 'That is just the way things are'."[37] The theist's ultimates become more and more meaningless as he proceeds further. Hence, to proceed beyond the empirical ultimates is progressively meaningless. Then we come to the third question. Is it correct to go beyond the ultimates of empirical explanation? Hume explains: "In such a chain too, or succession of objects, each part is caused by that which preceded it, and causes that which succeds it. Where then is the difficulty? But the *whole*, you say, wants a cause . . . Did I show you the particular causes of each individual in a collection of twenty particles of matter, I should think it very unreasonable, should you afterwards ask me, what was the cause of the whole twenty."[38] Similarly, the Buddhist would say that once the empirical facts have been explained causally it would be positively wrong to ask the cause of the whole of it. That was why Buddhaghosa, as we saw above, maintained that the knowledge of the causal origin of things forestalls the theories of a creator God.

2.22 Now, coming to the second question of the theist, he can still ask "Why does anything exist at all?" The Buddhist can give four answers to this question. One is that, as he accepts the possibility of an everlasting cosmos, this question does not, in an important sense, arise to him. Here it should be emphatically stated that we should not drag in the idea of logical contingency into this context because it does not have any meaning as applied to empirical and factual contexts. Of existential propositions one can speak only of an empirical necessity. So, if the world is everlasting the fact that anything exists at all is an empirical necessity. One can *logically* think the world away, but it is not important at all because we are not talking about the realm of logic. The important thing is that one cannot *practically* think the world away because it exists as an empirical necessity. Therefore, to the Buddhist 'why does anything exist at all?' does not pose any problem. One might still insist on a logical kind of explanation in terms of the idea of necessity, but such an explanation would not mean anything and therefore would fail to be an explanation at all.

2.23 The Buddhist can give yet another answer to this question. The Buddha answers Sunakkhatta, the Wanderer: "What think you, Sunakkhatta? Whether the beginning of things revealed, or whether it be not, is the object for which I teach the Dhamma (norm) this: that it leads to the thorough destruction of ill for the doer thereof? . . . If then, Sunakkhatta, it matters not to that object whether the beginning of things be revealed, or whether it be not, of what use to you would it be to have the beginning of things revealed?"[39] The Buddha can give this answer because he starts from the fact that there is the world, as a given. (He did not preach the everlastingness of the cosmos *as a theory* about the origin of the universe etc., but only tried to explain certain moral problems with the help of this idea [*v.* 5.13]). The main concern of religion is salvation and he discovered that it could be found without delving into all the mysteries of the world. A Christian cannot give this form of answer because in the context of Christianity the ideas of salvation and creator God are essentially bound to each other. Objectively speaking, it is possible to think of a non-creator God of salvation as is found in the later theistic Samkhya system. But in Christianity the ideas of creation and salvation are inevitably bound together, or rather entail each other. Theologians like Tillich and Bultmann try to maintain that the idea of strict creation is not relevant for salvation. Tillich says that "The doctrine of creation does not describe an event. It points to the situation of creatureliness and to its correlate, the divine creativity."[40] According to Bultmann, "This, then, is the primary thing about faith in creation: the knowledge of the nothingness of the world and of our own selves, the knowledge of our complete abandonment."[41] Without clarifying the problem of the possibility of limitations upon God's power how can one, as they maintain, put absolute and unconditional faith in the salvific power of God? If the world can manage to exist from eternity it might be able to account for its own internal mechanism too. Tillich should not confidently maintain, "The doctrine of creation affirms that God is the creative ground of everything every moment."[42] Or, Bultmann cannot safely conclude that faith in creation is "faith in man's present determination by God"[43], because there can be other possible sources of man's determination other than God. Without ruling out these possibilities, i.e. withoug clearing the idea of absolute creator, one cannot keep an unconditional faith in the salvific power of an absolutely omnipotent God. A Mahayana cosmic Buddha or Bodhisattva might be quoted as an example to the contrary. However, they are not gods of salvation, they can only help and aid men to get their own salvation, and they have limitations which they know of and consequently they work very hard indeed. Out of compassion for suffering men Kwan Yin is supposed to be weeping all the time. In the later Samkhya it is not God, who openly accepts limitations, that matters in salvation but the following of the practical path as laid down in the Yoga. But in Christianity the unconditional faith in God's salvific power presupposes and therefore logically entails the factual truth of God as absolute literal creator and as all perfect unique Being. Or, as Crombie puts it, "Christianity, as a human activity, involves much more than simply believing certain propositions about matters of fact, such as that there is a God, that He created this world, that He is our judge. But it does involve believing these things, and this believing is, in a sense, fundamental . . .".[44] Though the Buddhist can hold that creation is not necessary for salvation, the Christian cannot claim so, and this conclusion makes Tillich's and Bultmann's attempts to ignore the problem of creation essentially wrong.

2.24 The Buddhist can give two more answers on the basis of the Buddha's teachings. The idea of 'necessary being' that is advanced as a solution to the problem of the contingent world is fundamentally a logical conception based on *a priori* reasoning because, as we discussed before, 'contingency' and 'necessity' are concepts denoting a logical relationship. The Buddha was very critical of assertions based on *a priori* forms of reasoning (*v.* 8.35). He maintained that though a piece of logical reasoning may be self-evident and valid it does not say anything at all about the truth or falsity of the claims made by that type of reasoning. A valid argument can be, according to the Buddha, either true or false and this cannot be decided on grounds of logical reasoning alone. Therefore, *a priori* reasoning about logical relationships cannot lead to making any factual assertions.

2.25 The fourth answer stems from the Buddha's ideas about the universe. As we shall see later (*v.* 5.13), the Buddha spoke of the possibility of an infinite universe. If the universe is infinite then nobody can know the nature of the universe as a whole, and without knowing the universe fully and wholly one cannot arbitrarily decide that the concept of causation can be applied to the universe as a whole. We know that there are areas where the concept of causality is not applicable. As F. Waismann says, "It is only when we descend to the atomic level that the question of causality can be put to the test; and here all the facts speak decidedly against it. The only theory known at present capable of connecting and unifying an enormously wide range of phenomena, quantum theory, is in sharp logical contradiction with it."[45] This in an important way shows that the sovereignty of causation is not all pervading. Therefore one cannot arbitrarily maintain that it should apply in each and every case of which we can think. If causality is not applicable to microcosmic entities like atoms, can we not conceive the possibility that it might not be applicable to macrocosmic phenomena as a whole? As in the case of atoms the universe may be an exception to the principle of causality. Because we do not know the universe as a whole, how do we know that it is not?

Chapter Three

GOD AS BENEVOLENT, OMNIPOTENT AND OMNISCIENT

3.1 The arguments against the existence of God as the Creator mainly depended on proving the consistency of a rival hypothesis, namely that the world could be everlasting, which would make God irrelevant or superfluous. Therefore it cannot be a strong disproof of the existence of God, as the everlastingness of the world cannot be conclusively established. If God, in fact, created the world, the burden of proof falls upon the theist, and if he cannot prove creation as an event but can only point to the facts that suggest its possibility, the consistency of the everlastingness hypothesis undercuts the significance of those facts. It follows, then, that the unsoundness of the creator hypothesis depends on the consistency of a rival hypothesis. It does not prove or disprove anything. The field is still open to anybody who advances a creator. But the Christian God is not only a creator, he is also benevolent, omnipotent and omniscient. Here, existing facts are directly relevant for deciding the issues involved, and the ideas of benevolence, omnipotence and omniscience expose the hypothesis of God to a more direct kind of test.

3.2 The problems involved in the conception of God as benevolent assume a central importance to the Buddhist because they concern some of the very important problems the Buddha tried to solve. The idea of a benevolent God suggests that the world is good and not evil. But the Buddha's central thesis was that the world was evil. So, if the existence of evil cannot be justified as the Buddha maintained, that would militate against the existence of a benevolent God.

3.3 The problem of evil has occupied the greatest attention of the theologians and theistic thinkers through the ages and many solutions have been suggested. These solutions have been subjected to various forms of criticisms by David Hume,[1] J.S. Mill,[2] J.E. McTaggart,[3] A. Flew,[4] H.D. Aiken,[5] J.L. Mackie,[6] C.J. Ducasse,[7] H.J. McCloskey,[8] Nelson Pike[9] and by many others. There is no point in repeating these criticisms here. We shall first note the general outline of some of the solutions of the problem of evil. The two aspects of the problem of evil, physical and moral, are related to the divine characteristics of omnipotence, benevolence and omniscience. The difficulty has been how to reconcile the existence of evil with the existence of God who possesses those attributes. Omniscience and omnipotence are supposed to clash with the existence of free will.

3.4 The theists have taken three major ways of solving the problem. One is by trying to redefine the nature of God. William James,[10] J.S. Mill[11] and Hume, through the mouth of Cleanthes[12], suggested that God may be finite and therefore not fully omnipotent. C. Gore tries to account for free will by saying that God is not really omniscient.[13] However, these ways of solving the problem would be an anathema to the traditional Christian doctrine of God.

3.5 The second way of solving the problem has taken the form of redefining the concepts involved so that it tends to avoid the problem altogether. Tillich redefines 'omnipotence' to mean that God is creative. "In popular parlance the concept of 'omnipotence' implies a highest being who is able to do whatever he wants. This notion must be rejected, religiously as well as theologically . . . Opposing such a caricature of God's omnipotence, Luther, Calvin, and others interpreted omnipotence to mean the divine power through which God is creative in and through everything in every moment."[14] And he defines 'omniscience' to mean the possibility of participation in divine being or knowledge. ". . .the divine omniscience is the logical (though not always conscious) foundation of the belief in the opennes of reality to human knowledge. We *know* because we participate in the divine knowledge."[15] Tillich argues, what omniscience means is that "Nothing falls outside the *logos* structure of being".[16] In his theology 'providence' assumes a new meaning. "In Christianity providence is an element in the person-to-person relationship between God and man; it carries the warmth of belief in loving protection and personal guidance. It gives the individual the feeling of transcendent security in the midst of the necessities of nature of history."[17] Though this way of interpretation makes sense within the theological system of Tillich, it does not at all face up to the problems involved in theodicy. The same argument applies to Fritz Buri who tries a more radical approach when he makes God a completely subjective concept and the doctrine of God a mere symbolology. ". . . for our rational thought which tends to unity are produced the tensions and ununitable elements in the concept of God. The establishing of these contradictions is thoroughly in order, so long as we are conscious that we are operating in the sphere of conceptual-objective knowledge."[18] He calls omnipotence and infinite-goodness 'the so-called attributes of God' and says, "In them we are not dealing with a scientific description of the nature of God, but rather with symbols of the faith for existence".[19]

3.6 The third way of solving the problem has been to tackle the problem of evil directly as it exists. Five main solutions have been attempted in addition to an attempt to redefine evil so that the problem may disappear. Four solutions try to justify the existence of evil on grounds of utility. 1. Physical good requires physical evil to exist at all; 2. Physical evil is God's punishment of sinners; 3. Physical evil is God's warning and reminder to man; 4. Physical evil increases the total good. In addition to the many criticisms made about these four theories, one can point to a single instance that eludes these four ways of justification: a newborn baby suffering from cancer. As Ivan Karamazov insisted the case of one child's suffering is sufficient to raise the problem of evil in its full strength. The fifth theory is the most important in that it tries to answer this problem and it maintains that the physical evil is the result of the natural laws, the operation of which are on the whole good. Ninian Smart, advocating Tennant's view, says that "In brief, then, a world which evolves intelligent beings must be a regular world; and yet regularity will mean that disasters to sentient beings will occur".[20] It is evident that two factors or two types of justification are involved in this argument. One is that mere regularity involves no evil. The other is that regularity with evil is justified on the ground of a purpose, namely, the evolution of intelligent beings, and perhaps, other forms of life as well that have come to be successful evolutes. In a way, therefore, this becomes a form of justification of evil in terms of design and purpose. There are two main defects in this argument. One is that the argument has a highly selective bias towards the successful evolutes. From the point of view of the animals that suffered enormously in the process of evolution, the evil has no justification at all. From the point of view of babies who die young, the existence of evil does not serve any purpose at all.

3.7 The second defect of the argument is that it only emphasizes the essential reality of the existence of evil, and the existence of evil is itself the problem involved. One can say that it supplies a justification for its existence, but it is only a 'physical justification', and what is necessary is a 'moral justification'. The physical justification cannot be a moral justification precisely because God is omnipotent. If it is non-contradictory to think of a world where there is no physical evil, then it is possible for God to have created a world like that. Here, going back to one of the former solutions, one can point to the significance of the utility of evil. Referring to suffering, Hawkins states, ". . . we must admit, however reluctantly, that it has a real and important place in the development of human character, and we may not improbably estimate that, if moral evil and its effects were absent, the amount of natural suffering which would remain would be the right amount for this purpose".[21] But when a baby suffers from cancer it cannot have any significance for the development of its character because the death will preclude that possibility. If it is a lesson for the others,then the enormous problem of using human beings as a means to teach ethical lessons to others comes up. If that is regarded as as solution at all, then the problem of the privileged human beings has to be solved. Thus even after due allowances have been made for the utility nature of evil we are still left with a vast amount of evil that has yet to be morally justified, or as Wisdom says, "It remains to add that, unless there are independent arguments in favour of this world's being the best logically possible world, it is probable that some of the evils in it are not logically necessary to a compensating good; it is probable because there are so many evils''.[22] Therefore the physical justification cannot be a 'necessary justification' because this world is not logically the best. If it were, the physical justification could have been a moral justification.

3.8 If regularity is a mechanical sequence that affects inorganic phenomena only, then God can leave it to its own mechanisms, but when 'regularity' starts to make human beings suffer for no morally justifiable reason, the problem of the existence of a benevolent God comes up. If God allows innocent human beings to suffer from the regularity he established, God could not be either benevolent or omnipotent. The Buddha criticized the existence of God precisely on this ground. His main argument was that God could have made the world otherwise than it is. ''If Brahma is lord of the whole world and creator of the multitude of beings, then why (i) has he ordained misfortune in the world without making the whole world happy, or (ii) for what purpose has he made the world full of injustice, deceit, falsehood and conceit, or (iii) the lord of beings is evil in that he ordained injustice when there could have been justice.''[23]

3.9 Here the Buddha is talking of both physical and moral evil. The standard argument for the justification of moral evil is, as Hawkins puts it, that ''To those who take free will seriously, moral evil does not present an insuperable difficulty.''[24] Here again the justification is done by appealing to the utility nature of moral evil. Both Flew and H.J. McCloskey have argued that God should have made human beings choose the right things or as the latter puts it, ''The real alternative is, on the one hand, rational agents with free wills making many bad and some good decisions on rational and non-rational grounds, and 'rational' agents predestined always 'to choose' the right things for the right reasons—that is, if the language of automata must be used, rational automata. Predestination does not imply the absence of rationality in all sense of that term. God, were He omnipotent, could preordain the decisions and the reasons upon which they were based; and such a mode of existence would seem to be in itself a worthy mode of existence, and one preferable to an existence with free will, irrationality and evil''.[25] But Smart has argued that without freedom to do moral evil, the idea of free will does not make any sense.[26] But the problem takes a different turn when one looks at certain aspects of moral evil. Hitler's killing of six million Jews can ultimately be traced to the free will of Hitler. Is that a justification? Hick tries to give a mysterious justification of moral evil in terms of free will:"The origin of moral evil lies forever concealed within the mystery of human freedom."[27] But does that furnish a justification for the suffering and death of six million Jews? Here the more important problem is the problem of suffering and death of six million rather than the free will of one man. Morally speaking, it is a very dubious explanation or justification to say that the safeguarding of one man's free will invloves the suffering and death of six million people. One can say that man himself is responsible for it, but as a justification it would be saying too much. From the point of view of those who suffered and died, what form of justification can they find for their destiny? It is here that moral evil starts to assume a great similarity to physical evil. From the standpoint of those who suffered and the dead, both an earthquake and Hitler's extermination campaign would look very much the same. If the earthquake follows from physical regularity and moral evil from mental regularity, both become only factual justifications. One cannot say that moral evil, here, admits of a moral justification, because the one who has suffered does not, and cannot, share the justification. The problem becomes important when God is regarded as all-loving and omnipotent. If God is such why does he allow the innocent to suffer at the hand of a mass-murderer like Hitler? Therefore, it is sensible to maintain, as the Buddha did, that moral and physical evils stand on a par in many respects and hence one can sensibly ask, why God did not, if he were good, create the world otherwise than as he has created it. It is not contradictory to think of such an alternative world. The relevant objection, here, that without moral evil free will becomes meaningless, loses much of its justificatory value when one thinks of the enormous evils such a freedom can lead to. That is why some, like McCloskey and Flew, have gone so far as to prefer a world with no evil to a world with free will. But again, as we did in the case of physical evil, giving due allowance to the utility of moral evil, one can still argue that God could have created a will less free, i.e. limited in several respects, that is, so that it would limit a man from perpetrating Hitlerian types of crime. Even now, though man is theoretically free, there are many things that he cannot actually do. Some things can be done only by a very few men, like knowing other peoples minds. Having telepathic powers can increase man's degree of free will in the sense that the degree of one's free will increases when a man knows more, because one is less free when one knows less. This is only an example to illustrate how it would be possible for man's free will to be limited by God to avert 'unnecessary moral evil' without making man completely devoid of free will. It would be, of course, a limited form of free will. To speak of practically realizable unlimited free will would be to talk of an unrealizable ideal. If the Christians think, to argue from within the tradition, that they can reconcile predestination and free will, there is every reason why God should intervene in man's free will to avoid morally unjustifiable evils that happen due to the existence of free will. It is encouraging to note that some Christians do, in fact, think that it is sensible to think this way. Hawkins says, "We can be grateful, however, if he does not always leave us to this full freedom but sometimes directs us infallibly to the right by a motion which is not an infringement of freedom in the more general sense."[28]

3.10 Another solution to the problem of evil has been to say that evil is only a 'privation' of good and the divine. For example, Barth tries this solution: "Metaphysical evil, as the sum and source of all others, is simply the essential non-divinity of the creature . . . God could not endow the world with absolute perfection except by making it another God . . . . It is not, then, a positive evil, nor should it be described as evil but only as a deficiency or 'privation' proper to the creature."[29] This argument becomes very interesting from a Buddhist point of view because for the Buddha the fundamental truth of the world was the truth of suffering. His main thesis was that "birth is a suffering, decay is a suffering, disease is a suffering, death also is a suffering and, in short, all the five forms of grasping lead to suffering (or non-satisfaction)". For the Buddha, the worldly forms of happiness were essentially temporary and leading to various forms of suffering or non-satisfaction. Happiness or good is always a 'privation' of evil or suffering. Sometimes theists, too, think in the way the Buddha did. For instance the Jesuit Father G.H. Joyce says: "The actual amount of suffering which the human race endures is immense. Disease has store and to spare of torments for the body: and disease and death are the lot to which we must all look forward. At all times, too, great numbers of the race are pinched by want. Nor is the world ever free for very long from the terrible sufferings which follow the track of war. If we concentrate our attention on human woes, to the exclusion of the joys of life, we gain an appalling picture of the ills to which the flesh is heir. So, too, if we fasten our attention on the sterner side of nature, on the pains which men endure from natural forces—on the storms which wreck their ships, the cold which freezes them to death, the fire which consumes them—if we contemplate this aspect of nature alone, we may be led to wonder how God came to deal so harshly with His Creatures as to provide them with such a home."[30] Hawkins too shares the same view with regard to the nature of evil in the world: "Returning to human suffering, we must remark that it would scarcely be intelligible apart from immortality. If death were the end of everything, we might have some grudge against the Creator for having situated our short existence in so unsatisfactory a world."[31] If evil is such a glaringly positive fact, it would be extremely wrong to say that evil is only a privation of good. Also, when one looks at the general nature of human society it tends to strengthen the positive sense of evil. McCloskey observes, "It may be the case that over-all pleasure predominates over pain, and that physical goods in general predominate over physical evils, but the opposite may equally well be the case. It is both practically impossible and logically impossible for this question to be resolved. However, it is not an unreasonable presumption, with the large bulk of mankind inadequately fed and housed and without adequate medical and health services, to suppose that physical evils at present predominate over physical goods. In the light of the facts at our disposal, this would seem to be a much more reasonable conclusion than the conclusion hinted at by Joyce and openly advanced by less cautious theists, namely, that physical goods in fact outweigh physical evils in the world."[32]

3.11 From Buddha's point of view, the very phenomenal existence itself is a form of suffering and evil and therefore the Buddha would hold the creator who created such a form of existence, as essentially responsible for creating this evil form of existence. God has, of course, given us the possibility of salvation. But many people, e.g., many primitive tribes, do not or did not have the idea of salvation. Also, when one sees that more of humanity suffers the anguish and evils of existence than are overjoyed at the possibilities of salvation (which is particularly subject to the arbitrary will and grace of God) one can clearly see the point the Buddhist would make as to a God who created such an existence that he would have to account for the misery of existence and therefore would not be a good God. One can argue that 'existence' is intrinsically good, particularly with the possibilities of good. But if we did not exist the whole problem of existence would not have arisen. We like to exist because we do exist. The argument from the intrinsic goodness of existence is always jeopardized by the ever present possibility of death. Therefore the apparently overwhelming value of existence loses much of its worth due to the existence of death which behaves extremely erratically. For the Buddha phenomenal existence was evil, and any other form of existence however exalted, as mere existence was meaningless and superfluous (*v.* 6.75). Therefore, it would be wrong to say that the Buddha rejected phenomenal existence only. One can say that the problem of the justification of existence partly rests with the motives of God that are hidden. But whatever the motives may be, the creation of the whole knotty problem of existence seems to have been created, from a Buddhist point of view, not by a good God.

3.12 Before we leave the problem of evil, we have to look at another form of solution. Karl Barth advocates another extremely mysterious answer to the problem of evil. For Barth the problem of evil is completely negligible from the point of view of the faith in God. Every problem is silenced in terms of the *a priori* axioms and postulates of the doctrine of God. No phenomenal or empirical fact or proposition can stand on a par with the propositions about divine matters. Therefore, any and every empirical proposition that is contrary to divine propositions can be reconciled in any mutilated form, with the existence of God. Propositions about God are logically and therefore necessarily true. ". . . God loves because He loves; because this act is His being, His essence and His nature".[33] The tautologous nature of the propositions is immediately evident. Again, the propositions about God become immune to any empirical criticism or analysis becuse they are necessarily transcendent. "So in the highest and the last degree . . . the concept of God's love surpasses and oversteps the common concept of love that we ourselves can produce and presuppose. . . . In this connection especially, we must beware of an unreflecting inversion and therefore of a definition of the divine love on the basis of a common concept of love."[34] According to that, the love of God cannot have any discernible clear meaning in the human context. Though we cannot understand God's love, Barth thinks that His love can help us to understand human love. ". . . we can truly understand all other life, love and being only in virtue of His creation and therefore as the reflection and echo of His life and love."[35] But Barth, inconsistently enough, tries to make God's 'patience' meaningful with the help of 'love' in the usual sense.[36] Here, he cannot, of course, help contradicting himself when he wants to make his own discourse meaningful. However, according to his central thesis, God's love has no clear meaning in that it can embrace any form of evil, even the worst of evils: "God could be gracious and merciful in such a way that His love would consume His creature."[37] In this way, Barth can and does construct a system of *a priori* propostions of divine attributes. But if *a posteriori* facts have no relevance to those propositions then the idea of God ceases to have any relevance to problems of human existence.

3.13 To come to one last point, when one thinks of the usefulness and significance of the Christian way of justification of evil on the grounds of utility, one can see that it can, if it is strictly interpreted, lead to disastrous results. And it has, for as McCloskey observes, "The theist's argument is seen to imply that war plus courage plus the many other moral virtues war brings into play are better than peace and its virtues; that famine and its moral virtues are better than plenty; that disease and its moral virtues are better than health. Some Christians in the past, in consistency with this mode of reasoning, opposed the use of anesthetics to leave scope for the virtues of endurance and courage, and they opposed state aid to the sick and needy to leave scope for the virtues of charity and sympathy. Some have even contended that war is a good in disguise, again in consistency with this argument."[38] But if evil is accepted as a fundamentally positive fact and cannot in any way be justified, then the destruction of evil, in every form, becomes absolutely necessary. The Buddha's emphasis of this point makes his central preoccupation, the extinction of suffering, in every form (*dukkha nirodha*), very meaningful. The Christian cannot make the idea of the extinction of suffering very meaningful if he accepts the utility theory of suffering because the existence of evil has its own justification. Even on the 'regularity' theory of evil one can put forward an argument to the effect that it is wrong to change the order of regularity established by God, by medical means, etc.

Christianity necessarily demands a justification of evil. But any form of justification of evil carries grave implications which may lead to disastrous consequences.

3.14 Another ground on which the Buddha rejected theism was that if there were an omniscient creator God, then the moral discourse in the world would become impossible and meaningless. He was emphatically criticizing the idea of omniscience because he saw the existence of free will as a fact. The Buddha denied that he was omniscient, and, according to him, any form of omniscience would necessarily involve determinism. He therefore stated that "there is neither a recluse nor a brahamin who at one and the same time can know all, can see all—this situation does not exist".[39] But Flew thinks that foreknowledge does not necessarily involve determinism. ". . .foreknowledge alone is not necessarily incompatible with free will, in an untechnical sense. The fact that we knew a couple would get married does not imply, what is too often the case, that they had to get married. Nor is the possibility of predicting the outcome of some election sufficient by itself to show that that one will not be free. The problem really begins with omnipotence."[40] Flew's idea rests on a mistaken view of foreknowledge, particularly of divine foreknowledge. His mistake is that he does not realize that the foreknowledge of God, or of anyone who claims a superhuman or supernormal form of foreknowledge, is infallible while human foreknowledge is always fallible. When we say that a couple would get married what we mean is that we know of enough present evidence or facts of the type that have usually preceded many marriages. Therefore we conclude that because under similar circumstances many marriages have taken place, the present circumstances may also lead to a marriage. Likewise, usually our knowledge of the future or the predictive capacity is always based on inductive generalizations. We claim them only a high degree of probability. Particularly with regard to that couple getting married, one cannot have any certainty because the possibility of something unexpected happening is always there, e.g., one or both of them might die before marriage or they might out of their free will decide not to marry. In either case, our foreknowledge of their getting married will turn out to be incorrect. But with a person who claims foreknowledge with certainty, such foreknowledge is infallible. Particularly with God such knowledge is true and infallible in an *a priori* and necessary manner. As Nelson Pike says, " 'If a given person is God, that person is omniscient' is an *a priori* truth.''[41]

3.15 The real crux of the problem is exposed when Hawkins explains the nature of God's foreknowledge. ''The real solution is that God does not exist in time at all. His eternity is simultaneous perfection of being which altogether transcends the distinctions of past, present and future. God's point of view is an eternal now which is not our now. To it all times, past, present and future, are equally present. Hence God knows our future free acts simply as present in the now which, from our point of view, is not yet but will be theirs. This offers some difficulty to the imagination, but intellectually it is entirely clear.''[42] In short, God knows the future as we know the present. The future is actualized for God. The future event 'X' exists now for God and therefore he can know it. Hawkins clarifies this idea further when he refers to Aquinas. ''St. Thomas employs in this connection the useful image of a man walking along a road and unaware of those who come after him, whereas someone who is looking down on the road from a height sees the whole succession of travellers at once at their different positions along the road. So we, at our point of time, have some knowledge of what is before us and are, ignorant, except where inference from the present is possible, of what comes after us. God, on the other hand, looks down from his simultaneous eternity on the whole of time.''[43] Here the man on the height sees the whole succession of travellers as existing in the present. Smart says that God ''knows all at once''.[44] If God knows the future 'X' as existing in the present, and if his knowledge is essentially infallible, then the 'X' is bound and necessarily bound to happen and so a strict determinism follows. Nelson Pike explains the matter: ''Last Saturday afternoon, Jones mowed his lawn. Assuming that God exists and is (essentially) omniscient . . . it follows that (let us say) eighty years prior to last Saturday afternoon, God knew (and thus believed) that Jones would mow his lawn at that time. But from this it follows, I think, that at the time of action (last Saturday afternoon) Jones was not *able*—that is, it was not *within Jones's power*—to refrain from mowing his lawn. If at the time of action, Jones had been able to refrain from mowing his lawn, then (the most obvious conclusion would seem to be) at the time of action, Jones was able to do something which would have brought it about that God held a false belief eighty years earlier.''[45]

3.16 The Buddha was strongly against this type of conclusion because he maintained that if it were so, the whole of our discourse would have to be translated in a way that would make the moral discourse essentially meaningless. He illustrates this by taking the example of a religious teacher (of whom the Buddha makes a caricature), who claims foreknowledge. "As to this, Sandaka, some teacher, all-knowing, all-seeing, claims all-embracing knowledge-and-vision, saying: 'Whether I am walking or standing still or asleep or awake, knowledge-and-vision is constantly and perpetually before me.' He enters an empty place, and he does not obtain almsfood, and a dog bites him, and he encounters a fierce elephant, and he encounters a fierce horse, and he encounters a fierce bullock, and he asks a woman and a man their name and clan, and he asks the name of a village or a market or a town and the way. He, being one who asks, 'How was this?' answers, 'I had to enter an empty place, therefore I entered; I had to obtain no almsfood, therefore I obtained none; (someone) had to be bitten by a dog, therefore I was bitten by one; (someone) had to encounter a fierce elephant, horse and bullock, therefore I encountered them; (someone) had to ask a woman and a man their name and clan, therefore I asked; (someone) had to ask the name of a village and market town and the way, therefore I asked."[46] The particular way in which the Buddha clarifies the problem here throws into relief the fact that omniscience implies a universal kind of determinism in every minute detail. For example, as the Buddha clarified it, if I am determined to ask a question from someone then that person is determined to be asked a question by someone. Thus what the Buddha emphasizes is that if anybody accepts the possibility of any kind of super-normal foreknowledge, then no moral discourse would be permitted in his field of discourse. Thus moral discourse could be translated in two ways: from the point of view of mine or from the point of view of the other person or persons in either of which cases the idea of personal responsibility is completely left out of the picture. Thus what the Buddha emphasizes is that if anybody accepts the fact of any kind of super-normal foreknowledge then no moral discourse would be permitted in his field of discourse.

3.17 When one sees the translation of moral discourse as the Buddha clarified it, it is easy to understand how such a translation would leave free will completely out of the picture. But many theologians still insist that foreknowledge can be reconciled with free will. The Roman Catholic Church's official doctrine is that God's foreknowledge covers all human behavior and is not incompatible with man's freedom.[47] Emil Brunner makes the reconciliation, in a very mysterious way, by making God's foreknowledge dependent on man's free will. "God knows that which takes place in freedom in the future as something which happens in freedom."[48] But unfortunately the full implications of this doctrine are very disappointing. We shall look at a more explicit version of this doctrine as put forward by Molina. "It was not that since He foreknew what would happen from those things which depend on the created will that it would happen; but, on the contrary, it was because such things would happen through the freedom of the will, that He foreknew it; and that He would foreknow the opposite if the the opposite was to happen."[49] According to this, divine omniscience becomes completely unfalsifiable and therefore without any sensible significance. And also it becomes a meaningless concept because 'divine foreknowledge' becomes identical in meaning with free will. One cannot also solve the problem by saying, as Gore does, that 'God is not really omniscient' (*v.* 3.4).

3.18 Mark Pontifex tries to solve the problem of God's responsibility by advocating an extremely inconsistent, both logically and morally, theory of responbisility. "A failure to act, being as such merely negative, requires no cause, and can therefore originate in the creature who fails, without our needing to trace it further. . . . In so far as he chooses a positive good his action is caused by God; in so far as he chooses less good than was possible and a course that leads to frustration his action is due to himself alone. Hence God is always the cause of good, but the creature alone is responsible for evil."[50] The inconsistency of the argument is only too apparent, and it is also doubtful whether a Manichean dichotomy, in this sharp form, whould make any sense even within the tradition of Christianity itself. In providing apologies for his theory of responsibility, Pontifex goes on to advance a theory that can have very serious effects on God's omnipotence. "Even though a man can fail without this being due to a lack of causation in the world around him, yet surely his failure must be due to a lack of causation on God's part?

"Here we come to a very important point, and my suggestion is this. Of course the failure must be due to lack of causation on God's part, but this in its turn is due to the creature. The creature is able to exercise a negative priority—logical, and not temporal—over God's causal action upon him, so that God's causality is modified as a result of the creature's failure, and not vice versa. Unless, indeed, we agree to this, there seems no conceivable answer to this objection. Unless the creature can initiate failure, failure must be due to God and then God is responsible for sin. We are saying that God is not God.

"But can we agree to this negative priority on the part of the creature, and still hold that God is the first cause? It seems to me that we can. Whatever happens to the creature, and whatever the creature does, cannot affect God in Himself."[51] Once Pontifex has argued that creature can modify God's causality, he cannot, of course, decree that it cannot affect God.

3.19 One cannot solve this problem except by accepting that omniscience involves determinism. It is a logical implication. *Doctrine in the Church of England* clearly exposes the logical nature of the conclusion. ". . . the whole course of events is under the control of God . . . logically this involves the affirmation that there is no event, and not aspect of any event, even those due to sin and so contrary to the Divine will, which falls outside the scope of his purposive activity."[52] Here one can see the concept of the 'controller of events' as closely accompanying the idea of foreknowledge. Barth emphasizes the identity of the cognitive and conative aspects of God's will. "Everything that God knows He also wills, and everything that He wills He also knows."[53] "It is not that God knows everything because it is, but that it is because He knows it."[54] Even man's self-determination is preceded by and essentially conditioned by God's pre-determination. "Self-determination comes about when God is honoured by the creature in harmony with God's pre-determination instead of in opposition to it."[55] When thus the idea of the creator is related to the idea of foreknowledge, the problem becomes aggravated a thousandfold. If God, in his foreknowledge, creates man, then the whole of man's moral and spiritual progress becomes meaningless, and the ideas of good and bad lose their meaning because nobody is responsible for anything. In fact, during the Buddha's time, there were some theistic recluses and thinkers who, consistently enough, accepted this outcome. But the Buddha criticized them on the grounds that if their thesis was true their whole efforts in recluseship were clearly absurd. He says, "There are recluses and brahmins who hold and teach this view:—Whatsoever weal or woe or neutral feeling is experienced, all that is due to the creation of a Supreme Deity. . . . Then I say to them: 'So then, owing to the creation of a Supreme Deity, men will become murderers, thieves . . . and perverse in view.' Thus, for those who fall back on the creation of a Supreme Deity as the essential reason, there is neither desire to do so, nor effort to do so, nor necessity to do this deed or abstain from that deed. So then, the necessity for action or inaction not being found to exist in truth and verity, the term 'recluse' cannot be reasonably applied to yourselves."[56]

3.20 Further, if the theist's doctrine implies that God creates and designs the world with his foreknowledge, he has to bear the ultimate responsibility for every action done by the creature. So, the Buddha argues, "If God designs the life of the entire world—the glory and the misery, the good and evil acts—man is but an instrument of his will and God (alone) is responsible."[57] It is interesting to note that, here, the Buddha means that the existence of physical evil and good has a bearing upon man's free will. Good and evil physical circumstances, situations and facts, can have a significant influence upon man's free will, and they can condition it to a very great degree. As we explained above, if God designs the world, he is responsible for the existence of physical evil and good. What the Buddha says here is that if that is so, it has a significant bearing on limiting or conditioning man's will and that will, in turn, militate against the existence of free will.

3.21 When one thinks about the grounds on which the Buddha criticized theism, one can see that he was not merely arguing against the existence of God. He had much more in mind. He meant that the idea of an omniscient creator God was essentially harmful for the facts of morality in the world. The ideas of morality and morally responsible beings could not, according to him, at all be made meaningful in a world created by an omniscient creator God. Here it is important to note that the Buddha maintained his argument as equally applying, in a different way, to the theory which holds that 'everything is caused by past deeds (*kamma*)' (This theory is popularly believed to be the Buddha's). He states, "If one experiences happiness and misery as a result of past actions, a person is paying off the debts of his past sin and being a payer off of past debts, is not responsible for his evil actions."[58]

3.22 The other reason is that the ideas of religion and salvation lose their meaning in a theistic universe. When the implications of theism are fully drawn, with the doctrines of predestination and grace etc., the ideas of finding means of salvation and spiritual struggle and therefore the idea of religion as a way of salvation loses all its meaning. The conviction of feeling of divine security could dull man's spiritual sensibilities. The Buddha's arguments against an omniscient and benevolent creator God were directd to point out that theism could be positively harmful to moral and religious ideals.

Chapter Four

GOD AS THE GOOD

4.1 Traditionally, the existence and nature of morality has been an argument for the existence and nature of God, although the situation has undergone some remarkable changes in recent times. However, even today many thinkers believe in the moral argument, in its traditional sense, for the existence of God. The important change in recent times has been that some contemporary theologians and philosophers of religion do not attach the same nature and status to morality as the traditionalists did. For them morality does not prove the existence of God, or may not even suggest, as e.g., the cosmological argument may tend to do, the existence of any such Being, but the idea of God and its implications can reinforce the claims of morality thus adding a new dimension or depth to morals. The most remarkable change has been the claims of some thinkers that Christian theology can be completely translated without any residue into moralitiy. Nevertheless the translation is effected necessarily within the Christian context.

4.2 These positions can be interestingly compared with Buddhism which maintains that morality can be made completely meaningful from the point of view of humanistic ideals which are regarded as logically leading to the goal of salvation.

4.3 The traditionalists' arguments take various forms. One of the standard formulations of the traditionalist position is that of

H.P. Owen. Unfortunately, he does not develop his main argument or arguments very consistently, and so in his book *The Moral Argument for Christian Theism*, many types of formulations of the moral argument have been attempted, but with very little concern for consistency. One of the central points of his argument or arguments is the objectivity of morals. In developing this point, the logical connections between his arguments become obscure. To comment in advance, it is noteworthy that the inconsistencies he commits in his theory also point to the difficulties one encounters in advocating an objectivity theory of morals.

4.4 He starts with an account of the transcendent objectivity of values. "When we speak of values possessing 'objectivity' we can mean that they exist in an absolute form outside the world of sense-experience. 'Objective' in this sense signifies 'independent'. Values exist (or subsist) independently of their instances in a purely spiritual realm. Plato thought of them as existing 'on their own', without any further ground. The Christian interprets them as attributes of God."[1] Sometimes he speaks of this objectivity as normative objectivity, in which case it would not be a descriptive objectivity. "Sometimes we use the word 'objective' in the sense of 'universal'. An objective standard, ideal, or norm is one which everyone does, or ought to, recognize. So it could be held that kindness and loyalty are 'objective' in the sense of being ideals of conduct at which all persons ought to aim. This view of ethical objectivity implies that all men have (potentially if not actually) a common moral nature."[2] But he immediately changes his view rather drastically when he says that ethical objectivity is very much the same as empirical objectivity. "When we apply a moral attribute we may do so either objectively or subjectively. If we do so objectively we mean that the attribute inheres objectively in the person, act, or state of affairs to which it is applied. 'Goodness' or 'rightness' belongs to X as objectively as X's physical properties belong to it."[3] Though he says here that 'goodness' is very similar to physical properties, he goes beyond a Moorean standpoint when he speaks of a fundamental difference between the two. "Goodness, I submit, is neither a simple property distinct from the qualities that act as its criteria; nor does it refer merely to a pro-attitude that these qualities evoke; it exists in and through the latter which are its modes of operation".[4]

4.5 To start with, the idea of objectivity is not clear. In the further developments of his theory Owen makes the situation still more obscure. One of the obvious forms of objections to an objectivity theory of morals would be an argument from anthropological findings of the diversity of moral standards. Owen, in answering the question, "since different social groups acknowledge different moral norms how do we know which norms are in fact objective?, says, "The only answer . . . is that we 'know' by intuition. The final principles of morality, like those of metaphysics, are self-authenticating or self-evident."[5] Here he is talking of another kind of objectivity. According to this sense, in a social group moral norms need not be objective, yet we can say that they are. The objective manifestation is not necessary or is irrelevant to the objectivity of moral values. Here, 'objectivity' becomes very mysterious and therefore he posits the analogously mysterious way of knowing it: intuition.

4.6 Another problem arises from the discussion of the notions of self-authenticity and self-evidence. These terms cannot retain the meaning normally attached to them because their self-evidence and self-authenticity cannot withstand the problems raised by the existence of contrary standards of moral values. Therefore, Owen's ideas of self-evidence and self-authenticity remain very ambiguous. However, he goes on to say, still further confusing the situation, "Yet morality is not self-sufficient. Moral facts are not in the last resort self-authenticating; they require religious justification."[6] Here he is making a distinction between self-sufficiency and ultimate self-evidence and between self-authenticity and ultimate self-authenticity. Notwithstanding the fact that these distinctions are superfluous, to speak of further justification for self-authenticating and self-evident values is plainly redundant. Sometimes, he goes on to speak of 'explanation' instead of justification and it seems that he does not want to distinguish the two from each other. "Morality is autonomous in so far as we recognize the meaning and validity of the right and the good without recourse to the idea of God; but the autonomy is derived in so far as moral claims and values cannot be explained until they are seen in the light of the divine origin".[7] To speak of explaining self-evident truths would amount to explaining self-explaining truths.

4.7 He then goes on to say that he is introducing theological concepts not as a justification but as an additional factor that can be seen in the moral realm. It is like seeing design in order. Thus we are immediately aware of moral claims and values as facts existing 'in their own right'. They have their own distinctive meaning and validity. It needs additional perception to see in them the imprints of the God from whom they are derived. The task of the philosopher is to prompt this perception by pointing to those aspects of morality that demand a religious explanation. His aim is to show that what is first in the order of knowing is second in the order of being.

"There is, as Ewing observes, a parallel to this procedure in the argument from design. The behavior of organisms appears at first sight to be self-explanatory. When the biologist gives further 'explanations' he does so in terms of finite causes. But the theologian points to aspects of organic activity that demand the postulation of a divine Intelligence as their Final Cause."[8] If this argument is correct then it will only suggest theological concepts rather that presuppose them. Further to suggest 'design' in morality is as difficult as to suggest design in the physical realm because one feels the enormity of the problem, especially when one thinks of the great variety of moral standards and values prevalent in various types of human societies that have been found through the researches in this field by anthropological sciences. The objectivity theory is open to another significant objection. One can safely argue that such a theory does logically lead to the objectivity of immoral concepts. Here, the standard solution is to say that immoral concepts are, in fact, moral concepts with privations. But the analogous objectivity of immoral 'values' and their independent strength and the powerful force of attraction might be strong points against the privation theory. The Zoroastrians were consistent enough to posit two objective standards, moral and immoral, though this view has its own problems.

4.8 However, it should be noted that moral objectivity as such need not necessarily carry any theological implications. The earliest strata in Vedic philosophy contain a belief in the existence and complete supremacy of an objectively existent Moral Law (*Ṛta*). Even the gods were supposed to have been born from it (*Ṛta-jāta*). Only later did it start to attract theological conceptions when it was said that the god *Varuṇa* was the guardian of it (*Ṛtasyagopā*).

4.9 But, in Christianity, the moral objectivity is essentially related to strong theological implications. Christianity would grant the Vedic objectivity of morality but would deny its full validity on the grounds of it being not 'justified' by theological conceptions. It is in this sense that the argument from the objectivity of moral standards and values, though not much favored by some contemporary theologians and philosophers, still dangerously threatens non-theistic moral systems. It does so in two ways. One way is to say that non-theistic moral systems are not really moral or do not contain proper moral values because they are not grounded on necessary theological concepts. But this way would be difficult because non-theistic morality is nevertheless supposed to be moral. Hence the need for a second way of attacking it. This way is to say that non-theistic morality, in so far as it is morality, is really crypto-theistic morality. John Baillie maintained that atheists who acknowledge the existence of unconditional obligation possess 'unconscious faith' and they confess God 'in the bottom of their hearts' though they deny him with 'the top of their minds'.[9] Maritain asserts that 'the good pagan' is a 'pseudo-atheist' who unconsciously 'knows' without 'recognizing' God.[10]

4.10 It is in the light of the objectivity of morals and the allegations of being crypto-theistic that Buddhist ethics can be an easy target for Christian criticisms. Buddhism, though it is a religion of salvation, denies any transcendent ethical values or any independent ethical objectivity. Without going into all the details, we shall try to give a very summary account of Buddhist ethics and look at it in the light of the charges that could be made by the Christian moralist. This will facilitate our task of examining Christian ethics from a Buddhist point of view.

4.11 The Buddha accepted a utilitarian system of ethics. It was an 'act' utilitarianism as opposed to 'rule' utilitarianism, and it was also an ideal utilitarianism rather than a hedonistic, because the ultimate end of ethical endeavor went beyond the pleasure-pain principle. It is significant to note that Nirvana as the ideal of salvation, is very often characterized by negative ethical predications. The three fundamental (negative) ethical features of Nirvana are "absence of greed, absence of malice and absence of ignorance". Accordingly, the actions, mental and bodily, are termed 'good' and moral only in so far as they tend to go towards attaining this ideal.

Another significant aspect to be noted in Buddhist ethics is that the term for 'good' and 'moral' is '*Kusala*' which means 'efficient, able, capable', therefore any action that is capable of attaining the spiritual ideal will become good. Consequently any action that leads one away from the ideal will become a 'bad' or an 'immoral' action. In ethical discourse two factors assume fundamental importance. One is the 'end' in terms of which the action is done. The spiritual end can, and does, justify the means. The other factor, the intention (or motive) with which the action is done, is of predominant importance, particularly in terms of responsibility. The Buddha was very clear on this point. "Bhikkus, I call the intention to be the (good or bad) deed."[11] This does not mean that the nature and effects of actions can be disregarded. In the Buddha's teachings, the word '*Cetanā*' is a very complex term that covers both that which is technically distinguished, e.g., by Sidgwick, as 'intention' and 'motive' and the action as a consequence of the motive (or intention). With regard to actions that are bad though the end-motive is good, e.g., stealing money to give for charity, the Buddha would regard them as proceeding from two 'motives' and consequently as two actions.

4.12 Now, good and bad actions are defined in terms of Nirvana, the attainment of which also constitutes the 'summation' of all ethical values. Ethical values, with other intellectual values, generically effect Nirvana (*v.* 4.44). In that sense, Nirvana is the direct generic consequence of good actions. In Buddhism, merits are good consequences in the sense of *Kusala*. The Buddha defines good accordingly: "There are three roots of merit. What three? Absence of greed, absence of malice, absence of delusion is a root of merit. Whatever the absence of greed, that is merit. Whatever the non-greedy one performs with body, speech and thought, that is merit. What the non-greedy one, not overwhelmed by greed, whose mind is controlled, does not do to another by unjustly causing him suffering through punishment, loss of wealth, abuse, banishment, on the grounds that 'might is right'—that also is merit. Thus these good, meritorious conditions born of non-greed, conjoined with non-greed, arising from non-greed, resulting from non-greed, are assembled together in him."[12]

4.13 In contemporary terminology, Buddhism preaches a prescriptive theory of ethics. A Buddhist ethical proposition can be analyzed into two parts as a factual component and a value component. The factual component is extremely important because the Buddha strongly believed that 'ought' did not imply 'can'. This was because of his central thesis that any judgment, value or otherwise, should be based on a theory of facts as they are (*yathābhūta*). In that sense, the theory of reality logically precedes the theory of morality. As an example, a Buddhist ethical proposition can be analysed as follows: "Everybody dislikes punishment or harming, and everybody is afraid of death"—(The factual component) and therefore, "Taking oneself as an example, one should not harm and kill others"—(The value component).[13] When the Buddha speaks of specific ethical rules or regulations he makes the prescriptive component more explicit. One of the rules he formulated for monks was that they should not eat any solid food after midday until the following morning. This was made meaningful in regard to the end in view, namely that it will be conducive to a light physique which will in turn facilitate a good medium for meditation, the immediate aim of monkhood. But the Buddha also said that if one cannot have a light and a comfortable physique due to some form of illness, etc., then even after midday one should take nutritious and concentrated light food like ghee, but not bulky food. In this way, all Buddhist ethical rules gain their value and validity in terms of the ultimate spiritual ideal. Every ethical rule is a prescription to achieve or approximate that ideal. It is significant to note that in Buddhist literature, the Buddha is very often referred to as a 'physician'.

4.14 Therefore, the Buddhist theory of ethics maintains that morality is always hypothetical, for if the reality or the circumstances were to change, the ethical values would necessarily change, too. So, Buddhism becomes strongly opposed to any theory of objective values. Here, one can object that if that is so, then Buddhist ethics will lead to an extremely egoistic as opposed to an altruistic position. However, it should be emphasized that the Buddha does not make this pseudo-distinction between altruism and egoism, and we shall shortly see why. The illusion of objective values arises mainly due to a wrong conception of values. Very often we act non-egoistically with no discernible benefit for ourselves in view. Then we tend to think that we are trying to conform to some objectively existing intrinsic values. The Buddha, however, shows in two ways how these other-regarding values originate in terms of the origin of society. He accepts a social contract theory. Once the Buddha explained to Vasettha the origin of social morality in terms of a mythical story of the origin of society. The Buddha explains how the people in their earliest phase of society lived happily together. But as time went on the situation started to change. They had to divide plots of land between them so that the private ownership of property appeared. Then the Buddha goes on to explain, "Now some being, Vasettha, of greedy disposition, watching over his own plot, stole another plot and made use of it. They took him and holding him fast, said: Truly, good being, thou hast wrought evil in that, while watching thine own plot, thou hast stolen another plot and made use of it. See, good being, that thou do not such a thing again! Ay, sirs, he replied. And a second time he did so. And yet a third. And again they took him and admonished him. Some smote him with the hand, some with clods, some with sticks. With such beginning, Vasettha, did stealing appear, and censure and lying and punishment become known.

"Now those beings, Vasettha, gathered themselves together, and bewailed these things, saying: From our evil deeds, sirs, becoming manifest, inasmuch as stealing, censure, lying, punishment have become known, what if we were to select a certain being, who should be wrathful when indignation is right, who should censure that which should rightly be censured and should banish him who deserves to be banished? But we will give him in return a proportion of the rice.

"Then, Vahettha, those beings went to the being among them who was the handsomest, the best favoured, the most attractive, the most capable, and said to him: Come now, good being, be indignant at that whereat one should rightly be indignant, censure that which should rightly be censured, banish him who deserves to be banished. And we will contribute to thee a proportion of our rice.

"And he consented and did so, and they gave him a proportion of their rice.

"Chosen by the people, Vasettha, is what is meant by Maha Sammata . . . (The Great Elect)".[14] Here, for their mutual benefit people start to respect one another. The ethical principles they respect may seem to somebody as possessing some value of their own. But in fact, they have any value only in so far as they cater for people's needs. So they derive their value from people.

4.15 How do people get their value? Here the Buddha clarifies the second way of the origin of other-regarding values. In the *Anumāna Sutta*, he states that the basis of the other-regarding principle is an inference from oneself to another. The inference works in two ways. The first way is thinking of oneself in terms of others. According to the Buddha, the sense of the value of oneself or of one's own personality is derived from others. Therefore, 'personality' itself being a value concept, if one is to become a 'person' in the proper sense it has to be necessarily done in a social medium. For that one should be considerate of the value of others. Man's personality is largely a product and an item of the society around him. One becomes good or derives any value to one's personality only through the society. That is why one has to consider and respect others. One does not become oneself without the help of the others. Here the so-called distinction between altruism and egoism breaks down. The Buddha states his inferential principle: "Therein, your reverences, self ought to be measured against self thus by a monk: 'That person who is of evil desires and who is in the thrall of evil desires, that person is displeasing and disagreeable to me; and similarly, if I were of evil desires and in the thrall of evil desires, I would be displeasing and disagreeable to others'."[15] The dichotomy between egoism and altruism breaks down again when he repeatedly emphasizes the necessity of other-regarding virtues for one's development as a person, not only on a social level, but even on the spiritual level where progress is impossible without cultivating the other-regarding virtues. Referring to a prerequisite for meditation it is stated, "He dwells, having suffused the first quarter with a mind of friendliness, likewise the second, likewise the third, likewise the fourth; just so above, below, across; he dwells having suffused the whole world everywhere, in every way, with a mind of friendliness that is far-reaching, widespread, immeasurable, without enmity, without malevolence. He dwells having suffused the first quarter with a mind of compassion . . . sympathetic joy . . . equanimity . . . that is far-reaching, widespread, immeasurable, without enmity, without malevolence."[16] The Buddha preached that one's attitude towards other living beings should be similar to a mother's attitude towards her one and only child: "Just as a mother looks after her one and only child as her own life, one should look after all the living beings with an unlimited compassion."[17] A mother's love for her child is neither egoistic nor altruistic.

4.16 The second way of inference is considering others in terms of oneself. "For a state that is not pleasant or delightful to me must be so to him also: and a state that is not pleasing or delightful to me—how could I inflict that upon another? As a result of such reflection he himself abstains from taking life or creatures and he encourages others so to abstain, and speaks in praise of so abstaining. Thus as regards bodily conduct he is utterly pure."[18] (The Buddha goes on to elaborate that one should think similarly with regard to other moral principles too). Here he is suggesting the intrinsic value of other persons. And he proves the intrinsic value of other persons, in the only way that is possible to do it, namely, through empathy or sympathetic feelings. It is only an ethical justification and it seems to be the only way of justifying the so-called altruistic feelings.

4.17 One of the main arguments for the objectivity theory of values stems from this intrinsic value of persons. To make this argument the objectivists make a big leap from ethical justification to a completely different type of justification: logical justification, in the sense that it is absolutely final and necessarily justified because the value of the person is related to the source of ultimate and perfectly intrinsic values, namely God. So, this shows another aspect of the Christian search for logically necessary answers to empirical problems. Owen states this view: "We must therefore interpret the relation between human persons and the moral Absolute in terms of Christian theism. Their worth consists in the fact that they are created, loved and destined for eternal life by God. The value we attach to them is the value bestowed on them by God; so that, in A.M. Farrer's words, 'what claims our regard is not simply our neighbor, but God in our neighbor and our neighbor in God'. Human beings are 'sacred' because they are subject to the operations of God's holy will."[19] If one succeeds in proving the existence of logically necessary intrinsic values, then the next step is the objectivity theory.

4.18 Emil Brunner says that without a theological context one cannot see the intrinsic value of a person. Referring to a person who accepts a non-theistic morality, Brunner says that it "hinders him from seeing the other person as he really is, and prevents him from hearing the real claim which his neighbour makes on him."[20] Austin Farrer says that "the personal claim which meets him on every hand is exerted not simply by men, but by God''.[21] But the problem is that when a person makes a claim he makes it as a person. Therefore it is on this level that the claim must be accepted and respected. One can adopt a theistic perspective, but if we ask why one should adopt this perspective at all, the answer will be, as we shall see later, that to do so is morally effective. This, however, is a pragmatic justification, in which case we have to start from proving the intrinsic value of persons from a non-theological perspective. So we are back at the same problem. The Buddha tried to do this in the only possible way to do it, i.e., by appealing to the principles of empathy, sympathy or generalized benevolence.

4.19 Another intriguing factor for the objectivists has been the sense of obligatoriness exercised by 'good'. Owen says, ''when we consider the ideal of goodness under its obligatory aspect we are compelled to regard it as existing independently''.[22] We saw above as to how the ideas to do good and to be good mainly comes from society. Similarly, in man's higher stages of ethical development, the sense of obligatoriness comes not only from social standards but also from his own spiritual requirements. The Buddha clarifies: ''Monks, if a monk should wish: 'By the destruction of the cankers, having realised by my own super-knowledge here and now the freedom of my mind, and freedom through wisdom that are cankerless, entering thereon, may I abide therein', he should be one who fulfills the moral habits, who is intent on mental tranquility within, who does not interpret (his) meditation, who is endowed with vision, a cultivator of empty places. That of which I have spoken thus was spoken in relation to this: Fare along, monks, possessed of moral habit, possessed of the Obligations, fare along controlled by the control of the Obligations, possessed of right conduct and resort, seeing danger in the slightest faults; undertaking them rightly, train yourselves in the rules of training.''[23] Therefore, the Buddha would say that the sense of obligatoriness of the 'good' is perfectly accountable and comprehensible in its social and spiritual context and hence to posit the independence of 'good' would not only be unnecessary and superfluous but also it will pervert or misinterpret the sense of the good by taking it away from its contexts in terms of which alone it gets its meaning and significance.

4.20 The objectivity theory in Christian ethics is a search for the absolutely intrinsic justification of values in the sense of a logical justification. This can be very easily related to theological concepts. That is why W.R. Sorley emphasizes the necessity of an 'eternally valid' moral order and then thinks that the moral law should be in an eternal mind.[24] But the methodological principles behind the objective theory are even theoretically impermissible because here again is the confusion made between the empirical justification and logical justification. One can never find objective value schemes because value systems are always contingent. As the Buddha explained, social morality is necessarily related to ultimate social utility. Social and individual utility decides and makes moral values. Spiritual utility decides what other moral values are necessary for spiritual progress. In fact, this is the only way one can explain the variety of moral standards operative in various societies, primitive and modern. What may seem bad to us is good for them, yet from the point of view of their system of needs and values all their 'good' actions get full justification within that system. To take an example, in many primitive societies the idea of free moral choice is absent, morality being largely coercive. But this framework is justified in terms of the need for social survival. Without an integrated and regimented form of group behavior their survival would be at stake. Here the objectivist can argue from the fact of moral progress. For example, freedom in moral choice is better than a coercive morality and therefore he can point to a moral progress here. This way of arguing is unsatisfactory for two reasons. One is that we are trying to judge their system of values in terms of ours. The other is that 'free' morality is better not in their society but only in our society. In our society the whole system of needs essentially differs. If our society gets the system of needs of a primitive society then we too will need a coercive morality. In fact, something very similar to this happens in times of war. Some primitive tribes are in a perpetual state of war against other tribes or nature, which justifies a coercive morality. Those practices illustrate the idea that morality is based on social and individual needs. Certain moral values, though they seem to differ among societies may agree fundamentally with each other. To take an example, in some nomadic tribes killing old and invalid people is supposed to be good. Here the intrinsic value of the old person is challenged. But killing is recognized as good, and justified on the ground that invalid old age is a suffering to the individual as well as to the community. At this point one can say that living even with suffering is always better than dying and therefore such killing is bad. But the argument becomes suspect when one considers that even in modern societies an attempt is made to justify euthanasia. The nomadic tribes and modern societies have one factor in common: their inability to alleviate certain forms of suffering. The nomadic tribes appeal to this fact to justify their killing and members of the modern society appeal to the same fact to justify euthanasia.

4.21 However, from this type of agreement on moral values, it would be meaningless to deduce any objectivity theory because all it proves is the existence of the 'instinct' of self-preservation. Of course, it is a truism to say that due to the common biological features of men they tend to have a basic set of common values, again based on common needs. But to argue from this to an objective theory would mean nothing, for, as Strawson states, "some claim on human succour, some obligation to abstain from the infliction of physical injury, seem to be necessary features of almost any system of moral demands. Here at least we have types of moral behavior which are demanded *of* men as men because they are demanded *for* and *by* men as men."[25] It is also dangerous to appeal to abstract notions like 'justice' as shared by all human societies because what is meant by the term in different societies varies from society to society. For example, tooth for tooth is not justice to us, but for some it is. Abstract notions can be untrustworthy pointers to an objective theory.

4.22 What the above shows is the contingency of moral values, and so it is meaningless to argue about an objective value scheme, or logically necessary values or of any values proceeding from a source of intrinsic values. And we tried to show that one of the sources of this erroneous conception was a confusion made between ethical and logical justification. Once the move to an objective and necesssary value scheme has been made, it starts reinforcing the idea of the necessity of logical justifications in all aspects of manifestation of values. For example, for a complete justification of the intrinsic value of persons the objectivists proclaim objectively necessary values which will in turn start rejecting, normatively, various other forms of values unless the latter conform to or embrace the objectivity theory. So a vicious circle starts. In other words, the objectivity theory can very easily become an axiom or a presupposition of morality. Once the contingency of values is understood, the circle breaks down.

4.23 Another aspect of Christian morality is the theory that moral precepts and values are God's commands. Morality has value because its principles are God's commands. While some advocate this theory in an extreme form others do not go so far. Patterson-Brown advocates the extreme position when he says that "For Christians . . . to be moral *is* to adhere to the will of God. Things, actions, persons and so on are good and evil, right or wrong, according to whether God approbates or condemns them; this is the logic of Christian morality. If God exists, then the good is denoted by what he esteems, and the evil by what he damns."[26] There is absolutely no need to verify them independently as good because they are by definition good. Indeed it would be positively wrong to do so. Patterson-Brown goes on to say, "I maintain that one of the prerequisites for being a Jew or Christian is that one accepts God's decrees as taking moral precedence over whatever conflicting considerations. So that 'God is perfectly good' serves for such persons, not as a moral judgment made in the light of some ulterior standard, nor yet as a definition of terms, but rather as itself the ultimate moral criterion—just as the metal bar in Paris is not judged to be a metre long by comparison to some further rod, nor by verbal definition, but rather itself constitutes the standard whereby all lengths are to be measured."[27] The criticism has been made by A.C. Ewing when he said that if 'being obligatory' means just 'willed by God', it becomes unintelligible to ask why God wills one thing rather than another and if one starts adducing reasons then one would be making judgments about the good, independent of the will of God.[28] Here two initial criticisms can be made from the Buddhist point of view. One would be that if people act according to commands only, then they cannot be responsible and free moral agents because their commitment to the moral principle was completely irrational. One cannot give reasons for one's choice and there cannot be, therefore, any intellectual and moral discernment in the situation. Hence it would not be a moral action in the usual sense of the term. The other criticism is that even if it is called morality, it would be a superfluous morality because the so-called moral actions cannot be made meaningful in terms of an immediate or mediate end which is directly related to the moral action (*v.* 4.42). Therefore morality again loses its meaning because it can never be made contextually meaningful. However, Patterson-Brown's main thesis is that one has to make a commitment to theism in a moral vacuum. If that is so, then it would be the height of irrationality. As Keith Campbell points out, to make a commitment to theism in itself involves or requires a moral evaluation. So, to start with, the commitment to the word of God cannot take place in a moral or evaluational vacuum.[29]

4.24 There are two insurmountable problems involved in this idea of God's commands. One is to decide which are actually God's commands. The easiest way is to appeal to tradition via the Bible. But here, in the Biblical tradition, there are various conceptions and disagreements among differing strands of the tradition. It can become difficult to decide the correct tradition. The problem becomes really acute because the application of independent criteria becomes even theoretically impossible. The second difficulty is what the tradition or what God commands may be either socially beneficial or socially harmful, i.e., as a matter of fact, either right or wrong, in a particular social situation, e.g., the commands about birth control. Therefore, the tradition can be either badly or well remembered or can be either right or wrong. Here the Buddha makes a criticism which is very relevant to this context, though he makes it particularly with regard to epistemological problems. He addresses Sandaka: "Sandaka, some teacher here depends on report, holds to report for his 'truths', he teaches *dhamma* according to report, according to hearsay and tradition, according to the authority of the collections. If a teacher, Sandaka, depends on report, holds to report for his 'truths', he remembers (part) well and he remembers (part) badly, and is both right and wrong"[30] (*v.* 8.20). Here, one of the basic objections of the Buddha is as to how to determine which are the commands of God. The other objection is the problem of criteria. What the Buddha emphasized was that the criteria of objective truth are necessarily prior to accepting any kind of tradition or teaching. Kai Nielsen emphasizes the same point when he says that morality is prior to religion. "Only if we independently knew what we would count as 'good', 'righteous', 'just', etc., would we be in a position to know whether this Being is good or whether his commands ought to be obeyed."[31] And he concludes that "A moral understanding must be logically prior to any religious assent."[32]

4.25 Ewing has proposed a solution to this dilemma. He says that unless we assume that God is morally perfect, unless we assume the perfect goodness of God, there can be no necessary "relation between being commanded or willed by God and being obligatory or good".[33] Here, there should be, at least, some way of making the idea of goodness of God meaningful, or otherwise the 'goodness of God' would be a completely meaningless concept. One can say with certainty that if God commanded a mass slaughter or if all his commands involved killing and harming people, then a God who commanded such principles would be really bad. One of the reasons why we call an existing morality good is that it leads to a happy and harmonious social and spiritual life. One may say that moral principles are good because God is good. It makes sense to us because we can understand the meaning of 'good' in terms of its beneficial effects. If there is no way of making the idea of good meaningful in the human context, then the word loses its meaning completely.

4.26 So, if we try to look at God's actions and commands as they manifest themselves in the human context we encounter certain very interesting problems. It is true that the morality as operative in society is good, and agreeing to act accordingly leads to beneficial results. Therefore, to take and analyze a normal moral principle as a command of God would be begging the question. So we shall try to look at some of the problems the good-God theory has to face. We can make three main objections. One is, as we discussed earlier, that the Buddha maintained from the fact of the existence of evil that a God who created such evil cannot be good. If evil is a fact and not an illusion then it, obviously, threatens the idea of a good God. One way out of this problem is to go back again to the will and commands of God. Patterson-Brown tried this way when he defined good and evil in terms of the commands and will of God. However, this is only a redefinition of terms and therefore does not make any difference to the problem involved. Suffering and all kinds of evil as we know, do exist in the world and, as we explained before, the problem is that their existence is not morally justified. If human evil can be good from God's point of view, then that will exactly be the objection the problem of evil holds against the existence of a good God. What all this suggests is that if we take God's actions as a criterion for determining his goodness we have to face some very awkward problems.

4.27 Now we can turn to the Christian tradition and make a second objection. This tradition speaks of various actions of God. Aquinas says that "in order that the happiness of the saints may be more delightful to them and that they may render more copious thanks to God, for they are allowed to see perfectly the sufferings of the damned . . . the Divine Justice and their own deliverance will be the direct cause of the joy of the blessed, while the pains of the damned will cause it indirectly . . . the blessed in glory will have no pity for the damned."[34] Also Luther: "This the acme of faith, to believe that He is merciful . . . that He is just who at His own pleasure has made us necessarily doomed to damnation, so that, as Erasmus says, he seems to delight in the tortures of the wretched, and to be more deserving of hatred than love. If by any effort of reason I could conceive how God could be merciful and just who shows so much anger and iniquity, there would be no need for fatih."[35] These opinions make it very difficult to see how, for example, the moral principles of kindness and pity can be ultimately based on the will of God.

4.28 The third objection can be made from God's commands. For instance, when God commanded Abraham to sacrifice Issac, God was contravening ordinary morality. It was, of course, only a test. But the intention God generated in Abraham was bad even as a test, from the point of view of human morality. If Abraham had decided to sacrifice his salvation for the sake of his son's life and had decided not to kill Isaac what would the situation have been? From the human point of view, Abraham's intention would have been a noble one, but not from the point of view of God. From this point on, the answers to this question will revolve round a God-centered morality. Kierkegaard drew the full implications of this situation by saying that the religious sphere transcends the moral sphere, so that it can follow that the demands made in the religious sphere may seem immoral from the point of view of the moral sphere, though not always. What Patterson-Brown is trying to do is in fact to justify the existence of evil in the moral sphere from the point of view of the religious sphere. The justification is effected by confusing the two standpoints. This evident when he says, "If God causes or allows to exist things which are evil, i.e., which he himself condemns, then it is good for him to do so—or else he would not be God. Whatever God does is good, and this includes his creating things which he censures."[36] On the other hand, another solution would be to dub the will of God as mysterious and to say that the ways of thinking of God are incomprehensible to humans. But this would be to follow an ethical ideal which is a mystery, from which nothing sensible follows.

4.29 Now, the important thing to emphasize is that from divine morality no secular morality can be derived. If suffering without a moral justification is good from the point of view of God, then to inflict such suffering on human beings would be good in the human context. According to the traditional view of God and the saints, the enjoyment of other people's suffering would be good if we were to emulate the action of God and the saints. To take his commands, sacrificing one's own salvation for the sake of another's life would not be good in a Christian context. What all these examples clarify is that to follow and emulate God would not be necessarily moral or would be, sometimes, grievously immoral. God's will, therefore, cannot be a consistently good guide to morality. In other words, following God's will will, sometimes, have socially damaging and harmful results. Another point can be mentioned at this juncture and that is if suffering and killing are said to be good from a divine point of view then the meaning of the world 'morality' completely loses its meaning, because the whole of our morality is based on the principle that harming and killing others is immoral. Therefore if one is trying to base morality on God's will, in its full implications, such a morality cannot become consistently good. If God's morality is distinguished from secular morality then, again, one cannot base the latter on the former. On all these grounds, God's will cannot be either the *criterion* or the *nature* of morality. If 'morality' is defined in terms of God's will then the word 'morality' loses its meaning because there cannot be any discernible coherent criteria for moral and immoral actions.

4.30 There is another aspect to the command theory. Bonhoeffer states it when he says that the idea of commands is basically necessary for morals. Otherwise it cannot be proper morality. He says that the summit of authority is God, whose "commandment is the only warrant for ethical discourse".[37] "In ethical discourse what matters is not only that the contents of the assertion should be correct, but also that there should be a concrete warrant, an authorization of this assertion. It is not only what is said that matters, but also the man who says."[38] This situation has been clearly analyzed by Nowell-Smith when he says that because the Christian ethics emphasizes the necessity of commands, it is an infantile morality. Referring to Piaget's findings about the attitude towards the rules of games, of children from five to nine years old, Nowell-Smith says, "During this stage, says Piaget, 'the rules are regarded as sacred and inviolable, emanating from adults and lasting for ever. Every suggested alteration in the rules strikes the child as a transgression.' "[39] The other problem is that if Bonhoeffer's theory is valid, then the distinction between commands and morality gets blurred. Usually, obeying commands absolves one from one's responsibility for one's actions. Therefore Bonhoeffer's theory becomes inconsistent with a sensible theory of moral responsibility. The command theory can be expressed in yet another way. Crombie appeals to a necessary relation between God's will and morality on the ground that for moral rules to be fully valid, they should be universally valid, which only God can know. He says that God commands universal obedience to action-rules because they happen to be morally expedient. But, it should not be said that God commands it because it is independently right. "For to say that something is independently right might seem to mean that we can see it to be right out of our own resources. But it is difficult to see how we could ever come to be sure that in the case of some definite action-rule universal obedience to it is the only right answer. Our judgment has suggested that a man might, not unreasonably, decide to uphold some definite action-rule universally, but it has not even tended to suggest that he could *know* that he was right to do so, in the sense that it would be wrong to do otherwise. At this point we can no doubt appeal to the divine omniscience and say that, what man cannot know, God can, namely that in the case of the action-rule in question, universal obedience to it is in fact morally the best course in that it does most to promote those things which we ought to try to promote. (Therefore) the definite action-rules, which, *ex-hypothesis*, we are required to conform to universally, are not arbitrary. . ."[40] This is really a camouflaged version of the objectivity theory because it appeals to God's knowledge and will to establish the universality of moral rules. However, the Kantian myth of the universalisability of moral principles is not a necessary feature of moral principles. As we tried to explain above, moral principles are always contextual. This type of contingency precludes the possibility of a sensible universality. Contextual universalisability is, of course, a possibility. But this proves, again, only a contingency of moral principles. Also, one can appeal to abstract notions like Justice as the evidence for universality. But from this, as Strawson says, nothing meaninful follows: "What is universally demanded of the members of a moral community is something like the abstract virtue of justice; a man should not insist on a particular claim while refusing to acknowledge any reciprocal claim. But from this formally universal feature of morality no consequences follow as to the universality of application of the particular rules in the observance of which, in particular situations and societies, justice consists."[41]

4.31 Another reason for maintaining the relationship between morality and God is the argument from the existence of conscience. Paul Lehmann calls conscience a "theonomous conscience".[42] Referring to moral awareness in a theological context, H.D. Lewis states, "There is thus a very important sense in which the voice of God is to be heard especially in our moral awareness . . ."[43] According to A.E. Taylor, the witness of conscience to the active reality of the living God is the evidence of *fact*. It converts belief in God from a mere 'theistic hypothesis' into the faith which is the *evidence* of things not seen.[44] However, the theory of conscience shares many problems with the objectivity theory of morality, because conscience is the subjective manifestation of an objective moral principle. As in the case of the objectivity theory, the varying natures of differing consciences in varying cultures is the best refutation of the existence of a common conscience. If one does not accept that there is anything common in conscience, then the conscience-theory ceases to have any significant value and sense. If the psychological authoritativeness is supposed to suggest anything in favor of the conscience theory then it will be easily explicable in terms of psychological facts. Here, Freud's theory of super-ego as a product of parental and socio-cultural environments makes a meaningful case against the theory of the relationship between the individual conscience and God.

4.32 The Buddha was very concerned about the problem of conscience, but he maintained that conscience can be a bad guide to action, and so he emphasized that though the conscience should be consulted, that was not enough. According to him one should consult three things before one decides on an action. One is conscience (*attādhipateyya*), but it should have two checks. Therefore, the second is the opinion of the world (*lokādhipateyya*) and the third is the Buddha's teachings, moral and factual (*dhammādhipateyya*). If one does not pay attention to these three things, the Buddha said, one will have to suffer in three ways as the direct consequences of the actions done. So, if one does bad actions, he maintained, "the self upbraids the self therefor. On seeing it the wise blame him. An ill report of him goes abroad. He dies with wits bewildered. When body breaks up after death he is reborn in the Waste, the Way of the Woe, in the Downfall, in Purgatory."[45] Buddhaghosa clarifies the terms involved, "In the second triad that practised out of self-regard by one who regards self and desires to abandon what is unbecoming to self is virtue *giving precedence to self*. That practised out of regard for the world and out of desire to ward off the censure of the world is virtue *giving precedence to the world*. That practised out of regard for the Dhamma and out of desire to honour the majesty of the Dhamma is virtue *giving precedence to the Dhamma*."[46] Therefore, according to the Buddha, conscience is always fallible and can be positively immoral if it is morally perverted, and hence cannot be a good guide to morality.

4.33 Some thinkers try to map out another type of relation between God and morality. They maintain that if morality is couched and put in a theological language and context such a morality can have much more depth and significance than a secular morality. Their main interest is in how the theological setting and language can affect man's moral behavior. Therefore, theirs is more a phenomenological analysis of theological morality. Two main advocates of this theory are Smart and Ian T. Ramsey. Smart says, "Sacrifice is a religious ritual which is fairly closely linked, for a number of reasons, with worship. But, like other rituals, it can become mechanical and indelicate; so that, by way of protest, it is said: The sacrifice of God are a broken spirit. Here already there is a wide extension of the concept beyond its specifically religious use, leading to the notion that good conduct, or at least the dispositions leading thereto, are a kind of sacrifice."[47] " . . . moral conduct aimed at the production of other's and one's own happiness is considered to involve some degree of giving up. This is the path open for an extension of the notion of sacrifice so that a man's life or stream of conduct can count as a holy and living sacrifice to the Lord."[48] And Smart maintains that the theological context can give a different flavor to morals. "The superimposition of religious upon moral concepts as illustrated above gives the latter a different flavour . . . because the solemnity of moral utterances becomes considerably increased: it is not merely that murder is wrong, but that life is *sacred*; a bad action is *sinful* and impious . . . marriage is more than a fine institution, it is a sacrament''.[49] Referring to value claims, Ramsey states, ''Now such a claim disclosed through and around plain facts has been traditionally spoken of by terms like 'Duty' or the 'Moral Law' and a theological interpretation arises as and when such terms are theologically contextualized. The possibility of theology affording a 'lateral enrichment' of ethics, or theology 'adding a new tone' to ethics, of 'God' being partially a moral term, or of speaking of apprehending God in moral obligation—all these possibilities arise because moral judgments have the characteristic of being responsive, and in having this characteristic acknowledge a value-claim to which they express response. What a theological interpretation does is to set this value-claim in a wider context''.[50] ''. . . the theological interpretation in no way modifies the value-claim or otherwise comprises it. In so far as it is intrinsically justified it simply provides us 'with a wider context which sites the value-claim in relation to other, chiefly non-moral, features of the Universe.''[51] And he concludes that this theological dependence on disclosures ''affords the reason why there can be a legitimate theological account of morality . . .''[52] Another expounder of this theory is Austin Farrer who says, ''The impact is through the way things are. The unbelieving mind acknowledges the way things are, but not the divine impact. We try to explain how our view of the way things are is illuminated by our acknowledgment of the divine impact.''[53] These thinkers have a good case for justifying a relationship between morality and God. They do manage to give real depth to ethical values. Particularly, for example, the idea of an omniscient God can be an extremely effective deterrent to immoral actions or even to immoral thoughts themselves, because the idea of omniscience implies that God can see everything and therefore nothing can be hidden from God.

4.34 But the problem is that this is only one side of the picture. The theological context does not stop by giving depth to morality but also raises the host of issues that we have been discussing so far. Particularly, this theory strongly presupposes some kind of command and an objectivity theory. The theological context can drive certain ethical values to a deontological extreme that would lead to a harmful system of morality. To take an example, if marriage is regarded as a 'sacrament' too, it would make divorce impossible in cases where it is genuinely needed. The idea of *sin* and *impiety* can lead to the idea of divine commands which would be incompatible with free and responsible moral choices. The idea of omniscience has its difficulties, as we saw in a previous chapter. Likewise, the theological dimension of morality, when its full implications are drawn, can lead us back to the unresolvable problems of the theories of objectivity, commands and conscience. The idea of the proponents of this theory was, of course, to show how theological notions can affect moral discourse in enriching it. There is no doubt that the way they *affect* it can be extremely beneficial. This beneficial side is achieved at the expense of leaving the logical and ontological status of the theological notions unexamined and it is the latter aspect that creates the real trouble.

4.35 A radical attempt has been made to relate morality to God in a completely different way. An exemplary instance of that attempt can be seen in Paul van Buren. For van Buren, theology centers purely around Christ. The whole conception of God is drastically reduced to the person of Christ in his charismatic and moral behavior, charismatic behavior, that is, defined and made meaningful in terms of moral behavior. In a sense, van Buren reduces theology to a matter of ethics and morality, and he is happy about it because, according to him, that is the only way in which theology can make sense. Van Buren says, "we shall not properly speak of God unless we have first learned to speak of Jesus, not the reverse. Jesus . . . now takes the place of ontological priority."[54] The charismatic character of Christ is analyzed in terms of the discernment one would get by reading the Gospel as giving a new perspective to life. This discernment situation and its implications are analyzed in terms of the moral behavior of the person. Van Buren thinks that this type of morality is the only possible type of theology. He asks, "Have we not reduced theology to ethics? Our answer takes the form of another question: In a secular age, what would that 'more' be? . . . If this is a reduction in the content of theology, it is the sort of reduction which has been made by modern culture in many fields. Astrology has been 'reduced' to astronomy . . ."[55] He is confident that he has faithfully interpreted Christian theology. "Although we have admitted that our interpretation represents a reduction of Christian faith to its historical and ethical dimensions, we would also claim that we have left nothing essential behind."[56]

4.36 Van Buren's theory is interesting in the sense that it points to two funamentally different kinds of morality in Christianity and he advocates one to the exclusion of the other. The one is morality based on what God said and commanded, etc. The other is based on what God (Christ) did, and Christ's personality and moral behavior are taken as worthy of emulation and imitation. 'Follow what was done' has a much more practical moral relevance and avoids many of the theoretical problems involved in 'Follow what was said'. But, how and why should one commit oneself to follow Christ? It is here that the neo-Barthian elements enter into van Buren's thought. To the question 'how', van Buren says it is just only a 'blik'. "This interpretation of Christian faith is related to Hare's concept of 'blik'. The language of faith expressed in the Gospel may be understood if it is seen to express, define, or commend a basic presupposition by which a man lives and acts in the world of men."[57] Like Barth, he would say that one has only to wait for one's 'blik'. "The language of faith, by referring to a transcendent element, indicates that something has happened to the believer, rather than that he has done something."[58] As to the question 'why', van Buren does not see the possibility of any rational answer. This is, of course, suggested by the 'blik' theory. The question can be rationally answered only if van Buren sees a 'justification' for the moral perspective one gains through imitating or following Christ. But he does not see any. "Christians have never been able, however (and when they were at their best have not tried) to *prove* the 'superiority' of their historical perspective over other perspectives."[59] Therefore he does not see any grounds for adopting a particularly Christological perspective. "I said that 'we have grounds' for seeing things as we do. Let me confess that I am not at all clear about just what that means and that I am unable to give an account of this claim or its supports."[60] Hence he concludes that there should not be any reason why one should follow or imitate one morally good character rather than any other. "There is no empirical ground, however, for the Christian's saying that something of this sort could not happen to a disciple of Socrates."[61] If van Buren's initial remarks about the reducibility of theology to ethics are valid then one can easily find reasons, for imitating or following Christ or any moral character, in ethics itself. Therefore the approach to ethics via Christ becomes redundant or irrelevant because Christ himself gets a value purely in terms of moral values. If so, morality becomes independent of theology.

4.37 Now, if Christ is to be followed and imitated on moral grounds then there is one particular point that is worth clarifying. It is that the central aspect of Christ's moral behavior, i.e., sacrifice, becomes meaningful only within a Christian context. A typical objection from the Buddhist tradition would be to say that if the world contains suffering and misfortunes etc., then one should do one's best in one's lifetime to reduce as much as possible the amount of suffering and misfortune. But if sacrificing oneself voluntarily is the only possible solution, then that would be one of the greatest moral virtues to do so. It is in this sense of sacrificing himself for the sake of others that Christ becomes one of the greatest moral personalities in the world history. But if non-theological moral criteria are applied, then Christ's sacrifice does not assume the significance that it does under theological morals. A Buddhist can ask two questions about Christ's sacrifice. One is, can such a sacrifice reduce man's plight in any form? The second is, has Christ's sacrifice, in fact, made a difference to the situation of humanity? Or has there been a marked difference in the human situation since Christ? All these questions can be perfectly answered within a Christian context. But the point is whether the sacrifice or the central moral significance of Christ can be made meaningful outside the tradition of Christianity. If it cannot be made so, then van Buren is necessarily wrong to emphasize the great moral and religious significance of Christ without putting the latter in a full theological context that requires a thoroughgoing doctrine of God. Van Buren starts from the wrong end when he tries to reduce theology to Christ. If the central moral act of Christ cannot be made meaningful outside the theological context, then one of the central aspects of Christ's moral significance cannot be made universally meaningful. It is, of course, true that the sacrifice does not exhaust the moral significance of Christ and that his enlightened moral system makes him one of the great moral teachers of the world. But still, a Buddhist cannot make any sense out of Christ's sacrifice, or he would say that Christ did the wrong thing when he allowed himself to be taken. If the ideas of sacrifice and divinity are taken away as not very essential then Christ becomes a *primus inter pares* with many other moral teachers.

4.38 Another way of relating morality to Christianity has been attempted by Braithwaite. With Braithwaite, Christianity is a matter of a big story. In that sense, all religions are, according to Braithwaite, sets of stories. Even a fiction can be a religion according to him, because sometimes fictions can advocate moral standards rather effectively. He says, "Next to the Bible and the Prayer Book the most influential work in Christian religious life has been a book whose stories are frankly recognized as fictitious—Bunyan's *Pilgrim's Progress*; and some of the most influential works in setting the moral tone of my generation were the novels of Dostoevsky."[62] The logical priority of morality is clearly accepted by Braithwaite when he agrees with Matthew Arnold in saying "wisdom and goodness, they are God."[63] Therefore, the Christian stories become meaningful and important only in so far as they reinforce the accepted moral values.

4.39 According to Braithwaite, following a religion means following a set of stories. "On the assumption that the ways of life advocated by Christianity and Buddhism are essentially the same, it will be the fact that the intention to follow this way of life is associated in the mind of a Christian with thinking of one set of stories (the Christian stories) while it is associated in the mind of a Buddhist with thinking of another set of stories (the Buddhist stories) which enables a Christian assertion to be distinguished from a Buddhist one."[64] Braithwaite's remarks about Buddhism can be true only if Buddhism shares the problems of Christian theology, which, in fact, it does not. For Buddhism, moral perfection is the ideal in the sense that it leads to spiritual perfection. Morality, as we shall see later on, is generically related to the spiritual ideal. In Buddhism, morality is based on two fundamental *facts*. One is that humanity has a set of basic needs and the other is that moral values generically effect a spiritual perfection. The validity of Buddhist morals depends on these two *facts* and therefore if these two facts are false, then the morality becomes necessarily invalid. But stories of fictions can never be falsified. Therefore it would be a grave misinterpretation to say that in Buddhism to follow a religious morality is to act in conformity to a collection of stories. However, it should be pointed out that there is an important place for fictions in Buddhist morality. The Buddha had preached stories of his past lives for the moral edification of his followers. He had in mind the psychological impact those stories could make on his followers and therefore utilized them to reinforce and support the moral system he was preaching. These stories have always belonged more to the popular stratum of Buddhism than to the intellectual. They have no credal significance in Buddhism.

4.40 We have been discussing the various aspect of Christian morality with the view of making the relationship between God and morality clear. They all depend on the idea of God as the Good, though this idea is not very explicit in some of the theories we have been discussing. The theories attempted various ways of relating morality to God. They were treating morals as objectively existent facts, as commands, as conscience, as imitation of a divine personality or as a divine standard of behavior or morals as a result of the stories centering around the idea of God. The main problem with Christian ethics is that the moral values are always justified in terms of something completely external to morals. Therefore one cannot *see* the justification, but one can only *invoke* the justification. We can also look at the situation from another perspective. In fact, Christian ethics can be given a utilitarian justification too. Here one can make an initial distinction between Christian moral principles and the Christian moral system. Though Christian moral principles may be deontological, the Christian moral system is essentially built upon a utilitarian justification precisely because the religion is logically prior to the moral system. Because the system of ethics is based on a utilitarian justification, this justification can, in turn, relate to particular principles—thus making the latter as ultimately based on a utilitarian justification. Thus Christian moral principles can be re-stated as 'If you want God's love or salvation, then you must follow such and such moral proposition or propositions'. Here the external justification is clearly evident. Following moral values is meant to please God, and thereby attain salvation. One can also say that when one is highly evolved morally, then God grants one salvation, here grace depending on morals. In that case, morality is related to salvation via a Kantian God. In either way, morality cannot be directly made meaningful in terms of its ideal, God. The ideal is something that is external and foreign to morality. One can object that this is a trivial consideration because Christianity means salvation through God, but this triviality should be emphasized in the context of morality and moral justification for two main reasons. One is that morality, here, is not justified in terms of anything that is perceptible or comprehensible because the justification is not generically related to the moral principles. The second reason, which is related to the first, is that Christian morality cannot be a universal morality because the Christian system of morality can find justification only within the context of Christian theology and never outside it.

4.41 It is in this context that the main Buddhist criticism of Christian morality should be analyzed. For the Buddhist, a moral principle should have its justification as generically related to the moral principle. Wittgenstein meant the same thing when he once made an admirable attempt to clarify this point. "When a general ethical law of the form, 'Thou shalt . . .' is set up, the first thought is: Suppose I do not do it?

"But it is clear that ethics has nothing to do with punishment and reward. So this question about the consequences of action must be unimportant. At least these consequences cannot be events. For these must be a *kind* of ethical reward and of ethical punishment but these must be involved in the action itself.

"And it is also clear that the reward must be something pleasant, the punishment something unpleasant."[65]

4.42 The Buddha always found the justification of moral values in the consequences they generically produced. As we saw above, the Buddha condemned bad actions on three grounds: (i) the self upbraids the self, (ii) society condemns the evil-doer, (iii) the evil-doer will be reborn in a bad form of existence. Here, one can argue that in Buddhism, too, morality becomes meaningful only in its religious context because another religionist who does not accept rebirth cannot make full sense out of Buddhist morality. In fact, the Buddha has pointedly answered this question when he formulated his *moral wager*: If one believes in effective (i.e., moral) action (as involving rebirth), then one will be praised here and as well be born in good conditions. So one has victory in two ways. If one does not believe in effective action one loses in both the ways.[66] He elaborates this elsewhere. "If I do good, 'If there be a world beyond, if there be ripening of fruit and ripening of deeds done well or ill, then, when body breaks up after death, I shall be reborn in the Happy Lot, in the heavenly world . . .' 'If, however, there be no world beyond, no fruit and ripening of deeds done well or ill, yet in this very life do I hold myself free from emnity and oppression, sorrowless and well'."[67] What the Buddha is trying to show is that Buddhist ethics and moral values can be meaningful even outside the religious context of Buddhism. Therefore, here, moralitiy logically precedes religion in two ways. One, the Buddha accepted that morality does make perfect sense even outside the strict religious context. The other is that moral values are values that society in general and men in particular do actually follow. To be moral is to be a happy person as an individual. The Buddha states, "It is the guilty dread, housefather, which he who kills begets in this very life, as a result of his killing: it is that guilty dread about future life, which he who kills begets: that feeling of painful dejection felt by him, that guilty dread, is allayed in him who abstains from killing".[68] "He possessed of the Ariyan (noble) body of moral habit, subjectively experiences unsullied well-being."[69] The Buddha goes on to emphasize that man's moral actions make him what he is and it is in this sense that morality has a value. If someone does an action, one "is of one's own making, the heir to deeds, deeds are the matrix, deeds are the kin, deeds are the foundation; whatever one does, good or bad, one will become heir to that".[70] The distinction between individual and social morality be comes blurred from the Buddhist point of view. Buddhaghosa commentated: "Furthermore, on account of his unvirtuousness an unvirtuous person is displeasing to deities and human beings, is uninstructable by his fellows in the life of purity, suffers when unvirtuousness is censured, and is remorseful when the virtuous are praised. Owing to that unvirtuousness he is as ugly as hemp cloth. Contact with him is painful because those who fall in with his views are brought to long-lasting suffering, the states of loss. He is, worthless because he causes no great fruit (to accrue) to those who give him gifts. He is as hard to purify as a cesspit many years old. He is like a log from a pyre, . . . He is always nervous, like a man who is everyone's enemy. He is as unfit to live with as a dead carcass. Though he may have the qualities of learning etc., he is as unfit for the homage of his fellows in the life of purity as the charnel-ground fire is for that of brahmanas. He is as incapable of reaching the distinction of attainment as a blind man is of seeing a visible object."[71] These moral values get related to religion in the way that they are, as a matter of fact, causally conducive to attaining the spiritual goal. This is the central point where the Buddhist morality sharply differs from the Christian.

4.43 Buddhist morality can be subjected to another sharp criticism from Christian moralists. Brunner emphasizes that any non-theological morality is selfish. "Every form of natural ethics is anthropocentric—man desires the *summum bonum* because it is 'good' for him . . . Even the ethic which takes duty very seriously is an ethic of self-righteousness . . . The moralist who lives by duty also seeks himself, his moral satisfaction, by his own moral dignity . . . Natural ethics is dominated by the principle of self-seeking and self-reference . . . In it, man . . . expects the good as the result of his own efforts . . . This is the root of that which the Bible calls 'sin' . . . It is precisely moraltiy which *is* evil."[72] This passage epitomizes the search for external justification for morality in Christianity. On the other hand, it is not clear how Brunner establishes his conclusion. If any non-theological moral system becomes a selfish one by definition, then he is not really saying anything. If he is stating a matter of fact, then as we saw above, a Buddhist theory of morals would give two answers to Brunner's criticism. One is that the distinction between egoism and altruism is highly superficial and therefore not tenable. The other is, even if the distinction is correct, a Buddhist theory can very meaningfully formulate the principles of altruism. Coming to the other problem raised by Brunner, if self-seeking and self-reference is bad, then how can Brunner himself explain the motivation in Christian salvation? Any theory of salvation is necessarily egoistic ultimately. If one is not worried about oneself, then there is no reason why one should obey God's commands and rules.

4.44 In Christianity the justification of morality comes from outside, but in Buddhism it comes from something that is generically produced by morality. We saw above how the Buddha explained this relation in the social-individual dimension. Now we turn to the religio-spiritual dimension. This is how the Buddha clarifies it to Ananda: "So you see, Ananda, good conduct has freedom from remorse as object and profit; freedom from remorse has joy; joy has rapture; rapture has calm; calm has happiness; happiness has concentration; concentration has seeing things as they really are; seeing things as they really are has revulsion and fading interest; revulsion and fading interest have release by knowing and seeing as their object and profit. So you see, Ananda, good conduct gradually leads to the summit."[73] Without moral training spiritual perfection is impossible (*v.* 6.101).

4.45 Sometimes in Christianity, morality or obeying God's will is regarded as helping one attain union with God or a heavenly existence. (This can, of course, be interpreted in many ways, as we shall see later. *v.* 6.14ff.) Here morality is used to attain a different kind of end, in the sense that the religious end is not viewed in terms of moral perfection as leading to a spiritual perfection. For example, this is the idea behind Kierkegaard's thesis that the religious sphere transcends and sometimes contravenes the moral sphere. The Buddha strongly criticizes any form of generic differentiation between the means and end of morality. "Monks, a monk fares the religious life aspiring after some class of gods, thinking: 'By this moral habit or custom or austerity or religious life I will become a god or one among the gods', his mind does not incline to ardour, to continual application, to perseverance, to striving."[74] However, it should be emphasized that the Christian idea of union with God is not exactly the same as becoming a god in the Buddhist sense, because the Buddhist god is similar to a man at a carnival with plenty of money to spend. But the point to be emphasized here is the antipathy of the Buddha against any form of generic difference between the means and end of morality.

4.46 There is another aspect too to Christian morality. This aspect is closely related to the ideas of God as the Good and the objectivity of morals, the deontological nature of ethics as underlying the two. Here, moral principles are regarded as ends in themselves. Moral values become a system of objectively existent values. But the Buddha disagrees with this kind of conception of morality. In Buddhism, morality always caters to needs, social and spiritual. Therefore, in attaining the final spiritual perfection, though one has to use morality to attain it, at the end one has to overcome the need for morality. One who has attained spiritual perfection is one who has overcome the distinctions of good and bad. In other words he is by nature, by disposition, moral. To make a very crude analogy, an ordinary citizen is not called moral because he does not murder (though negatively we call him immoral if he murders and then we deprive him of the rights of an ordinary citizen). It is his nature, his disposition, not to murder. He has overcome the distinction between non-human and human and has become fully human. Also there is no conflict between good and evil thoughts about murder and therefore he does not find himself particularly moral in every situation where he comes across persons he does not like. When a man tries to perform a great act of charity or make a great sacrifice, he is trying to do something that an ordinary man is not usually inclined to do. And he struggles between contrary inclinations and then, he finds himself to be moral and others, too, call him so. The Buddha maintained that only when one triumphs in moral struggle can one be called good or bad. "Even so, monks, some monk here is very gentle, very meek, very tranquil so long as disagreeable ways of speech do not assail him. But when disagreeable ways of speech assail the monk, it is then that he is to be called gentle, is to be called meek, is to be called tranquil."[75] When one is spiritually perfect one does not have moral struggles, so one has gone beyond good and evil. In the *Sutta Nipata*, the Buddha describes the saint as one who has gone beyond good and evil. ". . . the noble man who does not cling to what has been seen, or heard, to virtue and (holy) works, or to what has been thought, *to what is good and to what is evil*, and who leaves behind what has been grasped, without doing anything in this world, he does not acknowledge that purification comes from another."[76] In the *Nettippakarana* this idea is again emphasized. "By good deeds one goes to heaven, by bad deeds to purgatory. By the destruction of (good and bad) deeds one attains cessation with a liberated mind, like the flame with the cessation of fuel."[77] Once the Buddha, speaking of Sariputta, says, "He has attained to mastery, he has attained to going beyond in the noble moral habit, he has attained to mastery. . . ."[78] In this way, the Buddha would criticize the Christian conception of morality as a very immature conception for it cannot go beyond the principles of good and evil, because the ultimate Christian idea, God, is still The Good.

4.47 Two points have to be mentioned. One is that a Christian can point out that in Christian literature there are many passages that would closely parallel the Buddhist passages we have been quoting in this chapter. They do look similar and closely parallel when they are taken out of their theological context. What is important is the theological context in terms of which all Christian morality derives its validity and meaning. One way to show the similarities between Buddhist ethics and Christian ethics is to compare Buddhist moral ideas with Christian moral teachings taking the latter out of their context. But it would not, in any sense, be going to the heart of the matter, and further, it would only distort the nature of both the religions involved. Here, we have been trying to analyze Christian morals in their proper context. The other point to be mentioned is that one can object to the Buddhist's case by saying that the Buddhist ethics cannot be any more universal than the Christian because, e.g., the Eskimos cannot adopt Buddhist morals and therefore it is operative only within the religious framework of Buddhism. This objection had already been answered by the Buddha (*v.* 4.42). In addition, it can be pointed out that the Buddhist ethics can be universal in two more senses: in the sense that it is utilitarian and in that it does not presuppose any extra-human notions, the commitment to which is a necessary prerequisite to appreciate the nature and status of morality.

4.48 We have been trying to analyze the idea of God as The Good from a Buddhist point of view. The Buddhist would make the following concluding observations about such an idea of God. One way to make such an idea meaningful is in terms of morality and moral values. But one could show how and why such an extraneous hypothesis is not necessary to justify moral values, and how and why such an extraneous justification cannot be a justification. Because moral values can be properly appreciated without such a justification, the idea of God as the source of moral values becomes unnecessary and redundant. If that idea is used as a fiction or a story to give depth or tone to morality (e.g., Braithwaite), then such a depth or tone would be morally misleading because it tends to conceal the true nature and status of moral values.

4.49 Whatever the theoretical problems involved, there are certain important aspects of Christian morality. When the Buddha was discussing his contemporary religions, he made a distinction between two types of religion, viz. unreligious 'religions' (*abrahmacariyavāsa*)[79] and unsatisfactory religions, (*anassāsika*).[80] The religions that were condemned as unreligious were: (i) Materialism; (ii) religions denying moral values (i.e., there are no good and bad actions); (iii) religions denying moral responsibility) i.e., there is no cause—*hetu*—for moral degeneration, regeneration or salvation and, (iv) religions denying free will.[81] The other type was unsatisfactory but not unreligious. The Buddha maintained that though a religion is based on authority, it may not be unreligious because it may attempt to promote moral values. In so far as the Vedic seers had attained moral perfections, the Buddha respected them. Although the Buddha criticizes the ancient seers for their lack of knowledge, he has the highest regard for them as virtuous men and says, "the ancient seers were restrained ascetics."[82] Referring to certain seers who had comprehended the nature of their desires and had eliminated them, thus attaining salvation, the Buddha says, "I do not declare that all these religious men are sunk in repeated birth and decay."[83] This shows that moral perfection and salvation can be achieved in religions other than Buddhist. When such phenomena occur in the contexts of theistic religions like Christianity, we have to make certain important qualifications as to the nature of their religious concepts, as we shall see later in detail (*v*.6.55, 56). Thus the theistic conceptions can, in a pragmatic sense, lead to a promotion of moral values. Therefore a Buddhist would say that in so far as it aids and promotes moral welfare Christianity should always be distinguished from non-religious 'religions'. However, it still remains an unsatisfactory religion because we have to keep in mind the various problems involved in the context of Christian beliefs.

Chapter Five

GOD, COSMOS AND EVOLUTION

5.1 The idea of God as the cosmos and evolution presents a different aspect of Christian theology. It is different from the other characteristics we have been discussing so far. For example, the idea of God as the Creator could be a rational proof or a suggestion for the existence of God as well as an interpretation of the world in terms of the idea of God. But in the case of the idea of God as cosmos and evolution, it always tends to be much more a speculative interpretation of the world than an attempt at a rational justification of the belief in God. It may, of course, in the light of the plausibility of the rational considerations of the process of evolution, if any, suggest a rational hypothesis in terms of God. But, here, the possibility of a strong rationality is precluded for two important reasons. One is the that the doctrine is always presented in terms of a future event. One can say that an interpretation in terms of a future event need not be irrational. The second reason answers this objection. Theologians who advocate the evolutionary theory make a dramatic break between rational and theological considerations. Therefore, the future even is always presented in terms of the language of faith and revelation. From the point of view of rational considerations, the doctrine of God is poetically speculative and has, sometimes, therefore, correctly been called a mystical interpretation of the world. It is true that even in the other conceptions of God, e.g., God as the Creator, the revelationary strand plays an important part ultimately. But the point is that in the evolutionary theory, the whole theory is made meaningful in terms of the revelationary strand. Therefore, with the evolutionary theory, we face a new situation. Here the interpretation of the world becomes consciously and primarily important. It should not be forgotten that objective rational problems about the truth or falsity of the doctrine are also posed in these theories. And we have to discuss them on that basis in so far as they are presented in that form. But the more important problem here is to discuss the validity and significance or the relevance of the evolutionary interpretation of the world in so far as it is related to the problems of religion and salvation. In terms of relevance and significance, the problems about the objective truth of these theories becomes subservient to their religious significance, or we might come across a different, or the the possibility of a different theory of truth which might need a different form of justification.

5.2 The evolutionary theory has two steps. The first step is to make the cosmos or the world intimately related to God. The second is the teleological process. Hartshorne and Cobb give more prominence to the relationship between God and the cosmos while attempting to give a subtle teleological explanation. The important evolutionists are those like Teilhard de Chardin, Karl Rahner and the Death of God theologians. Though the first two are clear evolutionists in the usual sense the last group advocates an evolutionary theory in a different form which may be called more consistent than that of Chardin and Rahner.

5.3 Compared with the cosmic evolutionists, Buddhism stands at the opposite pole. For Buddhism the problems of religion and salvation are essentially man centered and therefore a cosmic interpretation of the religious situation is irrelevant to the problems of religion. It is from this point of view that we are going to analyze the cosmic evolutionary theories of contemporary theologians.

5.4 The theology of Hartshorne and Cobb is based on the philosophy of Whitehead, and can be claimed to have much relevance to the contemporary world because it exhibits an openness to science and is an attempt to give a theological interpretation of the world by starting from its very constituent basis as exposed by modern science: atomic and sub-atomic phenomena. Hartshorne suggests a strong panentheism and Cobb develops all its implications including its evolutionary tendencies. Though the theology of Hartshorne and Cobb is based on an independent metaphysical doctrine as developed by Whitehead, it can also be appreciated on its own merits, as we shall see later, by trying to look at what it is attempting to point at fundamentally. The particular importance of their theology lies in their claim that if the idea of God is to be significant, then the world must be made necessarily an aspect of God.[1] This is also one way to avoid some of the problems that come up with the idea of creation, particularly those related to the idea of a beginningless and everlasting universe. Cobb goes on the say that one should thus identify the world with God, for two reasons. One is that "If God is an actual entity, then it is appropriate to attribute to him the structures characteristic of other actual entities".[2] The other is that the Order in the world requires a designer and this designer could work best if he could work from within rather that impose the Order from outside.[3] This also answers the problem of how God becomes the Creator in terms of continuous creation.[4] Thus, because the world is a part or an aspect of God, "Whitehead's philosophical reasons for affirming God and his attempt to show that God is not an exception to all the categories appear to me philosophically responsibile and even necessary".[5] To illustrate how God is related to the world, Cobb gives the analogy of a person. "The easiest way to understand this would be to regard God, like human persons, as a living person. A living person is a succession of moments of experience with special continuity."[6] Cobb draws out the evolutionary implications of the situation when he points to the subtle evolutionary process going on in the cosmic order. "Since God does exist, and since he aims at the maximum strength of beauty, he will continue to exist everlastingly. The necessity of his everlasting existence stems from his aim at such existence combined with his power to effect it."[7]

5.5 Chardin is a worldly evolutionist rather than a cosmic evolutionist. For him, the world is in evolution, and this evolution has to be understood in a strongly theistic sense. The world evolves into God and this theory is meant to be understood in an objectively factual sense because his theory is, partly, based on the objective scientific data. The evolution is emergent. "We are now inclined to admit that at each further degree of combination *something* which is irreducible to isolated elements *emerges* in a new order".[8] The evolution has so far progressed up to the stage of the noosphere and the important point is that the process has not stopped. "We have seen and admitted that evolution is an ascent towards consciousness".[9] The point of culmination cannot be an impersonal principle. "The Future-Universal could not be anything else but the Hyper-Personal—at the Omega Point."[10] In Chardin's theology, the world becomes a part or an aspect of God in terms of the evolutionary process. He differs from Hartshorne and Cobb in that with the last two God-and-Universe is one unit from the very beginning while with Chardin, God enters into the world only at the noospheric phase of evolution. Christ plays a vital part in it. "As early as in St. Paul and St. John we read that to create, to fulfill and to purify the world is, for God, to unify it by uniting it organically with himself. How does he unify it? By partially immersing himself in things, by becoming 'element', and then, from this point of vantage in the heart of matter, assuming the control and leadership of what we now call evolution."[11]

5.6 Karl Rahner is very much indebted to Chardin in advocating his evolutionary theory. In addition, he borrows the Heideggerian terminology of Being. He talks of an existentialistic appropriation of the propositions of faith and finds God in the abyss of existence. ". . . this salvation is God himself whom man does not create but always find already there in the ground and abyss of his existence."[12] This theistic existentialistic project is attempted from an evolutionary perspective. God is the climax of cosmic evolution. Matter evolves into life and life into spirit.[13]

5.7 Evolution is not an accidental process. There is a vital principle active within the process of evolution itself. 'Being' is this vital principle and in the context of Rahner's theology it resembles the Holy Spirit or God himself.[14] In order to prevent this doctrine from falling into a kind of pantheism he tries to make a distinction that is difficult to explain. ". . . It is impossible to explain here how being is both absolutely the most interior and yet the most foreign factor of this movement and how, in this dialectic of its relationship to the finite evolving spirit, it can support the whole of this movement and yet allow it to be the movement of this spirit itself."[15] The movement of God in this process is a result of God's grace. God's self-communication in terms of grace takes the form of God participating himself withing the process.[16] The divinization of the world starts with Christ: ". . . the Incarnation appears as the necessary and permanent beginning of the divinization of the world as a whole.''[17]

5.8 Thus, Hartshorne and Cobb give prominence to the idea of world being an integral aspect of God, with its implied evolutionary notions, while Chardin and Rahner give prominence to the amalgamation of the world with God which is made meaningful in terms of an evolutionary process. So these theologians try to make the idea of God meaningful in two ways. First, in terms of the world and secondly in terms of the evolution of the world where the idea of teleology plays a dominantly important part.

5.9 How can a Buddhist understand, analyze and interpret these theologies? Two ways are open. One is to take them as objective and factual or semifactual assertions. The other way is to take them as a religious explanation of the world.

5.10 Let us take up the first way of looking at them. Sometimes, in the way they are presented, these theories look quite like factual assertions. Here, particularly Chardin's account has strikingly factual connotations. His theory of evolution up to the Omega Point is based on true and factual assertions about the evolution of matter up to the noospheric stage. Rahner incorporates Chardin's factual framework in his theory. If we take this factual validity and significance of these theories, a Buddhist can make some factually significant comments on them.

5.11 The Buddha's idea of the universe was significantly different from the theories of Chardin or Rahner, because he conceived the world to be much vaster and greater in scale. G. P. Malalasekara and K. N. Jayatilleke summarize the Buddha's view: ''In this vastness of cosmic space are located an innumerable number of worlds. 'As far as these suns and moons revolve, shedding their light in space, so far extends the thousand-fold world-system. In it are a thousand suns, a thousand moons, thousands of earths and thousands of heavenly worlds. This is said to be the thousand-fold minor world-system. A thousand times such a thousand-fold minor world-system is the twice-a-thousand middling world-system. A thousand times such a twice-a-thousand middling world-system is the twice-a-thousand major world system.' ''[18] Malalasekara and Jayatilleke identify these systems with the galactic systems. The Buddha states his conception: "As far as moons and suns move in their course and light up all quarters with their radiance, so far extends the thousand-fold world-system. Therein are a thousand moons, a thousand suns, a thousand Sinerus, lords of mountains: a thousand Rose-Apple Lands, a thousand Western Ox-Wains, a thousand Northern Kurus, a thousand Eastern Videhas; four thousand mighty oceans, four thousand Mighty Rulers, a thousand Four Great Rulers, a thousand heavens of the Thirty-Three, a thousand Yama worlds, a thousand heavens of the Devas of delight, a thousand heavens of the Devas that delight in creation, the same of those Devas that delight in Others' creations, and a thousand Brahma worlds. This, Ananda, is called 'The system of the thousand lesser worlds'. A system a thousand-fold the size of this is called 'The Twice-a-thousand Middling Thousand-fold World-system'. A system a thousand-fold the size of this is called 'The Thrice-a-thousand Mighty Thousand-fold World-system'."[19] And the Buddha says that the universe extends even further.

5.12 These galactic systems are always subject to change internally and externally. Externally, these are in the process of contraction and expansion (*saṃvaṭṭamāna vivaṭṭamāna*). For a time, they go on contracting and then expanding.[20] This idea is similar to the modern theory of the oscillating universe. "But the time, we are told, is not the same everywhere for fifty earth years are equivalent to one day and night in one of the heavenly worlds, while in another a day and night is equivalent to no less than 1,600 years."[21] "The span of life of mortal men is insignificantly small in comparison with cosmic time and may be compared in its duration to a line drawn in water."[22] There are varieties of living beings living in these world-systems. As Malalasekara and Jayatilleke summarize, "Several attempts are made to classify this vast array of beings. One such classification speaks of human beings, as well as some of the higher and lower beings, as falling into the class of beings who are different and distinguishable from each other in mind and body. There are other classes where the beings are different in body but one in mind. Yet others are alike in body but different in mind, while there are some who are alike both in body and in mind. A further set of four classes of beings are mentioned who are formless. All these are described as the several stations which the human consciousness can attain (*viññāṇaṭṭhiti*), and find renewed existence after death. Another such classification puts beings into the several classes of the 'no-footed, the two footed, the four-footed, the many-footed, those having or lacking material form, the conscious, the unconscious and the super-conscious'. The human worlds are always represented as standing midway in the hierarchy of worlds. Life in these human worlds is a mixture of the pleasant and the unpleasant, the good and the evil, while the pleasant and good traits are intensified in the higher worlds and the unpleasant and evil in the lower."[23]

5.13 Here two ideas emerge. The 'Universe' is not a 'closed' concept. Therefore, no *significant factual meaning* can be attached to a concept that is made meaningful in terms of the universe. That was why the Buddha did not want to assert the infinity of the world as a fact or as a theory. When the other thinkers and his followers asked the Buddha whether the world was infinite and everlasting, he did not answer these questions because, according to him, they were unanswerable. Therefore he did not assert them, deny them, did not assert a combination of the assertion and denial and did not deny the negation of both the possibilities either. He did not want to theorize or make factual assertions about the *duration* and the *limits* of the universe because, here, the universe of discourse tended to be empty of significantly verifiable pheonmena. This situation is a peculiar problem that comes up particularly with the nature of the universe. Kant found the assertions, temporal and spatial, about the universe, as leading to antinomies. The Buddha maintained the infinity and everlastingness of the universe on practical grounds, on the grounds of practical impossibility to find the spatial and temporal ends to the universe. He said that even if one moves with the swiftness of an arrow in any direction and travel for a whole lifetime, one can never hope to reach the limits of space.[24] One can say that the cosmos may be and can be finite. But, as Kant would say, it is even theoretically impossible to conceive of this possibility though it is theoretically possible to conceive its infinity. Therefore, any attempt to make any concept, like God, meaningful in terms of the 'open' concept 'universe', as Hartshorne and the theistic evolutionists do, cannot carry any significant meaning mainly because their theories about the nature of the cosmos do not and cannot exhaust the nature of the cosmos as we do not fully know the cosmos, not to speak of its nature and the processes acting within it. Here, one can say that, e.g., for Chardin, what is relevant is that this earth is leading towards an evolution and this earth being a closed concept, the rest of the cosmos is irrelevant to the situation involved. It is here that the second idea that emerges from the Buddha's theory of the universe becomes relevant. The Buddha maintained that in the cosmic context the earth assumes an extremely insignificant position and therefore it follows that if the nature of the earth as a whole has to be understood it should necessarily be done in a cosmic context. The theistic evolutionists maintain that individual salvation can be understood only within the context of the worldly evolutionary process because the world is a part or an aspect of God. In that case, if the individual salvationary process cannot be understood without relation to the larger whole of the world, then the worldly evolutionary process cannot be understood without fully understanding its relation to its larger whole: the cosmos. There, innumerable numbers of variabilities may be awaiting. To advocate one dogmatic theory against all the cosmic odds does not explain anything. But once the concept of salvation is taken outside the boundries of the individual the problem assumes cosmic proportions. A half-way solution stands condemned by the very terms of the evolutionist's axioms and postulates which claim that the problem of salvation assumes a worldly dimension. But to meet the cosmic character of the problem is even theoretically impossible because of the peculiar nature of the cosmos.

5.14 When one talks about the evolutionary process of the world, another problem comes up. This stems from the nature of time that the Buddha mentioned. In terms of the cosmic time scale, the time on earth seems so insignificant that to talk of an evolutionary climax in terms of the world seems completely insignificant. It still leaves room for somebody to ask very meaningful questions. One such would be to ask about the nature of the earthly evolution in the context of cosmic evolution, and cosmic time scale. One may seem to see a teleological process in the world when viewed from within the world thus assuming a narrow perspective because of the ignorance of the nature of the vast cosmos. Thus, the main Buddhist objection to the evolutionist's theory would be that to attempt to give a cosmic explanation to the problem of salvation is both impossible and irrelevant.

5.15 However, one can still say that a religiously sufficient and relevant evolutionary process can be worked out in terms of a worldly evolution. If this can be the case, then we have to look closely at the cosmic and evolutionary theories as expounded by these theorists and see how far they succeed in making their theories meaningful. Cobb's suggested theory of evolution is too speculative and remote to mean anything in practice. Cobb says that God exists everlastingly in order to achieve the maximum strength of beauty (*v.* 5.4). This was exactly what Kant said when he maintained that moral perfection requires immortality. In other words, it is to say that the ideal is unattainable. Similarly, Cobb's idea does suggest a religiously very disappointing evolutionary process, in two ways. One is that it implies a morally deficient deity and the other is its practical unattainability.

5.16 There are other problems too. Hartshorne feels the tension between the God of Christianity and the God of his reductionism. So he tries to make a distinction that blurs the picture he is trying to paint. Because God is in the process of evolution, to make up for the deficiencies it involves with regard to the Godhead, Hartshorne has to make nearly two Gods. One is the contingent actual God. "That God exists is one with his essence and is an analytic truth . . . , but how, or in what actual state of experience of knowledge or will, he exists is contingent in the same sense as is our own existence."[25] The other is the primordial God. "But the individual essence of deity (what makes God, God, or the divine, divine) is utterly independent of this All, since any other possible all . . . would have been compatible with this essence. The divine personal essence in this fashion infinitely transcends the de facto totality. . . ."[26] Because there cannot be two Gods, even though the two are opposites, the two are made into one. ". . . God is not pure being but total actual being of a given moment, with all achieved determinations. Thus God is being in both its opposite aspects: abstract least common denominator, and concrete de facto maximal achieved totality."[27] This is the tension Hartshorne is bound to feel when he tries to relate a transcendent personal deity to the world of modern physics.

5.17 With Chardin and Rahner we see a much clearer and well expounded evolutionary theory. If we analyze Chardin's theory we can see the enormity of the problems he has to grapple with in advancing such a theory. His central theory is that the world, particularly the noospheric evolution, evolves towards a

Hyper-Personal Omega Point. Though Chardin, at times, speaks of the Omega Point as if it were an emergent evolute as is necessitated by the fundamental principles of evolution, he is very emphatic on its present existence. We must recognize and accept "not only some vague future existence, but also, as I must now stress, the radiation *as a present reality* of that mysterious center of our centers which I have called Omega".[28] The Omega-Point performs some very important functions in the present. "Expressed in terms of internal energy, the cosmic function of Omega consists in initiating and maintaining within its radius the unanimity of the world's 'reflective' particles. But how could it exercise this action were it not in some sort loving and lovable *at this very moment*?"[29]

5.18 The Omega is not an evolutionary climax. The process of evolution, at its end, meets Omega rather than evolving into Omega. It cannot be an emergent evolute because of its features that make it fundamentally and drastically different from the process and laws of evolution. "To satisfy the ultimate requirements of our action, Omega must be independent of the collapse of the forces with which evolution is woven. . . . while being the last term of its series it is also *outside all series*."[30] "If by its very nature it did not escape from the time and space which it gathers together, it would not be Omega."[31] "Autonomy, actuality, irreversibility, and thus finally transcendence are the four attributes of Omega."[32]

5.19 This places Chardin in a very queer position. If the Omega point goes beyond or transcends the principles of evolution how can evolution empirically, biologically, lead up to it? Nevertheless, he is forced, thus contradicting himself, to posit the Omega as an evolute because of the logical application of the experimental laws of evolution. Referring to the final end in Omega, he states, "That is the postulate to which we have been led logically by integral application to man of the experimental laws of evolution."[33]

5.20 There are other much more difficult problems that come up with the evolutionist theory of salvation. According to Chardin's scientific principles, evolution can be scientifically and biologically explained. Even biologically speaking, the process of evolution towards Omega is absolutely determined. ". . . in-folding of humanity upon itself; a process which is clearly apparent and which nothing can prevent, . . . it is a mark and an effect of biological super-arrangement destined to ultrapersonalize us",[34] and he refers to it as "a tide . . . cosmic in its dimensions".[35] "Having once become reflective it cannot acquiesce in its total disappearance without biologically contradicting itself."[36] He refers to the logic and coherence of facts involved in the process of evolution: "Yet if we try, as I have done in this essay, to pursue the logic and coherence of facts to the very end . . .".[37] However, he feels the determinism involved here and tries to safeguard against it. "*Man is irreplaceable*. Therefore, however improbable it might seem, *he must reach the goal*, not necessarily, doubtless, but infallibly."[38] But this is not enough of a safeguard against biological necessity. In his Christology, as we saw above, he makes the determinism a theistic one because Christ steers the process and Omega pulls evolution towards the goal. Whether it be theistic or natural determinism, this doctrine cannot stand on good terms with a doctrine of free will. But Chardin is an exponent of free will: "when intelligence, which originally, as has been well said, was simply a means of survival, became gradually elevated to the function and dignity of a 'reason for living', it was inevitable that, with the accentuation of the forces of free will, a profound modification should become discernible in the working of anthropogenesis, and one of which we are only now beginning to experience full effects."[39] Here Chardin thinks, contrary to his determinism, not only of the possibility of the emergence of free will but of its working as an added factor or force in the process of evolution. If free will enters into the field of evolution, any clear cut and definite program as to the future progression can hardly be envisaged because of the infinite possibilities implied in the workings of the free will. If the process of evolution inevitably forces upwards, it blunts free will, making man's freedom an absolutely meaningless concept. Here, the irony of determinism starts to work and makes man a passive creature waiting only to be carried forward by the necessarily-forward-marching process. Doctrines of free will, positive appeals, and moral exhortations to man prove absurdly futile in the face of any kind of determinism. Chardin's situation may be an echo of the deterministic implications of the omnipotent and omniscient Christian God and his position is worsened by the added doctrine of pantheism.

5.21 One can raise theoretical questions about his theory of evolution, too. Cannot evolution work in a circle? Considering man's scientific achievements, both good and evil, coupled with his untold potentialities for moral evil, cannot one envisage that the end of all this progress will be destruction? If one rules out these possibilities, it cannot be done on a purely *a priori* basis as Chardin wants to do. Biological evolution did progress because it followed a scientific and deterministic pattern. Here 'progress' is used in a partial sense because it was only the successful life forms that survived. From the point of view of those living beings that were eliminated in the evolutionary process, there was only utter chaos and absolutely no teleology, much less an evolutionary process. Therefore when we use the term 'evolutionary progress', we should note that it is always a biased term. Can one say that an evolutionary process that led to the cruel death and extinction of innumerable living beings had anything divine about it? However, even if we use the biased term 'progress', from the fact of deterministic biological evolution one can hardly predict any possibilities about the evolution of the psycho-social sphere precisely because it is not governed by any deterministic principles. When one considers man's potentialities and his free will that open up an infinite number of futures, it is really difficult to pin down *the* course he might take.

5.22 Biological deterministic evolutionary theory can be a dangerous basis for a religious theory of salvation. It can pose serious threats to religious ideals. Is Omega a part of the evolutionary process or is the evolution a part of Omega? According to Chardin's ideas, Omega should be a part of the evolutionary process because it is the logical end and climax of the process. But this is not possible because Omega is beyond time and space, while evolution is biological and spatio-temporal, features that do not harmonize with the Omega point if he treats it as an emergent evolute. Sometimes it looks as if evolution is part of God, i.e., evolution is necessary for the perfection of God. Chardin says, "We are constantly forgetting that the supernatural is a ferment, a soul, and not a complete and finished organism. Its role is to transform 'nature'; but it cannot do so apart from the matter which nature provides it with."[40] This, of course, raises grave religious and philosophical problems. How can a nonspatio-temporal and a transcendent object achieve perfection in terms of an imperfect spatio-temporal process? Religiously, a deficient God is not God. How can Omega be in a ferment and wanting to be a finished organism if it transcends all empirical features like space and time?

5.23 We shall turn to Rahner to see whether he makes any improvement on Chardin. On the contrary, we can see how he also meets with difficulties from the very beginning. As we saw above, he maintained that God has communicated himself to the world through Christ by divinizing the world. But he tries to make evolution meaningful taking this very idea of a future event. ". . . the goal of the world consists in God's communicating himself to it."[41] Here the problem is, if the world has already attained its goal, how can there be a further goal yet to be attained? However, he makes a distinction between two goals. ". . . in the very person of Jesus of Nazareth the history of the world has reached—not indeed its full and absolute perfection—but its unsurpassable final phase of perfection."[42] In fact, according to Rahner, what happened in Christ was much more than self-communication. If Christ's reality "is to be really the final and unsurpassable divine self-communication, then it must be said that it is not only posited by God but is God himself."[43] He wavers between these two goals. Is God the climax and end-point of this evolution? Was Christ God? If so, further evolution makes no sense. But the second may mean a final and absolute union with the Godhead, and Rahner speaks to that effect: "This final and absolute self-transcendence of the spirit into God must, however, be conceived as something which happens in all *spiritual* subjects."[44] But if the divination of the world has already taken place, it is difficult to understand how there can be any further goal to be achieved. Even from the point of view of salvation, man has already achieved the ultimate salvation. "In Christ God not only gives the *possibility* of salvation, which in that case would still have to be effected by man himself, but the actual salvation itself, however much this includes also the right decision of human freedom which is itself a gift from God."[45] The deterministic implications are clear. When 'the right decision of human freedom' itself is a gift from God, it does not leave any room for man's free will, and the whole process becomes thoroughly determined in terms of the will of God.

5.24 In Rahner's evolutionary theory, the deterministic ideas become much sharper. His theology requires the evolutionary process to be determined by God. "For Christianity, the history of this world is a history interpreted in a Christocentric sense. . . The world is the world created for the eternal Logos—by and for him. The world and its history has been designed from the very beginning with a view to the Word of God become flesh."[46] Referring to man, ". . . he and the reality surrounding him have structures and laws; these already existing realities, together with their determined structures, for the *a priori* law of what they become".[47] "It belongs to these convictions that these raw materials of Christian self-realization consist in the whole reality of the world created by God. This, however, makes the task of the Christian one which he does not freely choose himself but one which is pre-arranged for him—in short, the concrete existence, the historical hour, into which he is placed."[48] ". . . the future too is built out of materials with definite structures whose finite nature also sets internal limits to the possibilities of the future and renders them finite."[49] But this idea is contradicted immediately when Rahner makes a daring attempt to resurrect free will. ". . . the Christian as such is not given any clear prescriptions by the gospel as to how the future is to look or in fact will look."[50]

5.25 What is very clear from Chardin's and Rahner's accounts of the evolutionary theories is that such theories always tend to carry deterministic implications. In Rahner we can explicitly see the deterministic principles at work. This can be religiously the most devastating outcome of the theistic evolutionary theories. It can always be said that Chardin and Rahner were not formulating strict deterministic theories, the dangers of which they must have been fully aware of, but only suggesting the teleological nature of the universal processes. In other words, they may mean only that God has already made or shown a religious path to the individual. But the problem is that the mechanistic way in which they have propounded these theories opens them fully to the deterministic threat. If necessary, we can refer again to Chardin: he thinks that the process of evolution towards Omega is even biologically determined, ". . . in-folding of humanity upon itself, a process which is clearly apparent and which nothing can prevent . . . it is a mark and an effect of biological super-arrangement destined to ultra-personalize us," and he refers to it as "a tide . . . cosmic in its dimensions" (*v.* 5.20).

5.26 The Buddha was keenly aware of this type of deterministic threat to religion and he strongly criticized all forms of determinism including theistic determinism.[51] A criticism he leveled against nature-determinism, the fundamental principles of which are common to theistic determinism, can be relevant in this context. He says that if a deterministic theory is true, "happiness and pain are measured out (as) in a bushel; circling on has its limits fixed; there is not decline and growth, there is not high degree or low. Indeed, just as a ball of thread, when thrown down, unwinds itself as it rolls, ever so will fool and the wise alike, when they have run on and circled on, make an end of anguish."[52] It is difficult to conceive whether an evolutionary teleology can be formulated without implying some kind of determinism. If it is an evolutionary process, then there is always a necessity of the process as in the case of biological evolution where the process is determined and necessary in a biological sense. In the psychological sphere (or noosphere) any prediction about the future course of evolution becomes even theoretically difficult because of the overwhelming importance of free will. Here the only possible evolutionary theory will be a retrospective one.

5.27 So far we have been looking at evolutionary theories as statements of factual or semi-factual and objective or semi-objective theories. One cannot say that this way of looking at them is wrong, because they have been explicitly stated to be so, at times. Chardin's theory is based on a wealth of scientific objective facts, though faith and revelation play an important, a predominantly important, part. If these theories are defective as objective or semi-objective theories, can they be made meaningful in any other sense or dimension? We shall now turn to consider this possibility. It is here that the Death-of-God theologians become very important. Though they question, "Is it possible to conceive of a form of Christianity coming to expresssion without a belief in God?"[53] and say that their theology is "in effect, an attempt to set an atheist point of view within the spectrum of Christian possibilities",[54] their theology is much more theistic than they maintain or can maintain. They too propound an evolutionary theory, but with a strong emphasis on the historical aspect of Christianity. Though the Death-of-God theology is assumed to be a more heretical branch of Christian theology, their similarity with the theories of Chardin and Rahner is striking. Their central thesis is that the divinization of the world has taken place with the death of Christ as God, and this divinization has started a process. The death of God was a necessary thing to happen. "Can we not make the judgement that it is precisely this vision of the death of God in Christ that can make possible for us a realization of the deeper meaning of the Christian and eschatological symbol of the dawning of the kingdom of God?"[55] But this does not lead to pessimism.[56] This death of God signifies the final identification of God with humanity, thus destroying the chasm that existed between the two in terms of one transcending or separating the other.[57] ". . . by freely willing the dissolution of His transcendent 'selfhood', the Godhead reverses the life and movement of the transcendent realm, transforming transcendence into immanence, thereby abolishing the ground of every alien other".[58] The Word could not be real without the death of God. "Despite the Nicene formula, the Word cannot be fully God and fully man if, on the one hand, it continues to exist in an eternal form and, on the other, it is unable to move into the present and the full reality of history."[59]

5.28 As Altizer maintains, the Christian has no certainty of this death of God. It is, therefore, interpreted as a wager.[60] The other side of the wager "may very well be embracing a life-destroying nihilism . . . Who can doubt that a real passage through the death of God must issue in either an abolition of man or in the birth of a new and transfigured humanity?"[61] The new vision makes the profane 'radical'.[62] This view is, of course, different from orthodox Christianity. But, to them, it does not make any difference. "Nor can we expect the new revelation to be in apparent continuity with the old. Now that historical scholarship has demonstrated the chasm existing between the Old Testament and the Christian visions of Paul and the Gospel of John, might we not expect a comparable chasm between the New Testament and a new revelation?"[63]

5.29 Is God really dead for the Death-of-God theologians? This can be answered only by looking into the problems of how far God and the theistic implications are relevant to man and the world after the death of God. Altizer envisages the Word to be in movement towards an end. "We know this (Jesus') Word as a Word pointing to an eschatological future, and we must not be dismayed if it is no longer meaningful as a Word of the past."[64] This process of movement has great theistic and ontological importance. "Truly to pronounce his name—and for the radical Christian the names of Jesus and God are ultimately one—is to participate in God's death in Jesus and thereby to know God who *is* Jesus as the expanding or forward-moving process who is becoming 'one Man'."[65] "Waiting for God, expecting the transcendent and the marvellous. . . ."[66] We should pray for God to return. "Thus we wait, we try our new words, we pray for God to return . . ."[67] "Our ethical existence is partly a time of waiting for God and partly an actual Christology."[68] Furthermore, the movement is said to be voluntarily originated and guided by God.[69] In short, God is not dead but only transformed to a new form. And God is the life and source of the world, representing the 'totality' and 'the End' of the forward-movement of humanity.[70]

5.30 The importance of the Death-of-God theologians lies in the twist they try to give to their theory. According to them, the death of God and the evolutionary process have to be understood in a symbolical way as relevant to the problems of salvation and religious aspirations. "We might even say that Jesus is the Christian name of the totality of Experience, a new actuality created by the abolition of the primordial Being, whose death inaugurates a new humanity liberated from all transcendent norms and meaning."[71] Hamilton observes, "We are not talking about the absence of the experience of God, but about the experience of the absence of God".[72] He puts his case in an extreme form: "The plea for religionless Christianity is thus a plea to give up all claims for the necessity of religion generally".[73] In fact, in this picture, the death of God is more a logical death rather than historical. Historically, such a God did not exist and the so-called Christian God was only a metaphysical myth. The real meaning of God was something closer to the fundamental teachings of Oriental religions. ". . . the Christian idea of God is obviously a product of the fusion of the Bible with Greek ontology . . . When biblical faith is apprehended in its original form, it loses its radical uniqueness, and no longer exists at such a distance from the higher forms of Oriental religion."[74] "In the Orient, a fully dialectical form of faith, such as Madhyamika Buddhism, has inevitably dissolved all positive meaning, with the result that it has left behind the world of symbols, myths and dogmas. Is this the destiny that awaits the Christian faith?"[75]Altizer maintains that this is the scientific understanding of 'God'. ". . . to 'know' scientifically means to dissolve the ground of faith, and thus to will the death of God."[76] The eastern sense of the sacred is relevant to this understanding. ". . . we can encounter in the East a form of the sacred which

Christianity has never known, a form which is increasingly showing itself to be relevant to our situations.''[77] According to Altizer, theology is a dialectical understanding.[78] And he finds this in the mysticism of Madhyamika and Zen Buddhism. ''The language of Oriental mysticism is consistently all fully dialectical; it can speak of the sacred only by inverting the meaning of the profane . . . (Its language) is the language of silence.''[79]

5.31 However, we note a problem here. There are two strands of theological thinking, historical and mystical or religious. There is a tension between the two that Altizer and Hamilton feel throughout. This problem is very important in the Christian context because it points to a fundamental issue involved in the historical and mystical or religious ways of understanding Christianity. The latter way leads to a fully-fledged symbology which generates an enormous number of problems that are peculiar to Christianity. The Christian symbolist's main problem is to decide where the symbol ends and fact or history begins. The symbol is necessary to avoid the problems posed by the facts and to interpret experience, but the facts are extremely relevant to Christianity. This is the unresolvable problem in Christian theology. The Death-of-God theologians inherit this problem. For example, how the dialectical understanding of 'the present' ending up in a mystical experience involves a sense of history and a sense of a future universal consummation is not at all clear. The mystical experience as a self-authenticating experience ends up in itself. If this sense of the past and future should necessarily supplement the experience, such a necessity does not at all follow from the mystical experience. If the past as described in Christianity is to be accepted, it requires the usual faith in the traditional teachings of Christianity. If the future as the consummation of 'God in humanity' achieving the End is to be accepted, it necessarily involves strong faith in a living God and a teleological universe. This again illustrates the tension that exists between the historical facticity and the experiential relevance of the doctrines of Christianity.

5.32 The problem the Death-of-God theologians try to grapple with is important and significant. They emphasize the significance of the mystic's experience of reality but they run into difficulties when they try to relate the concepts of Christianity, in one form or other, to it. To facilitate this combination, they transformed God into process, movement, etc. Ironically enough, Altizer and Hamilton once argued against such an attempt. "... one is not free to give to the word 'God' whatever content one chooses, and that a desire to be relevant is no sufficient reason for the retranslation of God into 'process', 'depth', 'love', or 'future'."[80] In fact, this is exactly what Altizer and Hamilton have been doing throughout. Though they try to relate the transformed theism to mystical experience, they cannot see a necessary relation between the two. The fundamental problem that the Death-of-God theologians pose is how far one can reconcile the implications of theism with the mystical or religious experience. This problem is important because it is central to contemporary theology.

5.33 The significance of the Death-of-God theologians is that they emphasized the relation between interpretation and experience (This problem will be taken up in detail in a later chapter. *v.* 6.31). Their central thesis was that Christian theology is subservient to the mystical experience and therefore should be interpreted as a discipline that is relevant to that experience. In other words, they attempted to build up an interpretation of humanity in the context of Christian theology, as relevant to the mystical experience.

5.34 In fact, Chardin and Rahner also were entertaining ideas similar to those of Altizer and Hamilton. If their theories are looked at this way, they start to assume a different color. The factual problems recede into the background and the idea of the relevance of their theories to the religious context becomes more dominant or important. Chardin once thought that the interpretation of the world is done in terms of the relation to the religious situation. In this respect, Chardin, Rahner, Hartshorne and Cobb show an approach to theology that is somewhat different from the Death-of-God theologians. The latter explicitly emphasized the mystical experience. The former are more interested in giving a world-view or a rational metaphysics as relevant to the religious situation or context of Christianity (which may well include mystical experience too).[81] Thus, in a way, the Death-of-God theologians and the rest of the evolutionists show two differing approaches to the interpretation of theology.

5.35 Hartshorne and Cobb say that they are trying to build a rational metaphysics which will suit the idea of the basic religious concept of God as the holy. What is important is to make a 'religious' interpretation of the world.[82] . . . The word 'God' is so abstract, according to them, that it can and may mean anything provided the outcome is relevant to a theological interpretation of the world. This idea is clear from what Hartshorne states: "Only one individual can ever be divine. Here is an extremely abstract character which yet is the defining character of a self—or person. This character, though individual to God, is so abstract or non-specific that it can be correlated with any possible character you please in its correlate, the world."[83] The doctrine cannot lead to an abstract absolute because the religious hypothesis needs to be concrete. "The absolute is not more, but less than God—in the obvious sense in which the abstract is less than concrete."[84] Thus the whole doctrine of God can be manipulated in any way to suit the religious perspective one has. When one has got a particular theistic religious perspective, one may see God everywhere and in everything. Therefore, Hartshorne maintains that his doctrine is synonymous with pantheism. ". . . surrelativism and pantheism are logically the same doctrine with only a difference of emphasis."[85] In a way, theology becomes very similar to a poetic expression of a religious faith or an experience, and this poetic way can, in turn, aid and help the experience.[86]

5.36 The main criticism of Buddhism made by these theologians is that Buddhism does not build any rational metaphysics.[87] The evolutionists might say that the Buddha did not have the sense of time and history in the religious context. In fact, the Death-of-God theologians once made a similar objection to eastern mysticism. They maintain that eastern mysticism lacks an important factor: the progressive historical movement. "Whereas the prophetic faith of the Old Testament and the primitive faith of Christianity were directed to a future and final End, and thus are inseparable from a forward-moving and eschatological ground, the multiple forms of Oriental mysticism revolve about a backward movement to the primordial Totality . . ."[88] ". . . the way of the oriental mystic is a way *backwards.*"[89] ". . . the distinctiveness of Christian mysticism lies in its celebration of God or the Godhead as a forward-moving process."[90] But the problem is whether this sense of history is so much necessary or relevant to one's mystical experience. Altizer himself does not seem to think so. At the point of experience, according to him, the sense of time and world seem to collapse altogether. "A faith that could look forward to God's becoming all in all could rejoice in the imminent collapse of the reality of the world, thereby celebrating an End that is a repetition of a primordial Beginning."[91] "'Old Aeon' passes into 'New Aeon', Samsara is identical with Nirvana."[92] If these statements are to be made meaningful, these differences, for example, between *Saṃsāra* and Nirvana, should be interpreted purely as epistemological differences. Therefore in the context of Altizer's mystical notions the ideas of time, history and world seems to hold very little, if any, meaning.

5.37 Now, the central issue becomes the problem of relevance. Are rational metaphysics and evolutionary theories so relevant to the problems of salvation and spiritual welfare? In a sense, these theories can be relevant to a theistic religion, in helping and aiding to gain a God-orientated poetic existential relationship to, or a perspective of, the world. For example, it may induce a numinous attitude towards nature, thereby generating some form of religious experience. (The significance of this will be discussed later. *v.* 6.31). But, here, one big disadvantage is the enormous theoretical problems these interpretations lead to. If these interpretations are taken as religiously orientated poetic expressions, then they could be regarded as innocuous. But when one sees the amount of energy wasted on exactly these theoretical questions, it shows how easily theoretical theology can, and has, become an independent discipline of its own. On the other hand, to interpret Christian theology in an Upanisadic sense of 'All is Brahman' which means much more an orientation than an assertion of anything, would be a too much of a reductionism for Christianity because of the 'factual' nature of Christian doctrines.

5.38 Even if we take the relevance of Christian doctrines, bracketing their truth or falsity, in a phenomenological sense, still the idea of relevance can generate its own problems. The cosmic and evolutionary theories were supposed to be relevant in the sense that they give a 'religious' explanation of the world and time. But, as we have been trying to explain, they fail to give any form of explanation because of the nature of the subject they are dealing with. The concept of cosmos is too 'open' to be given satisfactory interpretation or an explanation. Hartshorne's and Cobb's cosmos is still unknown to any appreciable degree so that any edifying explanation becomes impossible. The evolutionist's theory is a fight against an unknown and innumerable number of future possibilities. Because they cannot be intellectually satisfying, and therefore fail in achieving their objective, they cannot be 'relevant' as explanations, to anything.

5.39 The Buddha's main criticism of this type of 'religious relevance' would be that these Christian theologians are misusing the term by extending it to the cosmic sphere. The Buddha too thought that the 'world' is relevant for religion, but only in the way it is relevant to religious and spiritual purposes, as it matters to an individual or as it affects him. If one goes beyond this point, then one faces a multitude of problems. That was why, when people asked the Buddha about the nature of the cosmos, he decided to be silent. One of his answers was that such questions were not relevant to religion. "The world is finite etc. . . . this, Vaccha, is going to a (speculative) view, holding a view, the wilds of views, the wriggling of views, the scuffling of views, the fetter of views; it is accompanied by anguish, distress, misery, fever; it does not conduce to turning away from nor to dispassion, stopping, calming, superknowledge, awakening, nor to Nibbana. I, Vaccha, beholding that this is a peril, thus do not approach any of these views."[93] In other words, he meant that one's wisdom sets limits to one's knowledge. (One can say that in theistic religions the situation is different in that the theists have to find ways of defining 'God' to include everything and every aspect of the world. But in that case, all systems of theology will become purely *a priori* definitions of God. However, even then, the problems of relevance can come in). The Buddha talked of the relevance of the world in an experiential way and maintained that it is the phenomenological world that matters to an individual and that the world is constituted by one's experience. "Friend, that there is a world's end where one neither is born nor ages nor dies nor passes nor reappears, which is to be known or seen or reached by travel—that I do not say. Yet I do not say that there is ending of suffering without reaching the world's end. Rather it is in the fathom-long carcass with its perceptions and its consciousness that I make known the world, and the way leading to the cessation of the world. It is utterly impossible to reach, by travel, the world's end; but there is no escape from pain until the world's end has been reached."[94] From a religious point of view, it is this world of experience that is relevant, not the infinite time and space of the outside cosmos. If 'religion' is defined to include the relevance of the latter then the theoretical problems we have been discussing emerge.

Chapter Six

GOD AS EXPERIENCE

PART ONE

6.1 The idea of religious experience has come to the forefront of contemporary philosophy of religion and theology as a fruitful method of making the main religious concepts meaningful. Particularly, Christian thinkers have welcomed this idea with the belief that as a last stronghold, here, the concept of God can be made meaningful in an experientially self-evident sense, thereby avoiding the pitfalls of the traditional rational argumentation. Therefore, John Baillie, rejecting logical arguments of any kind as helpful in knowing God, says that "our knowledge of God rests rather on the revelation of His personal Presence . . ."[1] H.H. Farmer believes that the experience of God is a normal function of a normal human capacity and, speaking of the compelling touch of God, says that "the capacity to become aware of God is part of normal human nature like the capacity to see light or to hear sound."[2] Smart maintains that beliefs are ultimately founded on the religious experience. "The strength of a strand ought to rest upon the strength of its bases . . . when the bases upon which rest belief in the Creator seem very weak, the strand is cut out altogether. But perception of the strength of the bases depends upon religious experience. The ordinary man, perhaps, will not be able to gain more than an inkling here; only the truly saintly and prophetic will be able to express such judgments of strength in new doctrines. At any rate, persuasion will have largely come from the conduct on the one hand which enlivens and lies behind the doctrines; and from the religious eloquence which points to the bases upon which the faith in these matters must rest."[3]

6.2 The word 'experience' is a vague concept in that it can mean things that are different in quality as well as in quantity. For example, within the same experiential dimension, the experience can differ quantitatively, like shallow and deep, etc. Quantitative distinctions, here, sometimes fade into qualitative distictions. There may also be experiences that are not open to any form of rational discussion. Barth's revelationary experiences are of that type. He says, "The decisive thing about the veracity of human knowledge of God is undoubtedly said when we remember the veracity of the revelation of God. The human knowledge of God becomes and is true because God is truly God in His revelation; because His revelation is true as such . . .".[4] As they are true by definition, we will not be discussing them in this chapter (*v.* 8.4). In this chapter, our main concern will be to analyze the various manifestations of religious experiences and to see whether they give any reason to believe in the existence, or in the possibility of the existence, of a deity or to see whether they throw any light in explaining or elucidating the concept of such a deity. In applying a Buddhist critique of the experiential route to the theistic beliefs, an examination of analogous concepts in Buddhist religious experience will be undertaken. This will be an attempt to compare and contrast the two sets of concepts to form the basis for critical evaluations.

6.3 Though our main concern will be with the 'deeper' types of religious experience or the mystical experiences, the religious experience, as we said, admits of varying degrees. Before going on to the deeper levels, a certain clarification has to be made about the non-deep or elementary types of religious experience. When a Christian experiences the objective world as a creation of God and feels the 'presence' of God in it, it becomes a religious experience for him. Hick illustrates this: "Consider the following imagined situation. I enter a room in a strange building and find that a militant secret society appears to be meeting there. Most of the members are armed, and as they take me for a fellow member I judge it expedient to acquiesce in the role. Subtle and blood thirsty plans are discussed for a violent overthrow of the constitution. The whole situation is alarming in the extreme. Then I suddenly notice behind me a gallery in which there are batteries of arc lights and silently whirring cameras, and I realize that I have walked by accident onto the set of a film. This realization consists in a change of interpretation of my immediate environment. Until now I had automatically interpreted it as being 'real life' as a dangerous situation demanding considerable circumspection on my part. Now I interpret it as having practical significance of a quite different kind. But there is not corresponding change in the observable course of events . . . let us now in imagination expand the room into the world, and indeed expand it to include the entire physical universe. This is the strange room into which we walk at birth. There is no space left for a photographer's gallery, no direction in which we can turn in search of new clues which might reveal the significance of our situation. Our interpretation must be a *total* interpretation. . .

"The monotheist's faith-apprehension of God as the unseen Person dealing with him in and through his experience of the world is from the point of view of epistemology an interpretation of this kind. . . ."[5]

6.4 Is there a rational explanation for this type of interpretation? Logically, there can be a rational explanation in terms of natural theology. But the problem is, if natural theology is invoked, then the rational problems about God discussed above recur. Therefore, the best way to avoid such a situation is to say that the interpretation is done from a faith-perspective. In that sense, a theistic believer will be defined as a person who views his experience that way. The situation will be definitional but it is, of course, the problem about the faith-circle. Hick accepts that there is no explanation for this interpretation. "The theistic believer cannot explain *how* he knows the divine presence to be mediated through his human experience. He just finds himself interpreting his experience this way."[6]

6.5 From this example of elementary religious experience we can make some observations. As will be shown later, this, in a way, is really an elementary prototype of the deeper forms of mystical religious experiences. But this can be easily subjected to an analysis because its experiential dimension is thinner than that of the mystical experience. An important point is, here, the experience-interpretation dichotomy is absent in a significant way. The dimension of experience is ordinary and normal and what makes it religious is the interpretation. There is nothing non-ordinary about the experiential dimension. What matters here most is the interpretation rather than the experience. Therefore, to put it in a rather paradoxical way, here, interpretation becomes an experience rather than the experience being interpreted. This idea can be clarified by contrasting it with visionary or/and mystical experience. In the latter, the experiential dimension changes completely. There is a separate and a different type of experience that can be, or has to be, according to the theistic believer, interpreted differently. This experience differs remarkably in its affective and cognitive qualities from ordinary experience. It is the intensity and powerfulness with which the subject feels it that demands a separate interpretation for it. Because the experience is so different and so intense and significant, the subject tries to make an interpretation of, or build an interpretation on, that experience. There, experience becomes the raw material or evidence for the theory. What matters is the experience more than the interpretation and therefore the interpretation comes as the value of the experience. However, here again, the interpretation can, in turn, reinforce the experience, thereby heightening its affective and intensive qualities. Thus, it is important to note this relationship between interpretation and experience because it can throw much light on the discussion which follows.

6.6 The mystical type of religious experiences poses at least five important problems.

1. Can one infer the existence of God or a being like God from this type of experiences?
2. Some may say that it is too radical and an extreme claim to make. If so, can such experience have any experiential relevance to the concept of God in the way of understanding what God is like, the existence of God being established on grounds other than religious experience?
3. Is the concept of God the best concept to evaluate and appreciate that experience?
4. Can we reverse the role and attempt to build a theology as based on the experience? If we can, how far can we go?
5. Can the behavioral accompaniments, if there are any, of the religious experience be taken as pointing via the religious experience, to anything divine?

6.7 First, we shall consider the quality of this experience. Mystical experiences are noted for being indefinable and inexpressible. Two points have to be made in this connection. One is that these qualities are common to all experiences in life. Nobody can define a headache but we all understand what is meant by headache, because it is a common experience or because most of us have experienced it. Why mystical experience is indefinable is only because it is not a common and general experience. One can object that mystic experience is indefinable mainly because of its intensity and richness. But when two LSD-users get together, they find their drug experiences no more indefinable than their headaches. To take a more responsible example, among the followers of the Peyote religion (a religion based on the experiences of a drug called Peyote, while accepting the belief-dimension of Christianity) the experiences that come from the drug are supposed to be common knowledge or they all know what happens under the drug, e.g., seeing Christ or God in his full majesty. Carlos Castenada, an anthropologist who underwent drug experiences under the guidance of the leader of a traditional Mexican drug religion, shows that, though the experiences were terrifying or majestic, they were common to him and to his leader, Don Juan. He calls these experiences "the reality of special consensus".[7] This brings us to our second point. Drug experiences have contributed much to an understanding of what happens in mystical experiences. Therefore it would be advisable to examine the findings of drug experiences with an idea of trying to delineate the criteria of peculiarly religious experiences.

6.8 The classic attempt to build up a system of criteria to determine religious experiences was made by Rudolf Otto. The feelings of *mysterium tremendum et fascinans* were supposed to be the paradigm features of mystic experience. According to Otto, these feelings suggested the idea of a powerful being standing behind these experiences. J.W. Harvey, writing an introduction to Otto's *Idea of the Holy*, says, "When, therefore Otto uses so frequently expressions like 'the numinous *feeling*', . . . he must not be taken to be merely repeating the claim of 'affect', subjective emotion, to a place in any genuine religious experience. But it would certainly have been better had he always preferred the alternative phrase 'the feeling of the numinous'."[8]

6.9 Otto's position has been very much affected by the findings of drug experiences. Drugs have produced exactly the same type of feelings Otto was advocating in support of theistic religious experiences. (Here we are dealing only with the experiential aspects rather than the theoretical and the interpretational dimensions, of which we will be speaking later on). Describing a mescaline experience he underwent, Huston Smith, Professor of Philosophy at the Massachussets Institute of Technology, says, "The accurate words are significance and terror—or awe, in Rudolf Otto's understanding of a peculiar blend of fear and fascination. The experience was positive in that it unfolded range upon range of reality I hadn't known existed."[9] About his LSD experience, Walter H. Clark, Professor of Psychology of Religion at Andover Newton Theological School, observes, "The experience recalls Otto's *mysterium tremendum*. It was awesome."[10] Elsewhere he maintains that "The drugs are simply an auxiliary which, used carefully within a religious structure, *may* assist in mediating an experience which, aside from the presence of the drug, cannot be distinguished psychologically from mysticism."[11]

6.10 Another form of important religious experience has been visions and voices. Since St. Paul's visionary experience on the road to Damascus, such type of experience has been treated in Christianity as carrying dramatic religious significance. As Underhill observes, many Christian mystics have treated visions and voices as an 'ineffable intuition of Reality'.[12] For example, the Crucifix which spoke to St. Francis of Assisi and the visions of the Cross experienced by St. Catherine of Genoa were dramatic starting, or turning points of their mystical careers.[23] St. Teresa is famous for being a visionary mystic. As Underhill says, "St. Teresa's mystic life was governed by voices: her active career as a foundress was much guided by them."[14] She took her visionary experiences with great seriousness as experiences of Reality or God. ". . . when St. Teresa saw only the Hands of God, she was thrown into an ecstasy of adoration by their shining loveliness."[15] St. Teresa claims that "His Majesty communicates Himself to us, and reveals His love for us by means of such wonderful appearances and visions."[16] Once she tells of a nun who had the experience of God: "To the person of whom we have been speaking the Lord revealed Himself one day, when she had just received Communion, in great splendour and beauty and majesty, as He did after His resurrection, and told her that it was time she took upon her His affairs as if they were her own and that He would take her affairs upon Himself; and He added other words which are easier to understand than to repeat.''[17] St.Teresa believed that as one near the climax of mystical experience or the Seventh Dimension of the Interior Castle such experiences become more and more reliable and important.[18] It is also to be noted that most of these mystical experiences were valued for the fact that they were useful in clarifying doubts, conferring convinced knowledge in certain matters etc.

6.11 The significance of intense and powerful visionary experiences has been very much called in question by the drug experiences. A dose of drugs is able to give one any type of visions one expects, e.g., a Christian will see God, Jesus, etc., and a Buddhist will see a universe of ever changing flux. People fond of hallucinations are known to have the habit of taking strong hallucinogens like strychnine which is in fact a poison. Drug literature is full of theistic type experiences of people who believe in God. If these comparisons with drugs seem too brash we can take examples from a religious context. The significant researches done into the Peyote religion by J.S. Slotkin has found much important material that sheds light on religious experience. Peyote religion accepts the beliefs of Christianity and the drug Peyote is used as a religious sacrament. Peyote is valued for the way it teaches spiritual and moral matters. Slotkin explains that one way of teaching by Peyote is by visions of God, Jesus, etc., and by communicating new teachings about matters of fact and morals.[19] In his classic study of Peyotism he describes the Peyote religious experience. ''The power absorbed from Peyote has spiritual effects . . . For the Peyotist, this occurs because he has put himself in a receptive spiritual mood and has absorbed enough of the Great Spirit's power in Peyote to make him able to reach that Spirit. This revelation often takes the form of a mystical rapture, the unification of all one's immediate experience with the Great Spirit himself. At other times the Great Spirit or one of his spirit representatives reveals some religious or ethical dogma to the Peyotist; it 'teaches' him 'how to live right'.

''The most notorious aspect of Peyote is the 'visions' produced by the plant. However, it is my impression that the more intelligent members of the religion tend to consider these, at best, a means of learning from Peyote; at worst, as distractions resulting from not concentrating on proper subjects, as well as from physical spiritual impurity. A scientific interpretation might be that the chemicals in Peyote diminish extraneous internal external sensations, thus permitting the individual to concentrate his attention on his ideas of God; at the same time affecting sight and hearing so that these ideas are easily projected into 'visions'."[20]

6.12 Some mystics, of course, would not attach much importance to visionary experiences. The foremost among such mystics were St. John of the Cross and Meister Eckhart. Even St. Teresa tries to give a criterion, though not very convincing, to define genuine visionary experiences when she said that such experiences can be identified by a "certainty which remains in the soul, which can be put there only by God."[21] St. John advocates that visions should be rejected because "the soul will become attached to them, cling to them and be hindered by them, as it will be by things of the world, if it know not how to renounce these as well as those".[22] And he gives additional reasons for rejecting visionary experiences. ". . . visions may cause deception even they be of God."[23] ". . . sometimes, although He answers, He is angered."[24] Or it may be difficult to understand the proper meaning intended by them.[25] But the important thing to remember is that St. John did not reject the visionary experiences completely. To start with, he distinguished between two types of visions and maintained that a visionary experience to be genuinely divine should be spiritual rather than corporeal. Referring to the visions that can be seen by bodily senses, he says that "we must never rely them or admit them, but we must always fly from them, without trying to ascertain whether they be good or evil; for, the more completely exterior and corporeal they are, the less certainly they are from God. For it is more proper and habitual to God to communicate Himself to the spirit . . ."[26] Later on he went on to say that sometimes even corporeal visionary experiences can genuinely be coming from God and he tried to formulate a criterion for their genuineness. ". . . corporeal vision, or feeling in respect to any of the other senses, or any other communication of the most interior kind, if it be of God, produces its effect upon the spirit at the very moment when it appears or is felt, without giving the soul time or opportunity to deliberate whether it will accept or reject it . . . this is a thing that is wrought and brought to pass in the spirit passively . ."[27] Therefore, St. John still believed in the truth of visions and also his criterion as very similar to St. Teresa's idea of conviction: ". . . visions that are of God penetrate the soul and move the will to love, and produce their effect."[28] However, the typical type of religious experience for St. John was the divine union or communication that happened at the hidden essence of the soul. Nevertheless, this should not make one blind to the fact that St. John did accept the validity and truth of some visionary experiences and therefore it is wrong to maintain, as Zwi Werblowsky does, that "Suffice it here to say that St. John clearly has no use for celestial interventions. There are no divine demonstrations in this world."[29] Even the union with the divine was still an experience, a very passive and a very effective one. ". . . the advice must be given to learn to abide attentively and wait lovingly upon God in that state of quiet, and to pay no heed either to imagination or to its working; not actively, but passively, by receiving that which God works in them."[30]

6.13 The mystic who made a strongly consistent attempt to reject visionary experiences was Meister Eckhart. But he did this at the expense of certain central doctrines of Christian theology. He did not believe in the essentially personal and unique nature of God. Reality, for him, was more an impersonal or a supra-personal transcendent state of existence, closely similar to, or practically identical with Sankara's *Nirguṇa Brahman* (unqualified Brahman). Therefore, he believed in the possibility of complete identification with that Reality and declared, "God is the same One that I am".[31] This shows a significant deviation from the orthodoxy which rightly branded him as a heretic. Eckhart believed in a state that even transcended the Holy Trinity. "In this way the soul enters into the unity of the Holy Trinity, but it may become even more blessed by going further, to the barren Godhead, of which the Trinity is a revelation. In this barren Godhead, activity has ceased and therefore the soul will be most perfect when it is thrown into the desert of the Godhead, where both activity and forms are no more, so that it is sunk and lost in this desert where its identity is destroyed."[32] Otto explains the theoretical structure of this experience. "Eckhart contrasts the 'Deitas' with 'Deus', the Godhead with God. God is for him the conscious, personal, tripersonal God of Church doctrine. This self-knowing, thinking, self-contrasting, and as such, strictly personal God, is 'God'. But 'God' becomes and disbecomes', says Eckhart. High above Him stands the pure Godhead. Out of the Godhead comes God . . ."[33] As Otto rightly points out, Eckhart's position comes very close to Sankara's *Ad-*

vaita philosophy and he explains how Eckhart's theology can be fully translated into a Sankarite terminology.[34] And Otto points out that this experience for Eckhart was still an experience of a unifying vision.[35] The experience was affective, too, because feelings played an important part in it. Eckhart says, "Without sound, for it is any inward immediate perception in pure feeling: without light, for it is an apprehension, beyond determination and opposites, of the 'nothing'. . . This '*is*' is the Oneness which is Being itself . . ."[36]

6.14 This Eckhartian type of mysticism has been thought by some to be the pure type of mysticism. As William James says, "the absence of definite sensible images is positively insisted by the mystical authorities in all religions as the *sine qua non* of a successful orison, or contemplation of the higher divine truths."[37] In his *Mysticism and Philosophy*, W.T. Stace advocates this type of mysticism or the unitive experience as the paradigm case of mystical experience. Walter Pahnke and William A. Richards built up a typology from Stace's analysis of mystic experience and to this they added what William James described as the characteristic features of a mystical experience.[38] These were the main features:

1. *Unity.* "Experience of an undifferentiated unity, we suggest, is the hallmark of mystical consciousness."
2. *Objectivity and reality.* "Intrinsic to this second category are two interrelated elements: (1) insightful knowledge or illumination about being or existence in general that is felt at an intuitive, non-rational level and gained by direct experience, and (2) the authoritativeness or the certainty for the experiencer that such knowledge is truly or ultimately real, in contrast to the feeling that the experience is a subjective delusion."
3. *Transcendence of Space and Time.*
4. *Sense of sacredness.*
5. *Deeply felt positive mood.*
6. *Paradoxicality.*
7. *Alleged ineffability.*
8. *Transiency.*
9. *Positive changes in attitude and/or behavior.*

6.15 With this typology in view, Pahnke and Richards performed an experiment by administering drugs in a religious setting. They report, "under the conditions of this experiment, those subjects who received psilocybin experienced phenomena that were apparently indistinguishable from, if not identical with, certain categories defined by the typology of mystical consciousness."[39] As Huston Smith says, this experiment has been widely recognized as meeting the strict demands of scientific rigor.[40] Ralph Metzner edits and explains that a theology student, under drugs, had an experience extremely similar to this typology. And this theology student claims that he underwent a dramatic change in his religious attitudes in becoming more spiritually devout towards God.[41] Rev. Mary Hart, a Protestant religious minister, reports another religious experience under drugs: "Oneness. All one. In-Goodness. Indescribable. Utmost. Emotionless. No self. No sensations . . . In God. All one. This seemed an eternity or in no time."[42]

6.16 The available evidence thus seem to indicate a close relation between drug and mystical experiences. Drug experiences are based on the fact that they make some chemical changes in the body.[43] The relationship is that similar chemical reactions precede the religious mystical experiences. Pahnke and Richards explain this relationship. "The medieval monk in his darkened cell and the hermit in the deep recesses of his cave, for example, used not psychedelic substances, but the tool of sensory deprivation, sleep deprivation, meditative disciplines, and fasting to elicit biochemical changes and unlock the door to unconscious levels of mind. The Hindu yogin uses similar methods in addition to autohypnosis and breath control, the latter increasing the amount of carbon dioxide in the blood and triggering unconscious levels of mind. Altered forms of consciousness often occur unexpectedly and spontaneously when one is undergoing great mental stress and is exhausted physically."[44] Therefore the obvious objection that the drug experiences are dependent on the drugs, while the religious mystical experiences are not dependent on anything, loses much of its force when it is seen that chemical changes in the body can be brought about by means other than drugs. Sydney Cohen elaborates, "Drugs are not necessary to induce profound states of altered awareness. The more traditional efforts have been varied but only sporadically successful. Breathing exercises change the chemical composition of the blood and provide a focus for rhythmic fixation of attention. Many other techniques employ rhythmicity, the hypnotic induction of a trance state, the use of chants, oscillating body movements in prayer, and the whirling of the Maulawiyah dervishes. Fasting, self-flagellation and other forms of mortification have been practised, not only to assuage guilt or prove devotion, but also to enhance mental awareness."[45]

6.17 We were maintaining above that even though some mystics discount the visionary experiences and advocate only the spiritual experiences like those of St. John or of Eckhart, e.g., the experience of unity, etc., still they were experiences. This needs elaboration. We call them experiences for two reasons. One is that, in an important way, they are mainly affective experiences. Feelings and emotions play an important part in them and we saw how Eckhart treasured this aspect. Their claims to the 'overwhelmingness of the experience' depend mainly on this affective quality. Particularly when the Ultimate Reality is conceived as a Person, these affective aspects can be enormously enhanced and this is emphatically evident in St. Teresa. The other reason why these are called experiences is that, because they are mainly affective experiences, they can be easily reproduced by and in drug experiences. We conclude, therefore, that as experiences, they have nothing particularly religious about them. This is shown by the fact that they can be reproduced by drugs in a completely secular context. So they are neither religious nor non-religious as experiences. They are just experiences as other experiences are.

6.18 Here we have to go back to the illustration quoted by Hick (*v.* 6.3). There our normal experiences of the world were neither religious nor non-religious. But that experience could be colored by the religious beliefs we hold. Then the ordinary experiences become 'religious' ones. There what matters is not the experience but the beliefs one holds. However, one can object that the typical religious experiences or the mystical ones differ because they form also a different dimension of experience. But what we tried to explain above was that these experiences were not different, in any important sense, from the other normal experiences. They may seem to differ rather dramatically, e.g., the experience of timelessness that accompany such experiences. But this difference is not very important mainly because the experiences are very easily reproducible. Sometimes they may occur quite spontaneously. A person who has not got any religious beliefs to hold on to, may have a spontaneous experience of this type, and to him it will be simply an abnormal experience. Arthur Koestler reports to have had such experiences but because he did not hold any religious beliefs, the experiences did not have any religious significance to him. The experiences, of course, took place when he was under stress. He had a series of mystical experiences which came upon him when he was imprisoned as a spy by the followers of Franco during the Spanish Civil War. One was as follows: "Then I was floating on my back in a river of peace under bridges of silence. It came from nowhere and flowed nowhere. Then there was no river and no I. The I had ceased to exist . . . When I say 'the I had ceased to exist' I refer to a concrete experience . . . The I ceases to exist because it has, by a kind of mental osmosis, established communication with, and been dissolved in, the universal pool. It is this process of dissolution and limitless expansion which is sensed as the 'oceanic' feeling, as the draining of all tension, the absolute catharsis, the peace that passeth all understanding."[46] Tennyson also had similar experiences: "A kind of waking trance—this for lack of a better word—I have frequently had, quite up from my boyhood, when I have been quite alone . . . All at once, as it were out of the intensity of the consciousness of individuality, individuality itself seemed to dissolve and fade away into boundless being, and this was not a confused state but the clearest, the surest of the sure, utterly beyond words—where death was an almost laughable impossibility—the loss of personality (if so it were) seeming no extinction but the only true life."[47] Stace comments, "the experiences of Tennyson and Koestler came to them spontaneously and unsought, whereas the classical mystics for the most part reached their experiences by rigorous disciplines involving religious exercises and the deliberate suspension of sensations, images and thoughts."[48] To say that these are just cases of nature mysticism and to dismiss them is only to silence an important problem. We have to accept the genuine similarities they have to religious mystical experiences. An experience extremely similar to so-called nature mystical experience can have very serious religious implications for a person who holds religious beliefs strongly. Brother Lawrence had such an experience which was "absolutely enduring in its results" as Lawrence claims. M. Beaufort reports what Lawrence said about his experience, "He told me that God had done him a singular favour in his conversion at the age of eighteen. That in the winter, seeing a tree stripped of its leaves, and considering that within a little time the leaves would be renewed, and after that the flowers and fruit appear, he received a high view of the Providence and Power of God, which has never since been effaced from his soul. That this view had set him perfectly loose from the world and kindled in him such a love for God that he could not tell whether it has increased in above forty years that he had lived since.''[49]

6.19 It would be very inaccurate to say that theistic mystic experiences come spontaneously as a proof of God's grace, because almost all Christian mystics have emphasized the necessity for contemplation, orison, sustained thinking of God and meditation as necessary prerequisites to an experience of divine truths. However, spontaneity is not a criterion of genuine religious experiences when one thinks of experiences like Tennyson's or Koestler's. After a long period of mental cultivation in relation to a certain system of beliefs with the accumulated mental tension when the mind is set, any event, as Lawrence's, can trigger off a depth-experience. Madam Guyon had a religious experience as a result of some words spoken by a Franciscan Friar: ''Madame, you are seeking without that which you have within. Accustom yourself to seek God in your own heart, and you will find him.''[50] When such experiences are not interpreted theistically they are said to be nature mysticism. Zen experiences are very often such experiences, which come after mental training. The so-called nature mystical experiences can, of course, be the results of meditating upon the beauty of nature, or deriving from many other causes like chemical changes in the body, in which case the experience seems much more spontaneous. Zen mysticism differs from 'nature mysticism' for being a controlled method of mental training. Therefore Zen comes much closer to Christian mysticism than to 'nature mysticism'. In Christianity the mind gets rigorously fixed on the idea of God and the whole personality gets centered on this central point of concentration. In Zen this one-pointedness of the mind is the technique of attaining *Satori*. If Lawrence did not hold Christian beliefs, he could very easily have been a Zen master, or a nature-mystic. Therefore, the attempts of those like R.C. Zaehner who in his *Mysticism Sacred and Profane* tries to make watertight distinctions between nature, Zen, monotheistic and monistic experiences, are only confused attempts to make meaningless distinctions. What makes those experiences different is the beliefs which the experiences hold. Therefore, one has to clarify and concentrate on the beliefs and make them meaningful because what is important is the beliefs, not the experience. The attempts of writers like Zaehner to make distinctions in the field of mystical or religious experiences is only a vain attempt as a last resort to make compensations for the lack of tangible and verifiable distinctions in their belief structures. Therefore, we are forced back to the belief dimension of Christianity as its crucially important part, if not the only important part.

6.20 An attempt has been made to justify religious experiences in terms of the belief dimension. This line takes up the Wittgensteinian or Austinian doctrine which maintains that concepts are meaningful only in their contexts. Therefore, a depth-experience becomes a Christian religious experience only within the context of the Christian belief structure. In this sense, Otto's treatment of religious experience can be seen as a skeleton analysis and therefore, as extremely defective. The most notable and consistent attempt at this has been made by Smart. He states that, "the occurrence of theistic-type experiences is no guarantee of the existence of God."[51] And "it does not at all follow that, because an experience is described as being of God, or is thought of by the participant as being of God, this guarantees its validity."[52] Therefore, "contemplative union requires something beyond contemplation. Or to put it another way: a purely contemplative faith has no need for anything more than eternity within the individual."[53] The Christian religious experience becomes a union with God in its belief and ritual context: "The contextual relation between ritual and religious experience cannot simply be interpreted a kind of causal relation, as though it is the practice of worship or yoga which causes the experience in question . . . More importantly, the nature of the experience is seen in relation to the contextual activity."[54] For instance, "the set of rules governing play constitutes the context of the concept of 'goal', and instances of goal-scoring occur in the context of play."[55] Therefore, "theistic mysticism only has a chance of being theistic as a result of the context of worship and *bhakti* surrounding and pervading it."[56]

6.21 However, this type of context-theory or game theory has several disadvantages and it can easily be a very dangerous theory of religion. When the idea of religious experience began to be emphasized in theology and philosophy of religion, there was the suggestion that it was thought of as a possible way of getting out of the belief circle, or the belief dimension (*v.* 6.1); religious experience as something that is at last tangible and verifiable as giving credence to the belief dimension. (This idea will be taken up in detail below). *But this game theory of religious experience leads only to a widening of the circle rather than to a getting out of it.* If beliefs give meaning to, or interpret, the experience then what is important is the belief dimension. The religious experience only reinforces the beliefs. The ultimate situation is that the beliefs validate the experience and the experience validates the beliefs and the vicious circle starts. As this theory accepts a 'coherence theory' of truth it can lead to a very tricky position in the field of comparative religion. All the religions in the world can invoke this theory and all can claim to be equally true. All sorts of fictional theories can claim truth. The context-theory is useful when one wants to explain and analyze the particular dimensions of a particular religion. But it becomes dangerous when it is used in the field of comparative religion as it justifies all competing claims. Different religions make competing claims and these claims are crucially important. Christianity is bsed on the ideas of soul and God while Buddhism is based on the ideas of no-soul and no-God. These competing claims are not contraries, but they are contradictories. These differences are decisive; as Voltaire said if God does exist, it is a crime not to accept him and if he does not exist it is a crime to invent him. The context-theory of religion cannot solve any of these problems. All it can do is to produce a 'fictional theory' of religion, but the competing claims made by religions do matter. One way to get out of this situation is to produce a diluted doctrine of the competing claims, thus making the differences as insignificant as possible. But the permissible degree of dilution is exactly the point of greatest dispute among the religionists.

6.22 However, is there any way to get out of the belief-experience circle? In fact four attempts can be made to get out of it, and some of them have been actually made.

1. Going back to the belief dimension.
2. Appeal to the epistemological certainty derived in terms of the experience.
3. Appeal to experience as a new form of evidence.
4. Appeal to behavioral accompaniments or resultants of the experience and take them as pointing, via the religious experience, to something divine.

6.23 (1) The first attempt is to go back to the belief dimension and appeal to natural theology again. That is, to maintain that certain beliefs, e.g., in a creator, can be rationally established, and therefore, to say that one can establish the existence of God on grounds other than experience and then by following the path prescribed by him and by rituals, etc., one can experience him. But even if the existence of God is rationally established, that does not guarantee the validity of the experience in which one supposes that one is experiencing *that* God. However, this is a different problem. If the existence of God can be rationally established, then that will be the best way of breaking the circle. But this possibility of getting out of the circle is barred by the inherent logical problems in the belief dimension, as we saw in our previous chapters.

6.24 There is another important problem that should be mentioned in this context. It stems from the lack of clarity of the belief dimension. The belief dimension is relevant to the experience in more than the way we just mentioned. In fact, the experiential dimension derives its meaning mainly and exclusively from the belief dimension. When one maintains that one is experiencing, God it means that one is in contact with a Person to whom a precise meaning, a precise denotation and a connotation, can be given. In other words, one must be theoretically clear about what one is claiming to be experiencing. C.B. Martin explains this point: "In reference to things other than our sensations of the moment knowledge is prior to seeming as if.

"The statement 'I seem to be looking directly at a chair' has meaning only insofar as I already *know* what it is like to look directly at a chair."[57] Therefore, in the case of religious experience, there occurs a very important shift of emphasis: "The conceptual weight is shifted from the experience to the previously established or assumed notion of the object of experience.".[58] So, the theoretical structure of Christianity becomes much more importantly relevant to the religious experience than it is usually assumed. By emphasizing the experiential side as a proof of validity of Christian beliefs and concepts one is only putting the cart before the horse. In this way, the possibility of getting out through the belief dimension is precluded by the inherent logical problems of the beliefs and also by the absence of a consistent theory and a conception of God. (*v.* also, chapter 7).

6.25 (2) There is another way to break the belief-experience circle, though it is not a very satisfactory solution. That is to invoke the experience as giving epistemological certainty to the beliefs one holds. Underhill says that there are some visionary experiences "experienced by the minds of great power and richness, which are crucial for those who have them. These bring wisdom to the simple and ignorant, sudden calm to those who were tormented by doubts. They flood the personality with new light: accompany conversion, or the passage from one spiritual state to another: arrive at moments of indecision, bringing with them authoritative commands of counsels, opposed to the inclination of the self: confer a convinced knowledge of some department of the spiritual life before unknown."[59] James H. Leuba explains with many examples that in conversions what happens is that a system of intellectual beliefs is accepted on the basis of a single experience.[60] Leuba refers to St. Augustine to show how 'experience' can triumph over intellectual problems. "Doubts vanished from the mind of St. Augustine at the moment he gave up the last impediment to a holy life: his unrighteous loves. Indeed, intellectual doubts played no part in the conversion to Christianity of this subtle dialectician. This inconsistent professor of intellectual conviction forgets his art when most needed, it seems, and receives bodily the Christian doctrines on the strength of a change of heart!"[61] Because of the irrationality of the experience, in the sense that it comes out of the blue in an unexplainable manner, any type of paradoxical or unsubstantial belief can be admitted to be true under the impact of this experience. Leuba explains this clearly: "St. Paul's conversion did not rest on speculations, but on affective experiences. Luther suddenly finds himself at peace relieved from the load of sin, which no amount of good works had been able to purge away, and then the scheme of salvation by faith, together with the related doctrines, become for him an unshakable reality . . . The more startling the affective experience, the less explicable it seems, the easier it is to make it the carrier of unsubstantial notions. The unwarranted support given to theological conceptions by the affective life is due to nothing else than to the universal and unavoidable proneness to connecting things as cause and effect for the only reason that they are together, or follow upon each other, in the mind. I fell once into a controversy with a very earnest and good man concerning the atonement as understood by a narrow church. As he was cornered by arguments pointing to the irrationality and immorality of the doctrine, he suddenly ceased arguing and exclaimed: 'It may appear so, but I cannot doubt it; *I have experienced it*'. He had experienced not only a change of heart, but also the transcendent doctrine of the atonement!"[62] The conversion experience can be triggered off by the explosion of any type of emotional tension. Leuba refers to a case of conversion of a drunkard. "The following quotation from Col. H.H. Hadley, well known in home-mission circles, the instrument of the reform of hundreds of drunkards, may interest the reader, if only by its picturesqueness: 'Men have been converted in the delirium tremens. It knocks all the theology higher than a kite! I don't understand it, but it is so. Take my own case—a big, bloated drunkard, had fifty-three drinks the day before I was converted, most of them brandy cocktails, and before me I saw the Lord crucified; I was converted.' I heard myself in a New York City Mission men tell me they had been converted while intoxicated, even to a considerable degree. I found satisfactory evidence that their story was correct, and that their conversion, judged by the newness of their life, was genuine. Subsequently similar facts came repeatedly to my knowledge."[63] It is notoriously known that in the drug experiences people get various types of enlightenments about cosmic truths and fundamental Realities.

6.26 The depth experiences only reinforce the beliefs one already holds, because of the high sensitization thse experiences generate. The Peyote religion is, in fact based on the idea that Peyote gives epistemological certainty to religious beliefs. Slotkin says that once a Commanche came out with the pointed remark: "The white man talks *about* Jesus; we talk *to* Jesus." And he quotes a leader of the Peyote religion a saying, "You respected the Bible, but you couldn't be sure which part was written by God, and which part by man. Nor even if any part of it was really written by God; you would have to accept it on faith, and might be wrong. But when you took Peyote, God spoke to you directly, and you found out for yourself, by your own experience."[65]

6.27 This shows how the belief dimension is given a high sensitization in the depth experiences. Cohen explains how this happens: "Despite the similarities, the spontaneous visionary experiences must have a much greater impact upon the person. If it is the culmination of a long period of abnegation or strenuous mental exercises, the psychological stage has been set for the awesome event. When it strikes a man like a bolt out of the blue, the conviction that it has an otherworldly origin is great. The message it contains carries more certitude. The spontaneous experience is, therefore, more likely to produce lasting changes in the chosen person."[66]

6.28 Therefore, the psychological certitude is only a part of the experience and can get attached to any type of beliefs one holds. What really happens here in the name of certitude of beliefs is that one values the experience one had with its overwhelming vividness. Consequently, it is the affective quality of the experience that matters and it has nothing to do with the meaningfulness or the truths of the belief. Leuba refers to a theology student who had such a spontaneous religious experience: "In this new state, discussion is no more possible, because, inasmuch as the ground of assurance is not rational, argumentation is irrelevant. The seminary student expresses this with pleasing ingenuousness: 'Strange to say, the arguments seemed not to enter into my thinking. There were no appropriate faculty and capacity for them in me. They stood apart from me. I could take the logical standpoint and could see that they were quite convincing, and yet my inward peace of belief was in no way disturbed.' 'Conviction' is, we see, a derived product, a mere causal off-shoot of the faith-state, having in itself no necessary worth. It is consequently a gross error to imagine that the chief practical value of the faith-state is its power to stamp with the seal of reality certain theological conceptions. On the contrary, its value lies solely in the fact that it is the psychic correlate of a biological growth reducing contending desires to one direction; a growth which expresses itself in new affective states and new reactions; in larger, nobler, more Christ-like activities. The strongest pillar of Christian 'orthodoxy' rests not on rational arguments, but on such experiences as those we have quoted. . . . When Biblical criticism, when historical and natural science, when psychology threatens the antique structure, it is in the regenerating power wielded by Christianity that the shaken believer finds shelter and rest. *The ground of this specific assurance in religious dogmas is then an affective experience.*"[67]

6.29 Therefore, the certitude of beliefs one gains in the depth experiences has really to be interpreted more as an emotional quality rather than as an epistemological quality. Because of the high sensitization featured in these experiences, they can increase the sensitivity to propositions which are immediately involved in the experience, so it is not at all surprising that a Christian should feel more certitude about beliefs, in the religious experiences. Such experiences need not be limited to feelings of certitude only. The depth experiences may add other dimensions to the beliefs. For example when one experiences Christ, one may also feel that Christ or God is the ultimate principle explaining everything such as the origin of the world, etc., etc. But these feelings have nothing to do with the beliefs. They are just features of the depth experiences. Arthur Koestler refers to a story George Orwell told him: "A friend of his, while living in the Far East, smoked several pipes of opium every night, and every night a single phrase rang in his ear, which contained the whole secret of the universe; but in this euphoria he could not be bothered to write it down and by morning it was gone. One night he managed to jot down the magic phrase after all, and in the morning it read: 'The banana is big, but its skin is even bigger'."[68]

6.30 (3) There is a third attempt that can be made to get out of the belief-experience circle. We suggested above that some Christian thinkers thought that appealing to religious experience was a way of giving evidence to the Christian beliefs. This possibility was mainly suggested by the intensity or the depth quality of those experiences. *In this respect*, we have to make a difference between the type of experiences Hick was speaking of (v. 6.3) and the depth experiences. In the latter their particular noetic and the depth quality is emphasized. We argued above that the intensity and the depth qualities of this type of experience do not separate them as particularly religious because of their easy duplicability. But still one can argue from the affective and illuminative qualities of these experiences for their possibility of giving credence to, or suggesting the possibility of, the facts asserted in the propositions of the belief dimension. Or one might argue that a positive metaphysics about Reality can be built upon the depth experience.

6.31 Such a theory can be suggested by an idea like this. The Judaic prophets first had overwhelming depth experiences. They were so impressed by the grand features of these experiences that they tried to interpret the universe and life in terms of these experiences. Particularly the illuminative and moral qualities of these experiences suggested that they were highly significant. Therefore, they projected the affective, noetic and moral qualities of these experiences to a transcendent person called God, the concept of God being easily borrowed from the existing polytheistic or animistic cults. Thus the experience comes first, then a theological accessory is attached to it so that it can give an overall religious interpretation of the life and universe. The kernel of truth lies in three central concepts: (i) an intensive depth experience, (ii) illuminative or enlightening qualities of this experience and, (iii) the moral accompaniments or resultants.

6.32 This is, of course a harmless theology to build, only if we remember to the very last how all this theology actually started. What can very easily happen is that we soon forget that theology started as a servant and start worshipping it instead. The process goes on unconsciously until the servant emerges triumphantly as the master—not unlike the computer in modern society. If Christian or Judaic theology actually started in the way we are discussing, then the present state of Christian theology is the best argument against even dreaming of such an attempt to build a theology on the depth experiences. However, in the light of this attempt, can we try to reinterpret Christian theology as subservient to religious experience? This can, of course, be done after manufacturing quite a few symbols. Christ would be a symbol, resurrection would be a symbol, atonement would be a symbol and even God would be a symbol, and his attributes like omniscience would be defined as harmless concepts only adding grandeur to the main symbol, God. The problem of evil would be defined as an aesthetic way of expressing man's moral deficiencies and so on and so forth. However, one thing is certain: it would not be Christianity any more.[69] And as it is beyond our scope we shall not go in to its details here.

6.33 To return to our main problem: can the grandeur and the moral perfections of the experience lend any support to Christian beliefs? We shall take the moral aspect later and now concentrate on the depth quality of the experience. On two grounds we can say that the grandeur of the depth experiences cannot lend any credence to Christian beliefs. One is that these experiences are not unique because of their easy duplicability and when the belief dimension is taken out, the illuminative or enlightening character of these experiences is without anchorage. And the other reason is that these experiences can accomodate any system of beliefs, as William James says: "The fact is that the mystical feeling of enlargement, union, and emancipation has no specific intellectual content whatever of its own. It is capable of forming matrimonial alliances with material furnished by the most diverse philosophies and theologies, provided only they can find a place in their framework for its peculiar emotional mood. We have no right, therefore, to invoke prestige as distinctly in favour of any special belief, such as that in absolute idealism, or in the absolute monistic identity, or in the absolute goodness, of the world."[70] Thus the attempt to emphasize the similarities between depth experiences and theistic beliefs only throws into clearer focus the need to clarify and establish, on other grounds, the beliefs which one entertains and which therefore, color the experiences one has.

6.34 It is not surprising to see the attempts made by drug followers to construct metaphysical theories based on drug experiences. Timothy Leary states, "I should like to advance the hypothesis that those aspects of the psychedelic experience which subjects report to be ineffable and ecstatically religious involve a direct awareness of the energy processes which physicists and biochemists and physiologists and neurologists and psychologists and psychiatrists measure."[71]

6.35 However, it should be emphasized that the peculiar nature of the depth experiences has made a deep impact on humanity in making various theoretical and affective observations about the world and society. Such attempts from the times of the Upanishads to the present day philosophies of religion testify to this fact. Particular mention should be made about the attempts to build religions based on drug experiences. Sometimes it is done within an accepted traditional religious framework, as for example in the Peyote religion. Or it is done outside any such religious framework, but within a socially integrated theoretical structure. Such a case of drug-based religion can be seen in Carlos Castaneda's *The Teachings of Don Juan: A Yaqui Way of Knowledge.* Some are trying even today to build religions based on drugs like LSD. Leary's attempts, with LSD prayers, etc., are well known. However suspect some may think this attempt to be, it should be accepted without any doubt that Leary and others are trying to start a religious movement based completely on the depth experiences produced by drugs. These attempts show the overwhelming psychological significance of the depth experiences and their 'attachability' to any type of suitable doctrinal or theoretical structure. When we think about such attempts, we can well understand why some Christian thinkers try to appeal to religious experience as giving credence to their belief structures.

6.36 (4) Now we come to the fourth way of getting out of the belief-experience circle. Almost all Christian mystics and philosophers have tried this way as their ultimate way out, though they have not consciously appreciated the immense value and importance of this way. Also, this way, if consistently carried out, is the only method of getting out of the circle. But once the mystic is out, he will find a different situation in front of him, because this way does not *necessarily* establish the existence of God or anything divine. Also, if this method is successfully carried out, it may well lead to making a radical transformation of man's relationship to God.

6.37 This way is to point to the ethical, moral and personality perfections that accompany or result from the religious experiences. The Christian position is that because the theistic religious experiences have such perfections as a result, it is a pointer to the fact that one is, in those experiences, experiencing God or the divine. Here, it is true, the moral criteria become the deciding factors. We discussed before how religious experiences were distinguished from other types of depth experiences by the fact that the former occurred within a religious belief-context. Thus, another distinguishing feature of such experiences is that they occur within the context of moral and ethical beliefs. If one needs to distinguish between nature and religious mystical experiences, this criterion could be very useful. Also, this criterion shows why Zen mystical experience is religious while nature mysticism is not.

6.38 It is only this criterion that gives grounds, if any, to distinguish religious experiences from drug experiences. The drug-followers have made many claims for the life-enhancing qualities of their experiences. But scientific researches into the field have made these claims very suspect. They claim that moral qualities like love and kindness are cultivated and increased in the drug experiences.

But a closer analysis shows that they are really chemically-induced abnormal mental reactions rather than rationally cultivated moral principles. Donald B. Louria, an authority on drug abuse, says: "One of the major claims of the proponents of the LSD experience is that it increases one's capacity to give or accept love. This too, of course, is almost impossible to measure accurately, but it seems to me very important to recognize that giving or accepting love connotes an in-depth relationship between two people, which mandates continuing communication between them. In many ways such a relationship is inconsistent with the LSD experience. LSD, more than any other illicitly used drug, places the individual in a very personal cocoon, spun out of illusion and hallucination. The experience is totally individualistic and self-centered, and therefore is diametrically opposed to the concept of love. This is not to say that after taking LSD one cannot have improvement in inter-personal relationships which appeared to be abrasive and unhappy prior to the use of the drug, but such apparently beneficial results do not, in most people, reflect an augmented capacity to love but rather diminished aggression and increased passivity."[72]

6.39 It is on the grounds of morals that the LSD religious experiences (like seeing God or experiencing the unifying vision under LSD) can be termed as religious hallucinations or illusions. (This should not be taken as cancelling the experiential validity of those experiences). This is clear from Louria's comments: "At the opposite end of the spectrum, the original notion that LSD could in some way circumvent tradtional religious experiences and permit the user to have immediate and direct communication with great religious leaders, with Christ or with God has for the most part not withstood the test of time. It certainly is true that LSD experiences are characterized by hallucinations and illusions which have religious overtones, but once the LSD experience is over, there is no evidence that the religious aspect of the experience has had any lasting beneficial effects on the user. By definition, a transcendental experience must have profound and long-lasting influence and effect specific and positive changes in behavioral patterns. Since this has not occurred under the influence of LSD, it would seem fair to conclude that the religious aspects of the LSD trip may well be pleasurable—and to certain individuals, especially those with religious training, meaningful—but they are not, in the conventional understanding of the the term, transcendental."[73]

6.40 But it should not be forgotten that within a proper context of religious and moral beliefs, the drug experiences can have a beneficial effect (This is not to recommend drugs in that sense, because the possible lethal and deadly effects of drugs are well known and proven). The experiment of Pahnke and Richards was carried out in a religious setting with students of religion and they report beneficial results: "renewed sense of personal worth coupled with, a relaxation of habitual mechanisms of ego defense . . . increased tolerance. . . . Changed or enlarged attitudes towards life are reported in the areas of deeper sensitivity to values that are felt to be eternal, increased sensitivity to an inner imperative that seeks expression through other-centred behaviour, increased vocational commitment. . . ."[74] Even Louria, who paints as black as possible a picture of the drug scene, commends this experiment. "This was an important experiment but its interpretation must be limited to students having formal training in religion, taking the drug during a traditional religious service. . . ."[75] However, it is true that a judgment on the behavioural changes cannot be made too soon. Pahnke and Richards say: "Although attitudinal and behavioural changes such as these are subjectively reported by psychedelic subjects . . ., the duration and permanence of such changes and the extent to which they are manifested in everyday existence are topics in need of extensive research. Only after such research is completed can the degree of correspondence between the positive changes claimed by psychedelic subjects and the effects of spontaneous life-enhancing mystical experiences be determined."[76] It is important to note that these comments are significant even in valuing the results of 'genuine' religious experiences, as we shall see.

6.41 If one tries to get out of the belief-experience circle through the way of moral perfection and personality perfection, this way has to be consistently and coherently pursued. The religious mystics appeal to moral criteria for the validity of their religious experiences. The supposition behind these appeals is that God is always good and therefore God always leads people to good. The genuineness of mystics and their claims is always proved by appealing to the moral and integrative features that characterize the personalities of the mystics.

6.42 St. Teresa very often makes moral criteria the deciding factor of genuineness of her mystical experiences. Often she wondered whether her visionary experiences were coming from Satan instead of God, but she decided that they were coming from God because, "I could not believe that Satan, if he wished to deceive me, could have recourse to means so adverse to his purpose as this, of rooting out my faults and implanting virtues and spiritual strength: for I saw clearly that I had become another person by means of these visions. . . ."[77] St. John of the Cross maintained that "with visions and experiences that are good: even though the soul desire it not they work their effect upon it. . . ."[78] Augustine Baker says: "Ecstasies that do not produce considerable profit either to the persons themselves or others, deserve to be suspected, and when any marks of their approaching are perceived, the persons ought to divert their minds some other way."[79] Underhill says that the worth of an ecstasy "depends entirely on the objective value of that idea or intuition"; otherwise "It is an abnormal bodily state, caused by a psychic state. . . ."[80] And she says that there is always a test for verifying the validity of visions and mystic experiences. "The test, . . . is . . . their life-enhancing quality. . . . They infuse something new in the way of strength, knowledge, direction; and leave it—physically, mentally or spiritually—better than they found it."[81] St. John says that one of the aims of religious life is "going forth from all things that are without, and from the desires and imperfections that are in the sensual part of man because of the disordered state of his reason"[82], and he speaks of the value of detachment and coveting nothing and of the resulting quiet and repose.[83] This shows the way they valued personality integration and perfection

6.43 However, the idea of moral perfection in the case of Christian mystics leads to some very complicated problems. We must try to analyze some of these problems. As we discussed in the chapter on God as The Good, morality assumes a peculiar nature in the Christian context. We saw that Kierkergaard was trying to point out a distinction between religious morality and ordinary morality and how he insisted that religious morality, when it contravenes ordinary morality, should be given preference over ordinary morality. This point is significant because this distinction is very important in the context of Christian mysticism. Very often the moral perfection of a Christian mystic is defined in terms of his affective relationship to God. To start with, the three fundamental moral virtues of mystical life are poverty, chastity and obedience.[84]

Poverty and chastity are aimed at controlling and perfecting oneself while obedience means obeying God's commands, moral and otherwise. Therefore, here again, morality is based on the idea of obedience. This way of taking morality, as we also discussed above (*v.* 4.28), can have bad implications and bad practical results.

6.44 It is true that Christian mystics have practiced love and charity towards humanity in many instances. In one instance, St. Teresa says: "What the Lord desires is works. If you seek a woman to whom you can give some help, never be affected by the fear that your devotion will suffer, but take pity on her, if she is in pain, you should feel pain too; if necessary, fast so that she may have your food . . .".[85] But the disturbing point about the Christian mystics is that all their salient moral ideals tend to center around the concept of God. This stems from the defects of Christian metaphysics. The ontological metaphysical Reality of God is always the Real and the Good state of existence. In relation to that, the world gets an inferior state of existence. This is an important value relation; the one is inferior to the other as contrasted with it. The world is less real and less important than something that is more real and more important. It is true that as creation the world is real, but that reality is essentially a derived reality; derived in relation to something that is fundamentally real. Therefore, the moral ideals tend to go towards the Transcendent Reality and so the relationships towards that Reality are much more important and significant than the relationships we have towards the world below. This is the idea that Kierkergaard was trying to give expression to. Eckhart speaks about the ontological relation between the world and God: "All this is created has no truth in itself. All creatures in so far as they are creatures, as they 'are in themselves' are not even illusion, they are 'pure nothing' . . .""All that is created is nothing . . . ""All creatures are one mere nothing. (Or:) There is no creature which is anything. (Or:) None of the creatures has being. What has no being—is nothing."[86] This type of metaphysics can have adverse effects on a theory of morality. We shall see how this happens in practice.

6.45 The Christian idea of love is more a reaching out towards the transcendent deity than a concern for the needs of man. As Underhill puts it: "Mystical Love is a total dedication of the will; the deep seated desire and tendency of the soul towards its source;[87] Love to the mystic, then, is (*a*) the active, conative, expression of his will and desire for the Absolute; (*b*) his innate tendency to that Absolute, his spiritual weight".[88] When the Reality is conceived as a Person to whom personal allegiance is to be offered, this type of relation can lead to certain dangerous extremes. As William James says, extreme devoutness can lead to fanaticism.[89] And he states: "An immediate consequence of this condition of mind is jealousy for the deity's honor . . . It is a partisan temper, and that is cruel. Between his own and Jehovah's enemies David knows no differences; a Catherine of Siena, panting to stop the warfare among Christians which was the scandal of her epoch, can think of no better method of union among them than a crusade to massacre the Turks; Luther finds no word of protest or regret over the atrocious tortures with which the Anabaptist leaders were put to death; and a Cromwell praises the Lord for delivering his enemies into his hands for 'execution'."[90] However much St. Catherine had to say about love towards human beings her relationship to human beings dramatically changed when she viewed them in terms of her allegiance to God and wished for the massacre of Turks. It is well know how St. Teresa hated the Lutherans and longed for the Church's triumph over them. Thus, the love towards God can sometimes lead to actions that contravene ordinary morality.

6.46 This type of love towards God can lead to another situation. James calls it the theopathic condition.[91] What were the fruits of strong and vivid revelations of Jesus and his love to the blessed Margaret Mary Alacoque? "She became increasingly useless in the convent, her absorption in Christ's love, which grew upon her daily, rendering her more and more incapable of attending to external duties. They tried her in the infirmary, but without much success, although her kindness, zeal, and devotion were without bounds, and her charity rose to acts of such a heroism that our readers would not bear the recital of them. They tried her in the kitchen, but were forced to give it up as hopeless—everything dropped out of her hands. The admirable humility with which she made amends for her clumsiness could not prevent this from being prejudicial to the order and regularity which must always reign in a community. They put her in the school, where the little girls cherished her, and cut pieces out of her clothes (for relics) as if she were already a saint, but where she was too absorbed inwardly to pay the necessary attention. Poor dear sister, even less after her visions than before them was she a denizen of earth, and they had to leave her in her heaven.''[92] James states: ''A lower example of theopathic saintliness is that of St. Gertrude, a Benedictine nun of the thirteenth century, whose 'Revelations', a well-known mystical authority, consist mainly of proof of Christ's partiality for her undeserving person. Assurances of his love, intimacies and caresses and compliments of the most absurd sort, addressed by Christ to Gertrude as an individual, form the tissue of this paltry-minded recital.''[93] In fact, most of the mystics' treatises like St. John's, contain voluminous praises of God and of His attributes rather than any considerations about human moral problems. That can very well be characterized as a mild form of the theopathic condition.

6.47 This love for God, which often results in making claims about the superiority of religious morals over and against ordinary morality, can sometimes lead even to ferocious extremes. Underhill says: ''From detachment such as that exhibited by the Blessed Angela of Foligno, who though *a true mystic*, viewed with almost murderous satisfaction the deaths of relatives who were impediments.''[94] St. Angela says: ''In that time and by God's will there died my mother, who was a great hindrance unto me in following the Way of God: soon after my husband died likewise, and also all my children. And because I had commenced to follow the aforesaid way, and *had prayed God that He would rid me of them*, I had great consolation of their deaths.''[95]

6.48 If mysticism can lead to this type of situation in the Christian context, it is difficult to argue for moral criteria in deciding the genuineness or validity of the mystical experiences, mainly because the moral criteria are not consistent or because they are, at times, completely anti-humanistic and anti-moral. In such situations, it is difficult to talk of a personality integration or perfection with regard to such mystics. Therefore, it is not a responsible statement to make when Stace maintains that ''The moral force of the Christian mystics is certainly more impressive'' than any other type of mystics; ''It is in this that the great strength of the Christian mystic lies.'' However, Stace adduces evidence for his statement though it is not at all convincing: ''. . . St. Teresa spent her life in founding or reforming monasteries [He says that this may not be impressive to a modern sociologist]. But this kind of activity was no doubt the medieval conception of the highest Christian virtue, and we have to take account of the times."[96] If St.Teresa was moved to this undertaking by her partisan temper, for which she was also noted, it could very easily be the reverse of a virtue from the point of view of human morality.

6.49 Some writers appeal to another distinguishing feature of Christian mystics to show that they were superior to other mystics. Underhill gives expression to this opinion. "In the mystics of the West, the highest forms of Divine Union impel the self to some sort of active, rather than of passive life: and this is now recognized by the best authorities as the true distinction between Christian and non-Christian mysticism."[97] But this distinction is not at all enlightening when one sees what she has to say about the active life of Christian mystics: "No temperament is less slothful than the mystic one; and the 'quiet' to which the mystics must school themselves in the early stages of contemplation is often the hardest of their tasks. The abandonment of bodily and intellectual activity is only undertaken in order that they may, in the words of Plotinus, 'energize enthusiastically' upon another plane. Work they must: but this work may take many forms—forms which are sometimes so wholly spiritual that *they are not perceptible to practical minds*. Much of the misunderstanding and consequent contempt of the contemplative life comes from the narrow and superficial definition of 'work' which is set up by a muscular and wage-earning community."[98]

6.50 In all fairness to Christianity, it should be admitted that Christianity has made an enormous contribution to the moral progress of humanity and some Christian mystics, like Eckhart and St. John, have achieved a personality perfection and serenity that implies a very high degree of moral and spiritual perfection. But the important thing we should not forget is that the Christian context very often has led to the contrary results. If the Christian context can contain anti-moral and anti-human tendencies, how can such a context lead to good results as well? This situation throws into light certain interesting facts about Christianity as it is practiced at times. This can be analysed in terms of the theistic theoretical strands and how they influence people's minds and personalities.

One can cultivate a loving kindness towards humanity by taking God as a supremely loving Person. But in the attempt to cultivate this attitude consistently one has to be oblivious to or ignore the other strand which shows from the fact of the existence of evil etc., that God is a bad person. Mystics and theologians have tried to explain away the existence of evil by many methods and means, e.g., by dubbing it as non-existent or as a privation of good, etc. (*v.* 3.10). But this is a cultivation of one strand to the exclusion of its accompanying strand which runs in contradiction to it. Many mystics have achieved personality perfection by meditation and other techniques thus insisting on the need for personal effort and the existence of free will. St. John says: "In order to reach this state, it will frequently need to make use of meditation . . .".[99] But this is to ignore the other doctrinal strands of predestination or omniscience or Grace which lead to a strong determinism (*v.* 3.15). As a unique moral character one may follow Christ though this uniqueness is not rationally established (*v.* 4.36). But such counter strands are dismissed on the grounds of faith. So, faith functions as a strong and impregnable bulwark in separating the theoretical strands and allowing one to choose now the loving strand, now the hating or punishing strand according to what one sees as the needs of the moment, without the slightest sense of contradiction (for examples of this almost schizophrenic condition *v.* 6.52; 6.45).

6.51 The idea of the world as a beautiful creation can lead one to appreciate nature and be thankful to God. This type of feeling of exhilaration and gratitude can generate noble sentiments and may make the person a great poet, a great musician like Bach, etc., etc. But, again, this is to be oblivious to the other strand (which, though logically necessary, may not appear in doctrine) of the theistic theoretical structure i.e., God as a bad person because of the existence of evil; and the world is not such an astonishingly beautiful place because of the existence of physical and moral evil. Here again faith is a strong foolproof mechanism to dispel the theoretical aspects of God that one does not want.

6.52 In a similar way, the bad theoretical strands also can influence human behaviour. In such cases they become only superficially bad because they get their justification from the religious morality (as distinct from ordinary and human morality) and become good and so may get into the doctrinal scheme as a doctrinal strand. The idea of God as a jealous person and as a person who hates or dislikes people of other faiths or religions can influence his followers to persecute other religions. Many 'religious' wars have been fought and many people of other religions persecuted on these grounds. We may condemn them now as wrong. But our argument is that such strands of theistic beliefs have led to such actions and are still doing so in some parts of the world. People who deviated from strict orthodoxy were burnt or persecuted. (The Islamic wars of persecution illustrate our point still more strikingly). In this type of behavior the idea that God loves everybody is ignored. One can always say that religious persecutions are bad and are always a misinterpretation of the Christian faith. But the persecutors may not find it difficult to find doctrinal support in the Bible and other religious writings to prove that God is a jealous person and hates or dislikes people who deviate from his teachings or follow other religions. St. Thomas Aquinas advocated that heretics must be "shut off from the world by death".[100]

6.53 However, the good results of the theistic faith depend on this way of using one (the good) strand to the exclusion of the other set that logically accompanies it. In the theoretical structure, the concept of God is contradictory because the ideas of omnipotence, omniscience and benevolence contradict each other. Omniscience also contradicts the existence of free will. These contradictions can be avoided if we take only certain strands to the exclusion of their logical counterparts. That is why though the idea of God is theoretically contradictory, it is not contradictory practically, or in practice. Therefore what happens here is that the believers choose the theoretical strands they want and ignore or explain away the others they do not want. But this is to take beliefs out of their proper context. The beliefs of a religion should be necessarily analyzed in their proper context in relation to the other ideas that are involved in the context. To a practicing Christian who chooses his strands, the Christian doctrinal scheme does not look contradictory. But to anybody who tries to view Christianity and its teachings *in their full* context, it will be clear that many of its strands contradict each other. (It is true that many have tried to explain rationally the undesirable strands. However, such attempts have not been successful, as we saw in the chapters above).

6.54 By choosing only the good strands of the Christian religion one might attempt to build up a consistent phenomenology of the doctrine of God. This can be done by seeing how in fact, the idea of God and Christ etc., affect believers behaviors, their moral ideas etc. If this is done in the proper cultural and historical context of Christianity, the possibility of the choice of only the good strands will be vitiated by the experiences like those of Angela de Foligno, etc. If these are avoided cleverly by appealing only to the healthy moral tendencies that Christianity has given birth to, then two consequences follow. One is that such a phenomenology of Christianity will be built necessarily upon humanist ethics and morality. Then morality becomes logically prior to theology which will be a devastating situation to Christianity. The other consequence is, such a phenomenology will essentially be an expurgated version of Christianity, not the Christianity with its full theoretical and practical implications in its historical and cultural context. Such attempts have been made by theologians like Tillich and Bultmann. But do they manage to get out of the predicament we have analyzed? Do they succeed in getting out of the problems of Christianity we have described? For Tillich, as well as Bultmann, ultimate salvation depends upon faith: "Faith is the state of being ultimately concerned." The important thing to note is that this faith cannot be created by man. "Faith cannot be created by the procedures of the intellect, or by the endeavours of the will, or by emotional movements. . . . in relation to God everything is by God."[101] ". . . in the moment in which the contents of the will to believe or of the obedience to order are sought, the shortcomings of the cognitive interpretation of faith reappear. For instance, if one is asked to accept the Word of God in obedience—and if this acceptance is called 'obedience of faith'—one is asked to do something which can be done only by one already in the state of faith who acknowledges the word heard to be the Word of God. The 'obedience of faith' presupposes faith but does not create it."[102] Thus, once the idea of faith is emphasized, the concept of a Personal God becomes the decisive concept. Does this mean that with Tillich we are going back to our old circle? Tillich rightly says: yes. "In accord with the circular character of systematic theology, the criterion of final revelation is derived from what Christianity considers to be the final revelation, the appearance of Jesus as the Christ. Theologians would not be afraid to admit this circle. It is not a shortcoming; rather it is the necessary expression of the existential character of theology."[103] Anyway, we are back in the old circle from which we have been trying to get out so far. Therefore, certain superficial terminological changes, such as Tillich makes in his theology, are not sufficient to solve the problems raised by Christianity. All that this can do is to make these problems lie dormant within the system. Another subtle attempt has been made by Wilfred Cantwell Smith when he says that there are no religions but only religious people, thereby trying to say that religions should be judged by the moral behavior of the 'religious' people.[104] But this way is really only a way of asking religions to commit suicide in the face of the threat of humanist ethics.

6.55 Any form of rehabilitation or a drastic reinterpretation of Christianity depends upon the choice of the good strands of Christianity. What happens when one chooses the strands one wants is that then one starts using these strands for the purposes one wants and likes. If one attempts moral perfection then one tends to utilize the theistic ideas and concepts that help one in attaining this ideal and tends to forget the contrary one that occur in the same context. Here morality precedes theology, and consequently, the concept of God may get transformed rather dramatically, in the sense that we tend to create the God we want. James explains how this has actually happened in the general theistic context: "Today a deity who should require bleeding sacrifices to placate him would be too sanguinary to be taken seriously. Even if powerful historical credentials were put forward in his favour, we would not look at them. Once, on the contrary, his cruel appetites were of themselves credentials. They positively recommended him to men's imaginations in ages when such coarse signs of power were respected and no others could be understood. Such deities then were worshipped because such fruits were relished.

"Doubtless historic accidents always played some later part, but the original factor in fixing the figure of the gods must always have been psychological. The deity to whom the prophets, seers and devotees who founded the particular cult bore witness was something to them personally. They could use him . . . In any case, they chose him for the value of the fruits he seemed to them to yield."[105] Referring to the modern context, Leuba says: "The feeling of freedom towards God has largely supplanted the duty-motive which the Catechisms continue to inculcate: action in obedience to God's commands is out of fashion; it is what is right and what is best which is now the favourite reason for conduct. Even a certain feeling of equality, monstrous as this may seem, has passed into the attitude of the people to God: awe, reverence, worship, appear only dimly and not as frequent as is assumed, in the religious consciousness of the democratic Anglo-Saxon."[106] This is what happens when one starts choosing or changing the various doctrinal and theoretical strands for one's particular purposes. Therefore, the concept of God as an experiential concept, is *fixed* mainly by one's temperament, outlook and socio-cultural environment. By projecting one's own chosen ideal on a chosen concept of God, one can make one's ideals divine. When such ideals become divine they are able to have a magnetic and attracting influence on the believer; in fact, more than Kant's Ideas can do. Therefore the phenomenological value of the concept of God depends, to a very high degree, on the choice of various strands implied in the concept and these may undergo various changes according to the believer's standpoint. This whole endeavor is necessarily dictated by the basic moral values one already accepts. Therefore, we can say that phenomenologically or experientially a concept of God can lead to morally beneficial results, but if one wishes to do that in the context of Christianity, then it involves sacrificing certain essential components of the Christian concept of God.

6.56 The use of particular strands or the changing of strands of the theistic beliefs for one's interests has been clearly illustrated by a survey carried out by Leuba. Referring to the collected material, he says, "The supremacy of the fundamental life-impulses over the directions of the intellect, of the unconscious over the conscious, affirms itself with uncontestable significance in these records: not what is objectively real or what is logical, but that which ministers to the approved needs and desires, is the 'religiously' true."[107] This makes the believer oblivious to many intellectual problems that surround the theistic doctrine. To illustrate, we shall quote Leuba again: ". . . preposterous as it may seem, it is yet true that he [the believer] cares very little who God is, or even whether He is at all. But *he uses Him*, instinctively, from habit, if not from a rational conviction in His existence, for the satisfaction of his better desires, and this he does ordinarily with the directness and the bluntness of the aggressive child of a domineering century, well-nigh stranger to the emotions of fear, of awe and of reverence. The truth of the matter may be put this way: *God is not known, He is not understood: He is used*—used a good deal and with an admirable disregard of logical consistency, sometimes as meat purveyor, sometimes as moral support, sometimes as friend, sometimes as object of love. If he proves himself useful, His right to remain in the service of man is thereby vindicated. The religious consciousness asks no more than that, it does not embarrass itself with further questions: does God really exist? . . ."[108]

6.57 So, to conclude, we can now see that for a Christian to get out of the belief-experience circle by appealing to moral and personality perfections is difficult because the results of Christian mystic life are not at all consistent. The presence of certain anti-moral tendencies in the Christian way of life was traced back to the inherent defects of the concept of God and its implied belief dimension. A Christian moral perfection was seen to be possible but at the expense of paying a critical price, i.e., by changing the doctrinal scheme to a very great and dramatic extent so that it ceases to be Christian or even theistic in the reverential sense. And we concluded by showing how a rehabilitated form of Christianity can be made. Any attempt to reformulate the concept of God, we saw, should be essentially based on humanistic moral values and as a consequence it establishes the necessary supremacy of humanistic moral values over and above the concept of God. This shows that the ultimate justification of any religion depends on its *consistent efficacy* in producing the moral perfection of man.

GOD AS EXPERIENCE - PART TWO

6.58 The analysis and the criticism of Christian religious experience in the preceding part of this chapter was carried out from an early Buddhist point of view, but the Buddhist basis of these criticisms was not examined in detail. The second part of this chapter, therefore, is devoted to such an examination, which will involve a discussion of the Buddhist idea of Nirvana and the ways of realizing it. To anticipate, our attempt in this part is to establish the following positions:

1. Nirvana is not a metaphysical or an ontological existent in any form.

2. The Buddha was completely against the establishment of the *existence* of any state of affairs purely or mainly on the basis of experience. The jump from experience to existence was emphatically criticized and rejected by the Buddha.

3. By going further still, we shall be seeing that Nirvana is *not* a mystical experience in the usual sense, that is, in the sense in which it is understood in the Christian tradition.

4. The Buddhist idea of Nirvana is completely translatable into categories of moral perfection and personality integration (in addition to extinction after death) and the Buddha believed that these two translations provided the ultimate justification of his teachings as a way of salvation.

6.59 Why should we discuss the idea of Buddhist Nirvana? Why is it so relevant to our discussion? It is relevant for some very important reasons. In the previous discussion we tried to show that the religious experience could not establish the existence of anything. To this some would say that in that case the Buddhist has a hard job to do, because the Buddhist, surely, posits the existence of Nirvana on the basis of experience. And the consensus of opinion of scholars and thinkers is that Nirvana is a state of existence or a transcendent existent. Also there is a common tradition among religious thinkers that there is 'a mystical truth' common to all religions. Underhill states this idea when she says that there is a mystical truth common to all religions though it may be obscured by various denominational colorings: "Hence its substance must always be distinguished from the accidents under which we perceive it: for this substance has an absolute, and not a denominational, importance."[109] This may suggest that Buddhism also shares in the adventure of mystical truths. Stace states this idea more clearly: " . . . the essence of the introvertive experience is the undifferentiated unity, and 'union with God' is one possible interpretation of it, which should not therefore be given as its definition. The same experience can be interpreted non-theistically as in Buddhism."[110] Otto goes to the extent of distinguishing the contents of mystical experiences. "Buddhism's very denial of atman only increases its mystical nature, for in so far as this final limitation is passed, the mystical, paradoxical character of Nirvana is revealed. Nirvana is an absolute, supernatural, mystic state to the same extent as is the *unio mystica* between the soul and the eternal God, and by virtue of that state both are forms of mysticism though with a very different content."[111] Even contemporary scholars like Trevor Ling state that Nirvana is clearly a metaphysical entity: "However, the explanation of some would-be etymologists, who used the simile of the going out of a lamp by blowing have caused some confusion about the meaning of the Buddhist term *nibbāna*, and this has led to the use of such English words as 'extinction' and 'annihilation'. This view of *nibbāna* is in fact refuted in the Buddhist canon as a mistaken opinion (*micchādiṭṭhi*) known as the Annihilationist View. As late a writer as Buddhaghosa makes it clear that *nibbāna* is so called because it means the complete end or dying down of passion and craving. In the Abhidhamma literature, *nibbāna* is regarded as an entity; it is a *dhamma* (entity) distinct from all other *dhammas*."[112] So, there is a very strong tradition of scholarship that maintains Nirvana to be a transcendent existent entity posited on the basis of a mystical experience. Our attempt, first, is to show why this tradition is wrong and how misleading it can be in the Buddhist context.

6.60 The term Nirvana literally means 'blowing out'. But even 'blowing out' can mean several things. Though the Hindus also used the term Nirvana, they used it in a different way from the Buddhists. It would be useful to clear up this confusion in order to clarify the Buddhist use of the term, particularly because some believe that the Buddhists borrowed the meaning as well as the term from the Hindu tradition. Frequent occurrences of the word Nirvan are found in the *Mahābhārata*. Berriedale Keith maintains: " . . . we must remember that in all likelihood the terms Nirvana as indicating the final end was taken over by the Buddhists from existing speculation, for the term is freely found in the philosophic parts of the *Mahābhārata* which, though late in their present form represent earlier doctrine . . . ".[113] In the *Bhagavadgītā* we find the following instances: "One reaches the Brahmanirvana; One is near the Brahmanirvana; The great bliss Nirvana".[114] In the *Anugītā* we find: "He gradually obtains Nirvana, like fire devoid of fuel."[115] Because the simile of fire was employed by the Buddha also, these instances seem to carry much weight.

6.61 But we must find out what was meant by 'the blowing out of the fire' when it was used by the Hindus. Keith and Schrader point out[116] that since ancient times the common Indian traditional view has been that an expiring flame does not really go out but is restored to that primitive, pure and invisible state of fire in which it rested prior to making its visible appearance. This view they illustrate referring to pertinent Upanisadic passages. *The Śvetāśvatara Upaniṣad* (vi. 19) speaks of Brahman as an expired flame: "A fire, the fuel of which has been consumed" and it (1.13) speaks of atman "as the form of fire when latent in its source is not seen and yet the seed is not destroyed". *Nṛsimhottarapāni Upaniṣad* (middle) states: "That Self is pure in spirit, like fire after it has burnt what it had to burn."[117] The third verse of the *Maitreyi Upaniṣad* runs as follows: "As fire for want of fuel comes to rest in its own birthplace, so from the cessation of its motions the thinking principle comes to rest in its own birthplace."[118] Schrader thinks that the Buddha too applied the simile of flame in this very same sense. If the Buddha did that, then he would have been in a peculiar position, because Buddhism arose from a criticism and a rejection of Hindu metaphysics. This rejection of Hinduism throws much light on the Buddhist use of the term Nirvana. As we shall see presently, a careful reading of the relevant passages of the Pali canon discloses that the Buddha used it in the sense of complete extinction. Herein lies the exact difference between the Nirvana of the Hindus and of the Buddha. Keith and Schrader have been misled by the apparently similar usage of the word without examining the subtle differences in the denotation of this word in the two traditions.

6.62 In order to clarify the question of Nirvana after death, the Buddha employed the simile of the extinction of fire. In the *Aggivacchagotta Sutta*, to a Brahmin who asks the Buddha as to what happens to a saint after death, the latter refuses any categorical reply. The simile illustrating the point at issue is a blazing fire, which, as the Buddha states, when extinguished, cannot be spoken of as having gone to any direction such as east, west, etc.[119] Here the utter extinction of fire is meant. That is why the question "where did it go?" becomes meaningless. If the Buddha meant it to indicate "a going back to a primordial fire" the question would not have been meaningless. *Sutta Nipāta* speaking of an Arahant states: "The old is destroyed, there is no arising of a new. Those whose minds are unattached to any future existence are destroyed of their seeds (of future existence) and their desires do not increase. The wise extinguish like this lamp."[120] Thus a newer existence in any form is clearly ruled out by the words "there is no arising of a new" (*navaṃ natthi sambhavaṃ*). The very same idea is emphasized again, in referring to the death of an Arahant: "Just as the bourn of a blazing spark of fire struck from the anvil, gradually fading, cannot be known as to have *gone anywhere*, so in the case of those who have rightly won release and crossed the flood of lusts that bind, and reached the bliss unshaken, they do not possess a *movement* (going anywhere) that can be pointed to."[121] The Commentator Dhammapala comments on "*paññāpetum gatī natthi*" as "gone into the state of not being able to be pointed at."[122] It is explicitly said in that instance, the five '*khandhas*' (component part of a person) being annihilated, the "consciousness reaches its end" (*viññānaṃ atthaṃ agamā*).[123] The commentary elaborates it as reaching "the end; destruction and stoppage".[124] When consciousness is destroyed there is absolutely nothing left to go anywhere, to return to any absolute source.

6.63 Many other instances to the same effect can be given. "As a flame blown out by the violence of the wind . . . O Upasiva, so said the Buddha, goes out, cannot be reckoned (as existing), even so Muni, delivered from name and body, disappears, and cannot be reckoned as (existing)";[125] "For him who has disappeared there is no form (measure), O Upasiva, . . . so said the Buddha, . . .

that by which they say he is, exists for him no longer, when all things (*dhamma*) have been cut off, all (kinds of) dispute are cut off."[126] The Arahant after death is said to have no measure because there is nothing left whatsoever that can be spoken of. One might argue then that the Arahant really becomes 'infinite' and 'measureless'. If so, then by the same token the extinguished flame also becomes 'infinite and measureless'.

6.64 An objection to our conclusion that Nirvana is absolute extinction might be made in terms of the Buddha's rejection of Yamaka's view "that an Arahant is broken up and perishes when the body breaks up, and becomes not after death."[127] It is said that the Buddha did not say so. The reason for this rejection is clarified when the problem is approached in exactly the same way as the question of the existence of the Tathagata (saint) after death. The question as to what happens to a saint after death has been treated as an 'unanswerable' question by the Buddha. Sariputta Thera explains that it is wrong to pose this question because "form, feelings etc., cannot be taken as the saint",[128] one cannot speak of a saint as existing in this very life in truth, in reality, and therefore, one cannot deny him after death.[129] According to this view the extinction or the annihilation (these two words are used synonymously) theory itself becomes meaningless because there is no 'person' to be annihilated.

6.65 Here, the 'two ways of speech' advocated by the Buddha become very relevant to our discussion. The person can be viewed in two ways. The first is the 'conventional way'. The other is designated in the commentaries as the 'absolute way'. It is said: "Just as much as the word 'chariot' is used when parts are put together, there is the use (*sammuti*) of the term 'being' (*satto*) when the (psycho-physical) constituents are present."[130] Buddhaghosa comments: "There is no 'being' here means that in the complex of conditioned things one does not obtain a 'being' in 'reality' . . .'Use' means that the 'being' is a conventional usage."[131] Thus, when viewed in the conventional way, there is a 'being' while in the absolute way one can see only the five-fold aggregates. The *Kathāvatthu* states the same when it says that "a person is not found in the real and the absolute sense."[132] Here K.N. Jayatilleke observes: "But although the commentaries speak of these two kinds of truth, it is necessary to note that they do not imply that what is true in the one sense, is false in the other or even that one kind of truth is superior to the other, notwithstanding the use of the term '*paramattha*' (absolute) does denote one of them. The commentary to the *Aṅguttara* says: 'The exalted one preaches the conventional teaching to those who are capable of listening to this conventional teaching and penetrating the meaning, discarding ignorance and acquiring eminence. But to those who are capable of listening to his absolute teaching and attaining distinction, he preaches the absolute truth. There is this simile on the matter. Just as if there were a teacher, who explains the meaning of the Three Vedas and is versed in the regional languages, to those who understand the meaning if he spoke in the Tamil language, he explains it in the Tamil language and to another who would understand (if he spoke) in the Andhra language, he speaks in that Language.'[133] We note that penetration of the truth is possible by either teaching, conventional or absolute; it is like using the language that a person readily understands and there is no implication that one language is superior to another. The commentary to the *Kathāvatthu* also emphatically says: 'But whether they use conventional speech, they speak what is true, what is factual and not false.'[134] Thus, according to the *Nikāyas*, it would be true to say, "a person exists in the present so long as one does not mean by 'person' a substance enduring in time. Convention requires that I use such words as 'I' or 'person' but so long as one is not misled by their implications (of a perduring entity) the statement is true."[135]

6.66 Thus, according to the absolute way, the annihilationist theory of Nirvana becomes meaningless. Nevertheless, even here, it can be made meaningful to a certain extent. According to the absolute way, only the factors like 'consciousness, feelings, form' etc, exist. What happens in rebirth is that the stream of consciousness becomes related to a newer existence or a birth. But, in the case of a saint, that consciousness reaches 'absolute stoppage'. The Buddha states it in exactly the same way when he says that the factors of personality (consciousness etc.) of a saint come to absolute stoppage, 'made of a nature not to spring up again in future time' (see below). Thus even in the absolute sense, though there is no person, the annihilationist theory can have meaning as the 'stoppage of the factors'. Viewed in the conventional way, of course, the 'person' is annihilated.

6.67 Another objection (*v.* 6.59) might be put forward by maintaining that Nirvana as absolute extinction may mean the 'annihilationist view' (*uccheda vāda*) which the Buddha rejected emphatically. Jayatilleke explains that this theory clearly and explicitly refers to the materialist view.[136] Therefore, what the Buddha meant by that view was the one held by the materialists who maintained that all men get fully extinguished soon after death. He rejected this view because he accepted the fact of rebirth.

6.68 Referring to the analogy drawn by the Buddha between the impossibility of speaking of the Tathagata after death and the impossibility of reckoning the sands of the river Ganges or the water drops in the ocean, Keith concludes that therefore the Tathagata is "real but ineffable".[137] But we have already seen how strongly the Buddha's ideas imply the extinction, in the fullest sense, of the Tathagata after death and how the impossibility of reckoning him is traceable to the fact that there was nothing left to be reckoned. The other simile also refers to the same impossibility. In that very context, too, it is clearly emphasized that the saint's consciousness (form, feelings etc.) "is abandoned, cut down at the root, made like a palm-tree stump, *made something that is not*, made of a nature not to spring up again in future time. Set free from reckoning as consciousness (feelings etc.) is the Tathagata, Maharaja, deep boundless, unfathomable like the mighty ocean."[138]

6.69 Here we have to face a problem. The Buddha has on many occasions spoken of Nirvana in various positive terms. In the *Udāna* it is said: "Monks, there is a not-born, a not-become, a not-made, non-compounded. Monks, if that unborn, not-become, not-made, non-compounded were not, there would be apparent no escape from this here that is born, become, made, compounded."[139] Some writers have taken this passage to indicate a positive and an ontological existence of Nirvana. But we should be careful to avoid taking words in their literal meanings particularly when they are not supported by any other positive evidence. Therefore we should interpret these words within the context of the Buddha's other teachings. What he meant to do by using these words was to emphasize the marked difference between *Saṃsāra* (the phenomenal cycle of existence) and Nirvana. he clarifies: "So I, monks, being liable to birth because of self, having known the peril in what is liable to birth seeking the unborn, the uttermost security from the bonds—Nirvana—won the unborn . . . being liable to ageing . . . won the unageing . . ."[140] It is important to remember here that the terms used in these passages have a very high value connotation and therefore one should not take them in a descriptive sense.

6.70 Rune Johansson, who has tried to make a detailed analysis of the psychology of Nirvana, maintains that Nirvana is not an ontological existent. Commenting on the above passage from the *Udāna* he says that the passage should be interpreted or translated really as "freedom from birth, freedom from death" etc.[141] Therefore he says that to regard Nirvana as an entity or a Reality is a 'misunderstanding',[142] as well as it is wrong to regard it as "a dimension of existence".[143]

6.71 But at the same time Johansson maintains that Nirvana is not annihilation either.[144] This is the root of Johansson's contradiction and this contradiction pervades his whole analysis of Nirvana. He thinks that "Nibbana certainly involves immortality in some form".[145] The contradiction is that if there is any form of existence after death of an Arahant, then Nirvana becomes necessarily an ontologically existent Reality. However, to prove his contention he says that *citta* (mind) and *viññāṇa* (consciousness) are different, *citta* is the fundamental thing while *viññāṇa* is only a process of *citta*,[146] and that what extinguishes at Nirvana is *viññāṇa* but not *citta* and therefore *citta* goes on after the death of an Arahant. It is *citta*, according to him, that attains Nirvana.[147] As evidence for his theory Johansson wrongly translates a canonical passage. Quoting ". . . *cittaṃ virattaṃ vimuttaṃ hoti anupādāya āsavehi vimuttattā ṭhitaṃ . . . apritassaṃ paccattaññeva parinibbāyati*",[148]he translates as ". . . *citta* is released from the obsessions without basis, then by its release it is steadfast . . . free from excitement it attains *nibbāna* by itself."[149] There is absolutely nothing in this passage to mean that "*citta* attains *nibbāna* by itself". "*Parinibbāyati*" means 'extinguishes' or 'blows out'. Also his distinction between *citta* and *viññāṇa* is completely unwarranted because all throughout the canon the two terms are used synonymously. Therefore to make such a radical distinction without even the slightest evidence for it is a very irresponsible step to take. Johansson obviously does not understand the gravity of the mistake he is making. This radical distinction between the *citta* and *viññāṇa* clearly leads to a theory of soul. His observations definitely lead in that direction. ". . .somebody should experience the function of *viññāṇa* and also experience that it has stopped: that is *citta*."[150] But this form of soul theory would be an anathema to the Buddha. Johansson refers to another instance to prove his view. With reference to the death of the Arahant Vakkali, the Buddha is said to have declared "with consciousness not established the noble-born Vakkali has attained *parinibbāna*."[151] Johansson gives a wrong interpretation to this when he says, "We can take these stories to mean that at least the Buddha himself was able to trace an arahant even after death."[152] In fact, what the Buddha advised about this type of situation is clear when he said that by asking whether there is or is not anything left after the death of an Arahant, "one makes difficulty where there is none."[153] In innumerable instances the Buddha has declared that Nirvana is the stoppage or extinction of *viññāṇa*.[154] Though the word 'extinction' has been put into disrepute[155] by scholars the simple fact is that the exact translation of the word '*nirodha*' is extinction. It is said that in Nirvana "there name and form stop without remainder: by the extinction of consciousness this also stops."[156] The eightfold path has been defined in terms of the extinction of consciousness: "This eight-fold path is the way leading to the cessation of consciousness."[157] This extinction of consciousness resembles the extinction of a flame: "To him who has won freedom through the cessation of *viññāṇa* and the destruction craving, the liberation of mind is like extinction of a lamp."[158] Sometimes the word 'cessation' is used, ". . . from the cessation of consciousness a Bhikkhu is completely extinguished."[159] The extinction of *viññāṇa* is necessary for the cessation of *dukkha*: "By the extinction of consciousness, there is no origin of pain."[160]

6.72 There is another important grammatical point that has been ignored by scholars. Nirvana is always said to be achieved. This idea is revealed in passages like '*nibbānaṃ sacchikaroti*'. But this idea of achieving Nirvana is used always with regard to the achievement of enlightenment while a person is living. Complete Nirvana is said to happen only at the death of the Arahant. When the death of an Arahant is referred to, a verb, *nibbāti* is always used. In such instances, scholars still speak of 'achieving Nirvana' etc., slightly suggesting that there is a 'state' to be achieved. In order to be precise, in such instances a precisely equivalent translation should be made. Thereby it would be emphasized that the idea of Nirvana appears not only in a nominal form but in a verbal form as well. Only by translating the verbal form with a verb can we do justice to the following instances: "Those who are free from defilements nirvanize"[161]; "By truly realizing the truth they have completely nirvanized"[162]; "By seeing what does the Bhikkhu nirvanize?"[163] (It is true that the word '*nibbuta*' is used for living Arahants but it is then used in the sense of 'cool' as in "*sītibhūtosmi nibbuto*"). The death of the Buddha or of Arahants is always referred to as '*parinibbāna*', '*pari*' meaning 'completely' or 'in every respect'. When we think that the meaning of Nirvana is blowing out, we can see that when it is used as a verb how precisely it expressed the idea of complete blowing out or extinction.

6.73 Another strong evidence for the idea that Nirvana is not an ontological state but only a psychological (a dispositional) state is seen when Nirvana is referred to as being able to be 'produced' by persons: *nibbānaṃ abhijāyati.*[164]

6.74 Most of the misconceptions about Nirvana as an ontologically existent Reality or an entity or as involving immortality arise from not taking Nirvana in the proper doctrinal context of Buddhism. The Buddha completely rejected the idea of a soul or anything similar to a soul, or any type of enduring entity in the human personality. Everything is conditioned necesarily. Therefore if anything persists after the death of an Arahant it has necessarily to be condtioned. And, anything conditioned is by definition impermanent. Therefore, even the slightest possibility of immortality is not admitted in the Buddhist context. When all the conditioned elements cease to exist, there is nothing in human personality that can come into contact with a permanently existing Reality. So the concept of an ontological Reality is a completely foreign concept to the Buddhist doctrinal context.

6.75 The idea of immortality is a particularly non-Buddhistic idea. If Nirvana means a further existence, in some form or other, it would be getting attached to another form of existence. In his teaching the Buddha rejects two forms of existence, *bhava* and *sambhava.*[165] Here by using *sambhava* in addition to *bhava* the Buddha was rejecting every form of new existence, even those other than *bhava*. A Christian can argue that the absence of the idea of immortality is a defect of Buddhism. Owen says that for the moral perfection, immortality is necessary and produces a Kantian argument. ". . . even those moral facts require another life, why should it be an *endless* life? would not man's end be reached in a life of limited duration? The answer is that a temporally finite life would still be morally incomplete. It would be infinitely less than the eternal end that could imagine, so that we should lack final happiness."[166]The main defect of this argument is that it makes moral perfection practically an unattainable ideal. For the Buddha, moral perfection was completely an attainable ideal (we shall discuss this later). However, the attempt to make the concept of immortality meaningful in terms of a theoretical and abstract idea of morality is not a very helpful way to understand immortality. The main problem about immortality is the justification of its existence. Why should there be immortality? 'Mere existence' does not have any specific significance. It is the quality of life that matters rather than its quantity. There can be various ways of justifying the existence of immortality. Owen tried one method, but at the expense of clarity and moral perfectability. A.E. Taylor tried another method in his *The Faith of a Moralist* where he appeals to the happiness that comes from enjoyment of the beatific vision.

6.76 Taylor's idea, however, does not make much sense for some important reasons. The most important reason was explained by the Buddha when he said that any form of affective experience was liable to change, and to be otherwise (*vipariṇāma aññathābhāva*), and strongly maintained that there could not be any form of static enjoyment. It is true that Taylor is talking about heavenly enjoyment which is different from ours. But, according to the Buddha, any form of affective experience was essentially conditioned (*v.* I.28). C.D. Broad's criticisms of Taylor's book can very easily be a commentary on the Buddha's position: "When we assert that to enjoy the beatific vision is man's greatest good, is there not a danger that we may be generalizing from the tastes and capacities of a very few exceptional men to mankind at large? Prof. Taylor's musical analogies will serve to illustrate my meaning. Musicians no doubt do derive a high and exquisite happiness from listening to great music well executed. It may well be that this kind of happiness is greater and better than any that the non-musical can enjoy. Still, to the vast majority of men, a concert of classical music would be a very fair earthly foretaste of Purgatory, to go no further. Frankly, I find it hard to believe that more than a tiny proportion of men would be capable of experiencing the beatific vision, or would view the prospect of an eternity occupied in it with anything but horror, unless they were so radically transformed by death as to be no longer themselves. Even if I assent to the doctrine that an eternity of beatific vision would be the highest good for *me*, I am not sure that my assent has not been gained under false pretenses. The fact is that I am well enough acquainted with temporal goods to see that they all have great drawbacks. By definition *these* defects would be absent in the beatific vision. But it might well have other defects of its own which I fail to envisage only because I know so little in detail about it. The defects of temporality, like those of representative government, are familiar to all of us, for we were all born and bred under it. For the same reason its merits tend to be taken for granted. We tend therefore to idealize eternity and autocracy, which at least are free from the old familiar ills. But autocracy has its castor-oil; and the denizens of eternity, if such there be, may for all we know have troubles of their own which do not affect the creatures of time."[167]

6.77 Therefore, both the ways of justifying immortality do not make much sense. A Buddhist would make another main and fundamental objection. It is that before proving even the possibility of immortality, the Christian has to prove the existence of a permanent, enduring soul. If the idea of soul cannot be made meaningful, to say nothing of being proved, then the idea of immortality becomes meaningless. Therefore immortality depends on the meaningfulness of the concept of soul (*v.* Chapter 1).

6.78 However, there is a parallel in later Buddhism. It is interesting to observe that in Mahayana Buddhism an idea of semi-immortality can be seen when it believes in the indefinite (not immortal) existence of the Buddhas or Bodhisattvas after their deaths. But the Mahayana Buddhists have clearly made this idea of semi-immortality subservient to an altruistic morality. Their argument is that, those Buddhas feel they are obliged to live on indefinitely to help all human beings to attain salvation. And they will attain complete Nirvana only after all the beings have attained salvation. This, of course, amounts, practically, to a doctrine of full immortality. But their reason for immortality can be a convincing justification for a semi- or a full immortality though, of course, it involves many other theoretical and practical problems. Further, it is interesting to observe that according to the Buddha, the justification for existence between the realization of Nirvana and the point of death was two-fold. One was that even to harm oneself was unethical and immoral and the other reason was that during that period the Arahants had to serve humanity for the latter's spiritual welfare and therefore, he advised the monks: "Monks, go on travelling for the spiritual welfare and happiness of humanity". But the Buddha did not go on to advocate the achievement of immortality on this ground because in the context of his teaching it was a meaningless concept.

6.79 So, we have seen that Nirvana does not involve the ideas of an ontological state of Reality or any form of immortality. We also saw that Nirvana, in its complete sense, means full extinction. But Nirvana is in many places characterized as a state of 'happiness' of a very high degree. If, as our interpretation goes, Nirvana means a person's extinction along with his body, how can it be termed as a happy state? This means that there are two kinds of Nirvana. These two kinds are explicitly mentioned in the canon. "Those two kinds of Nirvana have been declared by the Seer who is such and unattached. One is obtainable in this very life, with the base remaining but the stream of becoming cut off. The (Nirvana) without the base belongs to the future when all becomings cease utterly."[168] If so, what does this positive aspect of Nirvana mean? Does this realization of Nirvana mean a kind of experience? We criticized the Christian mystical experience for being an 'experience' on several grounds. With that criticism in the background let us see what the Buddhist analysis of 'Nirvana and religious experience' has to say about the Christian and other forms of depth experience.

6.80 In the Buddhist tradition, meditation is regarded as an essential way of preparing oneself for enlightenment. The main purpose of meditation is concentration and the personality integration that accompanies the higher stages of meditation, and the whole process ultimately leads to Nirvana or enlightenment. The most common meditational technique described in the canon starts with concentration as leading to four basic *dhyānas*. *Dhyānas* lead to four mental spheres which lead to the last stage that provides the background for enlightenment.

6.81 The central feature of Buddhist meditational techniques is that they emphatically refuse to pay any attention to the experiences that come to one in the course of meditation. The gradual rejection of experiences can be seen to be taking place progressively the first four *dhyānas*. The first *dhyāna* is accompanied by "initial thought and discursive thought, is born of aloofness and is rapturous and joyful. By allaying initial thought and discursive thought, ones mind is subjectively tranquilized and fixed on one point, one enters and abides in the second meditation which is devoid of initial thought and discursive thought, is born of concentration and is rapturous and joyful. By the fading out of rapture, one dwells with equanimity, attentive and clearly conscious, and experiences in his person that joy of which the Aryans say: 'Joyful lives he who has equanimity and is mindful', and he enters and abides in the third meditation (*dhyāna*). By getting rid of joy, by getting rid of anguish, by the going down of his former pleasures and sorrows, one enters and abides in the fourth meditation (*dhyāna*), which has neither anguish nor joy, and which is entirely purified by equanimity and mindfulness."[169]

6.82 There are two important things to note here. One is the gradual and progressive rejection of all affective experiences, even of happiness as a felt particular experience. The other important factor is the attitude or the reaction one has towards all types of experiences. In the first *dhyāna* a critical analysis of the experiences is carried out, and after their understanding the reaction to all experiences change. The new attitude is that of a neutral onlooker who views things with equanimity, or disinterestedness (*upekhā*). This stage shows a marked difference between the Buddhist tradition and the tradition of St. Teresa who based her mystic life on visionary experiences. The disinterestedness that is cultivated in the 3rd and 4th *dhyānas* becomes the central attitudinal reaction to all the experiences that are going to follow. Therefore the 4th *dhyāna* forms the most crucial junction in the Buddhist meditational techniques. After the 4th *dhyāna* one can, if necessary, progress straight into enlightenment, or follow one of several other meditational paths to enlightenment (*v.* 6.100). However, the standard practice has been the proceeding from the 4th *dhyāna* to the sphere of (the consciousness of) space. Here one enters into the mental sphere of space thinking that everything is space.

6.83 After the sphere of the consciousness of space, one enters into the sphere of consciousness thinking that everything is infinite consciousness. This stage is very important from our point of view because here the Buddhist is coming into contact with an infinite consciousness, the type of contact many Hindu mystics and Christian mystics like Eckhart and St. John of the Cross do claim. And, as those mystics claimed, the Buddha too declared it to be a very pleasurable state of experience. The Buddha says: "Again, monks, here we have a certain person who, by utterly transcending the sphere of infinite space, regarding the consciousness as infinite, reaches up to and abides in the sphere of infinite consciousness. He enjoys it, longs for it and finds happiness therein."[170]

6.84 But the Buddha refuses to accept this experience, because it is a mental experience. He says that one has to understand that it is really a mentally contrived and therefore a conditioned experience, and therefore is liable to vanish, change and end. Anything experiential is conditioned and therefore cannot stand the test of a fundamental Reality. The Buddha, referring to the meditator, explains why he refuses to accept the experience of the infinity of consciousness as an ultimate Realtiy: "He thus ponders: This sphere of the infinity of consciousness is just a higher product, it is produced by higher thought. Then he comes to know: Now even that which is a higher product, produced by a higher thought, is impermanent, of a nature to end."[171] He applies this criticism to all the stages of depth experiences.[172]

6.85 The Buddha maintained that anybody who has got a strong determination can produce such experiences with sufficient perseverence. What is necessary is sufficient concentration to 'will' such an experience. Here one can easily envisage how Eckhart and St. John, etc., could bring about such an experience because they were strongly 'willing' (making an effort of will) to experience the Infinite Consciousness of God. Talking about "the union and transformation of the soul with God", St. John says it "comes to pass when the two wills—namely that of the soul and that of God—are conformed together in one."[173] We saw how Eckhart emphasized the importance of feelings in the unitive experience. He conceives of this union as an embrace: "In this embrace all is dissolved in all; for all encloses all."[174] And he says that this unity in itself is unbounded: ". . . in itself (viz. the all-inclusive unity it is itself unbounded."[175] Buddhaghosa explains how, after the sphere of the infinity of space, one can attain the sphere of the infinity of consciousness, "When he wants to develop the sphere of infinite consciousness, he must first achieve mastery in the five ways in the attainment of the sphere of infinite space. Then he should see the danger in the sphere of infinite space in this way: 'This attainment has fine-material *dhyāna* as its near enemy, and it is not as peaceful as the sphere of infinite consciousness'. So having ended his attachment to that, he should give his attention to the sphere of infinite consciousness as peaceful, adverting again and again as 'Consciousness, Consciousness' to the consciousness that occurred pervading that space (as its object); He should give it attention, review it, and strike at it with applied and sustained thought. . .

"As he directs his mind again and again on to that sign in this way, the hindrances are suppressed, mindfulness is established, and his mind becomes concentrated in access. He cultivates that sign again and again, develops and repeatedly practises it. As he does so, consciousness belonging to the sphere of infinite consciousness arises in absorption with the (past) consciousness that pervaded the space (as its object), just as that belonging to the sphere of infinite space did with the space (as its object)."[176]

6.86 In fact, there were religious teachers during the time of Buddha himself who had achieved these spheres of consciousness and declared them to be the final attainment of the transcendent. For example, the ascetic Alarakalama declared the sphere of Nothingness, which comes after the sphere of infinite consciousness, as the final point of transcendent Reality, and Uddakaramaputta declared the next stage, the sphere of neither-consciousness-nor-unconsciousness as the final point.[177] But the Buddha, who first trained himself under those two ascetics, thought that they were enamored in the spheres of conditioned bliss. This also shows that anybody who perseveres in contemplation and control of mind can achieve these spheres of consciousness and those who have not any theistic beliefs already may try to build a religion based on these experiential states as Alarakalama and Uddakaramaputta did. A person, like a Christian, who has already got a theistic beliefs system about an Infinite God can very easily interpret these experiences as experiences of God and these experiences, in turn, have got certain characteristics of an Infinite Person, e.g., Consciousness, Infinity, Boundlessness, etc. Therefore, these experiences have got certain qualities that can very fittingly reinforce a theistic belief dimension. Also from these experiences, one can very easily argue for the existence of an immortal or a boundless or a non-spatio-temporal soul. The Buddha would reject such an argument as another mentally conditioned item of experience. These experiences by themselves are not important in any significant sense. The Buddha explains that even an evil man may be able to practice contemplation and reach up to the sphere of neither-consciousness-nor-unconsciousness.[178] This shows that it is not the experience that counts but the way one understands and responds to it. For the Buddha what was important was to understand and comprehend their nature. This requires non-committed cognition or an experience, because the mistake of the 'experientialists' was to get related to these experiences *affectively*. So Ananda explains how one should train oneself to view them, and he applies this principle to all levels of experience, beginning with sense experiences: " 'There will be just the eye, but no sensing of objects and the sphere thereof . . .'. When he had thus spoken, the venerable Udayin said to him: 'Is then he, who senses not a sphere, percipient, reverend Ananda, or impercipient?' 'He is certainly percipient, reverend sir, . . .'. 'But how can he be percipient and yet sense not the sphere?' '. . . consider the monk who, passing wholly beyond the sphere of space-infinity, enters and abides in the sphere of consciousness-infinity, thinking: " 'Consciousness is infinite'—he is this percipient, but senses not that sphere.''[179] This non-committed cognition is paradoxically stated again, ". . . though he pays no mental heed to . . . the element of earth . . . to the sphere of infinite consciousness . . . yet he does so . . .;[180]. . . he does not meditate dependent on the infinity of consciousness, yet he does so . . .''[181] This whole technique is explained in detail in the *Mūlapariyāya Sutta.*[182]

6.87 After the experience of the sphere of the infinity of consciousness, the person moves on to the sphere of nothingness or emptiness. And then to the sphere of neither-consciousness-nor-unconsciousness. These two spheres are also rejected exactly on the same grounds on which the sphere of the infinity of consciousness was rejected. Here, it is important to point out a misunderstanding committed by some scholars who equate Nirvana with Emptiness. In the early Buddhist literature the word used for 'complete emptiness' is '*akiñcana*' never the word '*suñña*' which was always reserved for the idea of no-soul or non-substantiality. According to the Buddha, the sphere of emptiness itself is a conditioned and a thought-out mental state. Therefore it was rejected as not having any further significance. Thus the Buddha maintained that all types of experiences that take place in depth experiences were mental imageries or mental creations due to the predispositions of the subjects. He would be strongly against positing the existence of anything on the basis that it was experienced so in the depth experience.

6.88 If these experiential states were of no value as such why should they be cultivated in such a systematic fashion? There are two explanations for that. One is that they are aimed, by techniques of concentration etc., at achieving a high degree of personality integration. The other is that the Buddha believed that the transcendence of all possible experiences would be a very conducive way to achieve moral and personality perfection. The value of these techniques is seen as giving a thorough exercise in and a deep understanding of all possible forms of experiences. In fact, the Buddha defines transcendence in this sense: "Udayin, a monk, by wholly transcending the sphere of infinite space, thinking, 'Consciousness in infinite', enters and abides in the sphere of infinite consciousness . . . But I, Udayin, again say, 'This is not enough', I say, 'get rid of it', I say, 'Transcend it'. And what is it transcending? As to this, Udayin, a monk, by wholly transcending the sphere of consciousness, thinking, 'There is not anything', enters and abides in the plane of emptiness. This is its transcending . . ."[183]

6.89 Therefore, this would be the Buddha's fundamental criticism of the Christian mystical experience. He would say that the Christian mystic finds happiness and satisfaction in his own mental constructions and fabrications. In fact, he once criticized the religions that are based on this type of dependent-happiness. In the *Sutta Nipāta* he observes: "He, who confusedly places in front of him the ideas that he had mentally constructed and therefore conditioned, and sees beneficial results in him as coming from that, contacts a bliss that is artificially fabricated and therefore dependent''.[184] He goes on to say that ''it is not at all an easy thing to shake off (speculative) beliefs once a person is deeply steeped in them''.[185] Therefore, any kind of bliss resulting from an experiential situation would be considered essentially as conditioned and therefore as lacking in any intrinsic reality. This basic argument of the Buddha becomes a sweeping criticism of all types of artificially induced mysticism like drug mysticisms, and mysticisms produced by austerities. The Buddha is emphatically against any form of 'cults of the mind'.

6.90 Because all forms of experientially induced bliss are of no ultimate significance, the Buddha says that one has to transcend all of them by the cessation of all forms of experience. Hence, the last stage of the Buddhist meditational path is called 'the cessation of perceptions and feelings' (*saññāvedayitanirodha*). He says that this is better than the other formless spheres: ''cessation is calmer than the formless . . .''[186] Buddhaghosa explains why it is better, ''Being wearied by the occurrence and dissolution of formations, they attain it thinking, 'Let us dwell in bliss by being without consciousness here and now and reaching the cessation . . .''[187] According to the Buddha, this is necessary because Nirvana presupposes the tranquilizing of all forms of activities. To realize Nirvana one has to be ''free from attachment to all forms of feelings''; ''He who having conquered all sensations, . . . which are (known) to *Samanas* and to Brahmanas, is free from passion for all sensations, he is *Vedagū* (having passed sensations) after conquering all sensations''.[188] ''It is by the destruction of sensations that the destruction of pain takes place.''[189]

6.91 However, still one has not achieved Nirvana which can happen only after emerging from this cessation. By 'cessation' one does not automatically attain Nirvana. Paradoxically enough, 'cessation' of experiences is also another form of experience. However, it is distinguishable from others as a negative form of experience. Therefore, Nirvana cannot be achieved even by a negative form of experience because it is still an experience. N. Dutt is wrong when he says that 'cessation' is psychically identical with Nirvana.[190] 'Cessation' is only a transcendence of all possible forms of experience by a radical negative experience. The sense in which we call it an 'experience' should be clear. It is an experience only in the sense that the one who undergoes it can think of it afterwards.

It is not 'an experience' while it lasts. In fact, it is very similar to death. The Buddha once clarified the difference. "When a Bhikkhu is dead, friend, had completed his term, his bodily formations have ceased and are quite still, his mental formations have ceased and are quite still, his life is exhausted, his heat has subsided, and his faculties are broken up. When a Bhikkhu has entered upon the cessation of perception and feeling, his bodily formations (actions) have ceased and are quite still, his verbal formations have ceased and are quite still, his life unexhausted, his heat not subsided, his faculties are quite whole."[191] But the 'cessation' is not Nirvana and this is clearly stated when the Buddha refers to persons who attain the 'cessation' but not Nirvana. "Herein, monks, a monk who has achieved virtue, achieved concentration, achieved insight, may both completely enter the cessation of perception and feeling and may emerge therefrom—this is so: if here among visible things he does not attain gnosis, he will verily go beyond the deva-community that feed on solid food and arise in a mind-pictured body, provided he enter and emerge from the cessation of perception and feeling—this is so."[192]

6.92 Though Dutt is wrong in identifying the 'cessation' experience with Nirvana, there is a very important relationship between the two. The 'cessation' is extremely analogous psychically to the Nirvana as extinction. The cessation of all feelings and perceptions is psychically very close to the complete extinction one attains when one nirvanizes. Therefore, sometimes the 'cessation' experience is spoken of as a psychic analogue to the 'experience' of complete extinction. One can object that this form of transcendence of all experiences is psychically duplicable by drugs. One can say, for example, that this is very similar to an experience of unconsciousness which can be easily attainable with a dose of chloroform. But there are two significant differences in the Buddhist experience. One is that when one comes to this level of experience, one has gone through many spheres of experience which require high spiritual development. Here one can again say that the whole series might be duplicated though it is a rather complex procedure. It is here the second difference becomes important. The 'cessation' is not just an experience. It is a result of a deep understanding that all forms of experience are ultimately conditioned. Therefore, to understand that, one should have those experiences completely under one's control as producible by oneself and so as being conditioned. It is only as a result of this understanding that one produces the cessation experience which is a transcendence of all positive forms of experience. However, the cessation experience, in itself does not have any ultimate significance except for the understanding it can give that the cessation experience itself is a conditioned one, thus furthering one's knowledge of the conditionality of all experiences.

6.93 This transcendence of experience was, for the Buddha, the point of happiness, mainly because the bliss that results from this 'experience' is not dependent on anything. But, if it is cessation how can it be happy? In fact, the monk Udayin once asked the same question from Sariputta Thera: "But what, herein, reverend sir, is the happiness which herein is not felt?" Sariputta Thera replies: "It is, verily, just that happiness which here is not felt."[193] We can take a story from the Buddhist tradition to illustrate this point. A man who has an itch gets some pleasure by scratching it. But this is followed by pain soon afterwards. Thus from the itch one gets both pleasure as well as pain. But if he gets rid of the itch completely he gets a happiness of a completely new and of a superior kind. The worldly experiences are said to resemble the itch-experiences while Nirvana resembles the getting rid of the itch. Here, one can again argue that the Buddha was searching for this kind of happiness and therefore he was searching for an affective experience. To this three answers can be given. One is that Nirvana is not only a cessation of experiences, 'cessation' is always only a prelude to the realization of Nirvana. The second point is that even if this is regarded as an affective experience it would be a peculiar kind of affective experience because of its negative nature. It is not an affective experience as other positive experiences are; and it is these positive experiences that are a danger to the moral perfection according to the Buddha. The third point is that the Buddha did not search for a happy experience but he just found a kind of happiness in this type of experience. Once the Buddha himself explained this: "But the situation occurs, Ananda, when wanderers belonging to other sects may speak thus, the recluse Gotama speaks of the cessation of perception and feeling, and lays down that this belongs to happiness. Now what is this, how is this? Ananda, wanderes belonging to other sects who speak thus should be spoken to thus: 'Your reverences, the Lord does not recommend happiness for the mere feeling of happiness, but your reverences, the

Tathagata lays down that whenever, wherever, whatever happiness is found it belongs to happiness."[194] And the Buddha clearly explained that the religious life is not followed to achieve a happy birth: "No, Udayin, it is not for the sake of realizing a world that is exclusively happy that monks fare the religious life under me. There simply are, Udayin, other things superior and more excellent for the sake of realizing which monks fare the religious life under me."[195] Thus these relationships between Nirvana and the 'cessation experience' should be noted as significant points about the affective life of an Arahant.

6.94 Even though a person does not follow the gradual path to the cessation stage and takes a short cut from the first *dhyāna*, the realization of Nirvana is immediately preceded by this transcendence of positive experiences with the understanding that all forms of experience are ultimately conditioned: "He thus ponders: This first *dhyāna* is just a higher product, it is produced by higher thought. Then he comes to know: Now even that which is a higher product, produced by higher thought, is impermanent, of a nature to end. Fixed on that he wins destruction of the cankers. . . ."[196]

6.95 We said that one can realize Nirvana immediately after emerging from 'cessation'. Then, what is Nirvana and its realization? Nirvana means several things. We saw above, in detail, that Nirvana was complete extinction after death, thus stopping the rebirth cycle. But this is only one aspect of Nirvana. We also saw another aspect namely that Nirvana is realizable in this life. What we are interested in here is Nirvana in this life. Before proceeding further we have to clarify one point. The opinion of scholars is that Nirvana is a mystical experience. Smart sums up the general consensus of scholarly opinion when he says that Nirvana is a pure mystic experience. ". . . my contention is that Buddhist mysticism . . . can be counted *pure* mysticism".[197] It should be clear to us by now how seriously wrong this idea is. As we saw, realization of Nirvana is necessarily preceded by a complete transcendence of all types of positive experiences. Even if we take 'cessation experience' as analogous to Nirvana, though it is *not* Nirvana, it is not at all similar to any type of usual mystical experience because there is nothing experienced as it is a complete non-experience. The Buddha says clearly that he had to emerge from all those experiential states *before* he became enlightened: "And as long as I did not attain to and *emerge from* these nine successive states, both forwards and backwards, I did not completely, as one wholly awakened, realize the full perfect awakening."[198]

6.96 If Nirvana does not end in any form of mystical experience then what is it? As we said, Nirvana, in this sense too, can mean several things. First of all it is an intellectual enlightenment resulting in personality integration and moral perfection. What is this intellectual enlightenment? Immediately after the 'cessation experience' one turns one's mind to an understanding or a realization of the worldly reality as it is (*yathābhūta*). One is now proficient to take this step because one has undergone and understood the conditionality of all experiences and also achieved a unification of the mind. The nature of this reality is understood in three ways, as impermanent, as non-satisfying and as non-substantial. That this is mainly an intellectual achievement is emphasized by the use of the word 'wisdom' (*paññā*) or 'gnosis' (*aññā*) in all the places where this enlightenment is referred to. It should be noted that what is meant by '*paññā*' or '*aññā*' is always a deeper kind of understanding or a deeper kind of discriminating knowledge, not a mere theoretical kind of knowledge which is denoted by '*ñāṇa*'. In fact, theoretical kind of knowledge is viewed by the Buddha as more or less another form of view: "A noble person does not enter time, (or) the number of (living beings), (he is) no follower of (philosophical views), *nor a friend of knowledge.*"[199] '*Ñāṇa*, as compared with '*paññā*, is always classified with views: "One does not find purification by views, by tradition, or *by knowledge.*"[200] To illustrate this difference by a crude example: to know that smoking is bad is *ñāṇa*. But to realize that deeply and stop smoking would require *paññā* and this type of exercise of *paññā* implies an amount of self-discipline and self-control. Compared to this *paññā* we can see how easily *ñāṇa* approaches more towards the side of 'views' or *diṭṭhi*. Sariputta Thera states that "to be an end-maker one has to see and know the reality of the world".[201] Therefore the release attained in Nirvana is termed as release by gnosis (*aññāvimokkha*).[202]

6.97 The importance of this *paññā* is very much appreciated in the Buddhist context. The Buddha says one can get enlightened by *paññā* alone. This again shows the difference of Nirvana from a mystical experience. Such Arahants who had attained Nirvana by wisdom alone were referred to as those 'released by wisdom' (*paññāvimutta*).[203] But they were releases with a difference: they did not have any psychic powers. Once it is said how a rich merchant and his son Yasa attained Nirvana after only a short instruction without any knowledge of meditation.[204] Though such instances are rare, a person who has deep wisdom and can understand and realize the conditioned nature and the other features of reality can attain Nirvana by wisdom or insight alone. The commentary to the *Visuddhimagga* states: "The words 'insight alone' are meant to exclude, not virtue etc., but serenity (i.e., *jhāna*,) which is the opposite number of the pair, serenity and insight. This is for emphasis. But the word 'alone' actually excludes only that concentration with distinction (of *jhāna*); for concentration is classed as both access and absorption. . . . this . . . does not imply that there is no concentration; for no insight comes about without momentary concentration. And again, insight should be understood as the three contemplations of impermanence, pain and not-self; not contemplation of impermanence alone."[205]

6.98 It is important to notice a point that emerges from this discussion. In Buddhism the reality one understands is this worldly reality. The word for reality is *yathābhūta*, i.e., things as they are. In Christianity the reality is a noumenal ontological Reality that one has to realize. In Buddhism one becomes enlightened about worldly reality, the only reality for Buddhism. If one is to become enlightened one has to understand and realize it fully. Therefore for the Buddha the world is fully real and the perfect understanding of it is strong enough to give enlightenment. In Christianity, when the world is contrasted with a more important Reality or a state of affairs there is always an implied degradation of the value of the reality of the world (We clarified this in detail above, *v.* 6.44). We could see this happening, in practice, in the case of morality, particularly as practiced by mystics when they degraded worldly morality in terms of a divine morality. Also we saw how this can happen in the case of an ordinary level of morality (*v.* 4.28), i.e., other than the mystics' morality. Because the Buddha has no reality other than the worldly reality he insisted that full justice should be done to the reality of the world. That is why in the Buddhist context worldly morality has a much stronger validity than in the Christian context. The difference is that for the Buddha the world is fully real but for the Christian the world is less real.

6.99 Buddhist enlightenment should not be understood to be a mere intellectual achievement. It is meant to achieve two fundamental results. The main aim is moral perfection and the second aim is its accompanying personality integration. In a way, the comprehension of reality logically leads to moral perfection. The Buddhist theory of moral perfection is based on a theory of reality. For example, when one realizes that things are impermanent, non-satisfying and are non-substantial then the desire and craving for things vanish and when the attachment to things ceases then strong emotional reactions, like hatred, cease. Therefore moral perfections are closely related to intellectual perfections. The defilements or cankers destroyed at elightenment are called *āsavas*. The three main *āsavas* are those of ignorance, becoming and sensuality or craving. These three are supposed to be the three main morally harmful defilements.[206] At enlightenment all these *āsavas* are destroyed by *paññā*. It is explained: "Whoever sees this as it really is by perfect wisdom his desire for becoming disappears . . . , by the complete extinction of desires there is dispassion, cessation without remainder, Nirvana."[207] "The destruction of *āsavas* is done by *paññā*,[208] because "a mind trained by wisdom quickly frees from the *āsavas*".[209] Wisdom is supposed to be a moral virtue, therefore enlightenment dispells ignorance. The three virtues most commonly emphasized are wisdom, charity and compassion towards all beings. Therefore the destruction of their contraries is the main aim of enlightenment. "In a brother who has destroyed the *āsavas*, who can look upon his heart as released from lust, hatred and ignorance, there arises a release."[210] Therefore release is a release from these impurities. "Lust . . . is a fault. Hatred is a fault. Ignorance is a fault. In a brother who has destroyed the *āsavas*, these are abandoned, cut down at the root, made like a palm tree stump, made things that have ceased to be, so that they cannot sprout again in time to come. Therefore a brother who has destroyed the *āsavas* is 'faultless' . . . is called 'stream-cutter'."[211]

6.100 The importance and significance of moral perfection is emphasized when it is said that one can realize Nirvana by meditating first on moral virtues and then directing the mind to the understanding of reality. Here one first trains the mind in four moral virtues (*cattāro brahmavihārā*), friendliness (*mettā*), compassion (*karuṅā*), sympathetic joy (*muditā*), and equanimity (*upekhā*).[212] Thus there is a way to realize Nirvana through the moral path as well. Also, one can first cultivate the four *dhyānas*, then the *brahmavihāras* and through them realize Nirvana.[213] These various moral paths show the emphasis given to the moral ideals.

6.101 Johansson interprets this way of moral perfection as a form of repression. "For the Buddhist, repression is simply a method of control and purification."[214] To support his theory he again mistranslates the Pali word '*vinodeti*' as 'represses'. But *vinodeti* does not mean repression in any sense, it only means clearing away or discarding. Johansson's mistake is that he does not view the Buddhist moral perfection in the light and context of the Buddhist theory of reality. The Buddhist way cannot be repression for a very important reason. The theory of morality is based on a theory of reality. When one really understands and realizes that there are fundamentally no things but only a flux of evanescent changes of a non-satisfying nature then one realizes that there are no things in any way substantial to get attached to. When one sees an ugly woman and does not feel attracted to her one is not repressing one's desire. One just does not have any feeling of lust towards her. One may illustrate this point by a popular Buddhist story. Once, in ancient Ceylon, a meditative monk was making his begging rounds. He met a woman fleeing from her husband and this woman tried to attract the monk's attention by seductively smiling at him. The monk saw her teeth and getting a clue from seeing the teeth went on his rounds meditating on the human skeleton and attained enlightenment. The husband who was looking for his wife saw this monk and asked him whether he had seen a woman running on the road, to which the monk replied, "I didn't see a woman, but I saw a skeleton passing by". As this story illustrates, Buddhist moral perfection is based on a realization of the nature of reality. When lust is non-existent many other immoral feelings that accompany lust also get automatically extinguished. The Buddha explains to a Brahamin: "As to the saying 'Seen in this life is Dhamma', master Gotama, pray how far is Dhamma seen in this life? How far is it a thing not involving time, inviting one to come and see, leading onward, to be realized for themselves by the wise?" "Brahamin, one who is ablaze with lust, overwhelmed with lust, infatuated thereby, plans to his own hindrance, to that of others, to the hindrance both of self and others, and experiences mental suffering and dejection. If lust is abandoned, he no longer plans thus, no longer suffers thus. So far, Brahmin, Dhamma is seen in this life."[215] It should be mentioned that there are various meditational techniques to cultivate various moral virtues. For example, to cultivate compassion one has to meditate and concentrate on the equality of humanity and loving kindness and the cultivation of the four *brahmavihāras* is an indispensable part in attaining enlightenment. Therefore moral perfection is not based on repression but on a real understanding of the nature of reality. When one knows the reality, the feelings of lust, etc., just do not arise, not to speak of their repression. The positive moral virtues also have the same basis. "One should not kill or harm others because everybody dislikes pain and is afraid of death. By taking oneself as an example, one should not harm or kill others."[216] The Buddha advocated that one's attitude towards other living beings should be exactly like the love and regard of a mother towards her one and only child (*v.* 4.15).

6.102 This points to another important feature of Buddhist morality. Morality and moral perfection essentially depend on a correct and true theory of reality (*v.* 4.13). That is why *paññā* is emphasized as an important element in acquiring moral perfection: "When the mind is thoroughly developed through understanding, it is quite set free from cankers, namely from the cankers of sensuality, becoming, view and ignorance."[217]

6.103 Further, moral perfection leads to a personality integration. This comes as a transcendence of the world and its experience by wisdom. ". . . when I comprehended, as it really is, the satisfaction of the world as satisfaction, the misery as misery, and the escape therefrom as escape, then I understood perfectly and accepted the full-enlightened status, and the knowledge and vision arose in me: sure is the release of mind: this is my last birth. . . ."[218] ". . . freedom from pride, restraint of thirst, uprooting of attachment, cutting off of the cycle of existences, destruction of craving, freedom from desire, ceasing, Nirvana."[219] One acquires peace, "This is peace, this is the highest, namely, the calming of all the activities, the rejection of all attachment, the destruction of craving, the freedom from desire, Nirvana."[220] Ego-consciousness is gone, "Thinking there is no soul, he attains freedom from pride 'I am',

Nirvana in this life."[221] "The one who has attained Nirvana is wantless."[222] Nirvana is often described as "peace, happiness, security and kindness."[223] The Buddha says, "I have become cool and attained Nirvana."[224] "One who has attained Nirvana is cool like the waters of a lake."[225] Nirvana is "the purity, freedom from impurities, release and freedom."[226] Therefore Nirvana is described as "the highest happiness."[227] This is the Buddha's idea of perfect health: "This is the perfect health, this is Nirvana."[228]

6.104 There is another important aspect of Nirvana that has to be mentioned. The idea of Nirvana after death is grounded on another theory of reality: the theory of rebirth. Nirvana as making an end of non-satisfying existence is based on that. Buddha says: "Were there no birth . . . , then, there being no birth whatever, would there, owing to this cessation of birth, be any appearance of old age and death?"[229] The theory of rebirth is not a metaphysical theory. The fact that a theory of rebirth without a soul is a meaningful one is accepted even by the strongest of the positivists. A. J. Ayer says: "I think that it would be open to us to admit the logical possibility of reincarnation merely by laying down the rule that if a person who is physically identified as living at a later time does have the ostensible memories and character of a person who is physically identified as living at an earlier time, they are to be counted as one person and not two."[230] Memory was the basis of the Buddhist theory of reincarnation and the Buddha always appealed to the fact that some had "the knowledge of the memories of their previous births (*pubbenivāsānussatiñāna*)".[231] He advocated this theory on two grounds. One was a moral ground. Trying to account for the lowness and excellence seen among human beings, he explained it in terms of the good and bad deeds done in their past lives. The other ground was that of verifiability. He said that he could remember his past births and he maintained that anybody who developed the powers of paranormal vision could verify these truths. Normally these powers are achieved when one progresses on the meditational path. In modern times verious forms of experiments have been made to prove the existence of rebirth.[232] The most outstanding experimenter in this field is Ian Stevenson whose major work '*Twenty Cases Suggestive of Reincarnation*' tries to make a scientific case for the existence of rebirth. The Buddha makes definitely factual claims about the validity of Nirvana. Even if there were no rebirth, Nirvana would, of course, be well worth achieving. But at least half of the validity and value of Nirvana depends on the empirical truth or falsity of the theory of rebirth. Even with regard to Nirvana at the point of death Buddhism does not make any metaphysical claims, but instead it makes only empirical claims. Therefore Buddhism becomes a falsifiable religion, and therefore meaningful. Because the central idea of Buddhism is the stoppage of rebirth, if the fact of rebirth is disproved as an empirical fact the Buddhism becomes false as a means of salvation. Indirectly, if the existence of God and Soul are proved then also many of the central concepts of Buddhism stand falsified.

6.105 The implied criticisms of the Christian mystical experience of God should have become clear in the course of this analysis of the Buddhist concept of Nirvana. The Buddha rejects all experiential states as having no fundamental value because of the fact that they are necessarily conditioned. Therefore, a transcendence of all levels of experience as giving a deeper understanding into the real nature of things is advocated. The resulting wisdom is used to understand reality in all its aspects thereby achieving moral and personality perfection. Moral perfection with its resultants was the ultimate aim of the Buddha. In Buddhism, as we showed in a previous chapter (*v.* 4.44), morality generically leads to salvation. The relation between morality and salvation is therefore generic and logical. Even though Christianity too has moral and personality perfection as ideals these aims are not consistently attained because the doctrinal framework of Christianity very often tends to deflect a person from the main aims, leading even the saints to contrary vices.

6.106 Still, a Christian believer can maintain that there are certain features in Christianity that makes it preferable to a Buddhist type of religion. Smart says, "The devotee of *bhakti* might invoke counter-arguments. He might seek to establish the superiority of *bhakti* over *dhyāna*. He might, firstly, point out that *bhakti* overflows with the joy of God's goodness. Since God is Creator of the world, it follows that the world too is basically good, however much it may be vitiated by the incapacity to follow the beckonings of the divine vision. Thus *bhakti* consummates the satisfactions of the world. It does not flee from them, as does *dhyāna* so typically. Second, *bhakti* is the mother of commitment, Love God and do what you will—hence one does what is God's will. There is a beautiful and loving dynamism about *bhakti*. By contrast, *dhyāna*, in seeking knowledge of the Transcendent, is too much centred in contemplation rather than loving action in the world. Third, *dhyāna* is admittedly an act of oneself, at least where it occurs outside the context of *bhakti*. But this makes it over-methodical, over-rigid. It is a technique. But *bhakti* has a warmth and spontaneity lacking in such a detached technique. The very glory of *bhakti* lies in the fact that it is not due to meditation and preparation. The spirit bloweth where it listeth. Fifth, *bhakti* offers a direction and purpose to living, and sees this against the control of the cosmos by a loving Lord. Too often, by contrast, *dhyāna* is pessimistic. It is mere good fortune that the cosmos offers the chance of liberation through the methods of yoga. The *bhakti* view is consistent and glorious."[233]

6.107 In the light of what we have been discussing in this and previous chapters, the above paragraph hardly needs any comment. There also the theist makes the usual mistake of taking Nirvana for a mystical state, as a *dhyānic* state. He emphasizes only one aspect of God's goodness. The same joy can very easily drive one into a theopathic condition. The fact that the world is good is not an *a priori* conclusion that follows from God's goodness, but an empirical matter to be established by appealing to experience which might show that the world is also full of evils. *Bhakti*, in fact, degrades the world while Buddhism accepts the full reality of the world and its validity. The Buddha did not try to flee from the world but tried to change the attitude towards it to make it a more pleasant and a happy place. It is true that the ultimate aim of the Buddha was to get out of the world by stopping rebirth. But to get out of this world is also the aim of Christianity. The love of *bhakti* can be selfish and egocentric sometimes leading to theopathic condition or anti-human immoral behavior. Meditation for Nirvana involves many dynamic forms of moral contemplation. The Buddha was not a secluded contemplative, but a leader who tried to make radical and significant moral and social transformations by preaching an enlightened system of social and moral philosophy. He was an active adviser to kings in political and social matters. The Buddhist Sangha, even in later times, was a dynamic social institution playing its role in every strata of society. When one thinks of great scholars like Nagarjuna who tried to formulate new systems of thinking and of institutions like the Sangha in Asia in modern times, one can see that the Buddhist ideals do not breed only full-time contemplatives. The way to Nirvana is not necessarily a rigid technique. We have seen that there are a number of simpler ways or 'shortcuts' to Nirvana. However, any type of moral and intellectual training involves a high degree of rigor. The Buddha's kindness and humane attitude was not reserved only for human beings but also extended to other living beings as well. The Buddha's oft-quoted advice that one should treat all living beings as a mother treats her one and only son shows how much warmth of love the Buddhist ideal can emanate. It produces a high degree of empathy extending even to the realm of animals and all living beings. The enormous amount of faith, contemplation and orison required to experience God renders suspect the claim that the *bhakti* feeling of warmth is not due to meditation and preparation. If the full implications of that claim of the theist are worked out, then Christianity would be the most erratic religion in the world, wherein one would not be able to find any justification for God's grace unless one were to salvage Christianity by accepting a totalitarian ethics. Buddhism is not pessimistic. The attitude one has towards the world when one needs to transcend the world should not be interpreted as pessimism. Buddhism, by its respect for reality, is very much alive to the realities of evil in the world and because Buddhism does not try to explain evil away, it should not be taken to mean pessimism. Instead, it has more a realistic approach to the world. In fact, the Buddha insisted that if there were no dissatisfaction in the world, people would not be repelled by the world: "If there were no dissatisfaction in the world, beings would not be repelled by the world. But since there is dissatisfaction in the world, beings are repelled by the world."[234] Lastly, it is not only a good fortune but a logical certainty that a good Buddhist will necessarily achieve union with God, provided God exists and is good, as the Buddha explained to the brahmin Vasettha who desperately insisted that Brahma (God) exists: "And so you say, Vasettha, that the bhikkhu (Buddhist monk) is free from anger, and free from malice, pure in mind, and master of himself; and that God is free from anger, and free from malice, pure in mind, and master of himself. Then in sooth, Vahettha, that the bhikkhu who is free from anger, free from malice, pure in mind, and master of himself should after death, when the body is dissolved, become united with

God, who is the same—such a situation of things is every way possible!"[235]

Chapter Seven

THE NATURE AND EXISTENCE OF GOD

7.1 This chapter should have been at the beginning: however, we did not want to start with a definition of God because this concept was too complex for a precise definition. The best way to see what this concept means is to examine how people in fact have used it in various ways and contexts. And, as we did in our previous chapters, we can now see how difficult it is to give an exact definition of this concept. It is true that an exhaustive definition cannot be given of an *a posteriori* thing. For example, nobody can define a thing as simple as a chair. What we do is to build up a complex concept of 'chair' based on family resemblances. Similarly, one can try to give meaning to the concept of God by attempting to build up the concept from the various aspects we have been discussing. But, even an attempt dependent on the theory of family resemblances is made difficult by some problems that are peculiar to the concept of God. It is not essentially due to the obvious fact that God is transcendently different from a chair. The difficulty stems rather from much more serious and complicated contradictions.

7.2 A concept is delineated in terms of its attributes. For five main reasons the attributes of God lead to problems which make the concept of God practically meaningless. One is that many of these attributes do not have a field of discourse. Secondly, there are internal contradictions inherent in the attributes. The third reason is that the particular ontological status of some of these attributes leads to peculiar epistemological problems which create difficulties concerning the meaning of the concept of God. The fourth reason is based on the peculiar logical status of some attributes which makes grasping their meaning even theoretically difficult. The fifth reason stems from the unusual epistemological status given to these attributes.

7.3 We have shown clearly that the divine attributes are internally contradictory and how they contradict one another. We also saw the various attempts made to salvage these attributes from the contradictions. One important point emerges from these analyses. It is that Christian theologians have been placed in a very uncomfortable situation by attempting to relate an Ideal of Worship and Devotion to a world explanatory principle. Most of the problems of divine attributes are due to the failure to establish this relation successfully. As the devotional Ideal, God must be loving and benevolent, etc. But these attributes do not operate within a self-enclosed and exclusive divine circle. They must derive their meaning in terms of a human context such as is indispensably required for human intelligibility. But the appeal to the human context is made difficult by the fact that the human context is full of both happiness and unjustified suffering. From the opposite point of view, if the human context is supposed to throw light on the divine attributes, it shows that the affective relationship of the deity is composed of both love and hate, or liking or disliking. Therefore, the affective relationship of God as love cannot be made meaningful, because it does not have a consistent field of discourse. In other words, when an attempt is made to render these attributes meaningful in the only way possible, i.e., by reference to the facts of the human context, they are contradicted by the very facts of this context. Another such attribute is omniscience, which is contradicted by the presence of human free will. If free will is taken away to make room for omniscience, then the main purpose of positing the whole doctrine of God, i.e., the possibility of moral progress and salvation, falls to the ground.

7.4 Some attributes are internally contradictory in the sense that these attributes logically imply the very antithesis of the thesis they try to establish. Therefore they do not convey any clear meaning. For example, such an attribute is that of creator. This attribute is advanced on the principle that everything that exists needs to be created. But by the same logical principle, the creator also needs to be created. There can never be a creator who does not need to be created if the principle of creation is held as a logically consistent principle. The believer's obvious reply is that he feels that God is so perfect that He is self-sufficient and therefore uncreated. But here the important point is that it is 'the believer' who says that because he 'feels' so. The word 'feel' is used here because there is absolutely no reason, from the point of view of logic or common sense, to stop at God as the uncreated principle. It is the believer's faith or feeling that makes him stop his argumentation at God. Thus, in this argument, we can see two qualitatively different steps. The first step is logical and the second is emotional. If the believer is satisfied with an emotional justification of logical problems, then he should not have recourse to logic at the first step. Therefore, the principle of creation that 'everything that exists needs a cause' is not a rational principle for the theist. Even the principle of causality which the theist presupposes in the argument, is contradicted when an emotional justification supercedes the causal justification. If God's existence is self-explanatory or self-caused, then the basic argument is false, because God exists uncreated. On the other hand, it is yet to be established that God is self-explanatory. The term self-explanatory is only a descriptive term meaning various things. If God is self-explanatory in a tautologous or analytical sense, it becomes an utterly trivial thing because it rests on defining the term God to mean self-created. If God is self-explanatory in some other sense, then it has yet to be explained. One cannot here appeal to religious or devotional feelings for evidence because the word 'self-explanatory' is a term denoting a matter of fact. The believer may feel that God is uncreated, etc., but that does not establish any existential claim. Also, one cannot leave the theist with his self-evident feelings because his claim that there is an uncreated God is a categorical claim which is relevant to both believers and non-believers as an existent state of affairs. A factual claim is to be established on factual grounds. In the attempt to establish it as a factual claim there can be another insurmountable problem. Even if God is uncreated it becomes theoretically impossible to prove that he is uncreated because it requires looking back into infinite time to establish this point as a conclusive theory. Therefore, it is *logically impossible* to prove an uncreated creator.

7.5 The idea of creation surreptitiously changes into the idea of accounting for a contingently existing universe. Even then the same logical principle applies. There is no reason why God should not be contingent. Defining God to be necessary is an unsatisfactory solution. One has to show and prove how he becomes a necessary being. The word 'necessary' is a logical term invoked by the theologians themselves and therefore, in adducing reasons, one has to follow logically rigorous techniques. As we explained above, the tautological necessity is too trivial a sense because it is merely definitional. If it is different, then it shares the same logical problems as the uncreated creator. In addition, to prove that an existential entity is necessary, if this is a meaningful concept at all, one first requires not only the knowledge of an infinite past but also of an infinite future. Hence, again, it is logically impossible to prove the existence of a necessary being. If these ideas of 'uncreated creator' and 'necessary being' cannot be made meaningful in any intelligible sense, they cannot, as attributes, enlighten us about the nature of God. One can argue that these terms should be taken only in an analogical sense. It is true that we often use terms for purposes they were not exactly made for. But this is not a convincing excuse, for two main reasons. One is that they are very often used as genuinely descriptive terms. Christian thinkers ascribe a poetical meaning to these words, for example, only when challenged to make them properly meaningful. The second reason is that analogies cannot be made meaningful without a knowledge of the originals, as we shall explain later. Thus, however we try to make the attributes 'creator' and 'necessary being' meaningful, we always end up in a fundamental contradiction. They seem to have meaning to the believer because he does not want to see the full implications of these concepts and thus becomes oblivious to the contradictory nature of the concepts. It is also true that these concepts may be meaningful to the believer as emotional epithets to qualify his Ideal of Worship.

7.6 Some attributes have a very peculiar ontological status. For example, the attribute of eternity is fraught with problems because of this peculiar status. Eternity is distinguished from endless duration to show that God is timeless or is beyond time. This is one of the attributes that eludes ordinary understanding. One might show analogues in mathematical truths. Once again, their eternity as based on necessity is fully explainable by the fact that they are purely analytical and therefore trivial. But the divine eternity is a factual eternity. Not only is the concept incomprehensible but the way in which God is said to perform his actions leads to an internal contradiction as well. The theologians make matters much worse by attributing to God other actions that contradict the implications of an eternal God. Thus, though God is said to be eternal, he also is supposed to be intervening in temporal affairs. The first such intervention was the act of creation (*v.* 2.6, 7). After that he appeared and talked to several people. The doctrine of the Incarnation involves an extremely dramatic temporal intervention. Also, God is said to be looking after the world, helping the good, punishing the bad, answering prayers and so on and so forth. These are all clearly temporal functions. One can, of course say that though God lives beyond time, he can 'descend' into the temporal realm whenever he wishes, etc. But the important point to note here is that 'whenever he wishes' is a temporal term. God thinks, and decides and these are manifested in the temporal realm not in eternity but in a temporal sequence. God does not decide for eternity because he changes his decisions often, and here he is influenced by happenings in the temporal realm. All these considerations show that God is very often temporal in the usual sense. His actions, decisions, all follow the temporal sequence of the world. Therefore, 'eternity' as beyond time contradicts these ideas. In so far as God has been understood and talked about, a temporal terminology has always been used. When theologians want to talk about and prove the existence of God they always use this temporal terminology. But when the doctrine of God is challenged, they immediately make a dramatic move to clothe God in eternity and make him immune to many of the atheist's arguments. This makes one suspect that 'eternality' is a defense-term rather than a genuine attribute of God. If God is properly eternal, then it undercuts the whole field of natural theology, and even revealed theology in so far as it is based on the incarnation and revelations, etc. As we saw in the case of omniscience, when the idea of eternality is applied to analyze theological problems, the term is clearly meaningless. Let us look at the concept of omniscience again. To overcome the problem that omniscience involves determinism, the theist can say that God's knowledge is eternal and therefore he knows everything at once, and he can say that eternal knowledge means knowledge without determining the event. However, if we translate this into ordinary understandable terminology, knowledge prior to the event is simply pre-knowledge and if God knows event X prior to its happening, and if God's knowledge is infallible, then X is determined necessarily. The theologian might say that eternal knowledge does not imply this determinism because it is non-temporal. If so, how can one understand omniscience as a meaningful concept? On the other hand, the sequence of Xs was temporal and if God's knowledge is correct then he has to know it as a temporal sequence. Not to know it as a temporal sequence is not to know the sequence of Xs. But the theist would say that God knows the sequence, but in a way that does not involve determinism for Xs. Here we come to the crux of the problem. Now we can see why the theologian introduced the word 'eternal knowledge' at all. It was to avoid the idea of determinism while keeping the idea of pre-knowledge. But introducing the 'eternal' does not at all change the picture which still stands as it did before. Thus, in this context, eternality does not mean anything. Here the theist can say that, though it is meaningless to us, it is meaningful in the divine context as a divine attribute. This is to say that a meaningless term becomes meaningful in the divine context. But this argument can be applied to any meaningless term.

7.7 The fourth reason is due to the peculiar logical status of some attributes. We discussed some of these problems above. To take them separately, we can see difficulties particularly in attributes like 'infinite' and 'uncreated'. God is said to be infinite. First of all, it is difficult to conceive how a person could be infinite. Here the obvious answer is that God is a person only analogically, analogous to man. Even then the difficulty does not vanish. One can say that what is meant here is that God is inconceivable. But this answer is wrong because God is conceived of as a person. One can again say that he is a person only analogically. But the point is that man conceives God to the extent that he is able to see that God is analogous to man. Thus here the doctrine of analogy pushes the problem straight into one's face rather than avoiding it by circumvention. If God is a person to a certain extent, then the problem is how can a person like that or 'an analogous person' be infinite? Because if God is a person to a certain extent, then it means that he is not infinite since the term 'person' sets boundaries and limits to an item of discourse. Therefore, to say that God is a person is to say that he is not infinite in an important sense. Thus how God can be partly finite and partly infinite is a problem that has yet to be explained. However, even if we grant that God as a person can be infinite how can we ever make the term 'infinite' meaningful? It is even theoretically and logically difficult to verify an existential infinity. Therefore, to call God infinite is to apply a meaningless attribute to him. Is the situation made better by using 'infinite being' non-anthropomorphically? Kai Nielson answers, "Where 'infinite being' is being used non-anthropomorphically, there can, *logically* can, be no observing an infinite being. To understand this term in the only way we can understand it, is to understand that there can, logically can, be no way of indicating or identifying what it purportedly refers to."[1] We have found the same logical problems with the attribute 'uncreated'. One can make two objections here. One is that in this discussion we are missing the important point about the Divine attributes, because what is meant by them is to show how God is great and perfect, etc. But this is avoiding a problem by making it ambiguous, because what we exactly need to know is how and why God is called great and perfect. In answering this the theist would show God's attributes to be implying perfection and greatness in the course of which he would also mention infinite and uncreated, and so we come back to the same problem. The second objection may be that we are taking these attributes too literally when they are meant to be taken only analogically. To answer this we shall look at the problem of analogy.

7.8 At this point we encounter the fifth reason. The theists have always believed that the doctrine of analogy could answer some of the problems raised by non-believers. But actually the doctrine of analogy raises and emphasizes the real problems in the doctrine of God rather than solves any. Wittgenstein points out the central problem involved here. ". . . in the ethical and religious language we seem constantly to be using similes. But a simile must be the simile for something. And if I can describe a fact by means of a simile I must also be able to drop the simile and describe the facts without it."[2] Nielsen comments, "If . . . we can *only* talk about God in images, then we cannot intelligibly speak of faithful or unfaithful images any more than we can speak of married or widowed stones".[3] Therefore the doctrine of analogy does not improve the situation. The theist has to explain how the doctrine of analogy started and how its works. To do this he has to go behind the analogies, which he confesses to be unable to do even in principle. What this amounts to is that the doctrine of analogy, as used by the theist, is meaningless because he only knows and uses the analogies which do not serve any useful purpose without a knowledge of the original data.

7.9 In understanding the doctrine of God there are, in addition, other difficulties posed by various thinkers according to their philosophical standpoints. To make the concept of God more acceptable as an explanatory principle, thinkers have substituted other words for God like 'Absolute' and 'Being' and 'Being-in-itself'. But in this way one does not solve any problems and one always has to come back to the traditional problems as we saw in the case of Tillich (*v.* 6.54), and then grapple with them in the traditional way. If they try to carry on with these new terms without going back to the traditional themes and problems, then their new vocabulary ceases to have any sensible meaning. For example, Hartshorne uses the word 'Absolute' to clarify the meaning of the concept of God. He treats "God as Absolute yet related to all".[4] And he says that "we must agree with modern absolutism and orthodox Hinduism that the supreme being must be all inclusive."[5] Now the concept of God may be manipulated more easily than the term Absolute because it is more plastic and is less precise in meaning. So he can say: "Thus God is being in both opposite aspects: abstract least common denominator, and concrete *de facto* maximal achieved totality".[6] And he, of course, later says that God is more than the Absolute.[7] But the problem is that by saying that God is less than the Absolute, or is more than the Absolute is he saying anything sensible? Is the concept of the Absolute any more intelligible than the concept of God? Referring to people who maintain that we can have 'some understanding' of such phrases, Paul Edwards observes: "There is a sense in which I do have 'some understanding' of 'the Absolute is lazy'—a sense in which, for example, a Chinese, who does not understand English at all, has no understanding of it and in which I have no understanding of gibberish like '*promax robar dux*!' But to say that I have 'some understanding' of 'the absolute is lazy' in this sense means no more than that I am familiar with certain rules of substitution governing the relative employment of the words 'lazy' and 'industrious' etc. In *this* sense we certainly have 'some understanding' of 'something is the creator of the universe'. But this is trivial and irrelevant. Nobody who has seriously discussed the question as to whether we understand 'problematic' theological sentences has used 'understand' and related terms like 'intelligible' or 'meaningful' in this sense."[8]

7.10 Another suggested synonym for God is Being or Pure Being. As a term what does this mean? Descriptively it hardly means anything. If it does not mean anything descriptively, does it have any other function? Smart says, ". . . ontological expressions are devoid of descriptive content. Moreover, the uses of these words in mystical contexts is such that they do not occur in descriptive combinations. Thus while 'human being' is a descriptive combination ('being' here functioning merely as a grammatical place-filler), 'Pure Being' is insured, so to speak, against the possibility of its describing. For 'Being' is an ontological place-filler, and 'pure' is itself contentless, being what may conveniently be termed an intensifier (like 'very', 'supreme', etc.). Similarly with such combinations as 'Ultimate Reality'."[9] However, this passages poses another problem. If 'being' is used evaluatively, the problem is, evaluative of what? If it is an evaluation of the theist's relationship to the world and to God, then it becomes a qualifier or another attribute of God. If it does not go that far but stops as an emotional evaluation of the world, then 'being' becomes the expression of a poetic sentiment. But this is not intended to be merely poetic. Therefore if this poetic sentiment has God in the background, then it becomes an indirect qualifier of God. Thus 'being' is either an attribute or a synonym of God, and in either case the meaning is not clear. Many theologians have used the word 'Being' or 'Pure Being' as a synonym for God, as an expression of the nature of the fundamental Reality. This usage has been very common from the time of the Upanisads. It was Uddalaka in the *Chāndogya Upaniṣad* who first raised the question, "How can being come out of non-being?" and he posited 'Being' as the Ultimate Reality.[10] Later a Metaphysical Materialist school (*nāstikas*) maintained that "There is no destruction of Being and nothing can come from Non-Being" and so they advocated the ultimate reality of material elements as Being.[11]

7.11 The Buddha criticized the term 'being' not only as a meaningless term, but also as a grammatically illegitimate construction. He strongly maintained that "one should not overstep the limits of conventional usage"[12] and said that by confusing the usages of "is, was and will be" one can be led into intricate philosophical muddles. He says: "There are these three linguistic conventions or usages of words or terms which are distinct, have been distinct in the past, are distinct at present and will be distinct in the future and which are not ignored by the recluses and brahmins who are wise. Which three? Whatever material form there has been, which has ceased to be, which is past and has changed is called, reckoned and termed 'has been' (*ahosi*), and it is not reckoned as 'it exists' (*atthi*) nor as 'it will be' (*bhavissati*). . . . (It is the same with) whatever feelings, percepts, dispositions, consciousness . . .; whatever material form is not arisen, nor come to be, is called, reckoned or termed 'it will be' and it is not reckoned as 'it exists' or 'it has been' . . .; whatever material form has arisen and has manifested itself, is called, reckoned and termed 'it exists' and it is not reckoned as 'it has been' nor as 'it will be'. . . . Even the Non-Causationists, the Non-Activists and the Materialists (*nāstikas*) should think that these three linguistic conventions, usages of terms or words should not be flouted and violated. And why is that? Because of the fear of being blamed, found fault with and censured."[13] Jayatilleke comments on this: "The mention of the nastikas can possibly be a reference to the school of Metaphysical Materialists, whose existence was doubtful but who made use of the *a priori* premise of the reality of Being. The very concept of Being is not possible without a violation of the convention. If Being = what exists, then only the specious present has being, for the past and the future do not exist at the present moment. But when we talk of the concept 'Being' without a time reference, we violate this convention and assume that the past as well as the future has existence in the sense in which the present has existence."[14]

7.12 Therefore, the attempts to define God in terms of Being or Absolute do not mean anything because these terms themselves hardly mean anything. Another defect of these definitions of God is that they are not really improvements on the concept of God. This becomes clear when theologians always go back in turn to the traditional doctrinal structure to clarify these definitions. Dealing with the problems of how to know 'being-itself', Tillich invokes the whole traditional doctrine of divine grace etc., with all the problems that accompany it (*v.* 6.54). Therefore, we are not better with these definitions or new terminologies than without them because we have to grapple with the same problems whether we use these definitions or not. Hartshorne does not illuminate us about the doctrine of God by his use of the term Absolute because he keeps God as mysterious as ever by making him go beyond the Absolute. The word Absolute is confusing enough. One way of avoiding this confusion, it has seemed to Hartshorne, is to make God more than the Absolute. And so we are, at last, left with the usual old God. The point we are trying to make here is that all these definitions are actually regressive definitions. They necessarily go back to the *definiendum*. The definiens was introduced in order to clarify the definiendum. The definiens is already obscure. The obscurity is multiplied when it goes back to the definiendum again for the clarification of itself. This regressive character is seen with regard to all definitions of God and it is, in fact, an unavoidable outcome of the essential obscurity and meaninglessness of the concept of God itself. To clarify further the regressive character of definitions we can contrast it with the definition of Nirvana. We said that Nirvana was cessation. And cessation was explained as stoppage of consciousness and stoppage of birth, etc. Thus this is a progressive definition as contrasted with the definitions of God which are always regressive.

7.13 What is clear from all this discussion is that the nature of God as explained by theistic thinkers is essentially obscure. Mystics do no better at enlightening us. Mystical descriptions start by talking of God as very similar to a human person and progress to talking of God as a completely non-personal transcendent state. For example, St. Teresa spoke very often of God as closely resembling a human person and she even went on to suggest that God has a body for she spoke of seeing the hands of God (*v.* 6.10). Eckhart goes to the other extreme when he treats the personal God as only an illusory product of the Godhead which is really an impersonal transcendent state comparable to the Hindu Brahman (*v.* 6.13). If we take the results of the experiences of God in the lives of people as giving any guidelines as to the nature of God, we are more baffled still, for some mystics have exhibited extremely immoral behavior while others have lived very moral lives. This situation makes the doctrine of God still worse. Therefore, we have to conclude that the concept of God elaborated in terms of his nature and attributes is essentially contradictory, incoherent and meaningless. If we cannot formulate a meaningful concept of God, then it becomes a meaningless question to ask 'Does God exist?' because we do not know what is meant by God.

7.14 Some of the Buddha's comments on the meaningfulness of questions become very relevant in this context. He said that there were two types of questions: meaningful (*sappāṭihīrakataṃ*), and meaningless (*appāṭihīrakataṃ*). If one asks a question that is meaningless then, he said, there is no way to answer because one does not understand the question. The Buddha refers to a person who says: "'Whoever is the beauty queen of this countryside, I want her, I desire her'. Another man might say to him, 'My good man, do you know whether this beauty queen of the countryside whom you want and desire is a noble maiden or a brahmin or a merchant or a worker?' Asked this, he would say: 'No'. The other might say to him: 'My good man, do you know the name or the clan of this beauty queen of the countryside whom you want and desire . . . whether she is tall or short or of medium height, or dark or brown or sallow; or what village or market town or what town she belongs to?' Asked this, he might say: 'No'. The other might speak to him thus: 'My good man, do you want and desire her whom you know not, see not?' Asked this, he might say: 'Yes'. What do you think about this . . .? This being so, surely that man's meaningless talk does not prosper him?"[15]

7.15 The Buddha says that the people who talk about God (Brahma) and talk about ways of attaining union with God are making meaningless statements because nobody can make the concept of God meaningful in any way, nobody can give any criteria for discriminating God from other entities. To understand a concept one must have delineating criteria for making that concept meaningful. These criteria can be derived either from knowledge by acquaintance or from knowledge by description. The Buddha says that the theistic believers can furnish none of these criteria: "Then you say, Vasettha, that none of the brahmins, or of their teachers, or of their pupils, even up to the seventh generation, has ever seen God face to face. And that even the sages of the old, the authors and utterers of the verses, of the ancient form of words which the brahmins of today so carefully intone and recite precisely as they have been handed down—even they did not pretend to know or to have seen where or whence or whither God is. So that the brahmins versed in the three Vedas have forsooth said thus: 'What we know not, what we have not seen, to a state of union with that we can show the way, and can say: 'This is the straight path, this is the direct way which makes for salvation, and leads him, who acts according to it, into a state of union with God.' Now what think you, Vasettha? Does it not follow, this being so, that the talk of the brahmins, versed though they be in the three Vedas, turns out to be foolish talk? . . . In sooth, Gotama, that being so, it follows that the talk of the brahamins versed in the three Vedas is foolish talk. . . . Verily, Vasettha, that brahmins versed in the three Vedas should be able to show the way to a state of union with that which they do not know, neither have seen—such a condition of things can in no wise be! Just, Vasettha, as when a string of blind men are clinging one to the other, neither can the foremost see, nor can the middle one see, nor can the hindmost see—just even so, methinks, Vasettha, is the talk of the brahmins versed in the three Vedas but blind talk: the first sees not, the middle one sees not, nor can the latest see. The talk then of these brahamins versed in the three Vedas turns out to be ridiculous, mere words, a vain and empty thing!''[16]

7.16 When the concept of God is not meaningfully established, the Buddha said, it becomes pointless to build a religion or a religious language based on the concept of God. If the central concept is meaningless, then the whole edifice of religion and the path of salvation are equally meaningless. In so far as Christianity depends upon the concept of God for its meaningfulness and validity, to this extent, the meaningfulness and validity of Christianity as a religion are decisively affected by the meaninglessness of the concept of God. The Buddha shows how the path to God becomes meaningless because meaning cannot be attached to the concept of God. ''Just, Vasettha, as if a man should make a staircase in the place where four roads cross, to mount up into a mansion. And people should say to him: ''Well, good friend, this mansion, to mount up into which you are making this staircase, do you know whether it is in the east, or in the south, or in the west, or in the north? Whether it is high or low or of medium size? And when so asked, he would answer: 'No'. And people would say to him: 'But then, good friend, you are making a staircase to mount up into something—taking it for a mansion—which, all the while, you know not, neither have seen!' And when so asked, he would answer: 'Yes'. Now what think you, Vasettha? Would it not turn out, that being so, that the talk of that man was foolish talk? . . . In sooth, Gotama, it would turn out, that being so, that the talk of that man was foolish talk . . . And just even so, Vasettha, though you say that the brahamins are not able to point out the way to union with that which they have seen . . .''[17]

7.17 The Buddha maintained that the clear meaningfulness of terms and concepts was an indispensable factor for clear thinking and understanding of things. Without clear terms and concepts one could not think in any intelligible way. 'God' is the most central concept on which rests the whole philosophy and religion of Christianity. If that concept is surrounded by a mass of philosophical and religious problems which render it practically meaningless, it points to the fragility of the foundations of Christianity as a religion. The Buddha said that for right reflection the concepts employed must be essentially clear. Once, addressing Bharadvaja, he said: ''Testing the meaning Bharadvaja, is of much service to reflection on and approval of things. If one did not test that meaning, the things could not seem right for this reflection; but if one tests the meaning, then the things seem right for reflection; therefore testing the meaning is of much service to reflection on and approval of the things.''[18]

7.18 It is not surprising that the theological reflections of Christianity are essentially unclear and obscure. That is why no theologian can meet the famous 'Flew's Challenge'. Flew challenged anyone to point out a criterion that would make Christianity falsifiable. But the Christian doctrine of God is unfalsifiable because the concept 'God' can mean anything, 'God' is not affected by contradicting states of affairs. This is exactly because God does not have any precise meaning. If an attribute of God is challenged, the theologian goes on qualifying, qualifying, qualifying . . . until God dies the death of a thousand qualifications. The theologian starts by saying that God is loving, like a father loves a son. Then, when he is challenged with the problem of evil, he immediately goes on to qualify the attribute 'love' by saying ''God's love is not exactly like human love but only analogous, and really we can't understand and conceive God's love etc. etc.'' Thus ultimately 'love' loses its meaning, and so the idea of 'God who loves' becomes meaningless. This way of making frustrating qualifications is the theologian's method of avoiding the contradictions inherent in the doctrine of God. However, this type of avoidance mechanism, sophisticated though it may be, again leads us to the same conclusion: the doctrine of God is meaningless. These theologians' qualifications create a very unpropitious atmosphere for clear thinking. Paul P. Schmidt calls them 'frustrating strategies in religious discussion' and says, ". . . the suppositions about God are strange suppositions in which the logic of the concept has no standard. Because of this lack of a definite standard, discussions about God are bound to end in frustration."[19] That is why most of Christian theological thinking is very inconsistent. The theologians, when challenged, immediately start qualifying. They do not abide by their assumptions and the usual procedures of argumentation. The Buddha did not like this type of argumentation and he gave curt advice as to how one should treat such thinkers: "If this person on being asked a question does not abide by conclusion, whether right or wrong, does not abide by an assumption, does not abide by recognized arguments, does not abide by usual procedure—in such case, monks, this person is incompetent to discuss."[20]

7.19 A theistic thinker might still suppose that one can make a fresh start here, and talk about the existence of God. This line of thinking may be explored in terms of the famous ontological argument. The theist can say that God is the most perfect being in every respect and therefore, if he is the most perfect being then he should exist, because if he does not exist he is not perfect. This argument has made much sense to many contemporary thinkers.[21] Let us examine the contemporary version of this argument as formulated or explained by Norman Malcolm. His starting point is this: ". . .'God is the greatest of all beings', 'God is the most perfect being', 'God is the supreme being', are *logically* necessary truths, in the same sense that the statement 'A square has four sides' is a logically necessary truth."[22] However, as we can well understand by now, there are problems at this very starting point itself. It is true that believers think that God is the most perfect being. It means that God has all good attributes to perfection. Malcolm thinks that God can be defined in an *a priori* way like a circle, and he also thinks that the attributes of God can be made meaningful in an exclusively divine field of discourse. This is the basic fallacy of Malcolm's thinking. God's attributes, like 'loving' etc., derive their meaning only in an *a posteriori* manner. Therefore before one says

'God is perfect' one has first to do three things:

1. One has to show that the attributes of God are meaningful and not obscure.
2. One has to show that they do not contradict one another or are not inherently inconsistent.
3. One has to show that these attributes can be meaningfully established in terms of experience because most of these attributes refer to this world or imply claims about this world.

Therefore, God is not perfect in the sense that a 'triangle has three sides' but in the sense that 'this man X is a good and a kind person'. 'God is perfect' is not an analytical statement and it can never be so because his perfections do not belong to and operate in an exclusively divine realm or domain. One can, of course, arbitrarily *define* God as perfect etc., but this is a trivial exercise. Even then the attributes used cannot be made arbitrarily meaningful because words like 'love' and 'omniscience' are not *a priori* concepts. They are necessarily *a posteriori* terms and therefore they cannot be used in an *a priori* definition meaningfully. Without a descriptive and an *a posteriori* foundation the attributes do not mean anything because they do not specify what is meant by 'perfect'.

7.20 During the time of the Buddha there was a religious teacher who preached about the existence of 'the highest luster'. But the Buddha criticized him by saying that the highest luster does not mean anything if one does not specify what one means by 'the highest luster'. Once the Buddha had a conversation with one of the disciples of that religious leader:

Buddha: What, Udayi, is your teacher's teaching?

Udayi: Our teacher's teaching is that 'this is the highest luster, this is the highest luster'.

Buddha: What is that luster?

Udayi: That luster than which there is no other luster which is higher or better, is the highest luster.

Buddha: What is that luster than which there is no luster higher or better?

Udayi: That luster than which there is no other luster which is higher or better, is the highest luster.

Buddha: You say that the 'highest luster' is that than which there is no other, which is higher or better. But you do not specify that luster. It is like a person saying,

'I want and desire the beauty queen of this countryside . . . .[23]

7.21 What the Buddha meant was that before talking about 'perfect' things, one has to specify clearly what one is talking about. He says that the qualities are relative, and because they are relative the specification becomes extremely relevant. He tells Udayi,

Buddha: What do you think about this, Udayi? Of these two lusters, which is the surpassing and more excellent: that emerald jewel, of lovely water, cut into eight facets that, if placed on a pale piece of cloth shines and gleams and glows; or some glow-worm or fire-fly in the dense darkness of the night?

Udayi: Why, revered sir, of these two lusters, the surpassing and more excellent is the glow-worm or the fire-fly in the dense darkness of the night."

The Buddha goes on to show that an oil lamp is more excellent than a fire-fly, a great blaze of fire is more excellent than the oil lamp etc., etc.[24] The irony in the Buddha's example is that though the emerald jewel is supposed to be a perfect and precious object, when it comes to the point of luster the fire-fly can be better than the emerald jewel. The emerald jewel can be a precious thing, but when we come to the precise delineation of its attributes one might see that certain trivial things, like fire-flies, can possess a certain attribute more fully than emerald jewels. Therefore, the Buddha's point is that for an intelligible discourse one must have criteria for delineating the concepts one is using. Malcolm explicitly admits that he does not have any criteria for talking about God. "That God is omniscient and omnipotent has not been determined by the application of criteria: rather these are requirements of our conception of Him. The are internal properties of the concept, although they are also rightly said to be properties of God. *Necessary existence* is a property of God in the *same sense* that *necessary omnipotence* and *necessary omniscience* are His properties."[25] This is the basic error of Malcolm. He thinks that the attributes he is using are *a priori* and therefore do not require delineating criteria for establishing them. The result is a defective starting point, because he misconstrues an *a posteriori* proposition as an *a priori* one. Therefore, because God's attributes have to be established on *a posteriori* grounds, even if we grant that 'existence' is an attribute, 'existence' also has to be established purely on *a posteriori* grounds as do the other attributes. So, if we take the divine attributes and try to test their meanings in their proper contexts then, as we saw, the concept of God becomes a contradictory concept. If the doctrine of God is contradictory then, of course, one cannot even begin to use the ontological argument because the concepts used are meaningless. And Malcolm admits this possibility: "The only intelligible way of rejecting Anselm's claim that God's existence is necessary is to maintain that the concept of God, as a being greater than which cannot be conceived, is self-contradictory or nonsensical."[26] "Thus God's existence is either impossible or necessary. It can be the former only if the concept of such a being is self-contradictory or in some way logically absurd. Assuming that this is not so, it follows that He necessarily exists."[27]

7.22 However, there are some important and interesting problems about the idea of 'existence'. Therefore, for the sake of argument, let us grant that the concept of God is meaningful and see whether 'existence' or 'an existence' follows from that. First of all, we have to be clear about the sense of existence that Malcolm is talking about. Now it is no use arguing that existence is contingent and factual and therefore existence cannot be a predicate because Malcolm, at the very start, maintains that he is not talking about a contingent existence with regard to God; or God's existence is not the contingent type of existence. Therefore, though contingent existence cannot be a predicate, there is no reason why 'necessary existence' cannot be a predicate. Malcolm states: "What Anselm has proved is that the notion of contingent existence or of contingent non-existence cannot have any application to God. His existence must either be logically necessary or logically impossible."[28] "Although it is an error to regard existence as a property of things that have contingent existence, it does not follow that it is an error to regard necessary existence as a property of God."[29]

7.23 The idea of necessary existence is, of course, full of difficulties. How can we conceive this 'necessary existence'? Malcolm gives some clues in terms of which we might be able to conceive this possibility. ". . . once one has grasped Anselm's proof of the necessary existence of a being a greater than which cannot be conceived, no question remains as to whether it exists or not, just as

Euclid's demonstration of the existence of an infinity of prime numbers leaves no question on that issue.

"... Do we not want to say that *in some sense* it asserts the existence of something? Cannot we say, with equal justification, that the proposition 'God necessarily exists' asserts the existence of something, *in some sense*?"[30] It is true that 'existence' can mean various forms of 'existence'. But that does not necessarily mean that there are various forms of existence in the usual sense of the word existence. When we say 'exist' what we mean is that things exist independent of our awareness of them. We have to accept this definition necessarily because otherwise God would not exist without believers or God would die with the death of his believers. The usual meaning of the word existence is seen when we talk of the existence of chairs, tables, mothers, etc. Here what we mean is that those objects and people exist independent of our awareness. Does the existence of an infinity of prime numbers exist in the same sense? Can numbers exist independent of our awareness. They do not and cannot exist independent of our awareness. They can, of course, exist on paper as symbols, but this is a trivial sense. If so, why do we say that numbers 'exist'? We say so analogically because they share some features of existence. Those features are their apparent objectivity and meaningfulness. Here, a theist can object and say that God also can exist analogously. But this cannot be so for two reasons. One is that the idea of God is not meaningful and the second reason is that the apparent objectivity of an idea does not entail its actual existence. The numbers are apparently objective because, as contrasted with dreams and hallucinations, everybody can use and think about numbers once they are taught the principles and know how to think about them. (We are using the word 'apparently' here because of the subjective nature of the origin of their objectivity. In other words, they become objective only after learning them. In this sense, any fiction can be objective in the sense that everybody has learned about it and knows it.) Therefore, 'numbers exist' means that people can conceive of them and so use them. So, 'an infinity of prime numbers exist' means that people can *conceive* an infinity (or, to be precise, the possibility of an infinity) of prime numbers. Thus, here, 'existence' can be very easily translated into 'conceivability' which is the proper sense of the term 'existence' in the context of numbers. The possibility of conceiving an infinity of numbers follows from the fact that this possibility is analytically deduced from the basic axioms and postulates of Euclid. Therefore, conceivability does not mean actual existence. It is true that we use 'existence' with regard to numbers. But one must not be misled by common usages, as the Buddha emphatically remarked (*v.* 7.11). Though we use words like 'the sun rises and the sun sets', this does not mean that the sun actually rises and sets.

7.24 Let us look at the problem of the existence of numbers from another standpoint. According to Euclid's theory of numbers, one plus one equals two ($1 + 1 = 2$). We say this is true because when we add one pebble to another it makes two. But it only means that this deduction is consistent and is validly made according to the theorems of Euclid. Therefore though we use the word 'true', what we really mean is that the deduction is valid and only that. Because, though it may be valid, it may well be false too. For example, when we add one drop of water to another it makes only one drop of water not two. Consequently, another mathematician can start a theory of numbers according to which one plus one equals one ($1 + 1 = 1$). We may call this also true, but what we mean is that it is valid and consistent. Now we have two theories of numbers which are completely contradictory to one another but equally valid. If they are contradictory, can both these two systems *exist*? Therefore validity and consistency have nothing to do with existence. True things are always consistent, but that does not mean all consistent things are true. There can be several consistent and coherent systems that contradict each other. Some of them may, at times, happen to apply correctly to matters of fact, i.e., to reality. For example, one mathematical system can be correct with regard to pebbles and another with regard to water drops.

7.25 Thus, Malcolm's elaboration of Anselm's argument is defective on two counts. First, the starting point itself is hardly a meaningful proposition. Second, even if we grant the meaningfulness of the starting point, it does not follow that God exists. His new maneuver to make 'necessary existence' a predicate is not meaningful because we cannot understand what he means by that new kind of existence. The mathematical analogy he gives to illustrate this new existence leads to conclusions that would hardly be welcomed by Malcolm. He might still insist that God has a kind of 'necessary existence' that we cannot easily demonstrate or explain. Then, of course, he is playing the usual theological game of elusive qualifications. However, by just saying that God has an unusual kind of existence called 'necessary existence' one is hardly saying anything that we can understand. It is easy to coin new terminologies but the real job is to find meanings for them. It may be that Malcolm is saying that, to believers, God has a necessary existence. And this is clear when he says: "It is hardly to be expected that a demonstrative argument should, in addition, produce . . . a living faith". This requires an 'inclination' which "in Kierkegaard's words, is 'from emotions'. This inclination can hardly be an *effect* of Anselm's argument, but is rather presupposed in the fullest understanding of it."[31] So, believers may think that God has necessary existence because they already believe in him. Here, one can say that though we tried to show that the idea of necessary existence is illogical, still some people i.e., Christians, can believe in this type of necessary existence. However, this is not the only illogical belief that the Christians can entertain: they also believe in 'God can be both man and God', 'God can be incarnated in man', 'Christ resurrected from death' and so on and so forth. Therefore, from the standpoint of belief and faith, one can hardly attempt to prove the meaninglessness of 'necessary existence' because belief and faith can justify any illogicality, and *credo quia absurdum* was meant to be taken seriously. Therefore, if Malcolm says that believers can understand God's necessary existence then, of course, non-believers can only regard it as yet another divine mystery. If he thinks that the argument is meant for believers, then he has wasted his efforts in giving what amounts to a rational formulation of an absurdity.

7.26 However, the idea of necessary existence poses some interesting problems. For the sake of discussing these problems, let us grant that necessary existence is meaningful in some sense. We shall say that this sense is that God exists in some 'necessary' form analogous to 'necessity' in mathematics, i.e., necessity in the sense that God cannot cease to exist. If this is true, then the Death-of-God theologians' claims are false because they speak of the literal death of God. Can Anselm or for that matter, Malcolm maintain that God should be necessary in such a way that he cannot die? If they do so, they are trying to say too much about God because they are making a *normative definition* of God. In other words, they are trying to ask God to behave in a particular way. But this is a restriction of God's freedom. If God is omnipotent then he must be free to die or to commit suicide. If he can die then he is not necessary. We can illustrate this by a short description of the logical nature of the divine attributes. When we speak of God as loving, we can say that there is no necessity for God to love us, but because God chooses to love us it is an empirical necessity that God loves us. If we say that there is a logical necessity for God to love us, then we are saying that he is not omnipotent because he is subject to certain logical necessities. This is what Malcolm tries to do when he says that God necessarily exists. The other mistake Anselm and Malcolm make is to take 'existence' to be of intrinsic value. But this, again is only a theistic dogma. For the Buddha, on the contrary, non-existence is better than existence. Therefore, let us imagine (however difficult it may be!) that God decides to achieve Nirvana. Then for the Buddhist, the resultant non-existence of God would be, in some sense, more valuable than his former existence. Therefore, existence is not a universally valuable phenomenon. If God can achieve Nirvana if he so decides, then he is not necessary. For a Buddhist, a God who cannot attain Nirvana or non-existence would be an inferior God, inferior even to man who can attain extinction. Thus, because 'necessary existence' does not have a universal intrinsic value it is not a necessary perfection.

7.27 However, since the idea of the existence of God is the central belief in Christianity, we cannot leave the discussion here. The theist can still make moves to show that God happens to exist and he may try to make God's existence meaningful in other ways and in terms of other analogies. To take up these moves, let us go on to other non-mathematical realms of existence. For example, we talk of the existence of unicorns. They do exist in some sense, in the way explained by Malcolm. Particularly, for children, their existence is quite vivid and real. A 'unicorn' is a meaningful and an apparently objective being because unicorns exist in pictures, myths and stories. Thus, again, their existence means only conceivability according to an accepted pattern of rules. If one likes, one can say that unicorns have an phenomenological existence. But, again, this should not be confused with existence in the proper sense, i.e., in the sense of the existence of chairs, which exist independently of awareness. Phenomenologists have posited the phenomenological existence of various types of odd things. For example, Meinong maintained that square-circles exist because they are conceivable in the sense that they are conceptualizable, and meaningful because the concept of square-circle can be used in and for meaningful discourse and is not nonsense like abracadabra. Thus, though one can talk of a kind of existence from the fact of conceivability and apparent objectivity, that does not at all say anything about proper existence.

7.28 There is also another sense of existence that we have to discuss. We can illustrate this, as some have done, by referring to an example in nuclear physics. In physics, we talk of the existence of electrons. We say 'electrons exist'. But here the sense of 'exist' is rather peculiar. An electron is not directly perceivable. Its nature is not precisely determinable as to whether it is a particle, or a wave or a wave particle. Its spatial location cannot be precisely pointed out except by saying that it exists somewhere in the Wilson Cloud Chamber. Thus, its nature and location are not precisely determinable. But, in physics, it is said that electrons do exist. By referring to this a theist could argue that this clearly points to a different kind of existence and therefore shows the perfect possibility of divine existence assuming a dramatically different form from that of ordinary existence. Also, he can say that just as 'an electron exists' is meaningful only within the language game of physics so 'God exists' is meaningful only within the language game of religion.[32]

7.29 But this analogy does not carry us very far, for while the electron's indeterminability in nature and location is experimentally demonstrable; in the case of God, to say that the nature of his existence is different, is only to advance an hypothesis about the possibility of the existence of God. This is because the concept of electron is meaningful prior to the question of the nature of its existence, while the concept of God is not meaningful prior to the question of the nature of his existence. To explain further, in the case of the electron, though the nature of its existence is peculiar, we know that it is a meaningful concept because by accepting its existence we can see certain consequences follow that can be fully and completely verified experimentally. In other words, we posit the 'existence' of electron because certain very unambiguous, clear consequences follow from this position. We first see the consequences and then posit the 'existence' of the electron. Now, we can accept that 'God exists' but we cannot see any consequence at all which follows from that acceptance. Here we are back at the problem of the evidence of the proofs for the existence of God. Also, in the context of physics the concept of electron is a meaningful term, while in the context of religion God is not a meaningful term. Notwithstanding the characterizations of God as Being, Love, etc., which are too ambiguous to mean anything definite, the problems of the contradictory or the meaningless nature of the divine attributes insistently militate against the possibility of giving any meaning to the concept of God. Further, by the fact that 'electron' is meaningful only within the context of physics, it should not be understood that 'electrons' cease to exist if the science of physics ceases to exist. It is true that the terms 'electrons' ceases to exist, but the series of events denoted by the term 'electrons' do not cease to exist in any sense. On the other hand, if the theistic religious language game ceases to exist, the whole idea of God will cease to exist and no corresponding events will be left because the idea of God cannot be made meaningful in terms of any form of event. If the idea of God could be made meaningful in this way, then the theists could have easily met Flew's Challenge and shown the events that would falsify the belief in God. In fact, however, even such a possibility is precluded by the prior meaninglessness of the concept of God.

7.30 We discussed the possibility of the phenomenological existence of God in the minds of believers. Let us now discuss this form of existence of God. As we explained in detail in the previous chapter, this phenomenological God is made up of strands which at any one time will be consistent. This means that believers use the idea of God for any particular purpose they want, e.g., to denote particular sentiments, emotions or ideals. A member of a primitive tribe expressed the nature and existence of this type of God when he said that such gods owe their existence to their believers. Raymond Firth writes: "Many years ago, it is reported, a judge in a Maori Land Court in New Zealand was hearing a case in which control by spirit beings was adduced as evidence for longstanding ownership of a piece of land. The court showed no surprise at hearing gods cited to support a claim in the case. But when the name of one god was mentioned a witness said, 'That god is dead'. The court demurred, 'Gods do not die'. The witness replied, 'Gods die when people cease to believe in them'."[33] Thus, in the case of the phenomenological existence of God, the nature of the concept is always fashioned by the believers who decide which type of God they want to believe in. They may change their conception of God as they want and as often as they want. As Peter A. Bertocci writes: "Since my childhood I have given up several conceptions of God. Each time there was quite a wrench, for, in my own limited way, I had been walking with my 'living' God. In my philosophical and theological studies, I have been impressed by the fact that one deep-souled thinker found the living God of another 'dead'. And then I realized that a God is 'living' or 'dead' insofar as 'He' answers questions that are vital to the given believer."[34] If we try to look at the concept of God as believed in by believers, then we can never form a coherent or a consistent picture of the nature of God. Different believers believe in different Gods though they may use the same word God. Devout crusaders and persecutors might believe in a jealous God; theopathic mystics might believe in a God who disapproves of kindness to other human beings, and humanist Christians might believe in a kind, loving God (*v.* 6.47). These are the varieties of God that theists might believe in. If a theist objects by saying that we must really judge God in terms of scriptures and tradition then we are no better off, as we saw in the case of Abraham and Isaac, the traditions of God's punishments, and the expositions of St. Aquinas, etc., etc. If we turn to natural theology, the same problems arise. When we consider the existence of unjustified evil, which again creates the idea of a cruel God, while the existence of happy states of affairs support the belief in a good God. Thus any method we adopt to talk of God lands us in widely differing conceptions of God.

7.31 Now, to go back to the believer's phenomenological conception of God, the theist might say that the conceptions of God as jealous, antihuman, etc., are wrong and the real and correct conception of God is that of a kind and a loving person. The important point in this move of the theist is that he is making a normative judgement about the definition of God and the basis of this normative judgment is the principles of morality. In other words, he is applying moral criteria in delineating or contructing the concept of God. Or, he is trying to build a God on the basis of the requirements of morality. Then, what is important turns out to be morality, *not* theology.

7.32 This conclusion is important because it illuminates the nature and existence of God as it is being formulated by contemporary theologians and philosophers of religion. What is clearly evident from their attempts is that they try to formulate a new justification for the existence of God. From the nature of this justification, they attempt to build a doctrine of the nature of God. This new form of justification is moral justification. In other words, the existence of God is justified (*not proved*) on moral grounds; God is *needed*, or God *should* exist for the effects belief in him can exert upon the moral development of mankind. Now, we can see, that we have to qualify this new God as a moral and a good God, and *only* a moral and a good God. We say 'only', because the main emphasis is on the moral necessity of the concept of God which is required *only* for moral purposes. Therefore, all other attributes of God, creatorship, omniscience, etc., are taken out as irrelevant to the delineation of this new God. As William Hamilton says: "The God seen as a person, making the world, manipulating some people towards good, condemning other people to damnation—the objectified God, in other words—this is the God many have declared to be dead today. This is the God who must disappear, so that we may remake our thinking and our speaking about him. 'The courage to be', Dr. Tillich writes in one of his most elusive and profound statements, 'is rooted in the God who appears when God has disappeared in the anxiety of doubt'."[35] Also he believes that the traditional God should be killed for moral reasons because he has the "Nietzschean conviction that God must be dethroned and killed to make way for the proper evaluation and freedom of man".[36] Hamilton, it is true, is a Death-of-God theologian. But he is, here, putting the new situation into a dramatic but correct perspective. And what he says is substantially and fundamentally true. His is the view which underlies the use of attitudinal theories of religious beliefs. What these new theories claim to do is to observe and analyse how the concept of God does phenomenologically affect people's behavior and thoughts. However, in the light of the above discussion, we have to examine this claim more closely and in doing so we shall see that what they actually try to do is to show how people should *use* the concept of God (phenomenonologically) so that certain moral consequences will follow. Now we can see the fallacy they are committing: they are trying to reason backwards and attempting to show (or suggest) that because certain moral consequences follow from the concept of God he does actually exist.

7.33 Contemporary Christian thinkers have made two types of moves in the direction of the moral justification of God's existence.

1. The first type maintains that the idea of God gives a perspective conducive to a better moral atmosphere, and so to moral progress.

2. The second type tries to make the idea of God morally meaningful by taking only the latter half of Christian theology, namely Christology, thus completely abandoning the other half as leading to all the complicated problems of Christian theology.

7.34 D.Z. Phillips illustrates the first type well. He says: "In order to renounce one's power one must not fix one's attention on *how* people are: useful or useless for one, desirable or undesirable, morally deserving or undeserving, but on the fact *that* they are. This is a prerequisite of compassion. When it is achieved in the presence of suffering, the giver is able to give without feeling that he has done anything deserving of praise, and the sufferer is able to receive without feeling bought or degraded. It might be said that in this attitude, people are seen, not as the world sees them, but as God sees them."[37] "The believer, if his faith is at all deep, is not concerned with his rights. He is not concerned with receiving thanks for the good he does, or recompense for the harm he suffers. What he considers to be advantage, disadvantage, happiness or misery is determined by his relationship to the love of God."[38] ". . . without his belief he could not be said to have the same relationship or experience the same events."[39] "The reason why love of God is said to be *other than* the world, is, as I have tried to illustrate, because it entails dying to the world's way of regarding things. . . . The love of God is manifested in the believer's relationship to people and things. . . . To see the world as God's world, would primarily, be to possess this love. To say that God created a world would not be to put forward a theory, hypothesis, or explanation of the world."[40] Phillips is aware of the usual objection: "The . . . objection which is sometimes made against the way I have argued, is that it denies the objective reality of God. The term 'objective reality' is a hazy one. The objector may be suggesting that the believer creates his belief, or decides that it should be the kind of thing it is. This obviously is not the case. The believer is taught religious beliefs. He does not create a tradition, but is born into one. He cannot say whatever he likes about God, since there are criteria which determine what it makes sense to say. These criteria may develop or change partly as the result of personal decisions. But not anything can count as a religious decision or a religious development."[41] But his answer does not help the problem very much because it only pays a lip service to the problem of the existence of God. However, Phillips's answer is a very clever one. Actually, his answer suggests that the objective reality of God is to be established on the grounds of tradition. If Phillips means his answer to be taken seriously, then we have to accept the objective reality of unicorns too (and various types of superstitions in various societies [*v.* 7.58]) because they have behind them a strong tradition that gives criteria for talking about them. As we explained above, objective reality need not mean the same thing as existential reality. Probably, here Phillips is trying to take advantage of this confusion of meanings and hence his cleverness.

7.35 Hick is another thinker who tries to give a perspectival justification for the existence of God. He says: "Entering into conscious relation with God consists in large part in adopting a particular style and manner of acting towards our natural and social environments."[42] Man needs such an idea of God, says Hick: "In his article 'Anselm's Ontological Arguments' Norman Malcolm has suggested that, for instance, the idea of an infinite divine mercy forms itself out of man's sense of a guilt which, requires such a mercy for its healing, and that the concept of God has other similar connections with the various aspects of human nature and experience. I think there can be no doubt that in principle this is so. The thought of God as unlimited goodness, mercy, and the like fits and meets certain deep needs of the human psyche."[43] The perspectival relevance of God is well explained in one of Hick's passages we quoted before (*v.* 6.3).

7.36 Norman Malcolm is another contributor to this tradition. He writes: "One may have the feeling that unless religious belief somewhere involved empirical consequences which can provide verification or falsification of the belief, then it does not 'get a grip' on the world; it does not really deserve the name of 'belief'. But a belief can get a grip on the world in another way. The man who believes that his sins will be forgiven if he is truly repentant, might thereby be saved from despair. What he believes has, for him, no verification or falsification; yet the belief makes a great difference to his action and feeling."[44]

7.37 John Wisdom, in his article on 'Gods', enunciates the fundamental principle that lies behind these attitudinal theories of religion. He says: "The difference as to whether a God exists involves our feelings more than most scientific disputes and in this respect is more like a difference as to whether there is beauty in a thing."[45] J.L. Stocks illuminates us more on the nature of this perspectival approach. He believes in "the religious truth emerging in the religious act as the vision of the ordering principle of the whole."[46] He further illuminates us as to the slender nature of the existence of the God that is implied in this type of perspectival approach. "The proof of the existence of poetry is in the poetical act, performed by the maker or reader or hearer of the poem. And there are in fact in this world many people who, if they were sufficiently honest and clear-minded, would deny the existence of poetry as well as the existence of God, and on the same grounds, viz., because of the absence of extreme poverty of the appropriate activity in their personal experience."[47] Bertocci is an exemplary instance of how these thinkers try to suggest a doctrine of the nature and existence of God as based on this perspectival or attitudinal theory of religion. ". . . when the personalist says that God is a unity-in-continuity of knowing-willing-caring, he is asserting that the essential constitution of the world and the essential constitution of man are such that the highest good of man is realized in that kind of community in which persons respect and care for each other's growth."[48] "In knowing-loving he enters into a fuller relationship with a universe that responds to him in his growth as inspired by truth and love. Why not then conceive of the Unity-Continuity of the Cosmic-Knower as a loving Person?"[49]

7.38 The moral justification of God has been taken to its logical conclusion by Robinson. He tries to make the whole doctrine of God meaningful exclusively by a moral term: love. What he says is not that God is love but love is God. ". . . Love is the ground of our being, to which ultimately we 'come home'."[50] Here, 'Love' refers to the concrete manisfestations of it in interhuman relationships. ". . . theological statements are not a description of 'the highest Being' but an analysis of the depths of personal relationships—or, rather, an analysis of the depths of *all* experience 'interpreted by love'."[51] He identifies love with God. "To assert that 'God is love' is to believe that in love one comes into touch with the most fundamental reality in the universe, that Being itself ultimately has this character."[52] Robinson epitomizes the complete triumph of the moral terminology, or morality, over and against the God-terminology, or theology.

7.39 The second move in the justification of God's existence has been made mainly by the Death-of God theologians. They try to do this by emphasizing Christology to the exclusion of the doctrine of God. However, they put themselves thereby in a highly paradoxical situation (as we shall see shortly), because many ideas of the doctrine of God are presupposed or taken as undertones in constructing their Christology. We saw how Hamilton maintained that the traditional God should be killed to make way for the progress of morality and freedom. Consequently, theology or this new 'doctrine of God' is given a radically moral justification in terms of the moral behaviour of Christ. Thereby, they try to avoid the uncomfortable problems of theology, and to give a convincing proof for the relevance of Christian religion. Thus William Mallard says: "The relation of the Infinite to man has taken a new and decisive turn. God is now no longer the Abyss, nor an intermediate personal, 'anthropomorphic' Spirit, but the Logos of man's hopeful existence. To ask precisely the nature of that Logos, or Meaning, of man's history is not to inquire after a 'personal, spiritual Being', but to contemplate the essential Mystery of Jesus' ministry and suffering and Resurrection. And to inquire into that Mystery is necessarily to become not less than a follower of Jesus, as a way of decisively dealing with our fellow human beings."[53] Hamilton says the same: "To speak about God and to know him means, therefore, to shape everything that we say and pray into the pattern of Jesus the humiliated Lord."[54]

7.40 Robinson also tries to make his 'love' meaningful in terms of Christology. For him, Christ is the discloser of this love. He says, referring to Christ: "For it is in making himself nothing, in his utter self-surrender to others in love, that he discloses and lays bare the ground of man's being as Love."[55] We saw how

Braithwaite tried to reduce theology to morality as illustrated by Christ (*v.* 4.39).

7.41 These attempts to reduce theology to Christology, as we saw earlier (*v.* 4.36), also suffer from a very serious inconsistency. Their main idea is to formulate a moral justification for the existence of God based on the moral behavior of Christ, hence invoking Christology. The inconsistency is clear in this attempt itself. Christology is necessarily based on the doctrine of God, and therefore without explaining the full intricacies of the doctrine of God, one cannot hope to build a Christology. One cannot avoid these intricacies just by keeping the doctrine of God in a hazy background. This inconsistency is very apparent in the very statements of these theologians or thinkers. Hamilton says that God is non-existent or is absent. Without an existent God, how can one hope for an eschatological future unless this eschatological future is mechanistically conceived? ". . . to be Christian today is to stand, somehow, as a man without God but with hope . . . Faith is, for many of us, we might say, purely eschatological. It is a kind of trust that one day he will no longer be absent from us. Faith is a cry to the absent God; faith is hope."[56] He feels the inconsistency of this view of God and soon goes on to talk of a presently existing God whom we can meet through Jesus: ". . . we have further a decision of faith that Jesus is the Lord, the one through whom God meets us. But we do not know any separate divine essence by means of which we can define Jesus."[57] How can one talk of Resurrection and the other aspect of Christology without presupposing the traditional doctrine of God? But Mallard tries to do this: "Man's redemption effects precisely a reversal of his alienation through a full reorientation of all his relationships. The human form of his redemption is his acceptance of the Cross and Resurrection. Such acceptance is expressed by an articulate, intellectual act of 'belief', but is not an intellectual act in its essence."[58] This way of talking of Resurrection and faith involves and implies a full fledged doctrine of God. Therefore, to try to make the doctrine of God meaningful in terms of Christology is exactly a way of putting the cart before the horse. Without first establishing a fully meaningful doctrine of God, Christology can never be a meaningful doctrine. Thus, Christology being a subsidiary and later part of theology, it cannot illumine us about the nature of the premises. It is, of course, true that when we see that Jesus was good, this, to a certain extent, shows that God is good. But the statement 'God is good' ***asserts much more*** than what is meant by 'Jesus was good'. Also, the Christological argument does not make any sense to non-believers. Because the relation between God and Christ is only intelligible to believers who accept it on faith. For non-believers Christ was only one of the many good people who have lived on earth. Therefore, for non-believers Christology does not have any necessary relation with the doctrine of God. Some Christians might say that we can completely leave God out of the picture and follow Christ as a great moral figure. These Christians might even say that God is not necessarily relevant for Christianity. But if we want to follow Christ then we have to face other problems. For example, the greatest moral act of Christ, e.g., the sacrifice of himself, cannot be made meaningful without a doctrine of God. Outside such a doctrinal context, Christ's 'sacrifice' might be interpreted as an act of cowardice, as 'giving up', or as the fate of a political insurrectionist, etc., etc. If we want to take Christ as a great moral figure, then many people would put forward many great personalities in history who could claim that title equally or even better. The important point to note here is the shift of emphasis. That means, if we want to maintain that Christ was the greatest moral figure in history, then we have to decide that question on a historical basis using our moral criteria: out of so many great moral characters in the history of mankind, who can be taken as the greatest? The crucial thing to notice here is that we are back again on to morality as the ultimate justification.

7.42 Thus, the two forms of moral justification of God's existence do not touch upon the most pertinent problems: the nature and the independent existence of God. However, these new approaches enlighten us as to our main line of inquiry when we see that they are trying to say that God *should* exist on moral grounds, or for moral reasons, to serve moral ends. Therefore, what they are talking about is a *normative existence*, not a descriptive existence. The nature of that God is delineated by moral reasons, by ethical criteria or norms. In other words, this new God is created by morals, to serve the needs of morals. The point we are trying to establish here is that morals or morality is the ultimate value form we can think of and the ultimate form of justification.

7.43 Let us summarize our discussion so far. We saw that in

the full doctrinal context, the concept of God could not be made meaningful because the attributes and the nature of God were contradictory and not meaningful in any intelligible sense. But we saw that by taking some of the consistent strands together, we could make a concept of God. In the choice of these we are always dictated to by our, needs moral or immoral. Immoral needs build up an immoral God and moral needs build up a moral God. Moral fruits of Christianity are due to these moral strands in God. Because these Gods are built on needs and choices, we saw that God, in this sense, is a God who is used for one's particular purposes. God changes according to one's needs and norms, as Bertocci says. In this sense, we argued, God is conceivable. On the grounds of conceivability the theist could argue for the existence of God. Here we distinguish between two forms of existence: proper existence and phenomenological existence in the sense of 'conceivablility'. We argued that this phenomenological existence could not claim the same status as that of proper existence (existence independent of awareness) because then even unicorns and superstitions should also be accepted as existing. Here, a theist could try to say that we do not accept the existence of unicorns because the idea of their mythical nature is always built into the concept of unicorns. In other words, unicorns are defined as mythical beings. Therefore, this argument from unicorns is not a very strong one. To overcome this defect we mentioned superstitions where the people who believe them do not think their ideas are superstitious. For them superstitious claims are really true and what they claim to exist does really exist. The problem now is, can we show that the idea of God is a superstitious belief?

7.44 Ranford Bambrough makes a detailed explanation illustrating how the belief in God is logically similar and is related to ancient and primitive beliefs about the existence of supernatural beings. "The simplest cases are linked with the most difficult by a continuous series of intermediate cases. There is an absolute continuity that connects ancient and primitive theology with contemporary sophisticated theology, a continuity unbroken by any jumps, gaps or sudden mutations."[59] He says that this historical evolution is paralleled by the growth of theistic beliefs in any individual. "This historical continuity and this logical continuity can both be seen again in the development of every individual Christian, in his growth from a primitive and childish understanding of the affirmations of his faith, when he is a child, to more advanced and sophisticated understanding of them, when he grows up and puts away childish things." "Every Christian congregation has its shepherds as well as its wise men. Even many unbelievers share a conception of the nature of religious belief which links them more closely with the ancient Greek theologians than with the sophisticated and advance theologians of this or any age."[60] Elsewhere, he makes the same point more strongly: "This objection may be put in an even stronger form. It may be suggested that the difference between Sophocles and St. John the Evangelist is not a mere difference in complexity of development and degree of sophistication, but a radical difference of logical kind. It has sometimes been maintained that Christianity is logically unique, and that therefore Christian epistemology, or the philosophy of the Christian religion, must also be *sui generis*, incapable of being understood in terms of anything but itself.

"This is just what I want to deny."[61] Bambrough's argument here would seem to be that there is no fundamental difference between primitive and sophisticated theology. The essential theistic elements are present in both, and though there is progress from one to the other in the sense of an increasing refinement and subtlety there is no progress in profundity or spiritual value.

7.45 Although Bambrough's main thesis is correct, he does not realize that the modern theist can always reason backwards too, and, using the framework of Bambrough's analysis, draw very different conclusions from it. Bambrough wished to show the primitive and therefore, the superstitious nature of the idea of God by analyzing how it is intimately related to the primitive ways of thought which always tend to claim the existence of many superstitious (false) elements. The sophisticated Christian theologian, however, can say that though the primitives too had glimpses of the transcendent truth of the existence of God, expressing their realization crudely in primitive categories of thought, and though fundamentally this realization was similar to that of the contemporary sophisticated Christian, nevertheless, for lack of knowledge of Christ's Incarnation and Resurrection, all primitive theologies must remain imperfect and complete.

7.46 It is interesting to observe that not only a theologian's arguments, but even the findings of an anthropologist would be able to lead to a clarification of the relation between primitive theistic religion and modern theology. For this let us examine Evans-Pritchard's anthropological analysis of the religion of a primitive tribe called Nuer in the southern Anglo-Egyptian Sudan. The remarkable fact to notice here is that the fundamental structure of primitive theologies is essentially similar to that of any modern theology. In the Nuer religion, God is known as Kwoth and he is supposed to be a 'Spirit of the sky' and a 'Spirit who is in the sky', but, Evans-Pritichard says, "it would even be a mistake to interpret 'of the sky' and 'in the sky' too literally".[62] They have a doctrine of divine manifestations too. "God is Spirit, which like wind and air, is invisible and ubiquitous. But though God is not these things he is in them in the sense that he reveals himself through them . . . he is in the sky, falls in the rain, shines in the sun and moon, and blows in the wind. These divine manifestations are to be understood as modes of God and not as his essence, which is Spirit."[63] In fact, in their conception of God, the Nuer people are much more sophisticated than many contemporary Christians in that the Nuer strictly sticks to the non-anthropomorphic character of God. Evans-Pritchard says: "I have never heard Nuer suggest that he has human form . . . If he is to be spoken about, or to, he has to be given some human attributes. Man's relation to him is, as it is among other peoples, on the model of a human social relationship. He is the father of men."[64] "As Spirit cannot be directly experienced by the senses, what we are considering is a conception. Kwoth would, indeed, be entirely indeterminate and could not be thought of by Nuer at all were it not that it is contrasted with the idea of *cak*, creation, in terms of which it can be explained by reference to effects and relations and by the use of symbols and metaphors. But these definitions are only schemata, as Otto puts it, and if we seek for elucidation beyond these terms, a statement of what Spirit is thought to be like in itself, we seek of course in vain. Nuer do not claim to know. They say that they are merely *doar*, simple people, and how can simple people know about such matter? What happens in the world is determined by Spirit and Spirit can be influenced by prayer and sacrifice. This much they know, but no more; and they say, very sensibly, that since the European is so clever perhaps he can tell them the answer to the question he asks."[65] Perhaps they have not yet understood that with regard to theology the European is not so clever as they are.

7.47 Nuer also use God as an all-explaining principle, a being who explains everything they find difficult to explain. This use of God as an explanatory principle has a very high emotional value because it gives enormous consolation in the face of worrying problems. This exactly resembles the contemporary perspectival theory of Phillips and others because the adoption of this perspective has significant emotional and moral benefits. ". . . if a cow or an ox of your herd dies Nuer say that you must not complain if God takes his own beast. The cattle of your herd are his and not yours. If you grieve overmuch God will be angry that you resent his taking what is his."[66] If one's favorite ox dies, then they tell him: "God is good, he might have taken you, but he has taken your ox instead."[67] The moral implications of the concept of God are clear: ". . . if a man wishes to be in the right with God he must be in the right with men, that is, he must subordinate his interests as an individual to the moral order of society."[68] And "if a man does wrong God will sooner or later punish him."[69] The life-enhancing quality of the concept of God is really significant. "They are asking God for deliverance from evil, so that they may have peace, denoted by a variety of images with emotional and ideational relatedness—sleep, lightness, ease, coolness, softness, prayer, the domestic hearth, abundant life, and life as should be according to the nature of the person."[70]

7.48 Nuer also have paradoxes similar to those in contemporary theology. ". . . Nuer religious thought cannot be understood unless God's closeness to man is taken together with his separation from man, for its meaning lies precisely in this paradox."[71] Evans-Pritchard also thinks that certain Nuer religious concepts have Biblical parallels. ". . . all Nuer have faith in God, the word 'faith' must be understood in the Old Testament sense of 'trust' (the Nuer *Nagath*) and not in that modern sense of 'belief' . . ."[72] Therefore it is not at all surprising to see Evans-Pritchard quoting Biblical passages to illustrate Nuer theological concepts: referring to the Nuer attitude to the death of cattle, ". . . I cannot convey the Nuer attitude better than by quoting the Book of Job: 'the Lord gave , and the Lord hath taken away; blessed be the name of the Lord' (1.21)."[73] Also Evans-Pritchard shows how they have a highly elaborate system of symbolism.[74] This symbology can explain away many repulsive things these Nuer do. "If we regard only what happens in sacrifice before the eyes it may seem to be a succession of senseless, and even cruel and repulsive acts, but when we reflect on their meaning we perceive that they are a dramatic representation of a spiritual experience. What this experience is the anthropologist cannot for certain say. Experiences of this kind are not easily communicated even when people are ready to communicate them and have a sophisticated vocabulary in which to do so. Though prayer and sacrifice are exterior actions, Nuer religion is ultimately an interior state. This state is externalized in rites which we can observe, but thier meaning depends finally on an awareness of God and that men are dependent on him and must be resigned to his will. At this point the theologian takes over from the anthropologist.''[75]

7.49 Elsewhere, Evans-Pritchard shows that the same basic structure can be seen in the theology of another primitive tribe called Azande in Africa.[76] Morally, emotionally and epistemologically the reasons that sustain that theology are exactly similar to the reasons that sustain the Christian theology even in its highly developed form. Morally, because of their underdeveloped moral sensitivities,the Azande require the existence of God and therefore God has a moral justification for Existence. The moral implications of God (*Mboli*) are clear in the following prayer they make to Mboli: ''Father, as I am here, I have not stolen the goods of another, I have not taken the goods of another without recompense, I have not set my eyes after the goods of another, all men are good in my eyes . . . Mboli, it is indeed you who settle the differences between us who are men.''[77] Emotionally, God's consolatory power is vividly potent: ''A thing deteriorates among the Azande, maybe a pot, maybe a gourd, maybe a hut, maybe anything else, and the Azande says: 'It is the doing of *Mboli*. It is *Mboli* who has said that the thing must perish.''[78] Epistemologically, the concept of God performs an important function: ''If you take an Azande back step by step to the limits of his knowledge you will reach Mboli, whose name takes the place of understanding. He is the horizon that rounds off knowledge and tradition. He made the sun and the moon and the stars, the rivers and plains and mountains, men and beasts and birds and trees. When Azande do not understand something, it is vaguely explained by citing Mboli.''[79]

7.50 If we want to quote from within the tribal tradition itself, a contemporary Zulu witch doctor talks in much the same way about his God. ". . . the Most Ultimate God is much more abstract. He is everything in everything. Each tree, each blade of grass, each stone, is part of God, just as is every man and every beast. Each hair on your head is part of Him, and every flea in your hair. . . . You will want to know what the Most Ultimate God looks like but we do not know, and we must not even try to know, because He is beyond human comprehension."[80]

7.51 Thus we can clearly see that the basic structure and argumentation of primitive theologies are very similar to Christian theology in its highly sophisticated form. A not-so-sophisticated Nuer or an Azande theologian could easily argue that their theology is much superior to the Christian theology and they could really advance very convincing arguments for their claim. For example, they can claim that they clearly avoid the anthropomorphic pitfalls of Christian theology and most of all they do not harbor many divine illogicalities known as mysteries such as Incarnation, Resurrection etc., etc., and therefore they would be able to claim a greater rationality and consistency and therefore superiority over Christian theology. So here we have yet another conclusion which may be drawn from Bambrough's analysis of the logical relationship between primitive and modern theologies: primitive is superior to modern. And strangely enough it is not only anthropologists who draw this conclusion from the Bambrough approach but there is also one contemporary Christian whose writing tends in this direction. John Hick tries to illustrate certain contemporary theological conceptions in terms of primitive tribal theology, taking the latter state as the ideal state of affairs. "Now within the circle of faith the question, 'Does God exist?' does not arise. To ask that question, as a real question, is *ipso facto* to stand outside the circle of faith. For to be within that circle is to be convinced, with a conviction which affects one's whole life, that one is, sometimes at least, aware of God as a reality as indubitable as one's material environment or one's fellow human beings. To many of the Biblical writers, for example, God was apprehended as a will interacting with their own wills; a sheer given reality, as inescapably to be reckoned with as destructive storm and lifegiving sunshine, or the fixed contours of the land. The Biblical writers were (sometimes, though doubtless not at all times) as vividly conscious of being in God's presence as they were of living in the material world . . . And to such people the question 'Does God exist?' would be not less absurd than the questions: 'Does the perceived world exist?' and 'Do the members of my family exist.'''[81] The Zulu witch doctor says: "The Bantu believe that to deny or doubt the existence of God is the greatest form of madness that there is. The heart might just as well deny the existence of the body, or the hair the existence of the head."[82] "In fact, the Bantu religion pervades daily life much more than Christtianity, as we do not separate politics, medicine, and economic affairs from our spiritual beliefs, and it is perhaps for this reason that until very recently atheism was almost unknown among the Bantu."[83] Thus the Biblical writer's religion is that of any primitive tribe because they hardly distinguish a separate religious life, as Evans-Pritchard says: "Early European travellers among savage peoples generally related that they had little or no religion. Anthropological writers often give the impression that they have little else."[84]

7.52 One might be able to point out even closer and clearer relationships between superstitious types of thinking and theological thinking. Fundamentally, what the anthropological facts prove is that it is the ignorance and fear of primitive people that give rise to their beliefs in Gods. The Buddha expressed this human fact when he said that fear generates many forms of superstitious beliefs: "Men driven by fear go to many a refuge, to mountains, and to forests, to sacred trees, and shrines."[85] This fear is generated by the events and facts they cannot explain. Some events may be particularly awesome though this feeling of awe has nothing to do with spiritual needs. Let us look at an actual instance of the arising of the conception of God in a primitive tribe in Africa. A Zulu native describes how this happened in his own tribe. He says that the failure to understand the white man "and the consequent failure to understand many of the white man's simplest gadgets, have increased the tendency among the Bantu to regard the white man as a god. When the Bantu does not understand something, he tends to give it a supernatural explanation—in fact, he is so fond of finding supernatural explanations for everything, that he attaches them to events which are quite clearly in need of no particular explanation at all. If, for example, a chief visits a place and immediately after his departure rain falls, he is regarded as being a favorite of the gods and is thereafter worshipped. This honor befell Dr. Verwoerd when an unusual amount of rain fell in Ovamboland just after he had paid the Ovambos a visit. This is normally a very dry region, and the Ovambos, in their gratitude, renamed Dr. Verwoerd their 'Rain Father' and began carving fetishes of him."[86] If this event had happened at a time in the remote past, then by now some anthropologist or a theologian would be able to write a treatise on the theology of the Zulu God called Dr. Verwoerd or its Africanized equivalent. And one of this God's major attributes would be the whiteness which could be very easily interpreted as a symbol of purity and his manifestation related to rain as a symbol of giving prosperity etc., etc. But because this event happened in very recent times and we know its origin as being due to completely superstitious grounds, nobody will venture to build a theology with the help of symbols on this incident. However, one can sometimes imagine a theist arguing that even this incident can have some transcendent significance. The theology that can start from this incident can be interpreted like Nuer theology, though Dr. Verwoerd's theology might be cruder than that of Kwoth. The theist can, of course, invoke the argument that to explain the origin of an idea is not to explain away the idea. Some crude incident can give rise to a great idea. Therefore, the theology that Dr. Verwoerd's incident generated can have a transcendent significance, though the way it all started was rather crude. Thus, though we can see how the theist might still argue, we can also see that his arguments are far-fetched and sound incredible to a person who is rational enough to see Dr. Verwoerd's religion as starting from superstitious fear and ignorance.

7.53 However, from the discussion so far, one thing is clear. The ideas of the nature and existence of God are logically related to primitive modes of thinking and behavior. And we can term it superstitious because it is born out of fear and ignorance. Though we demonstrated this point with the help of an examination of primitive religious theologies, we could not be fully satisfied because there was a slight defect in our arguments which the theologian could always point out, however incredible and trivial the theologian's point may seem to be. Therefore, now let us try to prove the point that became clear to us in such a way that forestall any possible further criticism by the theologian. The point we wish to make is that Christian or theistic theology is logically related to superstitious beliefs and is born out of ignorance and fear and because it bears logical and essential similarities with superstitious beliefs, Christian or any other theistic theology is only a superstitious way of thinking.

7.54 We shall try to prove our thesis by illustrating our points in terms of witchcraft, which is unanimously accepted to be a form of superstitious and primitive thinking, and we trust that the theologian would not be able to find any transcendent significance in this field of superstition. Our thesis will be established by proving these points: Christian or any theistic theology and witchcraft are based on (1) the same types of thinking, (2) same type of arguments, (3) and therefore built upon the same epistemological grounds, and they both have (4) the same phenomenological objectivity and validity and (5) the same emotional and sentimental value and significance and therefore (6) they both have the same type of perspectival significance and value and also (7) they both share the same type of structure as belief systems and therefore, finally, (8) both of them originate from the same root: ignorance and fear.

7.55 As we explained in an earlier chapter, all the arguments in the whole of Christian natural theology boil down to an answer to one single question: 'Why is there anything at all?' We said that the Buddhist would give four replies to this question. 1. One is that it is the way things are. 2. The world can be explained on naturalistic grounds. 3. This question is unanswerable because the question is not meaningful. 4. Even if one tries to answer it, one would only fabricate an *a priori* piece of theoretical reasoning which really would not explain anything. But the theist's contention is that his question is meaningful because we can all see that something other than nothing exists. The theist would say that this question cries for an answer. He uses the word 'cry' because many people can see to a certain extent that there is some kind of mysterious meaning in it, even though a non-believer could not make any sense out of it because it is not a sensible question, as the Buddha said. Nevertheless, the theist could say that to raise this question is meaningful because the question is fundamentally enigmatic.

7.56 Let us compare this theistic argument with the argument used in witchcraft. Godfrey Leinhardt explains the basic epistemological argument that sustains witchcraft as an institution when he writes about the modes of thought of primitive people:

"They are not satisfied, however, to regard natural causes as the only causes; and from this point of view, their reasoning about causes is more searching than our own. We are usually content, in cases of death or trouble, to speak of 'accidents', often assuming that further questions are pointless. But the Azande do ask a further question—why should it happen that a particular man, and at a particular time, becomes ill or meets his death? Theoretically, another man might equally have suffered in his place; or the accident might not have happened. What, then, has placed that man in the very circumstances where he is killed?"[87] The important point to note here is that the question makes perfect sense. We shall illustrate this idea by referring to Evans-Pritchard's findings in Azande Witchcraft. He says, "I found it strange at first to live among Azande and listen to naive explanations of misfortunes which, to our minds, have apparent causes, but after a while I learnt the idiom of their thought and applied notions of witchcraft as spontaneously as themselves in situations where the concept was relevant. A boy knocked his foot against a small stump of wood in the center of a bush path, a frequent happening in Africa, and suffered pain and inconvenience in consequence. Owing to its position on his toe it was impossible to keep the cut free from dirt and it began to fester. He declared that witchcraft had made him knock his foot against the stump. I always argued with Azande and criticized their statements, and I did so on this occasion. I told the boy that he had knocked his foot against the stump of wood because he had been careless, and that witchcraft had not placed it in the path for it had grown there naturally. He agreed that witchcraft had nothing to do with the stump of wood being in his path but added that he had kept his eyes open for stumps, as indeed every Azande does most carefully, and that if he had not been bewitched he would have seen the stump. As a conclusive argument for his view, he remarked that all cuts do not take days to heal, on the contrary, close quickly, for that is the nature of cuts. Why, then, had his sore festered and remained open if there were no witchcraft behind it? This, as I discovered before long, was to be regarded as the Azande explanation of sickness. Thus, to give a further example, I had been feeling unfit for several days, and I consulted Azande friends whether my consumption of bananas could have had anything to do with my indisposition and I was at once informed that bananas do not cause sickness, however many are eaten, unless one is bewitched."[88]

7.57 "The boy who knocked his foot against a stump of wood did not account for the stump by reference to witchcraft, nor did he suggest that whenever anybody knocks his foot against a stump it is necessarily due to witchcraft, nor yet again did he account for the cut by saying it was caused by witchcraft, for he knew quite well that it was caused by the stump of wood. What he attributed to witchcraft was that on this particular occasion, when exercising his usual care, he struck his foot against a stump of wood, whereas on a hundred other occasions he did not do so, and that on this particular occasion the cut, which he expected to result from the knock, festered whereas he had had dozens of cuts which had not festered. Surely these peculiar conditions demand an explanation. Again, if one eats a number of bananas, this does not in itself cause sickness. Why should it do so? Plenty of people eat bananas but are not sick in consequence, and I myself had often done so in the past. Therefore my indisposition could not possibly be attributed to bananas alone. If bananas alone had caused my sickness, then it was necessary to account for the fact that they had caused me sickness on this single occasion and not on dozens of previous occasions, and that they had made only me ill and not other people who were eating them . . . I present the Azande's explicit line of reasoning—not my own."[89]

7.58 Thus, the empistemological basis of witchcraft looks essentially sound and meaningful. In fact, the question witchcraft asks is much more sensible than the central question of natural theology. Theology asks: 'Why is there anything at all'? We said that in certain ways we can show this question to be meaningless. Also, another explanation is to say that the world has a beginningless existence. It has been there forever. This theory of the everlastingness of the universe, as we saw before, can also make that theological question meaningless or irrelevant, because if things have been there forever then there is a kind of empirical necessity for things to exist. The theist can rephrase the question in terms of contingency, but this is to beg the question because it presupposes a 'necessary being'. As we noted, we cannot prove a necessary being from contingency as a fact. This is impossible because contingency is not a fact but only an attitude formed by an already existing presupposition, i.e., necessary being. Thus, the everlastingness of the universe can meaningfully silence the theist's question. But can we ever silence the witchdoctor's question? The only way to silence him is to show the meaninglessness of the whole structure of witchcraft, thereby trying to show that though the question seems to be meaningful, it is not actually meaningful because there are certain thought categories that the witchdoctor has to learn. These are the thought categories of chance, coincidence and the ability to conceive and appreciate the fact that 'this is just the way things are'. If the witchdoctor refuses to accept these new thought categories we brand him as stupid, primitive, ignorant, etc., etc. But interestingly enough, the theologian also asks exactly the same type of question: Why are things as they are? The Buddha might tell him that his question is meaningless for several reasons, and ask him to think in terms of new categories and appreciate the point that 'this is the way things are' and would advise him that if he goes beyond that point he will only end up in *a priori* superstitions. But the theologian will insist that his question is still meaningful because it sounds meaningful. If the witchdoctor is called superstitious and ignorant on the grounds that he refuses to accept the new categories of thought, it is difficult to see how the theologian can avoid attracting the same epithets. The theologian also is working within a system of limited thought categories and therefore his system of thought is what anthropologists call a 'closed predicament'. The theologian can forever ask this question until he is enclosed in a cocoon of his system of limited categories. Because he cannot get a sensible answer, he always insists that there is a sensible question that needs answering with the help of the idea of God. Here, we can see how the idea of God becomes a meaningless answer to a meaningless question. As witchcraft flourishes among the superstitious because of its unanswerable questions, theology also flourishes because of its unanswerable question.

7.59 We shall now turn to another epistemological feature that is common to both witchcraft and theology. This is unfalsifiability. We saw how the doctrine of God was, even in principle, unverifiable. The principles of witchcraft too are unfalsifiable. However, the reasons given for the unfalsifiability of witchcraft are much more convincing and comprehensible than those given in the case of theology. As Max Gluckman says, "If the African has had his village protected with medicines against storms and it is struck by lightning, he says the magician was bad, his medicines poor, or a taboo was broken . . ."[90] There are many officially recognized reasons why the principles of witchcraft are unfalsifiable. Among the Azande, oracles are consulted by poisoning a fowl and asking the poison to spare the fowl or kill the fowl if the case is so or not so. Sometimes these oracles give contradictory answers. Does it falsify the oracle? Evans-Pritchard says, "Azande is seated opposite his oracle and asks it questions. In answer to a particular question it first says 'Yes' and then says 'No'. He is not bewildered. His culture provides him with a number of ready-made explanations of the oracle's self-contradictions and he chooses the one that seems to fit the circumstances best. He is often aided in his selection by the peculiar behavior of the fowls when under the influence of the poison. The secondary elaborations of belief that explain the failure of the oracle attribute its failure to (1) the wrong variety of poison having been gathered, (2) breach of a taboo, (3) witchcraft, (4) anger of the owners of the forest where the creeper grows, (5) age of the poison, (6) anger of the ghosts, (7) sorcery, (8) use."[91]

7.60 Likewise, we saw that the theologian also has many techniques of qualifying theological propositions to avoid the possibility of falsification. As every contrary incident can be fully explained within the system of witchcraft, every contrary incident can be explained within the system of theological beliefs. If a man prospers, he thanks God for kindness; if he becomes poor, he thanks God for not destroying him completely and for helping him to manage somehow or other; if he falls ill, he thanks God for not killing him; if he dies, others thank God for taking him to heaven. Thus commences a countless number of maneuvers or moves which are well known to anyone who is familiar with theistic arguments and thinking. Let anything happen, it only proves the truth of theistic beliefs just as the contradictions of the oracle proves the truth of the beliefs surrounding witchcraft.

7.61 In theology, sometimes the verificatory procedures are claimed in terms of other realms of reality. They usually posit two such realms. One is the mystical realm. The other is the eschatological realm. As we discussed in the previous chapter, a theist could claim that the propositions about God could be verified in a mystical realm by the mystics. In terms of visions, manifestations, illuminations, etc., they claim, the mystics can experience the truths propounded and claimed by theology. Thus the theological truths are made meaningful in terms of another reality. Some thinkers like Hick[92] maintain that the claims of theology may be verified eschatologically. Thus, the realm of eschatological reality which is, of course, a future reality, also functions as another realm where the claims of theology are verified. It is to be noted that these realms themselves are posited by the theological claims. That is, the contents of the mystical realm are produced by the theistic beliefs and the eschatological realm itself is a theological claim. The mystical realm is more relevant to our discussion because though the contents are theologically produced, it exists in the present. Also, the theologians attach a great significance to this realm as giving meaning and verifiability to the theistic beliefs.

7.62 One can see the same thing happening in witchcraft too. Monica Hunter Wilson explains the realm of reality of witchcraft, in terms of the beliefs of the Nyakyusa people in Tanganyika. "The Nyakyusa believe that witches exist as pythons in the bellies of certain individuals. They are something tangible, discoverable at an autopsy, and inherited. The incentive to witchcraft is said to be the desire for good food. Witches lust for meat and milk—the prized foods of the group—and it is this which drives them to commit witchcraft. They delight in eating human flesh and gnaw men inside, causing death to their victims. The witches also steal milk, sucking the udders of cows, so that the cows dry up and later abort. All this happens in dreams. Nightmares of being throttled, of being chased, of fighting, and of flying through the air are taken as evidence of an attack by witches; and, if a man wakes up suddenly at night in fear and sweating, he knows that 'they'—the witches—have come to throttle him."[93] She illustrates this further by referring to the Pondo tribe who also have the same reality structure.[94]

7.63 This shows how both theology and witchcraft draw most of their verificatory meaning in terms of a separate reality structure which is, in fact, as we showed earlier, a product the very belief structure itself. Thus the realms of special realities of theology and witchcraft share the same features as to their origin, their relationship to the belief structure, and as to the ways in which they reinforce the belief structure.

7.64 There are many other epistemological features that are common to both theology and witchcraft. One is the circularity of the systems. Evans-Pritchard writes: "Let the reader consider any argument that would utterly demolish all Zande claims for the power of the oracle. If it were translated into Zande modes of thought it would serve to support their entire structure of belief."[95] We saw how this occurred at the point where we discussed the story of the man who thanks God whatever happens, and in that type of thinking, any contrary evidence advanced was utilized for the reinforcement of the same belief-structure.

7.65 Witchcraft is unable to understand and appreciate the contrary evidence because it denies the very thought forms or thought categories which give meaning to this contrary evidence: namely, coincidence and chance, etc. Thus, in natural theology too, the theologian does the same and denies the same thought categories—coincidence or the idea that it is just the way things are—and instead invokes God to explain many facts and events that do not require any further explanations than natural explanations. Therefore, because the theologian denies the very thought categories that give meaning to contrary evidence, he cannot appreciate the relevance of the contrary evidence.

7.66 Theology and witchcraft differ from the rational scientific attitude on exactly the same grounds. As Robin Horton says, the "underlying readiness to scrap or demote established theories on the ground of poor predictive performance is perhaps the most important single feature of the scientific attitude."[96] Both theology and witchcraft do not admit of any predictive possibilities because they regard their beliefs as unfalsifiable.

7.67 Theology shares the same reasons with witchcraft for its stability in societies, primitive and modern. Here we come to what the Perspectival or attitudinal theologians were trying to establish. If we look at the world from a theistic perspective, they say one can react to the world better. Also one gets an enormous amount of emotional and psychological security with the idea of a God who looks after men as a benevolent father. God explains and fills many gaps and thus gives an emotional kind of intellectual satisfaction as well. In this sense, God (or various conceptions of God) continues to exist phenomenologically in peoples' minds, rendering them a good service. J.D. Krige explains how the existence of witchcraft in primitive societies is justified exactly on the same grounds. "Among the Lobedu, just as of course among other Bantu people, witches and sorcerers so far from playing the role of unreason, make a rational contribution to the fulfillment of men's needs and purposes. This is almost immediately evident when we remember that witchcraft and sorcery are explanations of evil in the universe. They enable men to account for their failures and frustrations. Moreover, since evil operates only through the medium of human beings, it can also be brought under human control. The parts assigned to these characters, the witches and sorcerers, presuppose a just world, ordered and coherent, in which the evil is not merely outlawed but can be overcome by man-made techniques. In the result men feel secure and the moral order is upheld.''[97] Referring to Navaho witchcraft, Clyde Kluckhohn says, ''. . . it must be realized that witchcraft ideology gives a partial answer to the problems which disturb the Navaho as well as other peoples—stubborn illness without apparent etiology, death without visible cause. One of man's peculiarities is that he requires 'reasons' for the occurrence of events. One of the manifest 'functions' of belief in witchcraft is that such belief supplies the answers to questions which would otherwise be perplexing—and because perplexing, disturbing.''[98] In addition, just as the idea of God can contribute positive results by encouraging people to do better moral things, witchcraft too can do the same to primitive societies by changing the perspective of, or rephrasing the situation. Referring to the benefits that result from sorcery to Lobedu society, Krige says: "The population, e.g., presses hard upon the natural resources but the periodical threat of starvation, even the scarcity of relishes, is attributed not to the limited resources, but to some shortcoming in men such as indolence; and the virtue of rephrasing the difficulty in this way is that rivalries for the scarce things are obviated while the merit of, say, industry is stressed''.[99] Also, sorcery is ''the projection of rivalries into the magical world since it is disallowed in ordinary life''.[100] We explained above how the existence of God is justified by contemporary theologians and theistic thinkers on the grounds of moral and social requirements. This form of justification for existence can be invoked for witchcraft as well. Krige says that witchcraft and sorcery ''enable men to believe that their failures are due not to any fault of their own, but to the machinations of others; and it is very necessary, in a world in which the technology is inadequate for the satisfaction of the complex culturally created needs, that men should be able to compensate for their inadequacy and continue to feel that they are masters of their own fate.

Moreover, witchcraft and sorcery provide avenues of vicarious achievement to those who, because of their aggressive temperaments or disharmonious conditioning, find it impossible or extremely irksome to conform to the pattern of co-operativeness and reciprocity.''[101]

7.68 Thus we see that theology and witchcraft have the same type of origin, structure, nature and justification. So now we can establish our thesis that the doctrine of the nature and existence of God is fundamentally a superstitious doctrine. If it is superstitious, why and how can it survive in a scientific, rational age? This is not a difficult question to answer. As we explained in several places, the idea of God (or conceptions of Gods) fulfills many emotional and temperamental and social needs, and that is why many theologians attempt to make these needs an argument for the existence of God. Even purely superstitious modes of thinking, very often, arise and exist in our modern societies. A. Rebecca Cardozo, writing about 'A Modern American Witch Craze', explains that McCarthyism in the 1950s in the United States shared all the features of a witchcraze.[102] We also know that many people in our 'modern and rational' society still actively patronize many forms of witchcraft and sorcery. When we come to theology and theistic thinking and beliefs, we have to trace their stability and continuance mainly to the cultural and social factors that surround it. Christianity is well entrenched in the society, and culturally and traditonally sanctioned. Particularly, the material and political success of the nations associated with Christianity and theism are reinforcing factors for the enhancement of the 'truth' and validity of their cultural institutions like the Christian religion. Early indoctrinations and constant feedbacks from the environment are added impetus for the continuance of these beliefs. The theologians can also ask certain apparently meaningful questions which seem to lend rational support to their beliefs (*v.* 7.59). Unfalsifiability too works in the same way. When we see theology in relation to witchcraft, we can clearly see that the coherence theory of religious beliefs cannot establish the truth of religion because one can also advance a coherence theory of witchcraft. This shows that rationality in the sense of coherence or consistency can only explain the stability of a particular institution of beliefs but not its rational veracity.

7.69 Therefore, people can live and continue to live within

the circle of faith and belief. If it is superstition, why do they not breakaway from it as it is easy to do in this rational age? It is not, however, as easy to break away from a closed predicament as it may seem. Robin Horton explains this difficulty: ". . . the transition seems inevitably to be painful, violent and partial. Why should the transition be so painful? . . . the moving, shifting thought-world produced by the 'open' predicament creates its own sense of insecurity. Many people find this shifting world intolerable. Some adjust to their fears by developing an inordinate faith in progress toward a future in which 'the Truth' will be finally known. But others long nostalgically for the fixed, unquestionable beliefs of the 'closed' culture. They call for authoritarian establishment and control of dogma, and for persecution of those who have managed to be at ease in a world of ever-shifting ideas. Clearly, the 'open' predicament is a precarious, fragile thing."[103]

7.70 When we ask, 'If Christianity is superstitious, how can it survive today?', we are also making a mistaken assumption. We assume that people are rational and scientific in their modes of thinking. But this is hardly the case. Still, rationality or the scientific spirit exists only in institutionalized forms and is a minority phenomenon. As Horton says, ". . . however, the 'open' predicament has nothing like a universal sway. On the contrary, it is almost a minority phenomenon. Outside the various academic disciplines in which it has been institutionalized, its hold is pitifully less than those who describe Western culture as 'science-oriented' often tend to think."[104]

7.71 Finally, we come to our last question. Can the existence of this superstitious God be justified? We have to remember that when we ask this question we are using the word God in a dramatically new sense. We make or create this new God by putting together chosen, consistent moral strands, so it is made by morality to serve morality and has a morally justified phenomenological existence (in the mental realms of people). Then, what happens is that God becomes subservient to morality and morality assumes the most supreme value. If that is so, then what we should really do is to face the moral problems directly, as the Buddha said, without clothing them in any other language like theistic language or without looking at them from an unwarranted theistic perspective. Therefore, can the phenomenological existence of the new moral

God be justified on moral grounds? It cannot, because intellectual dishonesty itself is a form of immorality.

Chapter Eight

REVELATION AND REASON

8.1 Revelation is an extremely important subject in theology because it constitutes the main epistemological basis for the concept of God. Reason plays two roles in theology. One is to support the revelatory truths. The other is to clarify and reinterpret the revelatory truths. It is the latter role which plays a significant part in contemporary theology and philosophy of religion.

8.2 We shall first take the question of revelation. We will not be discussing here the internal theological question of revelation, such as whether revelation is trinitarian or not, but will be considering only those aspects of revelation that can enter into a philosophical discussion. The idea of revelation is complicated by the fact that theologians try to give it meaning in many ways. F. Gerald Downing, for example, tries to make revelation meaningful in a completely eschatological sense. He says: "We may believe, trust, that Christ has made the 'revealing of God' a possibility in some sort of future. It is surely nonsense, even pernicious nonsense, to pretend that it is a present fact."[1] Downing's argument is basically a case for using a different terminology. This is clear when he takes " 'salvation' as a more useful term than 'revelation' to summarize for Christians the purpose of God in Christ,"[2] However, this is to put the cart before the horse and beg the question of the epistemological basis of general and special revelation without which Downing's own claim would be at stake.

Compared with this type of inconsistent attempt, the traditional view about revelation is a much more coherent attempt to answer the problems of revelation. The traditional way was to take scripture as the basis of revelation. But some contemporary theologians try to relegate scripture to the background and emphasize the special revelation of Christ, taking scripture only as a commentary on the special revelation. Barth is an exemplary instance of this attempt. Daniel Day Williams states the new situation concisely: "In brief this is the new understanding of what revelation is. . . . Revelation as the 'self-disclosure of God' understood as the actual and personal meeting of man and God on the plain of history. Out of that meeting we develop our formulations of Christian truth in literal propositions . . . Revelation is disclosure through personal encounter with God's work in his concrete action in history. It is never to be identified with any human words which we utter in response to the revelation. In *Nature, Man and God*, William Temple described revelation as 'intercourse of mind and event, not the communication of doctrine distilled from that intercourse.'."[3]

8.3 However, this new situation raises some insurmountable problems even within the field of Christian theology itself. The Evangelicals, who still maintain the traditional view of revelation, emphasize these problems. As, for example, when James I. Packer says: "So the revealing facts of history are only accessible to those who are already sure that Christianity is true. And how do we become sure of this? . . . Before I can find revelation in history, I must first receive a private communication from God: and by what objective standard can anyone check this? There is no norm for testing private revelations. We are back in subjectivism with a vengeance."[4] Actually there is much to say for Packer's standpoint because there is absolutely no way of circumventing the need of the scripture in the Christian tradition. Packer clarifies this situation: "Only when we abandon the liberal view that Scripture is no more than fallible human witness, needing correction by us, and put in its place the Biblical conviction that Scripture is in its nature revealed truth in writing, an authoritative norm for human thought about God, can we, in principle, vindicate the Christian knowledge of God from the charge of being the incorrigibly arbitrary product of our own subjective fancy. Reconstructed liberalism, by calling attention to the reality of sin, has shown very clearly our need of an objective guarantee of the possibility of right and true thinking about God; but its conception of revelation through historical events and personal encounter with the speaking God ends, as we saw, in illuminism or mysticism, and is quite unable to provide us with such a guarantee. No guarantee can, in fact, be provided except by a return to the old paths—that is, by a renewed acknowledgement of, and submission to, the Bible as an infallible written revelation from God."[5] Packer is here pointing to an unavoidable problem in Christian theology. Every theologian who has tried to overemphasize the special revelation of Christ has got repeatedly entangled in this problem. Therefore what really happens with these theolgians is that they usually confuse the general and special revelations together and do not, in practice, stand up to their theoretical dogma of the exclusive predominance of the special revelation. Barth also exemplifies this dilemma when he says that the hearing of the Word of God "can only be attested in the realm of humanity by an appeal to proclamation through the Church, to Holy Scripture, to revelation. . . ."[6]

8.4 There are divergences of opinion as to the nature and status of revelation in theology. Some believe that though revelation is the main epistemological basis of theology it has to be, or can be, supplemented by reason. Others believe that revelation is the only exclusive epistemological means of making the concept of God meaningful. Karl Barth exemplifies this standpoint. For him, revelation is the all-important and exclusive means of knowledge in theology. In Barth's sense, revelation becomes a very vague concept when it is subjected to a philosophical scrutiny, because by its very nature, revelation eludes rational analysis and investigation. If it did not elude rational scrutiny then it would not be, by definition, revelation. Revelation has no special or particular empirical basis. It is made by God through the normal empirical world. "It is good for us that God acts exactly as He does, and it could only be fatal for us if He acted otherwise, if He were manifest to us in the way we should hold correct, directly and without any veil, without worldliness or only in that harmless transparent form of it *analogia entis*. It would not be greater love and mercy, it would be the end of us and the end of all things if the Word were addressed to us thus."[7] Barth elaborates: "Jesus Christ in fact is also the Rabbi of Nazareth, historically so difficult to get information about, and when it is got, one whose activity is so easily a little commonplace alongside many later representatives of His own 'religion'. And let us not forget that theology in fact, so surely as it avails itself of human speech, is also a philosophy or a conglomerate of all sorts of philosophy. Even the Biblical miracles do not burst these walls of worldliness. From the moment they took place they were interpreted otherwise than as proofs of the Word of God, and admittedly they may ever and anon be interpreted in a very different sense. The veil is thick. We do not possess the Word of God otherwise than in the mystery of its worldliness."[8]

8.5 Thus there are no objective and empirical criteria to determine the nature of revelation. As Barth says, "we cannot produce conditions, on the fulfillment of which hearing of the Word is assured".[9] Therefore the fact that revelation cannot be made meaningful in terms of rational categories is not a criticism of, or an objection to the idea of revelation because it is the nature of revelation to go beyond the possibilities of rational investigation. Thus the main objection itself (i.e., lack of a rational basis) becomes a complement to theology. In this way, Barth tries to build up an impregnable anti-rational stronghold for theology.

8.6 For the believer this may look like a self-sufficient and an exclusive system of theology, hence its great attraction to many today. This system by definition excludes the relevance of empirical criteria as it maintains that "were God to speak to us in a non-worldly way, He would not speak to us at all".[10] "The man who hears God speak and can still inquire about the act corresponding, would simply show thereby that he actually has not heard God speak."[11] This means that Barthian revelation has to work within a circular system. He accepts this position: "The real interpretation of its form can only be that which the Word of God gives itself."[12] There is absolutely no way of getting out from this circle because faith, which is the faculty for identifying or obtaining revelation, is also a gift of God himself: "The Lord who gives the Word is also the Lord who gives faith"[13] because "faith is the work of the Holy Spirit".[14] This tightly circular system of theology may apparently look like a self-sufficient system to the believer. It is of course a coherent system, but this coherence is gained at the expense of a series of circular definitions. Its key concepts, such as revelation and God, are defined in terms of each other. This gives it the look of self-sufficiency and self-evidence. It is this look that adds to the attractiveness of the Barthian system. One can say that for the believer, and hence for Barth, the system can be self-sufficient and self-evident. But this is a misunderstanding and it arises from not paying enough attention to the basis of the Barthian system.

8.7 The basis of the Barthian system is fundamentally indefensible because Barth, on the basis of revelation, makes a series of statements that are claimed to be or supposed to be objectively true and valid. For example, the existence of God is assumed as objectively valid and factual claims are made on the basis of that assumption. For him the revelation "is the Word of our Creator."[15] Here God is taken as the Creator of the world or, in other words, he maintains that the world was created by someone and this someone was God. This is a factual claim. Therefore the validity and the meaningfulness of the Barthian system depends to a large extent on these factual claims. One can say that here these ideas of creatorship, etc., for the Barthian system, need to be meaningful only within the revelational system of beliefs. But this is a misunderstanding, because the idea of creatorship goes beyond the self-enclosed revelational system and posits objective and factual claims. Therefore the Barthian system is defective in essence because his basic presuppositions stand outside the revelational system of beliefs. The creatorship is a factual claim about the world and such statements are logically prior to revelational beliefs. Before one starts to talk of revelation at all, one first has to make those factual claims meaningful. A Barthian can say that that is exactly what Barth tries to avoid doing, because Barth believes that statements about God cannot be made meaningful outside the revelational system. If so, then it shows the basic unsoundness of an exclusively revelational system of theology because the basic presuppositions of such a system can never be made meaningful within the system except in a question-begging way. This weakness shows up very clearly when it is faced with competing claims from other theistic theologies and particularly from non-theistic or antitheistic philosophies. Such a system may be meaningful to a believer, and to a believer, the idea that God becomes meaningful only in terms of revelation is of no interest whatsoever.

8.8 Nevertheless, Barth appeals to certain criteria as the basis of his theology of revelation. He says that hearing of the Word of God "can only be attested in the realm of humanity by an appeal to proclamation through the Church, to Holy Scripture, to revelation''.[16] Thus he makes an ultimate appeal to tradition and holy scripture as the criteria of his theology. This way of building up a system of beliefs on the basis of authority raises some very important problems which we shall take up later in detail.

8.9 Let us look at how another theologian tries to overcome these problems and see whether he succeeds in his attempts. Paul Tillich is aware of many of the problems inherent in the Barthian approach. He says, "different and perhaps contradictory examples of revelation are encountered by phenomenological intuition. What criterion is to govern the choice of an example? Phenomenology cannot answer this question."[17] "The question of the choice of an example can be answered only if a critical element is introduced into 'pure' phenomenology. The decision about the example cannot be left to accident. If the example were nothing more than an exemplar of a species, as is the case in the realm of nature, there would be no problem. But spiritual life creates more than exemplars; it creates unique embodiments of something universal."[18]

8.10 In his answer Tillich becomes very mysterious but nevertheless he tries to give some meaningful criteria. "Revelation is the manifestation of what concerns us ultimately. The mystery which is revealed is of ultimate concern to us because it is the ground of our being. In the history of religion revelatory events always have been described as shaking, transforming, demanding, significant in an ultimate way. They derive from divine sources, from the power of that which is holy and which therefore has an unconditional claim on us."[19] The meaningfulness of these criteria is gained at the expense of an enormous generalization. Many such psychological situations would be easily explainable on naturalistic grounds without the hypothesis of revelation. Many things that concern us ultimately, like a simple-minded person losing his job, can have shaking effects. Here, one can of course define the ultimate concern to mean God, but it would be a suicidal solution. Therefore Tillich's criteria become very vague. This vagueness increases when he generalizes still more: "There is no reality, thing, or event which cannot become a bearer of the mystery of being and enter into a revelatory correlation. Nothing is excluded from revelation in principle because nothing is included in it on the basis of special qualities. . . . This is the reason why almost every type of reality has become a medium of revelation somewhere."[20]

8.11 Sometimes, Tillich tries to be more specific. Even when he does so, he is not very helpful because he goes on to define revelation in terms of God. "A dependent revelatory situation exists in every moment in which the divine Spirit grasps, shakes, and moves the human spirit. Every prayer and meditation, if it fulfills its meaning, namely, to reunite the creature with its creative ground, is revelatory in this sense. . . . Speaking to God and receiving an answer is an ecstatic and miraculous experience; it transcends all ordinary structures of subjective reason."[21] This way of delineating revelation presupposes a clear and unambiguous doctrine of God because here revelation is made meaningful in terms of God. And Tillich accepts this conclusion. "The knowledge of revelation, directly or indirectly, is knowledge of God, and therefore it is analogous or symbolic. The nature of this kind of knowing is dependent on the nature of the relation between God and the world, and can be discussed only in the context of the doctrine of God."[22] But as we saw earlier, Tillich can scarcely be said to have a clear doctrine of God since he is forced to make his doctrine meaningful in terms of such vague concepts like 'being-itself', 'ultimate concern' and the like. Actually, this argument applies to any doctrine of revelation. In earlier chapters we saw how difficult it was to give any clear meaning to the concept of God. If the doctrine of God is basically meaningless, then any doctrine of revelation can hardly be expected to have any meaning.

8.12 If one cannot give any clear meaning to the concept of God, one way out of this difficulty is to define revelation and God in terms of each other, thereby effecting a circular situation. This is exactly what Tillich tries to do. Referring to the special revelation, he says: "The question, however, is how much a claim can be justified, whether there are criteria within the revelation in Jesus as the Christ which make it final. Such criteria cannot be derived from anything outside the revelatory situation. But it is possible to discover them within this situation. And this is what theology must do."[23] Tillich is not worried about the resulting circular character of theology, but instead he thinks that is the nature of theology. "In accord with the circular character of systematic theology, the criterion of final revelation is derived from what Christianity considers to be the final revelation, the appearance of Jesus as the Christ."[24] Thus finally, Tillich too comes back to the Barthian circle. Ultimately, the whole thing depends on faith. "The Christian church takes the 'risk of faith' in affirming practically and theoretically . . . that no new original revelation could surpass the event of final revelation."[25] Here we go back to the problems of authority, because authority is taken as the epistemological basis for revelation. (One cannot argue here, for reasons explained in detail in Chapter 6, that what is accepted on the basis of authority can be verified in experience and therfore authority, though it can be defective as a source of knowledge, can always be validated by experience.)

8.13 Bultmann tried to give meaning to revelation in a moral sense. According to him, there are moral resultants from an revelatory context. "Revelation does not mediate a world-view, but rather addresses the individual as an existing self. That he thereby learns to understand his now, the moment, as a now that is qualified by the proclamation."[26] "The man of faith understands his now as one who comes out of a sinful past and therefore stands under God's judgement, but also as one who is freed from this past by the grace that encounters him in the word. Thus he for the first time sees the other person as his neighbour and in understanding the neighbour understands himself."[27] Thus moral consequences can follow from adopting this perspective. But our question is why should anyone adopt this perspective at all? Or has one any grounds for adopting this view rather than another? Here Bultmann, too, enters the circle. He says that revelatory truths are meaningful only within the revelatory context. "It is *not* to be understood so long as one observes from the outside; for from that perspective these statements must look like a complete circle. Outside of faith revelation is not visible; there is nothing revealed on the basis of which one believes. It is only *in* faith that the object of faith is disclosed; therefore, faith itself belongs to revelation."[28] Sometimes, Bultmann too talks about criteria of revelation, but unfortunately his criteria are all eschatological. ". . . the New Testament not only says *what* revelation is, it also says *that* it is. Revelation is an *occurrence* that abolishes death, not a doctrine that death does not exist. But it is not an occurrence *within* human life, but rather one that *breaks in upon it from outside* and therefore cannot be demonstrated within life itself. 'Eternal life' is not a phenomenon of this life; it consists neither in immortality—Christians die like everyone else—nor in spirituality or inwardness. It is to be perceived neither with the eyes nor with the mind or feelings.

One can only believe in it. It will be attested in the resurrection of the dead; therefore, it is future and one only has it in hope."[29] However, this eschatological possibility of attestation itself is meaningful only under the presuppositions of revelation. Therefore, this form of attestation does not carry much significant sense because it is itself a part of what it is supposed to attest. The special revelation means nothing but faith in Christ and this does not involve any precise and articulate statements. "What, then, has been revealed? Nothing at all, so far as the question concerning revelation asks for doctrine. . . ."[30]

8.14 Richard Niebuhr is clear about how the ideas of revelation or a revealed ideal can work as the focus point of life giving meaning, unity and purpose to life. "As a rule men are polytheists, referring now to this and now to that valued being as the source of life's meaning. Sometimes they live for Jesus' God, sometimes for country and sometimes for Yale. . . . Being selves they as surely have something for which to live as selves as being rational they have objects to understand."[31] Christian revelation means giving meaning to one's life in terms of the focusing point, Christ.[32] The decision about the choice of this focus is again within the focus itself. "Because God and faith belong together, the standpoint of the Christian theologian must be in the faith of the Christian community, directed toward the God of Jesus Christ. Otherwise, his standpoint will be that of some other community with another faith and another God. There is no neutral standpoint and no faithless situation from which approach can be made to that which is inseparable from faith . . . Neutrality and uncommittedness are great delusions where God and gods of men are concerned."[33] Thus Niebuhr's position boils down to a matter of authority and faith. "There is no continuous movement from an objective inquiry into the life of Jesus to a knowledge of him as the Christ who is our Lord, only a decision of the self, a leap of faith . . ."[34]

8.15 Now we can see how revelatory theology can always be a self-enclosed and a circular system of beliefs. Here the theist's obvious answer is that it is not a defect of revealed theology but its proper nature. But the problem is not so easy as that; the answer cannot be so simple as that. One cannot be silent by relegating all theology to the revelatory circle and feel that theology is then safe from rational objections. This is mainly because even though the revelationists use theistic concepts within a circle of revelatory statements, those concepts are made meaningful in a wider circle of factual statements, as we explained before. Let us illustrate this tension with the help of Rahner's theology. At one point he says that revelation is meaningful only within the faith-circle. ". . . the definitive Reality which resolves history proper is already here that Revelation is 'closed'. Closed, because open to the concealed presence of divine plenitude in Christ . . . It is further to be observed that the 'closed' Revelation with which we are concerned here is a Revelation made to the believing Church, in possession of the revealed Reality itself. A sure knowledge of this reality of divine salvation can only be gained through the divine tidings and through the faith which comes from hearing and speaks in human concepts and human propositions."[35] Later, he goes on to say that natural knowledge and revealed theology supplement each other. ". . . the revealed Word and natural knowledge of God mutually condition each other. The revealed Word presupposes men who really know something of God in spite of being lying and lost through sinfully idolizing the world; and on the other hand, this concealed knowledge of God only becomes really conscious of itself when it breaks through men's hardness of heart and is released by the Word of the God who reveals himself as utterly beyond the world."[36] Thus revelation, general or special, and natural knowledge mutually condition each other. The theist can argue that the special revelation of Christ is particularly within revealed theology and has nothing to do with natural theology. This may be true to a certain extent because there is hardly any empirical fact to make the idea of the savior Christ meaningful, and therefore positively, its meaning owes much to revealed theology. But on the other hand, it gets very closely related to factual statements. The revealed figure of Christ depends on many objectively factual premises like "God created man and the world and Christ is his incarnation; Man has sinned; This sin is transmitted on a social scale; Christ did attain resurrection", etc., etc. And these statements are meaningful only within a doctrine of God and salvation which itself can be made meaningful only in terms of natural theology and factual statements. Thus, we can clearly see that revealed theology can hardly keep to itself as an independent branch of knowledge. Here, one can always say that revealed theology can be an independent branch of knowledge on a completely different epistemological basis. This is what Barth tries to do; God being completely transcendent and 'wholly other' he can be known only through his own revelations to us. This makes tradition and authority its own epistemological basis. Revealed theology has also been treated as supplementing natural knowledge or as supplying the basis for natural theology in the sense that natural theology is said to be trying to prove and clarify what revealed theology has already stated. Thus, revealed theology can assume a great significance, not only in its Barthian form, but also in its many other variations. Whatever the form it takes, it always bases itself on authority and tradition as its only epistemological basis.

8.16 When tradition and authority are taken as means of knowledge, some very serious problems in the philosophy of religion arise. The Buddha was critically aware of these problems and has paid detailed attention to them. During his time, the Vedic religion, the dominant religious tradition, was largely taken as a revealed religion. The Buddha spoke of revelationists when he said that "some claim salvation by revelation"[37] In the Buddha's teachings, the word for 'tradition and authority' was *anussava* which meant 'divine revelation', 'authoritative tradition' or a 'report' come from mouth to mouth.[38] He strongly criticized *anussava* as a means of knowledge, and once addressing the Kalamas, he summarized his criticisms: "Now look you, Kalamas. Be ye not misled by tradition or hearsay. Be not misled by proficiency in the collections of scriptures, nor by logic or standpoint, nor on the basis of agreement with a considered view, nor by reflection on reasons inadequate for knowledge, nor because it fits a context, nor out of respect for a teacher. But Kalamas, when you know for yourselves: These things are unprofitable, these things are blameworthy, these things are censured by the intelligent; these things, when performed and undertaken conduce to loss and sorrow, —then indeed do you reject them, Kalamas."[39]

8.17 In several places, the Buddha criticized the epistemological grounds of revelation itself. He said that nobody has seen God face to face, and if so, it is difficult to talk of the existence of a revelation given by God. A Brahmin asks the Buddha: "Good Gotama, that which is an ancient revealed tract of the brahmins according to hearsay and tradition, according to the authority of the scriptures and in regard to which brahmins inevitably come to the conclusion: 'This alone is the truth, all else is falsehood'—what does the good Gotama say about this?'

'But, Bharadvaja, is there even one brahmin among them who speaks thus: 'I know this, I see this: this alone is the truth, all else is falsehood'?'

'No, good Gotama.'

'But Bharadvaja, is there even one teacher of brahmins, even one teacher of teachers back through seven generations of teachers who speaks thus: 'I know this, I see this; this alone is the truth, all else is falsehood'?'

'No, good Gotama . . .'

'. . . Bharadvaja, it is like a string of blind men holding on to one another—neither does the foremost one see, nor does the middle one see, nor does the hindmost one see. Even so, methinks, Bharadvaja, do the words of the brahmins turn out to resemble a string of blind men: neither does the foremost one see nor does the middle one see nor does the hindmost one see. What do you think about this, Bharadvaja? This being so, does not the faith of the brahmins turn out to be groundless?' ''[40]

8.18 This is a strinkingly relevant criticism for the Christian tradition because any type of seeing God is, by definition, ruled out in the teaching of Christianity. In the Old Testament it is often said that no man has ever seen God, and indeed God is made to say: ''There shall no man see me and live'' (Exod. 33.20). This is taken up in the New Testament, but with an addition. St. John says: ''No man hath seen God at any time; the only begotten Son, who is in the bosom of the Father, he hath made him known'' (John 1.18). The Buddha's criticism is an express denial that the seers or prophets were experts whose testimony could be trusted in regard to what they said, by virtue of the fact that they themselves did not claim personal knowledge of the validity of what they asserted. This denial of any special insight to them is tantamount to a denial that they were competent persons whose testimony could be accepted (One can say that God can be experienced in many other ways than by seeing him in person. But this raises a host of issues some of which we discussed in detail in Chapter 6).

8.19 The Buddha goes on explaining why he rejects tradition as a means of knowledge. ''There are five things which have a twofold result in this life. What five? (Belief based on) faith, likes, *anussava*, superficial reflection and approval of a theory thought about . . . ; even if I hear something on the profoundest revelation (tradition or report) that may be empty, hollow and false, while what I do not hear on the profoundest revelation (tradition or report) may be factual, true and not otherwise. It is not proper for an intelligent person, safeguarding the truth to come categorically to the conclusion in this matter that this alone is true and whatever else is false."[41] At this, the Buddha's interlocuter asks: "To what extent, Gotama, is there safeguarding of the truth? To what extent does one safeguard the truth, we question Gotama on the safeguarding of truth?"[42] The Buddha replies: "If a person has heard (from a revelation, tradition or report) then in saying 'this is what I have heard' (from revelation, tradition or report), he safeguards the truth, so long as he does not as yet come categorically to the conclusion that it alone is true and whatever else is false."[43] Jayatilleke comments. "The right attitude to take is to suspend judgement regarding the truth of the assertion or proposition thus heard and say that 'I have heard p from *anussava*—but I do not claim to know p since p may be false!' This is clearly a rejection of revelation, tradition or report as *pramāna* or a valid means of knowledge. For the truth or falsity of such a statement is to be judged by factors other than that of its claim to be the most reliable or authoritative revelation, tradition or report."[44]

8.20 In another instance, Ananda reports another criticism of tradition made by the Buddha. It is said: "Herein a certain religious leader is a Traditionalist who holds to the truth of *anussava* and preaches a doctrine according to *anussava*, according to what is traditionally handed down, according to the authority of scripture. Now a teacher who is a Traditionalist and holds to the truth of *anussava* would have well-remembered it or ill-remembered it and it would be true and it would be false. On this an intelligent person reflects thus—this venerable teacher is a Traditionalist . . . so seeing that his religion is unsatisfactory, he loses interest and leaves it."[45] Jayatilleke says: "We find here a good reason why an assertion that was handed down as a revelation, tradition or report was held to be untrustworthy. For even assuming that its origins were reliable it may be well-remembered or ill-remembered and the lapses of memory on the part of people transmitting a revelational or authoritative tradition or report can seriously affect the content of it so that what was originally a true proposition may in the course of time be so badly distorted as to make it false or unreliable.''[46] What the Buddha says is that with regard to traditionally handed down beliefs there can always be four possibilities:

1. Well-remembered and true
2. Well-remembered but false
3. Ill-remembered but true
4. Ill-remembered and false

On the grounds of tradition, we can never decide which possibility is the correct one with regard to a particular tradition. The reliability in the transmission of a tradition, as the Buddha says, has nothing to do with the truth of its system of beliefs.

8.21 This of course raises the question of authority within Buddhism as a religion. Consistent with his principles ''the Buddha is said to have preached a religion not based on hearsay or tradition''.[47] ''The teachings of the Buddha are not based on hearsay or tradition.''[48] Also, the Buddha never claimed to be omniscient and therefore did not claim any authority on that ground. He emphatically rejected the idea of omniscience on logical grounds as meaningless (*v.* 3.14), and strongly disclaimed the title of omniscience for himself. ''Those who say that the Recluse Gotama is omniscient and all-seeing and professes to have an infinite knowledge and insight, which is constantly and at all times present to him, when he walks and stands, sleeps or keeps awake—are not reporting him properly and misrepresent him (as claiming) what is false and untrue.''[49] Asked how he should be correctly reported he says, ''in proclaiming that the Recluse Gotama has three-fold knowledge, one would report him properly and not misrepresent him.''[50] Among hundreds of titles used for the Buddha in the *Nikāyas* the title of omniscience is conspicuously absent.[51] It is true that in later times the writers tried to attribute to the Buddha the title of 'all-knowing' and 'all-seeing'.[52] However, even here one cannot be sure that what is meant by 'all-seeing and all-knowing' is the same as the Christian sense of omniscience because the popular Buddhist tradition defines 'all' as 'all that had to be known' meaning fundamental truths proclaimed by the Buddha, in which case it has nothing to do with the idea of omniscience. However, in the original teachings the Buddha has emphatically disclaimed any form of omniscience and, therefore any form of authority is based on the claim to omniscience.

8.22 Similarly, in Buddhism there is no room for faith in the sense we are using the term here. It is true that the word *saddhā* occurs in Buddhism. But it means something that is completely different from the Christian sense of faith. Jayatilleke who has made a critical study of this concept, says: "The *Jñānaprasthāna* (1.19) defines *sraddhā* as '*cetasah prasādaḥ* (appreciation of mind) and we find '*cetaso pasāda*' in the *Nikāyas* where we can expect *saddhā: yato yato imassa dhammapariyāyassa paññāya atthaṃ upaparikkheyya labheth'eva attamanataṃ labhetha cetaso 'pasādam,'* i.e., inasmuch as he examines with his intellect the meaning of this doctrinal passage he obtains satisfaction and a mental appreciation (of it) (*M.*, I. p. 114). We note here that *cetaso pasāda* is 'mental appreciation' or the 'intellectual joy' resulting from intelligent study and a clarification of one's thoughts. Lack of *pasāda* is likewise correlated with lack of understanding, e.g., *saddhammaṃ avijānato pariplavapasādassa paññā na paripūrati*, i.e., the wisdom of a person who does not understand the good doctrine and whose *pasāda* is fickle does not increase, *Dh.* 38. Similarly, *aveccappasāda* in the Buddha, his Doctrine and his Order (*Buddhe . . . dhamme . . . saṅghe aveccappasādena samannāgato hoti, M.*, I. p. 37) seems to mean 'faith based on understanding' since *avecca* seems to mean 'having understood', e.g., *yo ariyasaccāni avecca passati*, he who having understood sees the noble truths, *Sn.*, 229. Here the Comy. has *paññāya ajjhogahetvā*, 'having comprehended with one's intelligence'. . .'faith born of understanding (*aveccappasāda-*) is similar to 'rational faith (*ākāravatīsaddhā, M.*, I. p. 320)' which is said to be 'rooted, established, fixed and irremovable' (*mūlajātā patiṭṭhitā . . . daḷhā asaṃhāriyā,* loc. cit.). It is said that failure to investigate and understand results in lack of *pasāda*, e.g., *ananuvicca apariyogāhetvā pasādanīye ṭhāne appasādaṃ upadaṃseti,* i.e., one shows lack of faith in a situation in which one ought to have faith as a result of not investigating and understanding."[53] The rational faith thus generated is always contrasted with 'baseless faith' (*amūlikā saddhā*).

8.23 The Buddha goes on to say that the free inquiring attitude should be directed towards the Buddha himself by his disciples. He advocates a strict test that should be carried out to determine whether the Buddha himself has really attained enlightenment before accepting him as one's teacher. It is said that "an inquiring monk, who cannot read the thoughts of another, should examine the Tathagata to determine whether he is enlightened or not''[54] and thus "the Tathagata is to be examined in respectof two things, namely of what can be learned by observation and by hearing about him''.[55] One should observe that he does not have nor is reputed to have morally corrupt or mixed modes of conduct but only virtuous conduct. One should ensure that this is so for a long period and not merely for a short term. As Jayatilleke says: "We may see from this that doubt about the claims of the Tathagata is not condemned, but in fact plays a central role in the process of inquiry which is considered to be essential, prior to and for the generation of belief (or faith)''.[56] After this preliminary examination of the Tathagata, it is said that one would feel that it was worth listening to his teachings.[57] After that "he realizes with his own higher knowledge some of those doctrines and concludes that (they are true) and then reposes faith in the teacher, believing that the Exalted One was enlightened, his doctrine well-taught and the Order of good conduct''.[58] "The faith of him, which is thus fixed, rooted and established on these reasons, grounds and features is said to be a rational faith, rooted in insight, firm and irremoveable by recluse or brahmin, a god, Mara or Brahma or anyone in the world.''[59] As Jayatilleke says: "This rational faith which is a product of critical examination and partial verification is apparently contrasted with the '*baseless faith*' (*amūlikā saddhā, M.*, II, p. 170) which the brahmins have towards the Vedas and which the Buddha shows, does not bear critical examination.''[60]

8.24 The *Caṅkī Sutta* summarizes the process from belief to the realization of truth. "With the faith arisen, he approaches and associates with (the teacher); thus associating he gives ear, giving ear he listens to the doctrine, listening to the doctrine he bears in mind; then he examines the meaning of the doctrine he has borne in mind, thus examining the meaning he approves of it, approving of it the desire (to try it out) arises; with desire arisen he exerts himself, having exerted himself he considers it; having considered, he puts forth effort; putting forth effort, he himself experiences the highest truth and sees it having penetrated it with his understanding.''[61]

8.25 A dialogue between Nigantha Nathaputta, the leader of Jainism, and Citta, a follower of the Buddha, clarifies the Buddhist's attitude towards the Buddha and his teachings.

"Nigantha Nathaputta:	Do you *believe* in (*saddahasi*) the statement of the recluse Gotama that there is a jhanic state (trance) in which there is no discursive or reflective thought there and is a cessation of discursive thought and reflection?
Citta:	I do not accept this as a *belief*.
Nigantha Nathaputta:	See what an honest, straightforward and upright person the householder Citta is . . .
Citta:	What do you think? Which is better, *knowledge or belief?*
Nigantha Nathaputta:	Surely, *knowledge is better than belief*.
Citta:	(I can attain up to the fourth jhana) . . . *Knowing and seeing thus*, why should I accept this on the grounds of faith in any recluse or brahmin, that there is a trance in which there is no discursive or reflective thought . . ."[62]

Thus 'faith' in Buddhism resembles very much the faith a scientist reposes in a particular hypothesis. He has faith that the latter might work because of the credibility and reliability that is suggested by the preliminary observations. Faith in Buddhism works only as a starting point in the scientist's sense and therefore it has necessarily to be replaced later by direct personal knowledge. Consequently, an Arahant is described as 'one devoid of faith'[63] and it is often pointed out that the Arahant must be in a position to claim the highest knowledge without having to rely on faith.[64]

8.26 The Buddha respected the critical attitude to such an extent that even when he was just about to die, he reproved his attendant monk Ananda for trying to turn away a monk who came to question the Buddha on a doctrinal point.[65] His dislike for authority is shown again when he refused to appoint a person as his successor after his death. "There is no monk singled out by the Buddha so that he would be a refuge after his death."[66] After the death of the Buddha, the Order of Monks too decided not to appoint a head, thus precluding the possibility of there arising authoritative traditions in the Buddhist institutions.

8.27 Theologians have tried to support revelatory traditions in many ways. One has been to invoke popular acceptance and social approval over a long period of time. The Buddha was critical of that type of traditional support as well. Once when Saccaka was arguing with the Buddha, the former tried to invoke the opinion of the majority. Saccaka was quietly rebuked with the remark that the belief of the majority has nothing to do with the truth of the thesis in question: "What has the opinion of the majority to do here . . .try to extricate your own thesis."[67]

8.28 Austin Farrer tries to evolve a theory of revelation by using moral criteria as checkpoints. ". . . the history of revelation is largely the history of false prophecy and a sifting of much sand to find a grain of gold. A number of complementary filters have gradually operated: the 'discernment of spirits', or scrutiny of the effect produced by the supposed revelation on the man who utters it; efficacy, or the tendency of his message to produce godly states in his hearers; orthodoxy, or the mutual support of all prophecies commended on other grounds; rationality, or agreement with conscience and good sense, and above all, applicability to fact."[68] If, as he says, the priority is given to moral criteria, this raises many serious problems that carry possibly disastrous implications for theology (*v.* 6.57). However, Farrer goes on to say that even these checks should work within the revelatory tradition itself, thus completing the full circle. "But the operation of checks is, to the believer, as much a part of revelation as any other, since the whole process is in the hands of God. It is thus that the canon of Scripture, and the Catholic creeds, come to be perceived as summaries of revealed truth."[69] Thus ultimately his checks become of little value because it is the tradition that succeeds in the final court of appeal. Though Farrer starts his article as a rational inquiry into the problems of revelation, hence speaking of checks, etc., he ends up in the helpless position of a strict revelationist in the sense that you just have to accept that Christ was the Son because Christ claimed to be so: ". . . the recognition of revealing action begins with Christ; He first, and in Himself, acknowleges divine presence. And if he was in truth the Divine Son it seems absurd to ask how he knew it; how could he have been ignorant of it?"[70]

8.29 This shows the utterly helpless position one finds oneself in when one accepts tradition or authority as a source of knowledge. This brings Christian theological thinking still closer to the superstitious type of thinking that we were trying to illustrate in the last chapter. Particularly with regard to the acceptance of the special revelation of Christ, Christianity becomes one among thousands of many other millenarian cults that have sprung up as mushrooms all over the world and are still thriving among many primitive societies.[71] Christ's claims become indistinguishable from those cults because those claims are, as Farrer pointed out, taken to be self-validating, a feature shared by the leaders or founders of all millenarian cults.

8.30 Now let us examine the role of reason in Christian theology. We are not thinking of reason, here, in the sense of rational knowledge. In that sense, reason attempts to play an important part in natural theology and we have examined in previous chapters these parts in detail. Here we are concerned with reason in its strict sense, the sense of 'mere reasoning' or *a priori* reasoning. This plays a very important role in speculative theology. This type of reasoning is used in speculative theology mainly for the purpose of clarifying or reinterpreting the basic concepts, specially the concept of God, in theology.

8.31 *A priori* reasoning has been used in many ways in theology. Sometimes it is used as a clarificatory adjunct. Hartshorne is a good example of this. We saw how he used the concept of the Absolute in the sense of all-inclusiveness, and tried to show transcendence and immanence of God by saying how God goes beyond the Absolute while still embracing the Absolute. The concept of Absolute is an *a priori* manufactured concept without any precise meaning but with many conceptual connotations that can be manipulated in all sorts of ways (*v.* 7.9). We also saw another similar example with regard to the Ontological Argument as formulated by Anselm and later clarified by Malcolm. That was, again, to clarify the idea of God which the believer already had in mind. We saw in detail how this whole argument is based on a high degree of *a priori* reasoning and argument (*v.* 7.21).

8.32 Now, to come to a use of *a priori* reasoning somewhat different from the above examples, we saw how some theologians were using *a priori* formulated concepts as the basis of their theology. They tried to reinterpret the concept of God in the light of such new terms. An exemplary instance would be Paul Tillich and Bishop Robinson, who borrows the former's basic terminology. Tillich's main concept is 'being-itself'. Robinson likes this concept because nobody can doubt its existence; "God is, by definition, ultimate reality. And one cannot argue whether ultimate reality *exists* . . . Thus, the fundamental theological question consists not in establishing the 'existence' of God as a separate entity but in pressing through in ultimate concern to what Tillich calls 'the ground of our being'."[72] The idea that there is something that exists ultimately is an *a priori* assumption by itself and we explained in detail how the Buddha himself clarified how the ideas like 'Being' can arise from confusions made by *a priori* reasoning (*v.* 7.11).

8.33 The Buddha did not like the use of pure reason as a source of knowledge for several reasons. He warned many times that by confusing words and tenses one can end up in unnecessary philosophical problems. In his address to the Kalamas, quoted above, the Buddha refers to several ways of knowledge, that are related to reason for accepting a proposition, and rejects them as very unsatisfactory means. One should not accept a proposition because it is well-argued (*takka*), because it is a standpoint or a point of view (*naya*), because of reflecting on reasons that are not adequate (*ākāraparivitakka*),[73] or because one is convinced of some theory (*diṭṭhinijjhānakkhanti*). It is obvious why most of those reasons are unsatisfactory as means of knowledge.

8.34 The Buddha went on to a detailed criticism of the use of pure reasoning in system building. Reasoning was called *takka*[74] and the Buddha said that "people say two things 'true' and 'false' by employing *takka* on views".[75] The commentary states: "They (i.e., debaters) are led by and carried away by their reasoning, thinking and imagination or they declare and assert what is beaten out by logic and speculative inquiry and is self-evident to them."[76] Most of the theories thus constructed by logic were metaphysical theories that dealt with problems of transcendent realities (*v.* 7.10). Buddhaghosa distinguishes between different kinds of reasoners: "There are four types of reasoners, one who reasons on a premise based on tradition (or report), one who reasons on a premise based on retrocognition, one who reasons on a premise based on jhanic experience and the pure reasoner. In this connection, he who hears such a statement as 'there was a king named Vessantara' and argues on the basis of it that 'if Vessantara is identical with the Exalted

One, then the soul is eternal' and accepts this theory, is one who reasons on a premise based on tradition (*anussaviko*). One who remembers one or two (prior) births and argues that since it was he who existed in the past in such and such a place, therefore the soul is eternal, is one who reasons on a premise based on retrocognition (*jātissara-takki*). He who, because of his jhanic experience, argues that since his soul is happy in the present, it must have been so in the past and it will be so in the future, and accepts the theory (that the soul is eternal) is an intuitionist reasoner (*lābhī takkiko*). But a pure reasoner (*suddhatakkiko*) is one who accepts this theory on pure reasoning of the form if p is true, q is true or if p is true, q is not true."[77]

8.35 In the *Sandaka Sutta,* Ananda states the main argument against the views that are based on reasoning: "Herein . . . a certain teacher is a reasoner and investigator; he teaches a doctrine which is self-evident and is a product of reasoning and the pursuit of speculation. But in the case of a person who reasons and speculates, his reasoning may be good or bad, true or false."[78] As in the case of the critique of tradition, what is maintained here is that there can be four possibilities with regard to views based on reasoning:

1. Well reasoned and true
2. Well-reasoned but false
3. Ill-reasoned but true
4. Ill-reasoned and false

8.36 The second possibility may need elaborating. What Ananda says here is that one can argue correctly but come to wrong conclusions. The Ontological Argument we were discussing may roughly illustrate this point. What Malcolm was trying to do was show the coherence and validity of that piece of reasoning. But that, as we saw, has nothing to do with the truth or falsity of the conclusion. A better example would be the coherent theory of religion (*v.* 6.21) we discussed in the 6th chapter. There the philosopher was trying to show the coherence of a particular system of religious beliefs and then trying to make the fallacious move that, because a system is coherent, it must be true as well. This is exactly what Ananda is denying here. He is maintaining that a theory can be well argued, etc., and therefore valid and coherent, but false. He is making an extremely important distinction between validity and truth which many thinkers confuse even today. In the *Caṅkī Sutta* it is said that "even that which is well reflected upon or well thought out is liable to be baseless, unfounded and false, while that which is not well-reflected upon or not well thought may turn out to be true, factual and not false".[79] The Buddha emphatically denied that his theories were based on *a priori* reasoning[80], but he always accepted the limited value of reasoning.[81] Thus, if we take reasoning as a true means of knowledge, then nobody can decide on the basis of reasoning alone which of the four possibilities is the true one and this makes it imperative that one should have recourse to experience and verification to decide the truth or falsity of the views in question. If so, what is basically important is experience and verification about the truth or falsity of the claims made by various views.

8.37 This is why the Buddha emphasized the necessity of experience, verification and rational understanding in gaining knowledge and enlightenment. In his sermons he always appealed to objective and factual criteria in establishing his doctrinal claims. In his advice to the Kalamas, after condemning authority and reason, etc., as means of knowledge, he proceeds to enunciate his doctrines as follows:

"Now what think you, Kalamas? When greed arises within man, does it arise to his profit or to his loss?

To his loss, sir . . .

Now what think you, Kalamas? When freedom from greed arises in a man, does it arise to his profit or his loss?

To his profit, sir . . .

Now, Kalamas, he who is an Ariyan disciple freed from coveting and malevolence, who is not bewildered but self-controlled and mindful, with a heart possessed by goodwill, by compassion . . . —such an one abides suffusing one quarter of the world therewith . . ."[82] The meditational techniques, as we saw earlier (*v.* 6.88), are not any mystical and mysterious techniques but are practical methods and practices to achieve personality integration and enlightenment as to the real nature or the conditionality of the world and experience.

8.38 This brings us to the problem of the place of experience, verification and rational understanding in religion. We saw the contrasting situations of Christianity and Buddhism with regard to their respective means of knowledge. For Christianity the basic and fundamental, and sometimes the only, means of knowledge are grace, revelation and authority. This is why the theists have always insisted that religious beliefs go beyond rational understanding and therefore maintained for instance, *credo quia absurdum*. They were always fond of saying that reason stops where faith begins. Thus Christianity becomes anti-rational in its fundamentals. Here, some philosophers try to speak of a different kind of rationality when they say that as a consistent system of beliefs, Christianity is a rational religion. Or the Bible may be called rational in this sense, as Gordon H. Clark maintains: "... revelation is not only rational, but it is the only hope of maintaining rationality. And this is corroborated by the actual consistency that we discover when we examine the verbally inspired revelation called the Bible."[83] Actually, this is another confusion often made between coherence and rationality. Any two related fictional concepts are always coherent as as system, but it does not say anything at all about their rationality. Coherence may be a form of rationality, and what is actually meant by rationality here is clarity or coherence: it is always advisable to distinguish between rationality and coherence in such instances. Novels and fictional stories though coherent are hardly spoken of as being rational. This distinction is an important one and should always be made.

8.39 Buddhism emphasizes the necessity of rational understanding, experience and verification in the field of religion. This points to an important problem for the philosophy of religion. The Buddha spoke of his teachings as a system "which was to be realized individually by the intelligent person".[84] He also said that "This teaching is for the wise, not for the unwise".[85] The theist will argue here that this makes Buddhism an elitist and exclusive type of religion giving salvation only to a few people in the world. The Buddhist tradition accepts this situation wholeheartedly. The popular Buddhist compromise is that the majority must practice the Buddha's moral injunctions and try to achieve as much moral perfection as possible until they attain sufficient wisdom, in this or another life, to attain salvation. Therefore Buddhism is not elitist in any exclusive sense. However, the fundamental emphasis is always on the rational understanding of the truths of the Buddhist doctrines by wisdom or *paññā* (*v.* 6.99). This raises the question of the place of faith and rational knowledge in religion. Our preceding discussions show the disconcerting problems a religion raises when rational knowledge plays little, or no part in it. However, this problem is not peculiar to religion. So far, the history of humanity has shown that in all and every branch of knowledge it has always been rational knowledge and rational experience that have led humanity to progress. There is absolutely no reason why they should be undervalued only in the field of religion. Therefore, the progress of religion in humanity also necessarily depends on the pursuance of rational experience which results in wisdom, *paññā*.

Chapter Nine / Postscript

MORE PROBLEMS WITH THE CONCEPT OF GOD THAT REQUIRE OUR SERIOUS AND URGENT ATTENTION

9.1 Earlier in this book I examined and criticized the Christian concept of God as a primitive and undeveloped concept. What I want to explain in this section is that the Christian concept of God is a primitive and underdeveloped conception of the perfect and ultimate Reality. The Christian or the Western theistic conception of God has many more facets and many more problems than I envisaged in my earlier inquiry where I maintained that the concept of God was full of theoretical problems like the inner contradictoriness of the concept and the consequent emptiness of it as an explanatory principle. But there is another set of problems involving the practical implications of the concept of God and these problems require more serious and urgent attention, particularly in the contemporary context.

9.2 The concept of God is one of the most complex concepts in the field of human thinking because it has so many aspects, some even contradicting others. The concept is so elusive because it has been used as the ultimate concept to explain everything. There are two problems that come up with an ultimate concept:

(1) The ultimate concept is necessarily relative to the amount of knowledge the concept-holder possesses. Therefore, the concept can have gradations.

(2) The ultimate concept has often been portrayed as a no-concept, in the sense that it goes beyond all concepts. That is why the ultimate-concept holders say that it is inexpressible, and that makes the concept necessarily ambiguous.

9.3 Early Gods were born in primitive tribes who used them as a blanket explanatory term to explain everything they could not explain otherwise. The nature and quality of Gods evolved in relation to the amount of knowledge of their believers. The Christian God was born as a tribal God, jealous and narrow, and the the Christian believer's knowledge of the nature of the world was extremely primitive and narrow. Their basic premise was that God created man in his own image; the world as his environment was created for the use of that man, thus man was made the sole owner of the earth. It was this simple basic premise that led to the birth of the Western technological civilization, based on the exploitation of the environment by man with an inflated ego. And this exploitation was sacredly sanctioned by Western theism.

9.4 What is meant here is that the implied world view of the Christian Concept of God was morally disastrous. It was factually wrong and therefore morally misleading. Firstly, it preached a narrow and alienated view of man. Man was said to be essentially superior to all other creatures because he was created in the image of God. Thereby, man becomes logically qualitatively different from other creatures. This idea inflated and strengthened man's ego, thus alientating man from the rest of creation. Secondly, their concept of the world was too narrow as to mean only this earth, sun and moon revolving around it, and this world was meant for the use of man.

9.5 Here, one could say that this is an outdated description of the Christian view of man and world. But the important point is that these are the essential basic premises of Christian theology. It is obvious that to an ignorant and simplistic primitive tribe, this looks like the most sensible explanation of the world and God. However much the later theologians tried to rationalize this God to mean sublime and sophisticated religious ideals, those two premises may be unconsciously behind the general Western psyche.

9.6 To the Westerner, animals are mere objects of food or fun. Milan Kundera says,"True human goodness, in all its purity and freedom, can come to the fore only when its recipient has no power. Mankind's true moral test, its fundamental test (which lies deeply buried from view), consists of its attitude towards those who are at its mercy: animals. And in this respect mankind has suffered a fundamental debacle, a debacle so fundamental that all others stem from it."[1]

9.7 In the West, meat is the major diet, while vegetarianism is respected in the East where animals are given more consideration. (The cow is nearly deified in India, and beef-eaters are call 'mother-eaters'). The Buddha says, "Like a mother, a father, a brother, and other relatives the cows are our best friends, in whom medicines are produced. They give food, and they give strength; they likewise give (a good) complexion and happiness: having realised this great benefit (from the cows) they (the ancients) did not kill cows."[2] In the Sasa Jataka, a rabbit, who is always addressed as 'Pandit Sasa', is a Bodhisattva, who offers himself as food for a hungry person. The Jataka book is full of stories of the previous lives of the Buddha, where very often he was born as an animal, thus clearly suggesting that there are Bodhisattvas among animals. There, animals are portrayed as exemplary teachers of morality to human beings.

9.8 The kindest thing a Western theist could say about animals would be to talk of human beings as the 'superior' guardians of the animal kingdom: "He (God) has granted us the honor to have dominion over the beasts of the field. With this honor comes the responsibiltiy to guard them against cruelty and neglect."[3]

9.9 Kundera comments: "The very beginning of Genesis tells us that God created man in order to give him dominion over fish and fowl and all creatures. Of course, Genesis was written by a man, not a horse. There is no certainty that God actually did grant man dominion over other creatures. What seems more likely, in fact, is that man invented God to sanctify the dominion that he had usurped for himself over the cow and the horse. Yes, the right to kill a deer or a cow is the only thing all of mankind can agree upon, even during the bloodiest of wars.

"The reason we take that right for granted is that we stand at the top of the hierarchy. But let a third party enter the game—a visitor from another planet, for example, someone to whom God says, 'Thou shalt have dominion over creatures of all other stars' —and all at once taking Genesis for granted becomes problematical. Perhaps a man hitched to the cart of a Martian or roasted on the spit by inhabitants of the Milky Way will recall the veal cutlet he used to slice on his dinner plate and apologize (belatedly!) to the cow."[4]

9.10 The most striking feature that illustrates the essential primitivity of Western or Judaic theisms is the way in which they have, with a strong and profound insensitivity, absolutely ignored the environment, animals and plant life, nay, they have positively sanctioned and advised man to use it in any manner he wants. It was this conception that led to the technical explosion in the West.The resulting dire consequences are now said to be bringing an end to an epoch. It was the Western concept of God that was fundamentally responsible for the birth as well as the collapse of the Western civilization. It is in this sense that one could say that a particular conception of God (namely, the Judaic or the Western conception of God) is threatening the survival of a particular civilization in a particular planet, the earth.

9.11 Inflation of the ego and the treatment of the world as an object to be used are the two most central disasters of the contemporary Western civilization, and the Judaic views of God have contributed the major part to bring the humanity to the present frightful situation.[5]

9.12 In Western theism, God is always portrayed as personal (*pauruṣeya*),and therefore, as a limited and narrow concept. God is necessarily different from the world, so a duality between God and the world is created. Christianity goes further in confirming this personalistic and narrow concept of God when it characterizes this God by historicity and facticity. God is not a-historical, but His existence is illustrated and proved in terms of historical events. In other words, God is understood more in terms of awe-inspiring historical events rather than by His teachings.

9.13 Teachings of such religions are mostly limited to simplistic moral aphorisms and proverbial utterances and they exhibit a profound lack of deep analyses of man and the world. One could, as contemporary theologians do, interpret such moral utterances to have transcendental implications, but it is problematic whether the utterers of such statements were consciously aware of such implications, because their views of man and world were not at all enlightened.

9.14 Nature of historicity is remarkably illustrated by the event of Jesus. Jesus was more a charismatic figure than an enlightening teacher with profound teachings. He was only one of thousands of Messiahs that have appeared in various types of human societies from time to time. In Christianity, dogmatic importance is given to the event of Jesus in terms of faith. Incarnation of God in human form is limited only to one human being, namely, Jesus, and all other possibilities of incarnation are ruled out by definition. Theisms like Judaism and Islam completely reject the ideas of incarnation of God, thus further narrowing down God or alienating Him from man.

9.15 Many Western theists have tried to interpret their theism in lines similar to the Eastern religious concepts. But the real problem is whether Western theisms could be interpreted in that sense. Their God is, by definition, 'the other' and God's appearance in man, if it happens at all, is exclusive, as in Christ, and God is necessarily related to historicity somewhere. Western theism could hardly see the identity of man and the ultimate Reality. One man who tried to come close to this conception, Meister Eckhart, who said "I am God", was immediatley branded a heretic by the Church. A Muslim Saint who said "Anal Haq" (I am God) was brutally tortured and killed for saying so. This clearly illustrates the narrowness of the Western theism.

* * *

9.16 The belief in Jesus Christ is based more on faith than on any objective criteria. Being one of thousands of Messiahs that appeared on earth, there was nothing exceptional in Christ as a moral leader because he was only an ethnocentric moralist. The belief in his divinity is based mainly on the belief in his resurrection, a supposedly factual event. But the truth of this event is not beyond doubt and dispute. When such a transcendental idea is based on such dubitable grounds, it shows the irrationality of the Christian faith perspective. Another defective feature illustrated by the Jesus-event is the relation of Christianity to fact. When we go on to discuss the developed religions of the East, it will be clear that to talk of a relationship of religion or ultimate salvation to a specific factual event does not make any sense at all.

9.17 Even though Jesus Christ had an exemplary and admirable moral behavior, it was essentially an ethnocentric morality, never a universal morality. The Buddhist point is that without a combination of perfect wisdom (i.e. epistemology) and perfect (i.e. universal) morality one can never achieve the ultimate liberation.

9.18 An important thing to remember here is that western theisms have only a narrow and limited (i.e. human centered) morality and also they have no (religious) epistemology at all. By epistemology what is meant here is an epistemological bridge between phenomena and noumena. Eastern religions accept three levels of reality: the dream experience which is sublimated by waking experience which in turn is sublimated by the ultimate noumenal experience. In Buddhism, through a sustained epistemological analysis of the phenomenal experience, a path is clearly delineated to arrive at the Nirvanic level.[6]

* * *

9.19 Though the Judaic religions talked of an immanent God, they never consciously propounded a full-fledged unitary view of the world. They had a built-in narrowness which they make evident on the level of human beings themselves. For example, to Western theists, 'the believers',from their early tribal stages to the present day, are always 'the elect' and they are the only proper human beings and therefore intrinsically superior to other men. That was why, in holy wars, it was all right to kill people of other faiths because they were mere animals. In the contemporary world, again, this superiority is exhibited in missionary works.

9.20 This is evident in their 'third-world' attitude too. According to the West, the progress is equated with exploitation of nature by man, whose self is thereby inflated and confirmed. According to that definition, a man who minds his own business without disturbing or hurting nature or others is simply undeveloped or underdeveloped.

9.21 If Western theism is a primitive concept, how could it have risen to transcendental heights, as in some instances like the field of morality and art? As mentioned above, Western theism has a system of morality, though it is only a man-centered one. And the other feature is that it has a sense of transcendence. This is emphasized by its defintion of God as a necessarily transcendent being. It is this sense of transcendence that could infuse theists with sublime feelings. However, the sense of transcendence is common to all possible religions. The nature and content of this transcendence arises in proportion to the amount of knowledge of the believers. The fact that people have achieved spiritual development through Western theistic faiths like Christianity is no proof against their primitivity. The moral and proverbial teachings of such religions could be interpreted on many dimensions according to the dimensions of belief and knowledge of the followers. The important thing is that anything can be interpreted to mean anything. What is important is whether the interpretation is farfetched or justified in the belief context of a particular religion. Further, as the Mahayanists say, every being is potentially capable of full enlightenment. What is necessary is a cue to spark that ignition. Such cues could be found in many moral and proverbial utterances.

9.23 Can one say that a technological civilization is superior to say, an agricultural civilization, and therefore that the birth of such a civilization can be adduced as credit to the Western theism? But civilizations are neither superior nor inferior to each other. All civilizations are myths. When a particular human group shares a particular belief system about the nature of utility, that becomes their civilization. But civilizations could be more consistent or less consistent, or more moral or less moral. The philosophy implied in the Western technological civilization is factually wrong and immoral. That is why it is leading, not to the well being of all beings, but towards the destruction of human psyche and body. Therefore, the birth of the Western technological civilization is more a discredit rather than a credit to the Western theism.

9.24 Another significant problem with the concept of God is

its partriarchal implications. Considering the cumulative disastrous results of a patriarchal civilization, as witnessed in the contemporary world-context, the immoral implications of the concept of God are too clear and obvious. This is the main doctrine of the feminists who are, as a desparate solution and a revolt, turning to the worship of the Mother Goddess and witchcraft.[7] (This is not to advocate matriarchy as the solution because it could turn out to be as bad as patriarchy. Karen Lindsey says, ". . . I am not wholly comfortable with the goddess. The image has power for me, a reclaiming of the birth image men stole from us when they invented gods capable of reproducing from their own bodies (Zeus creating Athena and Dionysius from his flesh; God the Father digging Eve out of Adam's body and later planting Jesus in Mary's incubator womb). But I don't see it justified by any superior female goodness operating in the world. Female non-violence seems to me chiefly a function of being deprived of the tools of violence, and I'm not sure the Mother would end up being any less abusive than the Father has been. Whatever the creative force is, it's too large to be encompassed in human imagery.)"[8] Feminists make the significant point that the ultimate Reality has to be of a neuter gender[9] (i.e. something like the Dharma). It is interesting to note that in an ultimate sense, one can see only 'beings', male-female distinction being only a secondary, a largely conceptual development. In the Vimalakirtinirdesa Sutra, the distinction between male and female is subjected to a profund ridicule.[10] (In Mahayana tradition the highest ultimate reality (*prajñā*) is portrayed as a feminine principle: denoted by the goddess Prajnaparamita from whom issues all the Buddhas, who are its phenomenal manifestation (*upāya*), and these Buddhas are portrayed as masculine. The most prominent Bodhisattva of Mahayana Buddhism, Avalokitesvara, is androgynous. This analysis may suggest that the Dharma is the ultimate principle that goes still behind the duality phenomena, such as male-female, *prajñā-upāya*, and *ying-yang*).

9.25 I think the biggest and the most dangerous problem of the concept of God is its authoritative implications. As Friedrich Engels also maintained, the idea of God is a result of our projection of the human being's best qualities to an outside object, thus alienating the person from his/her most sublime qualities. Subjecting oneself to this authority thus, one utterly degrades oneself.

All theistic religions strongly show this tendency towards authoritarianism.

9.26 This authoritarianism has done immense damage to humanity. It can lead to very dangerous situations. One is, as explained in Chapter 4, treating the religious dimension as superceding the moral dimension. This has led to much religious persecution and holy war. The other is the abominable subjection of the human mind to religious leaders. The possible dangers of such a situation is best illustrated by the religious community of Jim Jones, who preached a form of Christianity, that lived in Jonestown. In 1978, faced with the dangers of getting his ulterior motives exposed to the world, this religious leader commanded (preached?) his followers to commit suicide by drinking cyanide, and 918 followers at once followed his command and committed mass suicide. Jim Jones obviously had the necessary justification of authority from his religion: Christianity. This can, of course, happen in any religion or belief system where authority is respected.

9.27 The most sublime feature of the Buddha's message is its absolutely anti-authoritarian attitude (as explained in Chapter 8). The Buddha respects the intrinsic value and integrity of each and every being, or in other words, the potential omnipotence, ominiscience and benevolence of each and every being. In the ultimate sense, no being is intrinsically superior to another in any sense. Everyone is completely capable of attaining the ultimate supreme perfection exactly as the Buddha did. "Everyone is a potential Buddha, not different form the original Buddha in any way".

9.28 Most religions, particularly all theistic religions, have followers. The Buddha explicitly and consciousy emphasized the fact that no one should follow him, or for that matter, any one else. I think humanity should be grateful to the Buddha for showing this very simple, but very profound, truth about ourselves. He left the door open to go beyond the Buddha himself. Here it is interesting to note that, though one can go beyond the Buddha, no one can, in a sense, go beyond the Buddha, because the Buddha has posited forever the principle of ultimate spiritual (religious) freedom.

9.29 In that sense, all religions that follow a religious leader would be seen by the Buddha as slave religions. It is exactly the same situation in authoritarian systems of thinking like Marxism, etc., too. By their dogma they block the whole possibility of the further progress of the humam spirit and thought, and we should be constantly aware of this menacing threat to the further evolution of the human psyche. If capitalism exploits man's body, followers' religions and thought systems could be said to be exploiting man's brain or mind by enslaving it and degrading it to the level of a mere follower, thus forever foreclosing the possibility of him becoming the Buddha, Marx or God Himself, or going beyond all of them. (It is of course true, and sad, that people started, in a sense, following the Buddha as well. But that is is exactly the human predicament that the Buddha was warning us about.)

* * *

9.30 The narrowness of the God-concept is best illustrated by Christianity. This is due to the unfortunate fact that it is only in Christianity one finds a fully developed doctrine of natural theology. Because of this natural theology God became a conceptually tangible object, exclusive and alien from the world.

9.31 While the Western God is narrow because of its tribal and primitve nature, the Eastern God could be called more developed and refined because it was born not out of ignorance of nature, but out of a deep philosophical realization of the truth about nature and life. The best expression of the Eastern God is found in the Upanishads. The Eastern concept of God is basically a no-concept because it does not mean anything specific. If a specific meaning should be given to it, it would best be translated as "everything" (*Sarvam Khalu Idam brahma, Upanishads*). Basically, it is the transcendental principle underlying everything in nature. He is a-historical. He is both personal and non-personal, and he is said to be neither of those as well. He has absolutely no relationship to fact. The Western God was a conceptual phenomenon, while the Eastern God was an intuitive experience. That is why the question about the proofs of God's existence never arises in Eastern philosophy. There is no natural theology in the East. For them, the God-concept carries only a phenomenological significance.

9.32 The best interpretation of the Eastern God has been done by Shankara. In this he was significantly influenced by the philosophy of Mahayana, especially by the dialectic of Nagarjuna. The main theme of Nagarjuna was the doctrine of the identity of *Nirvāna* and *Saṃsāra*, thus dissolving the whole distinction between the sacred and the profane. Therefore, what they meant by God was the ultimate principle of nature. This principle had three main aspects: it was existence (*sat*), it was conscious (*cit*), and it was bliss (*ānanda*). Taking the *Sat* aspect, it was called an impersonal and in that sense it was termed in neuter gender as Brahman (however, this had a high positive content), and when they wanted to emphasize the *Cit* aspect it was called a personal God, *Brahmā*. Its experiential aspect was denoted by the term *Ānanda*. It is significant that the concept of Brahman is related to *jñāna mārga*, while the concept of *Brahmā* is related to *bhakti mārga*. Here *Bhakti* is the way of the unintelligent common man, and Brahma is emphasized to be only an illusory device, a utilitarian point of concentration, for the devotee. (This standpoint makes the Christian God an illusory concept.)

9.33 The ambivalent nature of the Hindu God as both personal and impersonal created a confusion in Indian thinking. The idea of a personal God (in the form of *Shiva*, *Vishnu*, etc.) was emphasized by the faith-oriented followers and this tendency led in the direction of the natural-theological narrow conception of God, thus deflecting the attention away from the transcendental but experiential impersonal principle. This meant a delineation of a transcendent concept making room for conceptualization.

The Buddha's attempt was to rescue the ultimate principle from degeneration to the conceptual level and make it a thorough going non-conceptual experiential principle. That was why, at the beginning, the Buddha's treatment of the ultimate principle was essentially negative. Perhaps the Buddha knew that to make the slightest positive hint about the ultimate principle was to invite torrents of positive speculation about it. So, in early Buddhism he tried to be consistently negative in his approach to Nirvana.

9.34 Nevertheless, there are a few places in early Buddhism that suggest the acceptance of a positive existent ultimate principle. Examples would be the Udana 80 passage where he speaks of the existence of an "unborn, unmade" principle, and the statement that "the Mind is luminous, though it is stained with adventitious defilements." Also, when the Buddha says that "the Dhamma protects the one who follows the Dhamma", he seems to come very parallel to the Hindu doctrine of ***Brahman*** or ***Brahmā***. Dhamma can be taken as the most refined version of ***Brahman*** because Dhamma is one of those rare concepts with least conceptual content. Dhamma literally means 'the thing', while *Dhammatā* means 'the thingness'.

* * *

9.35 Still, even in Eastern theistic religions the most dangerous problem of religion remains, i.e. the idea that the religious dimension transcends the moral dimension. Here, the Eastern theisms may be more virulent because amidst their celebrated doctrines of *Ahimsa*, they fervently advocate the sacrifice of beings, including human beings, to God. The sacrifice of human beings to God has received its full religious authorization, justification and santification since the time of the *Ṛg Veda* where, in the *Purusha Sukta* of the tenth Mandala, even gods perform a human sacrifice (*puruṣa medha*), and it is devoutly practiced even today in India. India Today reports: "On Rajasankranti Day (June 15) three teenaged boys were enticed to a shrine to Durga atop a steep hill near Ranpur, 75 km west of Bhubaneswar, where they were brutally killed and their blood offered in a misguided [sic!] attempt to propitiate the goddess. . . . They were throttled and then their heads crushed either with rocks or against the wall so their blood could drip at the feet of the goddess.

"There are many legends of human sacrifice in the area. Villagers say the Raja of the erstwhile Ranpur princely state used to sacrifice people secretly, though none of them claims to have witnessed the deed. Tales still make the rounds of people maintained by Rajas expressly for sacrifice who were well looked after, as well as of a community of throat cutters. But the police say that since Independence not a single case of human sacrifice has come to light. However, suspicion lurks that many cases of alleged suicide and murder—three severed heads were found in Puri last year—were actually ritual sacrifices, disguised to seem like a more ordinary form of mayhem."[11]

The Hindu reports: "MAN SACRIFICES TWO DAUGHTERS. Berhampur, (Orissa), April 18, 1986 (PTI):

"A father allegedly beheaded two daughters to attain proficiency in witchcraft at Pudugeswari village near Aska, 40 km from here.

"Police said the 34 year old man, arrested on Sunday, had been caught by villagers when he was carrying the heads of the two children—Puni (5) and Tuni (3).

"The accused, a Harijan, had confessed to them of having committed the crime. He was carrying the heads for offering them at the altar of a goddess on nearby Taratarini Hills. He said he had been advised to do so by his guru, a resident of Berhampur town."

We must remember that it is this very same devotion and spirit that prompted Abraham, the founder of the Western theism, to sacrifice his son, Isaac, to God. Should we really wait until we literally see the gruesome murder scenes of these innocent children, to realize what crimes can be perpetrated under the express license of theism?

* * *

9.37 What our analysis shows is that the Christian or the Western concept of God is a much underdeveloped and unrefined conception of God compared to the Eastern concept of God. However, even the Eastern concept of God, as any concept of God, not only falls far short of the morally and spiritually perfect ideal of ultimate Reality, but also poses an ever present danger to the value and sanctity of life, the only real, tangible and intrinsic value available to us.

FOOTNOTES

CHAPTER ONE FOOTNOTES

1. Reinhold Niebuhr, *The Self and the Dramas of History* (London: Faber and Faber, 1956), p. 15ff.

2. James Richmond, *Theology and Metaphysics* (London: SCM Press, 1970), p. 129.

3. Jacques Maritain. *Redeeming the Time,* Tr. Harry Lorin Binsse (London: Geoffrey Bles, 1946), p. 238.

4. Ibid., p. 239.

5. Jacques Maritain, *Existence and the Existent*, Trs. Lewis Galantiere and Gerald B. Phelan (New York: Vintage Books, 1966), p. 81.

6. Jacques Maritain, *The Range of Reason* (London: Geoffrey Bles, 1953), p. 59.

7. *Rūpaṃ (vedanā, saññā, saṁkhārā, viññānaṃ) niccaṃ vā aniccaṃ vā ti? Aniccaṃ bhante. Yaṃ panāniccaṃ, dukkhaṃ vā taṃ sukhaṃ vā ti? Dukkhaṃ bhante. Yaṃ panāniccaṃ dukkhaṃ vipariṇāmadhammaṃ kallan nu taṃ samanupassituṃ: Etaṃ mama, eso'hamasmi, eso me attā ti? No h'etaṃ bhante. M.,* III, p. 19.

8. *M.*, I, p. 421.

9. Maritain, *The Range of Reason*, p. 55.

10. Karl Barth, *Church Dogmatics*, Eds. G. W. Bromiley, T. F. Torrance. Trs. Harold Knight, G.W. Bromiley, J.K.S. Reid, R.H. Fuller (Edinburgh: T & T Clark, 1960), Vol. III, 2, p. 394.

11. *Bṛhadāranyaka Upaniṣad* II, 4. 14.

12. *Nāhaṃ bhikkhave aññaṃ ekadhammaṃ pi samanupassāmi evaṃ lahuparivattaṃ yathayidaṃ cittaṃ. Yāvañc'idaṃ bhikkhave upamā pi na sukarā yāva lahuparivattaṃ cittan ti. A.,* I, p. 8.

13. *Mano attā ti (dhammā attā ti, manoviññānaṃ attā ti) yo vadeyya, tam na uppajjati. Manassa uppādo pi vayo pi paññāyati. Yassa kho pana uppādo pi vayo pi paññāyati, Attā me uppajjati ca veti cāti icc'assa evaṃ āgataṃ hoti. M.*, III, p. 283.

14. *Varaṃ bhikkhave assutavā puthujjano imaṃ cātumahābhūtikaṃ kāyaṃ attato upagaccheyya na tveva cittaṃ. Taṃ kissa hetu? Dissatāyaṃ bhikkhave cātumahābhūtiko kāyo ekaṃ pi vassaṃ tiṭṭhamāno. . . . vassasataṃ pi tiṭṭhamāno bhiyyo pi tiṭṭhamāno. Yañ ca kho etaṃ bhikkhave vuccati cittaṃ iti pi mano iti pi viñāṇaṃ iti pi, taṃ rattiyā ca divasassa ca aññad eva uppajjati aññaṃ nirujjhati. S.*, II, pp. 94-95.

15. *Vedanā saññā cetanā phasso manasikāro. Idaṃ vuccati āvuso nāmaṃ. . . Chayime āvuso viññāṇakāyā: cakkhuviññāṇaṃ, sotaviññaṇaṃ ghāṇaviññāṇaṃ, jivhāviññāṇaṃ, kāyaviññāṇaṃ, manoviññāṇaṃ. M.*, I, p. 53.

16. *Aññatra paccayā natthi viññāṇassa sambhavo. M.*, I, p. 259.

17. *Manañcāvuso paṭicca dhamme ca uppajjati manoviññāṇaṃ ti. Evam āvuso. Yo āvuso hetu yo ca paccayo manoviññāṇassa uppādāya so ca hetu so ca paccayo sabbena sabbaṃ sabbathā sabbaṃ apariseso nirujjheyya api nu kho manoviññāṇaṃ paññāyethā ti? No h'etaṃ āvuso. S.*, IV, p. 167.

18. Barth, *Church Dogmatics,* Vol. III, 2, p. 380.

19. Ibid., p. 378.

20. Ibid., p. 394

21. Ibid., p. 375.

22. Ibid., p. 401.

23. Ibid., p. 417.

24. Ibid., p. 393.

25. Ibid., p. 356.

26. *Puggalo upalabbhati saccikaṭṭhaparamaṭṭhena, rūpañ ca upalabbhati saccikaṭṭhaparamaṭṭhenā ti? Āmantā. Aññaṃ rūpaṃ añño puggalo ti? Na h'evam vattabbe. Ājānāhi niggaham: hañci puggalo upalabbhati saccikaṭṭhaparamaṭṭhena, rūpañ ca upalabbhati saccikaṭṭhaparamaṭṭhena tena vata re vattabe "Aññaṃ rūpaṃ añño puggalo ti" Yaṃ tattha vadesi "vattabbe kho 'puggalo upalabbhati saccikaṭṭhaparamaṭṭhena', no ca vattabbe 'aññaṃ rūpaṃ añño puggalo ti" michā. No ce pana vattabbe "Aññaṃ rūpaṃ añño puggalo ti", no ca vata re vattabbe "Puggalo upalabbhati saccikaṭṭhaparamaṭṭhena, rūpañ ca saccikaṭṭhaparamaṭṭhenā ti." Yam tattha vadesi "Vattabbe kho 'puggalo upalabbhati saccikaṭṭhaparamaṭṭhena rūpañ ca upalabbhati saccikaṭṭhaparamaṭṭhena,' no ca vattabbe' aññaṃ rūpaṃ 'añño puggalo ti', micchā. Kvu.* pp. 11-12; *Points of Controversy* (Trs. Shwe Zan Aung, C.A.F. Rhys Davids. [London: Pali Text Society, 1960], pp. 14-15. Also, p. 25).

27. *Puggalo upalabbhati saccikaṭṭhaparamaṭṭhenā ti? Āmantā. Puggalo saṁkhato ti? Na h'evaṃ vattabbe . . . Puggalo asaṁkhato ti? Na h'evaṃ vattabbe . . . Kvu.* p. 59; *Points of Controversy,* p. 54.

28. Maritain, *Existence and the Existent,* p. 82.

29. Maritain, *The Range of Reason,* p. 59.

30. *So evaṃ ayoniso manasikaroti: ahosinnukho ahaṃ attaṃ addhānaṃ, na nu kho ahosiṃ atītaṃ addhānaṃ, kinnu kho ahosiṃ atītaṃ addhānaṃ, kathannukho ahosiṃ atītaṃ addhānaṃ, kiṃ hutvā kiṃ ahosinnukho ahaṃ atītaṃ addhānaṃ; bhavissāmi nu kho ahaṃ anāgataṃ addhānaṃ, na nu kho bahavissāmi anāgataṃ addhānaṃ, kinnukho bhavissāmi anāgataṃ addhānaṃ, kathannukho bhavissāmi anāgataṃ addhānaṃ, kiṃ hutvā kiṃ bhavissāmi nu kho ahaṃ anāgataṃ addhānan ti. Etarahi vā paccuppannaṃ addhānaṃ ajjhattaṃ kathaṃkathī hoti: ahannukho'smi, kinnukho'smi, kathannukho'smi, ayannukho satto kuto āgato, so kuhiṃ gāmī bhavissatī ti. Tassa evaṃ ayoniso manasikaroto*

channaṃ diṭṭhīnaṃ aññatarā diṭṭhi uppajjati: atthi me attā ti vā'ssa saccato thetato diṭṭhi uppajjati. . . . Atha va pan'assa evaṃ diṭṭhi hoti: Yo me ayaṃ attā vado vedeyyo tatra tatra kalyāṇapāpakānaṃ kammānaṃ vipākaṃ paṭisaṃvedeti, so kho pana me ayaṃ attā nicco dhuvo sassato avipariṇāmadhammo sassatisamaṃ ṭath'eva ṭhassatī ti. Idaṃ vuccati bhikkhave diṭṭhigataṃ diṭṭhigahaṇam diṭṭhikantāraṃ . . . M., I, p. 8.

31. C.B. Martin, *Religious Belief* (New York: Cornell University Press, 1962), p. 106.

32. *taṇhāvicaritāni ajjhattikassa upādāya. A.*, II, p. 212.

33. *manasmiṃ, āvuso, dhamme manoviññāṇe manoviññāṇaviññātabbesu dhammesu yo chando yo rāgo yā nandi yā taṇhā ye upāyupādānā cetaso adhiṭṭhānābhinivesānusayā . . . M.*, III, p. 32.

34. *Upāyupādānābhinivesavinibandho khvāyaṃ Kaccāyana loko yebhuyyena, tañcāyaṃ upāyupādānaṃ cetaso adhiṭṭhānaṃ abhinivesānusayaṃ na upeti na upādiyati nādhiṭṭhāti attā me ti. S.*, II, p. 17. The Pali Text Society edition of the text reads '*Attā na me ti* [wrongly divided]. Commentary reads '*Attā me ti*'. See, *The Book of the Kindred Sayings,* Tr. Mrs. Rhys Davids (London: Pali Text Society, 1952), Vol. II, p. 13. fn. 1.

35. *Yathā hi aṅgasambhārā hoti saddo ratho iti, evaṃ khandhesu santesu hoti satto ti sammuti. S.*, I, p. 135. *Miln.* p. 28.

36. *hetu ca suddiṭṭho hetusamuppannā ca dhammā. A.*, III, p. 440.

37. *aññatarassa bhikkhuno evaṃ cetaso parivitakko udapādi: Iti kira, bho, rūpaṃ . . . vedanā . . . saññā . . . saṅkhārā. . . viññāṇaṃ anatta annatakatāni kammāni kaṃ attānaṃ phusissatī ti. M.*, III, p. 19.

38. *Upabhuñjake ca asati kassa taṃ phalaṃ siyā?. . .Tatridaṃ vuccati: Ekasantānasmiṃ hi phalaṃ uppajjamānaṃ tattha ekanta ekattanānattānaṃ paṭisiddhattā aññassā ti vā aññato ti vā na hoti. Etassa ca pan'atthassa bījānam abhisankhāro sādhako. Ambabījādīnaṃ hi abhisaṅkhāresu katesu tassabījassa santāne laddhapaccayā kālantare phalaviseso uppajjamāno, na aññabījānaṃ, nā pi aññābhisaṅkhārapaccayā uppajjati, na ca tāni bījāni abhisaṅkhārā phalaṭṭhānaṃ pāpunāti; evaṃ sampadam idaṃ veditabbaṃ. Vijjāsipposadhādīhi cā pi bālasarīre upayuttehi kālantare vuḍḍhasarīrādisu phalaṃ detī ti ayam attho veditabbo. Yam pi vuttaṃ: upabhuñjake ca asati kassa tam phalaṃ siyā ti? Tattha: Phalass'uppattiyā eva siddhā bhuñjakasammuti, phaluppādena rukkhassa yathā phalati sammuti. Yathā hi rukhasaṅkhātānaṃ dhammānaṃ ekadesabhūtassa rukkhaphalassa uppattiyā eva rukkho phalatī ti vā phalito ti vā vuccati, tathā devamanussasankhātānaṃ khandhānam ekadesabhūtassa upabhogasankhātassa sukhadukkhaphalassa uppāden'eva devo manusso vā upabhunjatī ti vā sukhito dukkhito ti vā vuccati, tasmā na ettha aññena upabhuñjakena nāma koci attho atthī ti. Vsm.* p. 555. Translation, *PP.* p. 640. [Translation slightly changed].

39. *Ettha c'etassa viññāṇassa purimabhavato idha anāgamane atītabhavapariyāpannahetūhi ca uppāde paṭighosa-padīpamudda-patibimbappakārā dhammā nidassanāni siyuṃ. Yathā hi paṭighosa-padīpa-muddā-chāyā saddādi-hetukā honti, aññatra agantvā va honti evaṃ eva idaṃ cittaṃ. Ettha ca santānabandhato n'atthi ekatā nā pi nānatā. Yadi hi santānabandhe sati ekantam ekatā bhaveyya, na khīrato dadhi sambhūtam siyā athā pi ekantanānatā bhaveyya, na khīrassādhīno dadhi siyā; esa nayo sabbahetusamuppannesu. Evañ ca sati sabbalokavohāralopo siyā, so ca aniṭṭho; tasmā ettha na ekantaṃ ekatā vā nānatā vā upagantabbā ti. Vsm.* p. 554. Translation, *PP,* p. 554.

40. *So karoti so paṭisaṃvediyatī ti . . . ayaṃ eko anto. Añño karoti añño paṭisaṃvediyatī ti . . . ayaṃ dutiyo anto. S.*, II, pp. 75-76.

41. *Evarūpaṃ pāpakaṃ diṭṭhigataṃ . . . idaṃ viññāṅaṃ sandhāvati saṃsarati anaññanti. Nanu mayā moghapurisa anekapariyāyena paṭiccasamuppannaṃ viññāṇaṃ vuttaṃ: aññatra paccayā natthi viññāṇassa sambhavo ti. M.*, I, p. 258.

42. *asampajāno va . . . kāyasaṅkhāraṃ . . . vacīsaṅkhāraṃ. . . manosaṅkhāraṃ . . . abhisaṅkharoti. A.*, II, p. 158.

43. Ryle would not accept that his is a reductionism because the bodily behavior to which we apply the term 'mental' has certain typical differences from other forms of bodily behaviour. And some might tend to think that Ryle, on the whole, comes very close to the Buddhist position. But a Buddhist would still maintain that Ryle's attitude is basically reductionist because he has not taken into account the important causal aspects of mind. The Buddha emphasized the causal efficacy of mind in many ways and particularly in the field of paranormal phenomena, e.g. psycho-kinesis.

44. Gilbert Ryle, *The Concept of Mind* (Harmondsworth: Penguin Books, 1963), p. 274.

45. Ibid., p. 279.

46. C.A. Campbell, 'Ryle on the Intellect'; And, A.C. Ewing, 'Professor Ryle's Attack on Dualism' in *Clarity is not Enough*, Ed. H.D. Lewis (London: Allen and Unwin, 1963), pp. 278-310 and pp. 311-338.

47. H.D. Lewis, *Philosophy of Religion* (London: E.U.P. Teach Yourself Books, 1965), p. 278.

48. H.D. Lewis, 'Mind and Body. Some Observations on Mr. Strawson's Views' in *Clarity is not Enough*, p. 387.

49. Ibid., p. 388.

50. H.D. Lewis, 'The Elusive Self and the I-Thou Relation' in *Talk of God*, Royal Institute of Philosophy Lectures, Volume Two, 1967-1968 (London: Macmillan, 1969), p. 168.

51. Ibid., p. 169.

52. Ibid., p. 171.

53. C.A. Campbell, *On Selfhood and Godhood* (London: Allen And Unwin, 1957), pp. 82-83.

54. Ibid., p. 83.

55. James Richmond, *Theology and Metaphysics*, pp. 140-141.

56. "*Sace pana maṃ bhante evaṃ puccheyyuṃ: Yo te ahosi atīto atta-paṭilābho, sveva te atta-paṭilābho sacco, mogho anāgato mogho paccuppanno? Yo vā te bhavissati anāgato atta-paṭilābho, sveva te atta-paṭilābho sacco, mogho atīto mogho paccuppanno? Yo vā te etarahi paccuppanno atta-paṭilābho, sveva te atta-paṭilābho sacco, mogho atīto mogho anāgato ti? Evaṃ puṭṭho ahaṃ bhante evaṃ vyākareyyaṃ: 'Yo me ahosi atīto atta-paṭilābho sveva me atta-paṭilābho tasmiṃ samaye sacco ahosi, mogho anāgato mogho paccuppanno. Yo vā me bhavissati anāgato atta-paṭilābho, sveva me atta-paṭilābho tasmiṃ samaye sacco bhavissati, mogho atīto bhavissati mogho paccuppanno. Yo me etarahi paccuppanno atta-paṭilābho, sveva me atta-paṭilābho sacco, mogho atīto mogho anāgato ti.' Evam puṭṭho aham bhante vyākareyyan ti . . ." ". . . Itimā kho Citta loka-samaññā loka-niruttiyo loka-vohārā loka-paññattiyo yāhi Tathāgato voharati aparāmasan ti." D.*, I, pp. 200-202.

57. Ian Crombie, 'The Possibility of Theological Statements', in *Faith and Logic*, Ed. Basil Mitchell (London: Allen and Unwin, 1958), p. 57.

58. Peter Geach, *God and the Soul* (London: Kegan Paul, 1969), p. 38.

59. Ibid., pp. 39-40.

60. Ibid., p. 38.

61. Ninian Smart, *Philosophers and the Religious Truth* (London: SCM Press, 1969), p. 174.

62. Ibid., p. 172.

63. C.B. Daly, 'Metaphysics and the Limits of Language' in *Prospect for Metaphysics*, Ed. Ian Ramsey (London: Allen and Unwin, 1961), p. 184.

64. Ibid., pp. 194ff.

65. James Richmond, *Theology and Metaphysics*, pp. 129ff.

66. Peter Geach, *God and the Soul*, p. 37.

67. Ibid., p. 38.

68. *Atha imassa purisassa aññā va saññā uppajjati aññā va saññā nirujjhati. Iminā pi kho etaṃ Poṭṭhapāda pariyāyena veditabbaṃ, yathā aññā va saññā bhavissati, añño attā ti. D.* I, p. 186.

69. P.F.S. Strawson, *Individuals* (London: Methuen, 1965), p. 89.

70. Ibid., pp. 104-105.

71. "The way in which we know God who has been called 'the Soul of the World', 'the Mind of the Universe', might also be compared with the way one knows the soul or mind of another creature." John Wisdom, *Paradox and Discovery* (Oxford: Basil Blackwell, 1965), p. 15.

72. Alvin Plantinga, *God and Other Minds* (New York: Cornell University Press, 1967), p. 271.

73. *Kinnukho bhante Bhagavā Vacchagottassa paribbājakassa pañhaṃ puṭṭho na vyākāsī ti . . . Ahañ c'Ānanda Vacchagottassa paribbājākassa natthattāti puṭṭho samāno natthattāti vyākareyyaṃ sammūḷhassa Ānanda Vacchagottassa bhiyyo sammohāya abhavissa ahu vā me nūna pubbe attā so etarahi natthī ti. S.* IV, pp. 400-401.

74. J.A.T. Robinson, *Exploration into God* (London: SCM Press, 1967), pp. 143-144.

75. J.A.T. Robinson, *Honest to God* (London: SCM Press, 1963), p. 47.

76. Ibid., pp. 48-49.

77. Ibid., p. 49.

78. Loc. cit.

79. Ibid., p. 50.

80. Robinson, *Exploration into God*, p. 140.

81. *Tassa tajjaṃ bhante, paccayaṃ paṭicca tajjā tajjā vedanā uppajjanti. Tajjassa tajjassa paccayassa nirodhā tajjā tajjā vedanā nirujjhantī ti. M.*, III, pp. 273-274.

82. Robinson, *Exploration into God*, p. 132.

83. Ibid., p. 72.

84. Ibid., p. 66.

85. Ibid., p. 68.

86. John Hick, *Philosophy of Religion* (New Jersey: Prentice Hall, 1963), p. 50.

87. John Macquarrie, *Studies in Christian Existentialism* (London: SCM Press, 1965), p. 62.

88. Ibid., p. 70.

89. Ibid., p. 75.

90. Ibid., p. 76.

91. Loc. cit.

92. Charles Hartshorne, 'Religion in Process Philosophy, in *Religion in Philosophical and Cultural Perspective*, Eds. J. Clayton Feaver and William Horosz (Princeton: Van Nostrand, 1967), p. 264.

93. Ibid., p. 260.

94. John B. Cobb, Jr, *A Christian Natural Theology* (London: Lutterworth Press, 1966), pp. 47-48.

95. Ibid., pp. 65-66.

96. *Sabba-bhava-yoni-gati-ṭhiti-nivāsesu hetu-phalasambandhavasena pavattamānaṃ nāmarūpamattam eva khāyati. So neva kāraṇato uddhaṃ kārakaṃ passati, na vipākappavattito uddhaṃ vipākapaṭisaṃvedakaṃ, kāraṇe pana sati kārako ti, vipākappavattiyā sati paṭisaṃvedako ti samaññāmattena paṇḍitā vohāran t' icc' ev' assa sammappaññāya sudiṭṭhaṃ hoti. Ten'āhu Porāṇā: Kammassa kārako natthi vipākassa ca vedako, suddhadhammā pavattanti ev'etaṃ sammadassanaṃ. . . .Phalena suññaṃ taṃ kammaṃ phalaṃ kamme na vijjati, kammañ ca kho upādāya tato nibbattate phalaṃ. Na h'ettha devo brahmā vā saṃsārass'atthi kārako, suddhadhammā pavattanti hetusambhārapaccayā ti. Vsm.* pp. 602-603 (Translation, *PP.* pp. 700-701).

97. Hartshorne, *Religion in Process Philosophy*, p. 254.

98. Cobb, *A Christian Natural Theology*, p.211.

99. Loc. cit.

100. Paul Tillich, *Christianity and the Encounter of the World Religions* (New York: Columbia University Press, 1963), p. 75.

101. *Asmī ti bhikkhave maññitam etaṃ, ayaṃ aham asmī ti maññitam etaṃ, bhavissanti maññitam etaṃ, na bhavissanti maññitam etaṃ . . . maññitaṃ bhikkhave rāgo maññitaṃ gaṇḍo maññitaṃ sallaṃ. S.* IV, p. 202.

102. *A.*, I, p. 44.

103. *Cakkhusmiṃ (jivhāya, kāyasmiṃ, manasmiṃ) so bhikkhave sati cakkhuṃ upādāya cakkhuṃ abhinivissa seyyo . . . sadiso . . . hīno'ham asmī ti vā hoti. S.*, IV, p. 88.

104. *Tass'imam kāyaṃ aniccato dukkhato rogato gaṇḍato sallato aghato ābādhato parato palokato suññato anattato samanupassato yo kāyasmiṃ kāyachando kāyasneho kāyanvayatā sā pahīyati. M.*, I, p. 500.

105. Maritain, *The Range of Reason*, p. 59.

106. Maritain, *Existence and the Existent*, p. 69.

107. Barth, *Church Dogmatics*, Vol. III, 2, p. 356.

108. *Assutavā puthujjano . . . viññāṇaṃ attato samanupassati, viññāṇavantaṃ vā attānaṃ attani vā viññāṇaṃ viññāṇasmiṃ vā attānaṃ. Tassa taṃ viññāṇaṃ vipariṇamati aññathā hoti, tassa vipariṇāmaññathābhāva viññāṇavipariṇāmānuparivatti viññāṇaṃ hoti, tassa viññāṇavipariṇāmānuparivattajā paritassanā dhammasamuppādā cittaṃ pariyādāya tiṭṭhanti, cetaso paridyādānā uttāsavā ca hoti vighātavā ca upekhā ca anupādāya ca paritassati—evaṃ kho, āvuso, anupādā paritassanā hoti. M.*, III, pp. 227-228.

109. *abalaṃ, virāgaṃ, anassāsikaṃ viditvā ye viññāṇe (rūpe . . .) upāyupādānā cetaso adhiṭṭhānābhinivesānusayā . . . M.*, III, pp. 30-31.

110. *Idh'ekacco evaṃ diṭṭhi hoti: mahā me attā ti. So sabbaṃ lokasannivāsaṃ tass'okāsabhāvena parikappetvā so kho pana me ayaṃ attā sabbasmiṃ ti maññati. Ayaṃ assa diṭṭhimaññanā. Tasmiṃ yeva pan'assa attani sinehaṃ taṃvatthukañca mānaṃ uppādayato taṇhā-mānamaññanā pi veditabbā. M.A.*, I, p. 38.

111. *Santo'ham asmi, nibbuto'ham asmi, anupādāno'ham asmī ti samanupassati. Tad api'massa bhoto samaṇabrāhmaṇassa upādānaṃ akkhāyati. M.*, II, p. 237.

112. *Passatha no tumhe bhikkhave taṃ attavādūpādānaṃ yaṃ sa attavādūpānānaṃ upādiyato no uppajjeyyuṃ sokaparidevadukkhadomanassupāyāsā? No h'etaṃ bhante. M.*, I, p. 137.

CHAPTER TWO FOOTNOTES

1. G.E.M. Anscombe and P.T. Geach, *Three Philosophers* (Oxford: Basil Blackwell, 1963), pp. 109, 117.

2. D.J.B. Hawkins, *The Essentials of Theism* (London: Sheed and Ward, 1949), p. 12.

3. ibid., p. 14.

4. Ninian Smart, *Philosophers,* p. 85.

5. Rudolf Bultmann, *Existence and Faith* (London: Fontana, 1964), p. 210.

6. ibid., pp. 261-262.

7. Smart, *Philosophers,* p. 89.

8. ibid., p. 84.

9. ibid., p. 87.

10. *Eke Samaṇabrāhmaṇā issarakuttaṃ brahmakuttaṃ ācariyakaṃ aggaññaṃ paññapenti. D.*, III, p. 28.

11. *Loko loko ti bhante vuccati. Kittāvatā nu kho bhante loko ti vaccati? Lujjatī ti kho bhikkhu tasmā loko ti vuccati. Kiñca lujjati? Cakkhu. . .rūpā. . . cakkhu viññaṇaṃ. . . jivhā. . .kāyo. . .mano. . .lujjatī ti kho bhikkhu tasmā loko to vuccatī ti. S.,* IV, p. 52.

12. *So ādito va iti paṭisañcikkhati: na tāv'idam nāmarūpaṃ; ahetukaṃ sabbattha sabbadā sabbesañ ca ekasadisabhāvāpattito; na issarādi-hetukaṃ, nāmarūpato uddhaṃ issarādīnaṃ abhāvato. Ye pi: Nāmarūpamattam eva issarādayo ti vadanti, tesaṃ issarādi-saṅkhātanāmarūpassa ahetukabhāvappattito, tasmā bhavitabbam assa hetupaccayehi: ke nu kho te ti? So evaṃ nāmarūpassahetupaccaye āvajjetvā imassa tāva rūpakāyassa evaṃ hetupaccaye pariggaṇhāti: . . .Tass'evaṃ nibbattamānassa avijjātaṇhā, upādānaṃ, kamman ti ime cattāro dhammā nibbattakattā hetu; āhāro upattham, bhakattā paccayo ti pañca dhammā hetu-paccayā honti. Vsm.* 598-599. Trans. PP. pp. 693-694.

13. Smart, *Philosophers,* p. 82.

14. ibid., p. 89.

15. loc. cit.

16. ibid., p. 90.

17. ibid., p. 91.

18. Hawkins, *The Essentials,* p. 104.

19. Smart, *Philosophers,* p. 93.

20. ibid., p. 104.

21. ibid., p. 97.

22. A. Flew, *God and Philosophy* (London: Hutchinson, 1966), p. 74.

23. Hawkins, *The Essentials,* p. 88.
24. Smart, *Philosophers,* p. 97.
25. Karl Barth, *Church Dogmatics,* Eds. G. W. Bromiley, T.F. Torrance. Trs. J. W. Edwards, O. Bussey, Harold Knight (Edinburgh: T & T Clark, 1958), Vol. III, 1, p. 14.
26. Hawkins, *The Essentials,* p. 63.
27. J.J.C. Smart, 'The Existance of God' in *New Essays in Philosophical Theology,* Eds. Antony Flew and Alasdair Mac Intyre (London: SCM Press, 1963), p. 38.
28. ibid., p. 39.
29. J.N. Findlay, 'Can God's Existence be Disproved?' in *New Essay,* p. 55.
30. I.M. Crombie, 'The Possibility of Theological Statements' in *Faith and Logic,* pp. 64-65.
31. *Katamo ca Paṭiccasamuppādo? Jātipaccayā . . . jarāmaraṇaṃ; uppādā vā Tathāgatānaṃ anuppādā vā Tathāgatānaṃ ṭhitā vā sā dhātu dhammaṭṭhitatā dhammaniyāmatā idappaccayatā. Taṃ Tathāgato abhisambhujjhati abhisameti; abhisambujjhivā abhisametvā ācikkhati deseti paññapeti paṭṭhapeti vivarati vibhajati uttānikaroti passathā ti cāha. S.* II, p. 25.
32. K.N. Jayatilleke, *Early Buddhist Theory of Knowledge* (London: Allen and Unwin, 1963), pp. 446 ff.
33. Hawkins, *The Essentials,* p. 106.
34. A. Schopenhauer, *On the Fourfold Root of the Principle of Sufficient Reason* (First Edition, Bohn, 1813. London, 1888), Sec. 20 Quoted in Flew's *God And Philosophy,* p. 96.
35. *samudayañānaṃ issara. . .ādīhi loko pavattatī ti akāraṇe kāraṇābhimānapavattaṃ hetumhi vippaṭipattiṃ. Vsm.* 511. Tr. PP., p. 584.
36. Flew, *God and Philosophy,* p. 83.
37. Martin, *Religious Belief,* p. 160.
38. David Hume, *Dialogues Concerning Natural Religion,* Ed. Henry D. Aiken (New York: Hafner Publishing Co., 1962), Part ix, p. 59.
39. *Taṃ kiṃ Maññasi Sunakkhatta? Paññatte vā aggañño apaññatte vā aggañño ass'atthāya mayā dhammo desito so niyyāti takkarassa sammā dukkhakkhayāti. . .ti kira Sunakkhatta paññatte vā aggañño appaññate vā aggañño yass'atthāya mayā dhammo desito so niyyāti takkarassa sammādukkhakkhayāyāti. Tatra Sunakkhatta kiṃ paññattaṃ aggaññaṃ karissati? D.,* III, pp. 4-5.
40. Paul Tillich, *Systematic Theology* (London: Nisbet, 1955), Vol. I, pp. 280-281.
41. Bultmann, *Existence and Faith,* p. 262.
42. Tillich, *Systematic Theology,* Vol. I, p. 301.
43. Bultmann, *Existence and Faith,* p. 262.
44. Crombie, *'The Possibility of Theological Statements,'* p. 31.
45. F. Waismann, *How I See Philosophy,* Ed. R. Harre (London: Macmillan, 1968), p. 250.

CHAPTER THREE FOOTNOTES

1. Hume, *Dialogues*, Parts x and xi.
2. J.S. Mill, *Theism,* Ed. Richard Taylor (New York: The Liberal Arts Press, 1957), p. 40ff.

3. J.E. McTaggart, *Some Dogmas of Religion* (London: Edward Arnold, 1906). pp. 212ff.

4. A. Flew, 'Theology and Falsification' in *New Essays,* pp. 96-99.

5. H.D. Aiken, 'God and Evil: Some Relations Between Faith and Morals' in *Ethics,* Vol. LXVIII, 1958, pp. 77ff.

6. J.L. Mackie, 'Evil and Omnipotence' in *Mind,* Vol. LXIV, No. 254, pp. 200-212.

7. C.J. Ducasse, *A Philosophical Scrutiny of Religion* (New York: The Ronald Press, 1953), Chapter 16.

8. H.J. McCloskey, 'God and Evil', in *The Philosophical Quarterly,* Vol. X, No. 39, 1960. Reprinted in *God and Evil* Ed. Nelson Pike (New Jersey: Prentice Hall, 1964), pp. 61-84.

9. Nelson Pike, 'Hume on Evil' in *The Philosophical Review,* Vol. LXXII, No. 2, 1963. Reprinted in *God and Evil,* pp. 85-102.

10. William James, *The Pluralistic Universe* (New York: Longmans, 1909), p. 311.

11. J.S. Mill, *Theism,* p. 45; *An Examination of Sir William Hamilton's Philosophy* (London: Longmans, 1872), pp. 111-135.

12. Hume, *Dialogues,* p. 71.

13. C. Core, *Belief in God* (Harmondsworth: Penguin Books, 1939), p. 122.

14. Tillich, *Systematic Theology*, Vol. I, p. 303.

15. ibid., p. 310.

16. ibid., p. 309.

17. ibid., p. 297.

18. Fritz Buri, *Theology of Existence* (Greenwood S.C.: The Attic Press, 1965), p. 41.

19. ibid., p. 42.

20. Smart, *Philosophers*, p. 154.

21. Hawkins, *The Essentials*, p. 142.

22. J. Wisdom, 'God and Evil' in *Mind*, Vol. XLIV, No. 173, 1935, p. 20.

23. *Sace hi so issaro sabba loke Brahmā bahūbhūtapatī pajānaṃ,* (i) *kiṃ sabbaloke vidahī alakkhiṃ kiṃ sabbalokaṃ na sukhiṃ akāsi. . .* (ii) *māyāmusāvajjamadena c'āpi lokaṃ adhammena kimatth'akāsi. . .* (iii) *adhammiyo bhūtapatī . . .dhamme satī yo vidahī adhammaṃ. J.*, VI, p. 208. Quoted and translated by Jayatilleke, E.B.T.K., p. 411.

24. Hawkins, *The Essentials*, p. 141.

25. A. Flew, 'Divine Omnipotence and Human Freedom' in *New Essays*, pp. 144-169; McCloskey, '*God and Evil*', p. 83.

26. Smart, *Philosophers*, p. 144; Also, Ninian Smart, 'Omnipotence, Evil and Supermen' in *Philosophy*, Vol. XXXVI, No. 137, 1961. Reprinted in *God and Evil*, pp. 85-102.

27. Hick, *Philosophy of Religion*, p. 43.

28. Hawkins, *The Essentials*, p. 134.

29. Karl Barth, *Church Dogmatics*, Eds. G.W. Bromiley, T.F. Torrance. Trs. G.W. Bromiley, R.J. Ehrlich (Edinburgh: T & T Clark, 1961), Vol. III, 3, p. 316.

30. Father G.H. Joyce, *Principles of Natural Theology*, Chapter 7. Quoted in McCloskey's '*God and Evil'*, p. 64.

31. Hawkins, *The Essentials*, p. 143.

32. McCloskey, '*God and Evil*', p. 64.

33. Karl Barth, *Church Dogmatics*, Eds. G.W. Bromiley, T.F. Torrance. Trs. T.H.L. Parker, W.B. Johnston, Harold Knight, J.L.M. Haire (Edinburgh: T & T Clark, 1964), Vol. II, 1, p.279.

34. ibid., p. 281.

35. ibid., p. 298.

36. ibid., p. 407.

37. ibid., p. 408.

38. McCloskey, '*God and Evil*', p. 75.

39. *N'atthi samaṇo vā brāhmaṇo vā yo sakideva sabbaññasati sabbaṃ dakkhīti, n'etaṃ ṭhānaṃ vijjatī ti. M.* II, pp. 127-8.

40. Flew, *God and Philosophy*, p. 46.

41. Nelson Pike, 'Divine Omniscience and Voluntary Action' in *The Philosophical Review*, Vol. LXXIV, 1965, p. 28.

42. Hawkins, *The Essentials*, p. 122.

43. ibid., pp. 122-123.

44. Smart, *Philosophers*, p. 104.

45. Nelson Pike, '*Divine Omniscience and Voluntary Action*', p. 32.

46. *Idha Sandaka ekacco satthā sabbaññū sabbadassāvī aparisesaṃ ñaṇadassanaṃ paṭijānāti: carato ca me tiṭṭhato ca suttassa ca jāggarassa ca satataṃ samitaṃ ñāṇadassanaṃ paccupaṭṭhitan ti. So suññam pi agāraṃ pavisati, piṇḍam pi na labhati, kukkuro pi ḍasati, caṇḍena pi hatthinā samāgacchati, canḍena pi assena samāgacchati, caṇḍena pi goṇena samāgacchati, itthiyā pi purisassa pi nāmam pi gottam pi pucchati, gāmassa pi nigamassa pi nāmam pi maggam pi pucchati. So: kim idan ti puṭṭho samāno: suññaṃ me agāraṃ pavisitabbaṃ ahosi, tena pāvisiṃ; pindam me aladdhabbaṃ ahosi, tena nālatthaṃ; kukkurena ḍasitabbaṃ ahosi, ten'amhi daṭṭho; caṇḍena hatthinā samāgantabbaṃ ahosi, tena samāgamaṃ; caṇḍena assena samāgantabbaṃ ahosi, tena samāgamaṃ; caṇḍena goṇena samāgantabbaṃ ahosi, tena samāgamaṃ; itthiyā pi purissasa pi nāmam pi gottam pi pucchitabbaṃ ahosi, tenāpucchiṃ; gāmassa pi nigamassa pi nāmam pi maggam pi pucchitabbaṃ ahosi, tenāpucchinti. M.*, I, p. 519.

47. See for instance, *Concilium Valentinum* (Contra Joannem Scotum) *de praedestinatione*, Can 2 [Denzinger, Enchiridion Symbolorum, Sec. 321]. Also *Concilium Vaticanum*, Sessio III, Chap. I [ibid. Sec. 1784]. Note especially in the latter '*Omnia enim nuda et aperta sunt oculis eius, ea etiam quae libera creaturarum actione futura sunt.* References as quoted by Flew in *New Essays*, p. 151, fn. 11.

48. Emil Brunner, *The Christian Doctrine of God: Dogmatics*, Tr. Olive Wyon (London: Lutterworth Press, 1962), Vol. I, p. 262.

49. Luis de Molina, *Concordia Liberti Arbitrii*, This passage translated and quoted by John Mourant, in *Readings in the Philosophy of Religion* (New York: Thomas Y. Crowell Co., 1954), p. 426.

50. Mark Pontifex, 'The Question of Evil' in *Prospect for Metaphysics*, Ed. Ian Ramsey (London: Allen and Unwin, 1961), p. 129.

51. ibid., p. 130.

52. *The Report on the 1922 Commission on Doctrine in the Church of England* (London: S.P.C.K. 1938), p. 47.

53. Barth, *Church Dogmatics*, Vol. II, 1, p. 551.

54. ibid., p. 559.

55. ibid., p. 674.

56. *Tatra bhikkhave ye te samaṇā brāhmaṇā evaṃ vādino evaṃ diṭṭhino—yaṃkiñcāyaṃ purisapuggalo paṭisaṃvedeti sukhaṃ vā dukkhaṃ vā adukkhamasukhaṃ vā sabaṃ taṃ issaranimmāṇahetūti. . .Tyāhaṃ evaṃ vadāmi: Tena h'āyasmanto pāṇātipātino bhavissanti issarāṇimmanahetu, adinnādāyino bhavissanti issaranimmāṇahetu. . .micchādiṭṭhino bhavissanti issaranimmāṇahetu. Issaranimmāṇaṃ kho pana bhikkhave sārato paccāgacchataṃ na hoti chando vā vāyāmo vā idaṃ vā karaṇīyaṃ idaṃ vā akaraṇīyan ti. Iti karaṇīyākaraṇīye kho pana saccato thetato anupalabbhiyamāne. . .na hoti paccattaṃ sahadhammiko samaṇavādo. A.*, I, p. 174.

57. *Issaro sabbalokassa sace kappeti jīvitaṃ iddhivyasanabhāvañca kammaṃ kalyāṇapāpakaṃ niddesakāri puriso issaro tena lippati. J.*, p. 238. Quoted and translated by Jayatillike, E.B.T.K., p. 411.

58. *Sace Pubbekatahetu sukhadukkhaṃ nigacchati, porāṇakaṃ kataṃ pāpaṃ tam eso muccate iṇaṃ, porāṇakaṃ iṇamokkho kuvidha pāpena lippati. J.*, V, p. 238 Quoted and translated by Jayatilleke, loc. cit. Also. A., I, pp. 173-174.

CHAPTER FOUR FOOTNOTES

1. H.P. Owen, *The Moral Argument for Christian Theism* (London: Allen and Unwin, 1965), p. 17.

2. ibid., p. 17.

3. ibid., p. 18.

4. ibid., pp. 20-21.

5. ibid., p. 24.

6. ibid., p. 34.

7. ibid., p. 35.

8. loc. cit.

9. John Baillie, *The Sense of the Presence of God* (Oxford: University Press, 1962), pp. 79-87.

10. J. Maritain, *Approaches to God* (London: Allen and Unwin, 1955), p. 84.

11. *Cetanāhaṃ bhikkave kammaṃ vadāmi. A.*, III, p. 415; *Kvu.* p. 393.

12. *Yad api bhikkhave alobho tad api kusalaṃ, yad api aluddho abhisaṁkharoti kāyeāna vācāya manasā tad api kusalaṃ, yad api aluddho lobhena anabhibhūto apariyādinnacitto na parassa asatā dukkhaṃ upadahati vadhena vā bandhena vā jāniyā vā garahāya vā pabbājanāya vā balav'amhi balattho iti pi tad api kusalaṃ. Iti'ssa'me alobhajā alobhanidānā alobhasamudayā alobhappaccayā aneke kusalā dhammā sambhavanti. A.*, I, p. 203.

13. *sabbe tasanti daṇḍassa sabbe bhāyanti maccuno, attānaṃ upamaṃ katvā na haneyya na ghātaye. Dhp.*, x. 1.

14. *D.*, III, pp. 92-93; S.B.B., Vol. 4, Part iii, pp. 87-88.

15. *Tatrāvuso bhikkhunā attanā va attānaṃ evaṃ anuminitabbaṃ: yo khvāyaṃ puggalo pāpiccho pāpikānaṃ icchānaṃ vasaṃgato ayam me pugaglo appiyo amanāpo; ahañceva kho pan'assaṃ pāpiccho pāpikānaṃ icchānaṃ vasaṃgato aham p'assaṃ paresaṃ appiyo amanāpo ti. M.*, I, p. 97.

16. *M.*, I, p. 38; *M.L.S.*, I, p. 48.

17. *Mātā yathā niyam puttaṃ āyusā eka puttamanurakkhe, evaṃ pi sabbabhūtesu mānasambhāvaye aparimāṇaṃ. . . .Sn.*, § 149.

18. *S.*, V, pp. 353-354ff, *K.S.*, V; pp. 308-309ff.

19. Owen, ibid., p. 56.

20. Emil Brunner, *The Divine Imperative* (London: Lutterworth Press), 1939, pp. 73, 79ff.

21. Austin Farrer, 'A Starting-Point for the Philosophical Examination of Theological Belief' in *Faith and Logic*, p. 29.

22. Owen, ibid., p. 77.

23. *M.*, I, pp. 35-36; *M.L.S.*, I, p. 45.

24. W.R. Sorley, *Moral Value and the Idea of God* (Cambridge: University Press, 1921), pp. 352-387.

25. P.F. Strawson, 'Social Morality and Individual Ideal' in *Christian Ethics and Contemporary Philosophy* Ed. Ian T. Ramsey (London: SCM Press, 1966), p. 291.

26. Patterson-Brown, 'Religious Morality' in *Mind*, Vol. 72, April 1963, pp. 237 and 240-1.

27. Patterson-Brown, 'God and the Good' in *Religious Studies*, Vol. 2, p. 275.

28. A.C. Ewing, 'The Autonomy of Ethics' in *Prospect for Metaphysics*, p. 39.

29. Keith Campbell, 'Patterson-Brown on God and Evil' in *Mind*, Vol. 74, 1965, p. 583.

30. *M.*, I, p. 520; *M.L.S.*, II, p. 199.

31. Kai Neilsen, 'Some Remarks on the Independence of Morality from Relilgion' in *Christian Ethics*, p. 146.

32. ibid., p. 151.

33. Ewing, ibid., p. 41.

34. St. Thomas Aquinas, *Summa Theologica*, Trs. Fathers of the English Dominican Province (Burns Oates and Washbourne: London 1926), III, Supp. (XCIV) 1-3. Quoted in Flew's *God and Philosophy*, p. 57.

35. M. Luther, *The Bondage of the Will*, First Edition, 1525. Tr. H. Cole, revision by E.T. Vaughan: London, 1823. Corrected by H. Atherton W. Eardmans and Sovereign Grace: Grand Rapids, Michigan and London, 1932), Section 23, Quoted in Flew's *God and Philosophy*, p. 107.

36. Patterson-Brown, '*Religious Morality*', p. 242.

37. D. Bonhoeffer, *Ethics* (London: SCM Press, 1955), p. 244.

38. ibid., p. 238.

39. Nowell-Smith, 'Morality: Religious and Secular' in *Christian Ethics*, pp. 95, 101.

40. I.M. Crombie, 'Moral Principles' in *Christian Ethics*, pp. 259-260.

41. Strawson, '*Social Morality and Individual Ideal*', p. 291.

42. Paul Lehmann, *Ethics in a Christian Context* (New York: Harper and Row, 1963), p. 350.

43. H.D. Lewis, 'The Voice of Conscience and the Voice of God' in *Christian Ethics*, p. 177.

44. A.E. Taylor, *Does God Exist?* (London: Macmillan, 1947), p. 120.

45. *Attāpi attānaṃ upavadati anuvicca viññū garahanti pāpako kittisaddo abbhuggacchati sammūṭho kālaṃ karoti kāyassa bhedā parammaraṇā apāyaṃ duggatiṃ vinipātaṃ nirayaṃ uppajjati. A.*, I, p. 57; *G.S.*, I, p. 52.

46. *Vism.*, 13-14, p. 14.

47. Ninian Smart, 'God, Bliss and Morality' in *Christian Ethics*, p. 21.

48. ibid., p. 23.
49. ibid., p. 24.
50. Ian T. Ramsey, 'Moral Judgements and God's Commands' in *Christian Ethics*, p. 167.
51. ibid., p. 167.
52. ibid., p. 168.
53. Farrer, '*A Starting Point*', p. 22.
54. M. Paul van Buren, *The Secular Meaning of the Gospel* (London: SCM Press, 1963), p. 103.
55. ibid., pp. 197-198.
56. ibid., p. 200.
57. ibid., p. 143.
58. ibid., p. 141.
59. ibid., p. 155.
60. M. Paul van Buren, *Theological Explorations* (London: SCM Press, 1968), p. 173.
61. Van Buren, *The Secular*, pp. 138-139.
62. R.B. Braithwaite, 'An Empiricist's View of the Nature of Religious Belief' in *The Existence of God*, Ed. J. Hick (New York: Macmillan, 1964), p. 247.
63. ibid., p. 248.
64. ibid., p. 64.
65. L. Wittgenstein, *Notebooks* 1914-16 (Oxford: Basil Blackwell, 1961), Section 30. 7. 16.
66. *M.*, I, p. 407; *M.L.S.*, II, p. 76.
67. *Sace kho pana atthi paraloko atthi sukaṭadukkaṭānaṃ kammānaṃ phalaṃ vipāko ṭhānaṃ ahaṃ kāyassa bhedā parammaraṇā sugatiṃ saggaṃ lokaṃ uppajjissāmīti. . .Sace kho pana n'atthi paraloko n'atthi sukaṭadukkaṭānaṃ kammānaṃ phalaṃ vipāko idāhaṃ diṭṭh'eva dhamme averaṃ avyāpajjhaṃ anīghaṃ sukhim attānaṃ pariharāmīti. A.*, I, 192; *G.S.*, I, p. 175.
68. *S.*, V, p. 387-388; *K.S.*, V, pp. 333-334.
69. *M.*, I, 180; *M.L.S.*, I, p. 226.
70. *A.*, III, p. 186. *G.S.*, III, p. 137.
71. *Vsm.*, 54. pp. 53-54.
72. Brunner, *The Divine Imperative*, pp. 68-71.
73. *Iti kho Ānanda kusalāni sīlāni avippaṭisāratthāni avippaṭisārānisaṃsān avippaṭisāro pāmujjattho pāmujjānisaṃso, pāmujjaṃ pītatthaṃ pītānisaṃsaṃ, pīti passaddhatthā passadhānisaṃsā passaddhi sukhatthā sukkhānisaṃsā, sukhaṃ samādhatthaṃ samādhānisaṃsaṃ, samādhi yathābūtañānadassanattho yathabhūtañāṇadassnānisamso yathābūtañāṇadassanaṃ nibbidāvirāgatthaṃ nibbidāviragānisaṃsaṃ, nibbidāvirāgo vimuttiñāṇadassanattho vimuttiñāṇadassanānisaṃso. Iti kho Ānanda kusalāni sīlāni anupubbena aggāya parentīti. A.*, V, p. 2. *G.S.*, V, pp. 2-3.
74. *M.*, I, p. 102; *M.L.S.*, I, p. 133.
75. *Evameva kho bhikkhave idh'ekacco bhikkhu tāvadeva soratasorato hoti nivātanivāto hoti upasantūpasanto hoti yāva na amanāpā vacanapathā phusanti; yato ca kho bhikkhave bhikkhuṃ amanāpā vacanapathā phusanti atha kho bhikkhusorato ti veditabbo nivāto ti veditabbo upasanto ti veditabbo. M.*, p. 126; *M.L.S.*, I, p. 163.

76. *Na brāhmano aññato suddhiṃ āha, diṭṭhe sute sīlavate mute vā, puññe ca pāpe ca anuppalitto, attañjaho nayidha pakubbamāno. Sn.* § 790; *S.B.E.*, X. p. 151.

77. *Subhena kammena vajanti suggatiṃ, apāyabhūmiṃ asubhena kammunā, khayā ca kammassa vimuttacetaso, nibbanti te jotiriv'indhanakkhayā. Netti.*, p. 184.

78. *M.*, III, p. 29; *M.L.S.*, III, p. 81.

79. *M.*, I, p. 517.

80. *M.*, I, p. 520.

81. *M.*, I, pp. 515-518; *M.L.S.* II, pp. 193-196.

82. *Sn.*,§§. 284 ff.

83. *Sn.*, § 1082.

CHAPTER FIVE FOOTNOTES

1. Charles Hartshorne, *The Divine Relativity: A Social Conception of God* (New Haven: Yale University Press, 1964), p. 79.

2. Cobb, *A Christian Natural Theology*, p. 174.

3. ibid., p. 172.

4. ibid., p. 214.

5. ibid., p. 176.

6. ibid., p. 188.

7. ibid., p. 212.

8. Teilhard de Chardin, *The Phenomenon of Man* (London Collins, 1961), p. 268.

9. ibid., p. 258.

10. ibid., p. 260.

11. ibid., p. 294. Also, p. 310.

12. Karl Rahner, *Theological Investigations*, Tr. Karl-H. Kruger (London: Darton, Longman & Todd, 1966), Vol. V, p. 191.

13. ibid., p. 168. Also, pp. 185, 166, 167.

14. ibid., p. 165.

15. loc. cit.

16. ibid., pp. 171-172.

17. ibid., p. 161. Also, pp. 174-175.

18. G.P. Malalasekara and K.N. Jayatilleke, *Buddhism and the Race Question* (Paris: UNESCO, 1958), p.32.

19. *A.*, I, 227-228; *G.S.*, I, p. 207.

20. *A.*, II, p. 142.

21. *A.*, IV, p. 256-257.

22. *A.*, IV, p. 138.

23. *A.*, IV, p. 39, 40; *A.*, III, p. 35.

24. *A.*, IV, pp. 429-430.

25. Hartshorne, *The Divine Relativity,* p. 87.

26. ibid., p. 89.

27. ibid., p. 88.

28. Chardin, *The Phenomenon of Man,* p. 268.

29. ibid., p. 269.

30. ibid., p. 270.

31. ibid., p. 271.

32. loc. cit.
33. ibid., p. 291.
34. T. de Chardin, *The Future of Man* (London: Collins, 1964). p. 254.
35. ibid., p. 255.
36. ibid., p. 296.
37. Chardin, *The Phenomenon of Man*, p. 258.
38. ibid., p. 276.
39. Chardin, *The Future of Man,* pp. 276-277.
40. T. de Chardin, *Le Millieu Divin* (London: Collins, 1961), p. 150.
41. Rahner, *Theological Investigations,* Vol. 5, p. 173.
42. ibid., p. 188.
43. ibid., p. 183.
44. ibid., p. 179.
45. ibid., p. 124.
46. ibid., p. 114.
47. ibid., p. 141.
48. ibid., p. 150.
49. ibid., p. 140.
50. loc. cit.
51. *M.*, II, p. 222.
52. *M.*, I, p. 518; *M.L.S.*, II, p. 198.
53. Thomas J.J. Altizer and William Hamilton, *Radical Theology and the Death of God* (Harmondsworth: Pelican Books, 1968), p. 9.
54. ibid., p. 13.
55. J.J.T. Altizer, *The Gospel of Christian Atheism* (London: Collins, 1967), p. 106.
56. ibid., p. 107.
57. ibid., p. 112.
58. ibid., p. 113.
59. ibid., p. 42
60. ibid., p. 145.
61. ibid., p. 146.
62. ibid., p. 148.
63. ibid., p. 28. Also, p. 54.
64. Altizer and Hamilton, *Radical Theology*, p. 135.
65. Altizer, *The Gospel of Christian Atheism*, p. 75.
66. Altizer and Hamilton, *Radical Theology*, p. 56. Also, p. 53.
67. ibid., p. 58.
68. ibid., p. 60.
69. Altizer, *The Gospel of Christian Atheism*, p. 89.
70. ibid., p. 90.
71. ibid., p. 73.
72. Altizer and Hamilton, *Radical Theology,* p. 40.
73. ibid., p. 122.
74. ibid., p. 27.
75. ibid., p. 28.
76. ibid., p. 31.
77. ibid., p. 33.
78. ibid., pp. 115-116. Also, p. 107.

79. Altizer, *The Gospel of Christian Atheism,* p. 37.
80. Altizer and Hamilton, *Radical Theology*, p. 10.
81. T. de Chardin, *Letters from a Traveller* (London: Collins, 1962), p. 127. Claude Cuenot, *Science and Faith in Teilhard de Chardin* (London: Garnstone Press, 1967), p. 52.
82. Cobb, *A Christian Natural Theology*, p. 169.
83. Hartshorne, *The Divine Relativity*, pp. 80-81.
84. ibid., p. 83.
85. ibid., p. 90.
86. Hartshorne, *A Natural Theology for Our Time* (Illinois: Open Court, 1967), p. 15.
87. ibid., p. 22. Also, p. 23.
88. Altizer, *The Gospel of Christian Atheism*, p. 35.
89. Altizer and Hamilton, *Radical Theology*, p. 132.
90. ibid., p. 133.
91. ibid., p. 145.
92. ibid., p. 146.
93. *M.*, I, p. 486; *M.L.S.*, II, p. 164.
94. *Na kho panāhaṃ āvuso appatvā lokassa antaṃ dukkhasssa antakiriyaṃ vadāmi. Api khvāhaṃ āvuso imasmiññeva vyāmamatte kalevare saññimhi samanake lokañ ca paññapemi lokasamudayañ ca lokanirodhañ ca lokanirodhagāminiñ ca patipadan ti. Gamanena na pattabbo, lokassanto kudācanaṃ, na ca appatvā lokantaṃ, dukkhā atthi pamocanaṃ. S.*, I, p. 62; *K.S.*, I, pp. 86-87.

CHAPTER SIX FOOTNOTES

1. John Baillie, *Our Knowledge of God* (London: O.U.P., 1949), p. 132.
2. H.H. Farmer, *Towards Belief in God* (London: S.C.M. Press, 1942), Pt. ii, p. 40.
3. Ninian Smart, *Reasons and Faiths* (London: Kegan Paul, 1958), p. 158.
4. Karl Barth, *Church Dogmatics*, Vol. II, I, p. 214.
5. John Hick, 'Man's Awareness of God' in *Religious Belief and Philosophical Thought*, Ed. W.P. Alston (New York: Harcourt Brace & World, 1963), p. 217.
6. ibid., p. 219.
7. Carlos Castaneda, *The Teachings of Don Juan: A Yaqui Way of Knowledge* (Harmondsworth, Penguin Books, 1970), p. 247.
8. J.W. Harvey, 'Introduction' in *The Idea of Holy* by Rudolf Otto, Tr. J.W. Harvey (London: O.U.P., 1957), p. xvi.
9. Huston Smith, 'Empirical Metaphysics' in *The Ecstatic Adventure*, Ed. Ralph Metzner (New York: Macmillan, 1968), p. 73.
10. Walter H. Clark, 'Shaking the Foundations' in *The Ecstatic Adventure*, p. 77.
11. ibid., pp. 75-76.
12. Evelyn Underhill, *Mysticism* (London: Methuen, 1962), p. 196.
13. loc. cit.
14. ibid., p. 276.
15. ibid., pp. 289-290.

16. St. Teresa, *The Complete Works of St. Teresa of Jesus*, Ed. E. Allison Peers (London: Sheed and Ward, 1957), Vol. II, p. 309.

17. ibid., p. 334.

18. ibid., p. 334.

19. Underhill, op. cit., p. 269.

20. J.S. Slotkin, 'Menomini Peyotism, A study of Individual Variation in a Primary Group with a Homogeneous Culture' in *Transactions of the American Philosophical Society*, New Series, Vol. 42, 1952, p. 569.

21. St. Teresa, op. cit., p. 251.

22. St. John of the Cross. *The Complete Works of Saint John of the Cross*, Ed. E, Allison Peers (London: Burns Oates & Washbourne, 1934), Vol. I, p. 13.

23. ibid., p. 144.

24. ibid., p. 148.

25. ibid., p. 151.

26. ibid., p. 102.

27. ibid., p. 104.

28. ibid., p. 105.

29. R.J. Zwi Werblowsky, 'On the Mystical Rejection of Mystical Illuminations' in *Religious Studies*, Vol. I, p. 184.

30. St. John of the Cross, pp. 113-114.

31. R. Otto, *Mysticism East and West*, Tr. B.L. Bracey and R.C. Payne (London: Macmillan, 1932), p. 12. As quoted by Otto.

32. Meister Eckhart, *Meister Eckhart* Tr. by R.B. Blakney (New York: Harper & Row, 1941), pp. 200-201. As quoted by W.T. Stace in *Mysticism and Philosophy* (London: Macmillan, 1961), p. 98.

33. Otto, *Mysticism*, p. 7.

34. ibid., pp. 10, 15.

35. ibid., p. 39.

36. Otto, *Mysticism*, pp. 179-180. As quoted by Otto.

37. William James, *The Varieties of Religious Experience* (New York: Longmans, 1935), p. 54.

38. Walter Pahnke and William A. Richards, 'Implications of LSD and Experimental Mysticism' in *Journal of Religion and Health*, 1966, 5, pp. 177-183.

39. ibid., p. 192.

40. Huston Smith, 'Do Drugs Have Religious Import?' in *Journal of Philosophy*, Vol. LXI, No. 17, 1964, p. 521.

41. John Robertson, 'Uncontainable Joy' in *The Ecstatic Adventure,* p. 87.

42. Rev. Mary Hart, 'The Oneness of God, the Vision of Christ, the Crucifixion' in *The Ecstatic Adventure*, p. 80.

43. Sydney Cohen, *Drugs of Hallucination* (London: Paladin Books, 1970), p. 23.

44. Pahnke and Richards, op. cit., pp. 194-195.

45. Cohen, op. cit., p. 31.

46. Arthur Koestler, *The Invisible Writing* (New York: Macmillan, 1954), p. 352.

47. Stace, *Mysticism*, p. 119. As quoted by Stace.

48. ibid., pp. 121-122.

49. Brother Lawrence, *The Practice of the Presence of God,* Tr. D. Attwater (London: Orchard Books, 1926), p. 9. As quoted by Underhill, pp. 190-191.

50. Underhill, op. cit., p. 184.

51. Ninian Smart, *The Yogi and the Devotee* (London: Allen and Unwin, 1968), p. 74.

52. ibid., p. 74.

53. ibid., pp. 49-50.

54. ibid., p. 56.

55. ibid., p. 57.

56. ibid., p. 75.

57. Martin, *Religious Belief*, p. 77.

58. ibid., p. 94.

59. Underhill, p. 269.

60. James H. Leuba, 'A Study in the Psychology of Religious Phenomena' in *The American Journal of Psychology*, Vol. VII, April, 1896, No. 3, pp. 309-385.

61. ibid., pp. 340-341.

62. ibid., p. 347. Also, p. 348.

63. ibid., p. 343.

64. J.S. Slotkin, 'The Peyote Way' in *Reader in Comparative Religion: An Anthropological Approach*, Eds. William A. Lessa & Evon Z. Vogt (New York: Harper & Row, 1965), p. 515.

65. J.S. Slotkin, '*Menomini Peyotism*', p. 579.

66. Cohen, op. cit., p. 81.

67. Leuba, op. cit., pp. 346-347.

68. Arthur Koestler, *Drinkers of Infinity* (London: Hutchinson, 1968), pp. 210-211.

69. This does not mean that theologians like Tillich and Bultmann are not Christian, for reasons explained below 6.54.

70. James, op. cit., pp. 425-426.

71. Timothy Leary, *The Politics of Ecstasy* (London: Paladin Books, 1970), p. 20.

72. Donald B. Louria, *The Drug Scene* (London: Corgi Books, 1970), p. 132.

73. ibid., pp. 135-136.

74. Pahnke and Richards, op. cit., pp. 182-183.

75. Louria, op. cit., p. 126.

76. Pahnke and Richards, op. cit., p. 183.

77. St. Teresa, *Interior Castle*, Tr. Fr. Benedict Zimmermann (London: Thomas Baker, 1930), p. 171.

78. St. John of the Cross, op. cit., p. 104.

79. Ven. Augustine Baker, *Holy Wisdom: or Directions for the Prayer of Contemplation*, Ed. Abbot Sweeney (London: 1908), Treatise III, Sec. iv, Chapter III. As Quoted by Underhill, p. 362.

80. Underhill, op. cit., p. 360.

81. ibid., p. 270.

82. St. John of the Cross, op. cit., p. 17.

83. ibid., p. 63.

84. Underhill, op. cit., p. 205.

85. St. Teresa, *The Complete Works*, p. 263.

86. Otto, *Mysticism*, p. 92. As quoted by Otto.

87. Underhill, op. cit., p. 85.

88. ibid., p. 86.

89. James, op. cit., p. 340.
90. ibid., p. 342.
91. ibid., p. 343.
92. Bougaud, *Hist. de la bienheureuse Marguerite Marie* (Paris, 1894), p. 267. As quoted by James, pp. 344-345.
93. St. Gertrude, *Revelations de Sainte Gertrude* (Paris, 1898), i. 44, 186. As quoted by James, p. 345.
94. Underhill, op. cit., p. 216. (My italics).
95. St. Angela de Foligno, *Le Livre de l'experience des Vrais Fideles*. Ed. M.J. Ferre (Paris, 1927), p. 10. As quoted by Underhill, p. 216 (My italics).
96. Stace, op. cit., p. 339.
97. Underhill, op. cit., p. 172.
98. ibid., p. 173. (My italics).
99. St. John of the Cross, op. cit., p. 128.
100. Aquinas, *Summa Theologica*, II-2 (XI) 3-4. Quoted in Flew's *God and Philosophy*, p. 92.
101. Paul Tillich, *Systematic Theology* (London: Nisbet, 1964), Vol. 3, p. 141.
102. ibid., p. 140.
103. Paul Tillich, *Systematic Theology*, Vol. I, p. 150.
104. Wilfred Cantwell Smith, *Questions of Religious Truth* (London: Victor Gollancz, 1967), pp. 99-123.
105. James, op. cit., p. 329.
106. James H. Leuba, 'The Contents of Religious Consciousness' in *The Monist*, XI, July, 1901, p. 538.
107. ibid., p. 537.
108. ibid., pp. 571-572.
109. Underhill, op. cit., p. 96.
110. Stace, op. cit., p. 341.
111. Otto, *Mysticism*, p. 143.
112. Trevor Ling, 'Buddhist Mysticism' in *Religious Studies*, Vol. I, 1965-1966, p. 165.
113. A.B. Keith, *Buddhist Philosophy in India and Ceylon* (Oxford: University Press, 1923), p. 68.
114. *Brahmanirvāṇaṃ ṛcchati; Abhito Brahmanirvāṇaṃ; Śantiṃ nirvāṇaparamāṃ. Bhagavadgītā.* Chapters, ii. 72; v. 26; vi. 15. As quoted by Keith.
115. *Śanai nirvāṇamāpnoti nirindhanamivānala. Anugitā*, iv. 13.
116. F.O. Schrader, 'On the Problem of Nirvana' in *Journal of the Pali Text Society*, 1904-5, p. 167.
117. *Ayaṃ ātmā cid-rūpa eva yathā dāhyaṃ dagdhvā'gnir.*
118. *Yathā nirindhano vahniḥ sva-yonāv upasāmyati tathā vṛttikṣayāc cittaṃ sva-yonāv upaśāmyati.*
119. *M.*, I, pp. 486-487.
120. *Khīṇaṃ purāṇaṃ navaṃ natthi sambhavaṃ, viratta cittā āyatike bhavasmiṃ tekhīṇa bījā avirūḷhicchandā, nibbanti dhīrā yathā'yam padīpo. Sn.*, § 235.
121. *Ayoghanahatass'eva jalato jātavedasso, anupubbūpasantassa yathā na ñāyate gatī, evaṃ sammā vimuttānaṃ kāmabandhoghatārinaṃ, paññāpetuṃ gatī natthi pattānam acalaṃ sukhan ti. U.*, viii. 10.
122. *Apaññattika-bhāvam evahi so gato ti attho. U.A.*, p. 435.

123. *U.*, viii, 9.

124. *Attham vināsam upacchedam. U.A.*, 435.

125. *Acci yathā vātavegena khitto, Upasīvāti Bhagavā, attham paleti na upeti samkham, evam muni nāmakāyā vimutto, attham paleti na upeti samkham. Sn.*, § 1074.

126. *Attham gatassa na pamāṇam atthi, Upasīvāti Bhagavā, yena nam vajju tam tassa natthi, sabbesu dhammesu samūhatesu samūhatā vādapathā pi sabbe. Sn.*, § 1076.

127. *S.*, III, p. 110.

128. *Rūpam tathāgato ti samanupassasīti?. . .No h'etam āvuso. S.*, III, p. 111.

129. *Ettha ca te āvuso Yamaka diṭṭheva dhamme saccato thetato tathāgato anupalabbhiyamāno kathan nu te tam veyyākaraṇam tathāham bhagavatā desitam ājānāmi yathā khīṇāsavo bhikkhu. . .S.*, III, p. 112.

130. *Yathā hi aṅgasambhārā hoti saddo ratho iti, evam khandhesu santesu hoti satto ti sammuti. S.*, I, p. 135.

131. *S.A.*, I, p. 194.

132. *Puggalo n'ūpalabbhati saccikaṭṭhaparamaṭṭhena. Kvu.*, I.

133. *A.A.*, I, pp. 94-95.

134. *Kvu., A*, p. 34.

135. *E.B.T.K.*, pp. 367-368.

136. ibid., p. 374.

137. Keith, op. cit., p. 66.

138. *Tam viññāṇam tathāgatassa pahīnam ucchinnamūlam tālāvatthukatam anabhāvakatam āyatim anuppādadhammam. Viññāṇa saṁkhaya vimutto kho mahārāja atthāgato gambhīro appameyyo duppariyogāho seyyathāpi mahāsamuddo. S.*, IV, p. 379.

139. *Atthi bhikkhave ajātam abhūtam akatam asaṁkhatam, no ce tam bhikkhave abhavissa ajātam abhūtam akatam asaṁkhatam nayidha jātassa bhūtassa katassa saṁkhatassa nissaraṇam paññāyetha. U.*, pp. 80-1.

140. *So kho aham bhikkhave attanā jātidhammo samāno jātidhamme ādīnavam viditvā ajātam anuttaram yogakkhemam nibbānam pariyesamāno ajātam annuttaram yogrkkhemam nibbānam ajjhagamam, attanā jarādhammo samāno jarādhamme ādīnavam viditvā ajaram anuttaram yogakkhemam nibbānam pariyesamāno ajaram anuttaram yogakkhemam nibbānam ajjhagamam . . .byādidhamme ādīnavam viditvā. . .abyādhim. . .pariyesamāno. . .M.*, I, p. 167.

141. E.A. Rune Johansson, *The Psychology of Nirvana* (London: Allen and Unwin, 1969),p. 134.

142. ibid., p. 111.

143. ibid., p. 113.

144. loc. cit.

145. ibid., p. 114.

146. ibid., p. 76.

147. ibid., p. 107.

148. *S.*, III, p. 45.

149. ibid., p. 62.

150. ibid., p. 83.

151. *appatiṭṭhitena ca bhikkhave viññāṇena Vakkali kulaputto parinibbuto ti. S.*, III, p. 119.

152. Johansson, op. cit., p. 63.

153. *appapañcaṃ papañceti. A.*, II, p. 162.

154. See also, 6.90.

155. See 6.59.

156. *Ettha nāmañca rūpañca asesaṃ uparujjhati, viññāṇassa nirodhena etth'etaṃ uparujjhati. D.*, I, p. 223.

157. *Ayaṃ aṭṭhaṅgiko maggo viññāṇanirodhagāminī paṭipadā. S.*, III, p. 61.

158. *Viññāṇassa nirodhena taṇhakkhayavimuttino pajjotass'eva nibbānaṃ vimokho hoti cetaso. A.*, I, p. 236.

159. *Viññānūpasamā bhikkhu nicchāto parinibbuto.* Sn., § 735.

160. *Viññāṇassa nirodhena n'atthi dukkhassa sambhavo.* Sn., § 734.

161. *Parinibbanti anāsavā. Sn.*, § 765.

162. *Te ve saccābhisamayā nicchātā parinibbutā. Sn.*, § 758.

163. *Kathaṃ disvā nibbāti bhikkhu. Sn.*, § 915.

164. *Nibbānaṃ abhijāyati. D.*, III, p. 251; *A.*, III, p. 385.

165. *So bhave na rajjati, sambhave na rajjati. A.*, IV, p. 70.

166. Owen, *The Moral Argument*, p. 100.

167. C.D. Broad, Review of A.E. Taylor's The Faith of a Moralist in *Mind*, Vol. 40, p. 372.

168. *Duve ime cakkhumatā pakāsitā, nibbānadhātu anissitena tādinā, ekā hi dhātu idha diṭṭhadhammikā, sopadhisesā bhavanetti saṁkhayā, anupadhisesā pana samparāyikā, yaṃhi nirujjhanti bhavāni sabbaso. It.*, pp. 38-9.

169. *M.*, III, p. 4; *M.L.S.*, III, pp. 54-55.

170. *Puna ca paraṃ bhikkhave idh'ekacco puggalo sabbaso ākāsānañcāyatanaṃ samatikkamma anantaṃ viññāṇanti viññ āṇañcāyāntanaṃ upasampajja viharati. So tad assādeti tan nikāmeti tena ca vittiṃ āpajjati. A.*, I, p. 267. *G.S.,* I, p. 246.

171. *So iti paṭisañcikkhati: Idam pi kho viññāṇañcāyatanaṃ abhisaṁkhataṃ abhisañcetayitaṃ, yaṃ kho pana kiñci abhisaṁkhataṃ abhisañcetayitaṃ tad aniccaṃ nirodhadhamman ti pajānāti. A.*, V, p. 346.

172. *A.* V., 343-347; *G.S.*, V, 222.

173. St. John of the Cross, p. 80.

174. Otto, *Mysticism*, p. 68. As quoted by Otto.

175. ibid., p. 68. As quoted by Otto.

176. *Vsm.* §§ 331-332. *PP.*pp. 360-1. Translation slightly changed.

177. *M.*, I, pp. 164-165.

178. *M.*, III, p. 37-44.

179. *A.*, IV, pp. 426-7; *G.S.*, IV, p. 286.

180. *na paṭhaviṃ. . .na viññāṇañcāyatanaṃ manasikareyya. . .manasi ca pana kareyyāti. A.*, V, p. 322.

181. *na viññāṇañcāyatanaṃ nissāya jhāyati jhāyati ca pana. A.*, V. p. 326.

182. *M.*, pp. 1-6.

183. *Idh'Udāyi Bhikkhu sabbaso ākāsānañcāyatanaṃ samatikkamma anantaṃ viññāṇan ti viññāṇañcāyatanaṃ upasampajja viharati, ayaṃ tassa samatikkamo. Idam pi kho ahaṃ Udāyi analan ti vadāmi, pajahathā ti vadāmi, samatikkamathā ti vadāmi; ko ca tassa samatikkamo: Idh'Udāyi bhikkhu sabbaso viññāṇañcāyatanaṃ samatikkamma natthi kiñcī ti ākiñcaññāyatanaṃ upasampajja viharati. Ayaṃ tassa samatikkamo. M.*, I, p. 455; *M.L.S.*, II, p. 128.

184. *pakappitā saṁkhatā yassa dhammā, purakkhatā santi avīvadātā, yadattani passati ānisaṃsaṃ, tan nissito kuppapaṭiccasantiṃ. Sn.* §. 784.

185. *Diṭṭhīnivesā na hi svātivattā. Sn.* §. 785.

186. *āruppehi nirodho santataro. Sn.* §§. 146-7.

187. *Vsm.* § 705, p. 828.

188. *Vedāni viceyya kevalāni, . . .samaṇānaṃ yāni p'atthi brāhmaṇānaṃ, sabbavedanāsu vītarago, sabbaṃ vedaṃ aticca vedagū so. Sn.* § 529.

189. *saññāya uparodhanā, evaṃ dukkhakhayo hoti. . .Sn.* § 732.

190. N. Dutt, *Aspects of Mahayana Buddhism and its Relation to Hinayana* (London. Luzac & Co., 1930), p. 167.

191. *M.*, I, p. 296.

192. *Idha bhikkhave bhikkhu sīlasampanno samādhisampanno paññāsampanno saññāvedayitanirodhaṃ samāpajjeyya pi vuṭṭhaheyya pi atth'etaṃ ṭhānaṃ no ce diṭṭh'eva dhamme aññaṃ ārādheyya atikkamm'eva kabaliṅkārāhāra bhakkhānaṃ devānaṃ sahavyataṃ aññataraṃ manomayaṃ kāyaṃ uppanno saññāvedayitanirodhaṃ samāpajjeyya pi vuṭṭhaheyya pi, atth'etaṃ ṭhānan ti. A.*, III, p. 194; *G.S.*, III, p. 143.

193. *G.S.*, IV, pp. 279-280.

194. *Ṭhānaṃ kho pan'etaṃ Ānanda vijjati yaṃ aññatitthiyā paribbājikā evaṃ vadeyyuṃ: saññāvedayitanirodhaṃ samaṇo Gotamo āha tañca sukhasmiṃ paññāpeti, tayidaṃ kiṃsu, tayidaṃ kathaṃ sū ti. Evaṃ vādino Ānanda aññatitthiyā paribbājikā evaṃ assu vacanīyā: na kho āvuso bhagavā sukhaṃ yeva vedanaṃ sandhāya sukhasmiṃ paññāpeti, api c'āvuso yattha yattha sukhaṃ upalabbhati yahiṃ yahiṃ tan taṃ tathāgato sukhasmiṃ paññāpetī ti. M.*, I, p. 400.

195. *Na kho, Udāyi, etassa ekantasukhassa lokassa sacchikiriyāhetu bhikkhū mayi brahmacariyaṃ caranti. Atthi kho Udāyi, aññe ca dhammā uttaritarā ca paṇītatarā ca yesaṃ sacchikiriyā hetu bhikkhū mayi brahmacariyaṃ carantī ti. M.*, II, p. 37.

196. See footnote 171.

197. Smart, *Reasons and Faiths*, p. 94.

198. *Yāvakīvañcāhaṃ imā nava anupubbavihārā samāpattiyo na evaṃ anulomapaṭilomaṃ samāpajjiṃ pi vuṭṭhahiṃ pi, neva tāvāhaṃ. . .sammāsambodhiṃ abhisambuddho paccaññāsiṃ. A.*, IV, p. 448.

199. *Na brāhmaṇo kappaṃ upeti saṁkhaṃ, na diṭṭhisāri na pi ñāṇabandhu. Sn.* § 911.

200. *na diṭṭhiyā na suṭiyā na ñāṇena. . .suddhiṃ āha. Sn.* § 839.

201. *yathābūtaṃ jānaṃ passaṃ antakaro hotī ti. A.*, II, p. 164.

202. *Sn.* § 1107.

203. *S.*, II, p. 119.

204. *Thera Gāthā*, p. 117.

205. *Paramattha-Mañjūsā, Visuddhimagga Aṭṭhakathā* (Commentary) *Mahāṭīkā*. (*Vis.* Chs. I to XVII), Vidyodaya Sinhalese Edition, pp. 9-10. As quoted in *PP.* p. 2, fn. 3.

206. *A.*, I, p. 165.

207. *Evam etaṃ yathābhūtaṃ sammappaññāya passato bhavataṇhā pahīyati, . . .sabbaso taṇhānaṃ khayā asesavirāganirodho nibbānaṃ. U.*, p. 33.

208. *Āsavānaṃ khayo paññāya sacchikaraṇīyo. D.*, III, p. 230.

209. *Paññāparibhāvitaṃ cittaṃ sammad eva āsavehi vimuccati. D.*, II, p. 123.

210. *S.*, IV, pp. 235-6ff.

211. *S.* IV. pp. 291-2ff.

212. *M.*, I, p. 38.

213. *D.*, III, pp. 79.

214. Johansson, op. cit., p. 126.

215. *Sandiṭṭhiko dhammo ti bho Gotama vuccati. Kittāvatā nu kho bho Gotama sandiṭṭhiko dhammo hoti akāliko ehipassiko opanayiko paccattaṃ veditabbo viññūhi ti? Ratto kho brāhmaṇa rāgena abhibhūto pariyādinnacitto attavyābādhāya pi ceteti paravyābādhāya pi ceteti ubhayavyābādhāya pi ceteti cetasikam pi dukkhaṃ domanassam patisaṃvedeti. Rāge pahīṇe n'eva attavyābādhāyapi ceteti. . .Evam pi kho brāhmaṇa sandiṭṭhiko dhammo hoti. . .A.*, I, pp. 156-157; *G.S.*, I, p. 140.

216. *Sabbe tasanti daṇḍassa sabbe bhāyanti maccuno, attānam upamaṃ katvā na haneyya na ghātaye. Dhp.*, x, 1.

217. *Paññāparibhāvitaṃ cittaṃ sammadeva āsavehi vimuccati, seyyathīdaṃ kāmāsavā bhavāsavā diṭṭhāsavā avijjāsavā. D.*, II, p. 81.

218. *Yato ca kho ahaṃ. . .evaṃ lokassa assādañca assādato ādīnavañca ādīnavato nissaraṇañca nissaraṇato yathābhūtaṃ abbhaññāsim. Athāhaṃ. . .anuttaraṃ sammāsambodhiṃ abhisambuddho paccaññāsiṃ, ñāṇañca pana me dassanaṃ udapādi: akuppā me ceto vimutti ayam antimā jāti. . .ti. . .A.*, I, p. 259.

219. *madanimmadano pipāsavinayo ālayasamugghāto vaṭṭūpacchedo taṇhakkhayo virāgo nirodho nibbānaṃ. It.*, p. 88.

220. *Etaṃ santaṃ etaṃ paṇītaṃ yad idaṃ sabba saṁkhāra samatho sabbūpadhipaṭinissaggo taṇhakkhayo virāgo. . .nibbānaṃ. A.*, V, p. 110.

221. *Anattasaññī asmimāna samugghātaṃ pāpuṇāti diṭṭh'eva dhamme nibbānaṃ. A.*, IV, p. 353.

222. *aniccho hoti nibbuto. Sn.* § 707.

223. *santaṃ, sivaṃ, khemaṃ, avyāpajjho. S.*, IV, p. 368.

224. *sītibhūto'smi nibbuto. M.*, I, p. 171.

225. *parinibbuto udakarahado va sīto. Sn.* § 467.

226. *suddhi, S.*, IV, p. 372; *asaṁkiliṭṭha, M.*, I, p. 173; *Mutti., S.*, IV, p. 372.

227. *nibbānaṃ paramaṃ sukhaṃ. Dhp.* xv. 8.

228. *Idan taṃ ārogyaṃ, idan tan nibbānan ti. M.*, I, p. 511.

229. *sattānaṃ tathattāya jātinābhavissa sabbaso jātiyā asati jāti nirodhā api nu kho jarāmaraṇaṃ paññāyethāti?. . .D.*, II, p. 57.

230. A.J. Ayer, *The Concept of a Person* (London: Macmillan, 1963), p. 127. Ayer says elsewhere, "The question of the possibility of reincarnation is comparatively straightforward. It is assumed that we are confronted with someone who satisfies the ordinary physical criteria of personal identity, and our problem is then only to consider whether we shall allow the continuity of memory to make him the same person as one who, if we went to the physical criteria alone, would be reckoned to be someone else. But when it comes to the possibility of a person's continuing to exist in a disembodied state, much greater difficulty arises." A.J. Ayer, *The Problem of Knowledge* (London: Macmillan, 1958), p. 221. Also, p. 219.

231. *M.*, II, pp. 20-21; *M.L.S.*, II, p. 220.

232. Three types of evidence have been put forward for the existence of rebirth: 1. Evidence from claimed memories of previous births, these memory claims being independently verified, e.g., *Twenty Cases Suggestive of Reincarnation* by Ian Stevenson (New York: American Society for Psychical Research, 1966). 2. Evidence from hypnotists' experiments, e.g., *Explorations of a Hypnotist* by Jonathan

Rodney (London: Elek Books, 1959). 3. Indirect evidence: From the findings of Edgar Cayce who successfully treated patients on the hypothesis of the law of good and bad deeds done in previous births, e.g., *Many Mansions* by Gina Cerminara (New York: William Sloan Associates, 1960).

233. Smart, *Yogi*, p. 84.

234. *No ce taṃ bhikkhave loke ādīnavo abhavissa nayidaṃ sattā loke nibbindeyyuṃ yasmā ca kho bhikkhave atthi loke ādīnavo tasmā sattā loke nibbindanti. A.*, I, p. 260.

235. *Iti kira Vāsseṭṭha avera citto bhikkhu, avera citto Brahmā. . .avyāpajjha citto bhikkhu, avyāpajjha citto Brahmā. . .asaṃkiliṭṭha citto bhikkhu, asaṃkiliṭṭha citto Brahmā; vasavattī bhikkhu, vasavattī Brahmā. Api nu kho vasavattissa bhikkhuno vasavattinā Brahmunā saddhiṃ saṃsandati sametī ti? Evam bho Gotama' Sādhu Vāseṭṭha. So vata Vāseṭṭha vasavattī bhikkhu kāyassa bhedā param maranā vasavattissa Brahmuno sahavyūpago bhavissatī ti ṭhānam etaṃ vijjatī ti. D.*, I, p. 252.

CHAPTER SEVEN FOOTNOTES

1. Kai Nielsen, 'On Fixing the Reference Range of God' in *Religious Studies*, Vol. 2, 1966-67, p. 36.

2. Ludwig Wittgenstein, 'A Lecture on Ethics' in *The Philosophical Review*, Vol. LXXIV, January 1965, p. 10.

3. Nielsen, '*On Fixing*', p. 30.

4. Hartshorne, *The Divine Relativity*, p. 60.

5. ibid., p. 76. Also, p. 143.

6. ibid., p. 88.

7. ibid., p. 143.

8. Paul Edwards, 'Some Notes on Anthropomorphic Theology' in *Religious Experience and Truth*, Ed. Sidney Hook (London: Oliver and Boyd, 1962), p. 245.

9. Smart, *Reasons and Faiths*, p. 138.

10. *Chāndogya Upaniṣad*, 6.2.1

11. *E.B.T.K.*, p. 97.

12. *samaññaṃ nātidhāveyya. M.*, III, pp. 230, 234.

13. *Tayo. . .nirutti pathā adhivacana-pathā paññatti-pathā asaṁkiṇṇā asaṁkiṇṇapubbā na saṁkīyanti na saṁkīyissanti appaṭikuṭṭhā samaṇehi brāhmaṇehi viññūhi. Katame tayo? Yaṃ hi. . .rūpaṃ atītaṃ niruddhaṃ vipariṇataṃ ahosī ti tassa saṅkhā ahosī ti tassa samaññā ahosī ti tassa paññatti. Na tassa saṅkhā atthī ti na tassa saṅkhā bhavissatī ti. . .vedanā. . .saññā. . .saṅkhārā . . .viññāṇaṃ. Yaṃ. . .rūpaṃ ajātaṃ apātubhutaṃ bhavissatī ti tassa saṅkhā . . .tassa samaññā. . .tassa paññatti. . .yaṃ rūpaṃ jātaṃ pātubhūtaṃ atthī ti tassa saṅkhā. . .tassa samaññā. . .tassa paññatti. Na Tassa saṅkhā ahosī ti na tassa saṅkhā bhavissatī ti. . . . Ye pi. . .ahetuvādā akiriyavādā natthikavādā te pi'me tayo niruttipathā adhivacanapathā paññattipathā na garahitabbaṃ na patikkositabbaṃ amaññiṃsu. Taṃ kissa hetu? Nindābyārosaṇā-bhayā ti. S.*, III, pp. 70-73.

14. *E.B.T.K.*, pp. 316-317.

15. *. . .puriso evaṃ vadeyya: ahaṃ yā imasmiṃ janapade janapadakalyāni, taṃ icchāmi taṃ kāmemī ti. Taṃ enaṃ evaṃ vadeyyuṃ: ambho purisa, yaṃ tvaṃ janapadakaḷyāniṃ icchasi kāmesi, jānāsi taṃ janapadakaḷyāniṃ: khattiyī vā vessī*

vā suddī vā'ti? Iti puṭṭho no'ti vadeyya. Taṃ enaṃ evaṃ vadeyyuṃ:' ambho purisa, yaṃ tvaṃ janapadakaḷyāniṃ icchasi kāmesi, jānāsi taṃ janapadakaḷyāniṃ: evaṃ nāmā evaṃ gottā iti vā'ti . . . dīghā vā majjhimā vā kālī vā sāmā vā maṅguracchavī vā'ti? Amukasmiṃ gāme vā nigame vā nagare vā ti? Iti puṭṭho no ti vadeyya. Taṃ enaṃ evaṃ vaddeyyuṃ: ambho purisa, yaṃ tvaṃ na jānāsi na passasi, taṃ tvaṃ icchasi kāmesi ti? Iti puṭṭho āmāti vadeyya. —Taṃ kiṃ naññasi Udāyi? Nanu evaṃ sante tassa purisassa appāṭihīrakatam bhāsitaṃ sampajjatī ti? M., II, pp. 32-33.

16. *D.*, I, p. 241.

17. *D.*, I, p. 243.

18. *Dhammanijjhānakkhantiyā kho Bhāradvāja, atthūpaparikkhā bahukārā; no ce tam atthaṃ upparikkheyya, nayidaṃ dhammā nijjhānaṃ khameyyuṃ; ca kho atthaṃ upaparikkhati, tasmā dhammā nijjhānaṃ khamanti, tasmā dhammanijjhānakkhantiyā atthūpaparikkhā bahukārā ti. M.*, II, p. 175; *M.L.S.*, II, p. 364.

19. Paul Schmidt, 'Frustrating Strategies in Religious Discussion' in *Religious Experience*, p. 296.

20. *Sacāyaṃ bhikkhave puggalo pañhaṃ puṭṭho samāno ṭhānāṭṭhāne na saṇṭhāti, parikappe na saṇṭhāti, aññavāde na saṇṭhāti, paṭipadāya na saṇṭhāti, evaṃ santāyaṃ bhikkhave puggalo akaccho hoti. A.*, I, pp. 197-8; *G.S.*, I, p. 179.

21. *The Many Faced Argument*, Eds. John Hick and Arthur McGill (London: Macmillan, 1968).

22. Norman Malcolm, 'Anselm's Ontological Arguments' in *The Philosophical Review*, Vol. LXIX, 1960, pp. 41-62. Quoted in *The Existence of God*, p. 52.

23. *Kin ti pana te, Udāyi, sake ācariyake evaṃ hotī ti? Amhākaṃ sake ācariyake evaṃ hoti: ayam paramo vaṇṇo, ayam paramo vaṇṇo ti. Katamo so paramo. vaṇṇo ti? Yasmā vaṇṇā añño uttarītaro vā panītataro vā natthi, so paramo vaṇṇo ti Katamo pana so vaṇṇo yasmā vaṇṇā añño vaṇṇo uttarītaro vā panītataro vā natthī ti? Yasmā vaṇṇā añño vaṇṇo uttarītaro vā paṇītataro vā natthi, so paramo vaṇṇo ti. Yasmā vaṇṇā añño vaṇṇo uttarītaro vā paṇītataro vā natthi, so paramo vaṇṇo ti vadasi; tañ can vaṇṇam na paññāpesi. Seyyathāpi puriso evaṃ vadeyya: Ahaṃ yā imasmiṃ janapade janapadakaḷyānī, taṃ icchāmi taṃ kāmemī ti. . .M.*, II, p. 32.

24. *M.*, II, pp. 33-34.

25. Malcolm, op. cit. p. 57.

26. ibid., p. 56.

27. ibid., p. 56.

28. ibid., p. 56.

29. ibid., p. 58.

30. ibid., p. 59.

31. ibid., *v*. 67.

32. Also, v. 6.20.

33. Raymond Firth, 'Gods and God' in *The Humanist Outlook*, Ed. A.J. Ayer (London: Pemberton, 1968), p. 31.

34. Peter A. Bertocci, 'The Person God Is', in *Talk of God*, p. 185.

35. William Hamilton, 'The New Essence of Christianity' in *Toward a New Christianity: Readings in the Death of God Theology*, Ed. Thomas J.J. Altizer (New York: Harcourt Brace and World, 1967), p. 269.

36. ibid., p. 272.

37. D.Z. Phillips, 'From World to God' in *The Proceedings of the Aristotelian Society:* Supplementary Volume XLI, 1967, p. 145.

38. ibid., p. 145.

39. ibid., p. 148.

40. ibid., p. 148-149.

41. ibid., p. 151.

42. John Hick, 'The Nature of Faith' in *Philosophy of Religion*, Eds. George L. Abernathy and Thomas A. Langford (New York: Macmillan, 1962), p. 266.

43. John Hick, 'Meaning and Truth in Theology' in *Religious Experience*, p. 207.

44. Norman Malcolm, 'Is it a Religious Belief that God Exists?' in *Faith and the Philosophers*, Ed. John Hick (London: Macmillan, 1964), p. 110.

45. John Wisdom, 'Gods' in *Philosophy and Psychoanalysis* (Oxford: Basil Blackwell, 1953),pp. 149-159. Quoted in *Philosophy of Religion*, p. 349.

46. J.L. Stocks, 'The Validity of the Belief in a Personal God' in *The Proceedings of the Aristotelian Society*: Supplementary Volume, VI, 1926, p. 73.

47. ibid., p. 71.

48. Bertocci, '*The Person God Is*', p. 196.

49. ibid., p. 197.

50. John A.T. Robinson, *Honest to God and the Debate* (London: SCM Press, 1963), p. 49.

51. loc. cit.

52. ibid., p. 53.

53. William Mallard, 'A Perspective for Current Theological Conversation' in *Toward a New Christianity*, p. 336.

54. Hamilton, '*The New Essence*', p. 281.

55. Robinson, *Honest to God*, p. 75.

56. Hamilton, '*The New Essence*', p. 276.

57. ibid., p. 279.

58. Mallard, ibid., p. 339.

59. Renford Bambrough, *Reason, Truth and God* (London: Methuen, 1969), p. 27.

60. ibid., p. 28; p. 39.

61. Renford Bambrough, 'Reason, Truth, and God', in *Religion and Humanism*, Ed. Ronald Hepburn (London: BBC, 1964), pp. 46-47.

62. E.E. Evans-Pritchard, *Nuer Religion* (Oxford: Clarendon Press, 1967), p. 2.

63. ibid., pp. 2-3.

64. ibid., p. 7.

65. ibid., pp. 315-316.

66. ibid., p. 13.

67. ibid., p. 13.

68. ibid., p. 18.

69. ibid., p. 17.

70. ibid., p. 27.

71. ibid., p. 4.

72. ibid., p. 9.

73. ibid., p. 13.

74. ibid., pp. 123-143.

75. ibid., p. 322.
76. E.E. Evans-Pritchard, *Essays in Social Anthropology* (Chapter on Azande Theology), London: Faber & Faber, 1962.
77. ibid., p. 168.
78. ibid., p. 168.
79. ibid., pp. 201-202.
80. Credo Mutwa, *My People: Writings of a Zulu Witchdoctor* (Harmondsworth: Penguin Books, 1971), pp. 176-177.
81. John Hick, '*Meaning and Truth in Theology*', pp. 208-209.
82. Mutwa, op. cit., p. 177.
83. ibid., p. 176.
84. E.E. Evans Pritchard, 'Religion' in *The Institutions of Primitive Society* (Oxford: Basil Blackwell, 1967), p. 1.
85. *Bahuṃ ve saraṇaṃ yanti, pabbatāni vanāni ca, ārāmarukkhacetyāni, manussā bhayatajjitā. Dhp., ix.* 10.
86. Mutawa, op. cit., pp. 227-228.
87. Godfrey Lienhardt, 'Modes of Thought' in *The Institutions*, p. 100.
88. E.E. Evans-Pritchard, *Witchcraft, Oracles and Magic Among the Azande* (Oxford: Clarendon Press, 1968), pp. 65-66.
89. ibid., pp. 67-68.
90. Max Gluckman, 'The Logic of African Science and Witchcraft' in *Witchcraft and Sorcery*, Ed. Max Marwick (Harmondsworth: Penguin Books, 1970), pp. 327-328.
91. Evans-Pritchard, *Witchcraft*, p. 330.
92. John Hick, 'Theology and Verification' in *Theology Today*, 17 (1960), pp. 12, 31.
93. Monica Hunter Wilson, 'Witch-Beliefs and Social Structure' in *Witchcraft and Sorcery*, p. 253.
94. ibid., p. 255.
95. Evans-Pritchard, *Witchcraft*, pp. 319-320.
96. Robin Horton, 'African Traditional Thought and Western Science' in *Witchcraft and Sorcery*, p. 237.
97. J.D. Krige, 'The Social Function of Witchcraft' in *Witchcraft and Sorcery*, p. 237.
98. Clyde Kluckhohn, *Navaho Witchcraft* (Boston: Beacon Press, 1967), p. 82.
99. Krige, op. cit., p. 242.
100. ibid., p. 243.
101. ibid., pp. 250-251.
102. A. Rebecca Cardozo, 'A Modern American Witchcraze' in *Witchcraft and Sorcery*, pp. 369-377.
103. Horton, op. cit., pp. 366-367.
104. ibid., p. 367.

CHAPTER EIGHT FOOTNOTES

1. F. Gerald Downing, *Has Christianity a Revelation?* (London: SCM Press, 1964), p. 238.
2. ibid., p. 241.

3. Quoted in 'Contemporary Views of Revelation' by James I. Packer, in *Revelation and the Bible*, Ed. Carl F.H. Henry (London: The Tyndale Press, 1959), p. 96.

4. Packer, ibid., p. 101.

5. ibid., pp. 103-104.

6. Karl Barth, *Church Dogmatics*, Tr. G.T. Thomson (Edinburgh: T & T Clark, 1936), Vol. I, p. 211.

7. ibid., pp. 192-193.

8. ibid., p. 188.

9. ibid., p. 209.

10. ibid., p. 192.

11. ibid., p. 163.

12. ibid., p. 190.

13. ibid., p. 208.

14. ibid., p. 211.

15. ibid., p. 161.

16. ibid., p. 211.

17. Paul Tillich, *Sytematic Theology*, Vol. I, p. 119.

18. loc. cit.

19. ibid., p. 123.

20. ibid., p. 131.

21. ibid., p. 141.

22. ibid., p. 145.

23. ibid., p. 148.

24. ibid., p. 150.

25. ibid., p. 160.

26. Rudolf Bultmann, 'The Concept of Revelation in the New Testament' in *Existence and Faith*, Tr. Schubert M. Ogden (London: Hodder and Stoughton, 1961), p. 86.

27. ibid., p. 87.

28. ibid., p. 79.

29. ibid., p. 72.

30. ibid., p. 85.

31. Richard H. Niebuhr, *The Meaning of Revelation* (New York: Macmillan paperback, 1967), p. 57.

32. ibid., p. 27.

33. ibid., p. 69.

34. ibid., p. 61.

35. Karl Rahner, *Theological Investigations*, Tr. Cornelius Ernst (London: Darton, Longman & Todd, 1965), Vol. I, p. 49.

36. ibid., p. 98.

37. *sutenāpi vadanti suddhiṃ. Sn.*, 1079.

38. *E.B.T.K.*, p. 182.

39. *Etha tumhe Kālāmā mā anussavena mā paramparāya mā itikirāya mā piṭakasampadānena mā takkahetu mā nayahetu mā ākāraparivitakkena mā diṭṭhinjjhāhakkhantiyā mā bhavyarūpatāya mā samaṇo no garū ti, yadā tumhe Kālāmā attanā va jāneyyātha—ime dhammā akusalā ime dhammā sāvajjā ime dhammā viññūgarahitā ime dhammā samattā samādinnā ahitāya dukkhāya saṃvattantī ti—atha tumhe Kālāmā pajaheyyātha. A.*, I, p. 189.

40. *M.*, I, pp. 169-170.

41. *Pañca kho ime . . . dhammā diṭṭhe va dhamme dvidhā vipākā. Katame pañca? Saddhā, ruci, anussavo, ākāraparivitakko, diṭṭhinijjhānakkhanti . . . Api ca svānussutaṃ yeva hoti tañca hoti rittaṃ tucchaṃ musā; no ce pi svānussutaṃ, tañca hoti bhūtam tacchaṃ anaññathā . . . Saccaṃ anurakkhatā . . . viññunā purisena nālaṃ ettha ekaṃsena niṭṭhaṃ gantuṃ: idaṃ eva saccaṃ mogham aññan ti. M.*, II, pp. 170-171. Translation by Jayatilleke, *E.B.T.K.*, p. 184.

42.*Kittāvatā kho pana, bho Gotama, saccānurakkhaṇā hoti? Kittāvatā saccaṃ anurakkhati? Saccānurakkhaṇaṃ mayaṃ bhavantaṃ Gotamaṃ pucchāmā ti.* loc. cit.

43. *Anussavo ce pi. . .purisassa hoti, evam me anussavo ti vadaṃ saccaṃ anurakkhati, na tveva tāva ekaṃsena niṭṭham gacchati: idameva saccaṃ mogham aññan ti.* loc. cit.

44. *E.B.T.K.*, p. 185.

45. *idh'ekacco satthā anussaviko hoti anussavasacco, so anussavena itihītihaparamparāya piṭakasampadāya dhammaṃ deseti. Anussavikassa kho pana . . .satthuno anussavasaccassa sussatampi hoti dussatampi hoti, tathā pi hoti aññathā pi hoti. Tatra viññū puriso iti paṭisañcikkhati: Ayaṃ kho bhavaṃ satthā anussaviko. . .So anassāsikaṃ idaṃ brahmacariyam ti iti viditvā tasmā brahmacariyā nibbijja pakkamati. M*, I, p. 520.

46. *E.B.T.K.*, p. 186.

47. *brahmacariyaṃ anītihaṃ. . .adesayī so Bhagavā. A.*, II, p. 26.

48. *dhammo anītiho. Th.*, I, p. 331.

49. *Ye te evam āhaṃsu: Samaṇo Gotamo sabbaññū sabbadassāvī, aparisesaṃ ñāṇadassanaṃ paṭijānāti: carato ca me tiṭṭhato ca suttassa ca jāgarassa ca satataṃ samitaṃ ñāṇadassanaṃ paccupaṭṭhitan ti, na me te vuttavādino, abbhācikkhanti ca pana man te asatā abhūtenā ti. M.*, I., p. 482. Translation by Jayatilleke, *E.B.T.K.*, p. 468.

50. *Tevijjo Samaṇo Gotamo ti. . .byākaramāno vuttavādi c'eva me assa na ca maṃ abhūtena abbhācikkheyya.* loc. cit.

51. *M.*, I, p. 386.

52. *sabbaññū, sabbadassāvī. Kvu.*, p. 228.

53. *E.B.T.K.*, p. 386.

54. *vīmaṃsakena bhikkhunā parassa cetopariyāyam ajānantena Tathāgate samannesanā kātabbā, sammāsambuddho vā no vā iti viññāṇāyā ti. M.*, I, p. 317. The key word in this passage '*ajānantena*' (By one who does *not* know) has been misprinted as '*ājānantena*' (by one who knows) in the P.T.S. edition. If this word is taken as '*ājānantena*' then the passage does not make any sense. Although the word is correctly given in all the Sinhalese and Nagari manuscripts and editions, Jayatilleke has, accidentally, followed the P.T.S. misprint. See, *Sūtra Piṭaka*, Ed. Kirielle Gnanawimala (Ratnapura: Sastrodaya Press, 1960), p. 317; Also *Majjhima Nikāya* (Nalanda Devanagari Pali Grantha Mala), Ed. P.V. Bapat (Pali Publications: Bihar Government, 1958), p. 389.

55. *dvīsu dhammesu Tathāgato samannesitabbo cakkhusotaviññeyyesu dhammesu, M.*, I, p. 318.

56. *Ye saṅkiliṭṭhā. . .vitimissā cakkhusotaviññeyyā dhammā na te Tathāgatassa saṃvijjanti. . .ye vodāta cakkhusotaviññeyyā dhammā saṃvijjanti te Tathāgatassā ti. M.*, I, p. 318; *E.B.T.K.*, pp. 392-393.

57. *evaṃvādiṃ. . .satthāraṃ arahati sāvako upasaṅkamituṃ dhammasavaṇāya. M.*, I. p. 319. Translation by Jayatilleke, *E.B.T.K.*, p. 393.

58. *tasmiṃ dhamme abhiññāya idh'ekaccaṃ dhammaṃ dhammesu niṭṭhaṃ agamaṃ, satthari pasīdiṃ: sammāsambuddho bhagavā, svākkhāto bhagavatā dhammo supaṭipanno saṅgho ti. M.*, I, p. 320.

59. *yassa kassa ci. . .imehi ākārehi imehi padehi imehi byañjanehi. . .saddhā niviṭṭhā hoti mūlajātā patiṭṭhitā, ayaṃ vuccati. . .'ākāravatī saddhā' dassanamūlikādaḷhā asamhāriyā samaṇena vā brāhmaṇena vā devena vā Mārena vā Brahmuṇā vā kenaci vā lokasmiṃ.* loc. cit.

60. *E.B.T.K.*, p. 393.

61. *Saddhājāto upasaṅkamanto payirupāsati, payirupāsanto, sotaṃ odahati, ohitasoto dhammaṃ suṇāti, sutvā dhammaṃ dhāreti, dhāritānaṃ dhammānaṃ atthaṃ upaparikkhati, attham upaparikkhato dhammā nijjhānaṃ khamanti, dhammanijjhānakkhantiyā sati chando jāyati, chandajāto ussahati, ussahitvā tūleti, tūlayitvo padahati, pahitatto samāno kāyena c'eva paramasaccaṃ sacchikaroti, paññāya ca taṃ ativijjha passati, M.*, II, p. 173.

62. *saddahasi tvaṃ samaṇassa Gotamassa atthi avitakko avicāro samādhi atthi vitakkavicārānaṃ nirodho ti?; na khvāhaṃ saddhāya gacchāmi; passantu yāva ujuko c'āyaṃ citto gahapati yāva asaṭho amāyāvi. . .; taṃ kim maññasi? katamaṃ nu kho paṇītataraṃ ñāṇaṃ vā saddhā?; saddhāya kho gahapati, ñāṇaṃ eva paṇītataraṃ; so khvāham evaṃ jānanto evam passanto kassaññassa samaṇassa vā brāhmanassa vā saddhāya gamissāmi, atthi avitakko avicāro samādhi. . .S.*, IV, p. 298.

63. *assaddho. Dh.*, 97.

64. *aññatra saddhāya. . .aññaṃ vyākareyya. S.*, IV, p. 138.

65. *D.*, II, p. 150.

66. *natthi. . .ekabhikkhu pi tena Bhagavatā. . .ṭhapito: ayaṃ vo mam'accayena paṭisaraṇaṃ bhavissatī ti. M.*, III, p. 9.

67. *kiṃ hi te. . .mahatī janatā karissati, iṅgha tvaṃ sakaṃ yeva vādaṃ nibbeṭhehi. M.*, I, p. 230.

68. Austin Farrer, 'Revelation' in *Faith and Logic*, pp. 105-106.

69. ibid., p. 107.

70. ibid., p. 102.

71. See, for example, Peter Worsley, *The Trumpet Shall Sound: A Study of 'Cargo' Cults in Melanesia* (London: Paladin, 1970), especially pp. 234-235.

72. Robinson, *Honest to God and the Debate*, p. 29.

73. *E.B.T.K.*, p. 275.

74. *Sn.*, §§ 885, 886.

75. *Sn.*, §886.

76. *takkena vitakkena saṁkappena yāyanti niyyanti vuyhanti. . .athavā takkapariyāhataṃ vīmaṃsānucaritaṃ sayampaṭibhānaṃ vadanti kathenti. . .Nd.*, I, p. 294.

77. *Tattha catubbidho takkī, anussustiko jātissaro lābhī suddhatakkiko ti. Tattha yo 'Vessantaro nāma rājā ahosī ti ādīni sutvā, tena hi 'yadi Vessantaro' va Bhagavā sassato attā ti takkayanto diṭṭhiṃ gaṇhāti, ayaṃ anussutiko nāma. Dve tisso jātiyo saritvā, 'aham eva pubbe asukasmiṃ nāma ahosiṃ, tasmā sassato attā' ti takkayanto jatissaratakki nāma. Yo pana lābhitāya, 'yathā me idāni attā sukhito atīte evam āsi, anāgate pi evaṃ bhavissatī' ti takkayitvā diṭṭhiṃ gaṇhāti, ayaṃ lābhī takkiko nāma. 'Evaṃ sati idaṃ hoti, evaṃ sati idaṃ na hotī, ti takkamatten'eva*

pana gaṇhanto suddha-takkiko namā. D.A., I, pp. 106, 107. Translation by Jayatilleke, *E.B.T.K.*, pp. 262-263.

78. *Idh'ekacco satthā takkī hoti vīmaṃsī, so takkapariyāhataṃ, vīmaṃsānucaritaṃ sayaṃ paṭibhānaṃ dhammaṃ deseti. Takkissa kho pana. . .satthuno vīmaṃsissa sutakkitam pi hoti duttakkitam pi hoti, tathā pi hoti aññathāpi hoti. M.*, I, p. 520.

79. *api ca. . .suparivitakkitaṃ yeva hoti. . .sunijjhāyitaṃ yeva hoti, tañ ca hoti rittaṃ tucchaṃ musā; no ce pi suparivitakkitaṃ hoti, no ce sunijjhāyitaṃ hoti, tañ ca hoti bhūtaṃ tucchaṃ anaññathā. M.*, II, p. 171.

80. *M.*, I, p. 68.

81. *S.*, I, p. 56.

82. *Taṃ kiṃ maññatha Kālāmā? Lobho purisassa ajjhattaṃ uppajjamāno uppajjati hitāya vā ahitayā ti? Ahitāya bhante. . Taṃ kiṃ maññatha Kālāmā? Alobho purisassa ajjhattaṃ uppajjamāno uppajjati hitāya vā ahitāya vā ti? Hitāya bhante. . .Sa kho so Kālāmā ariyasāvako evaṃ vigatābhijjho vigatavyāpādo asammūḷho sampajāno patissato mettāsahagatena cetasā. . .karuṇāsahagatena cetasā. . .ekaṃ disaṃ pharitvā viharati. . A.*, I, pp. 189-192.

83. Gordon H. Clark, 'Special Divine Revelation as Rational' in *Revelation and the Bible*, p. 41.

84. *dhammo. . .paccattaṃ veditabbo viññūhi. A.*, II, p. 56.

85. *paññavato ayaṃ dhammo, nāyaṃ dhammo duppaññassa. A.*, IV, p. 229.

CHAPTER NINE FOOTNOTES

1. Milan Kundera, *The Unbearable Lightness of Being*. London: Faber & Faber, 1984, p. 289

2. *Yathā mātā yathā bhātā, aññevāpi ca ñātakā gāvo no paramā mittā yāsu jāyanti osadhā. Annadā baladā ceta, vaṇṇadā sukhadā tathā, etamatthavasaṃ ñatvā, nassu gāvo hanimsu te.* Su., § 296.

3. Reuven Allon Maimon. 'Judaism versus Animal Cruelty', in *Jewish Press*, Fiday, May 23, 1986, p. 15.

4. Kundera, p. 286.

5. Gunapala Dharmasiri. "Buddhism and the Modern World", in *Fundamentals of Buddhist Ethics*, Golden Leaves, 1988.

6. Nanananda, *Concept and Reality*. Kandy, B. P. S.

7. Karen Lindsey. "Spiritual Explorers", in *Ms.* December, 1985, p. 89.

8. Ibid., p. 90.

9. Gloria Steinem. "Shirley MacLaine Talks About Spirit Vs. Action", in *Ms.* December, 1985, p. 100.

10. Robert A. F. Thurman. *The Holy Teaching of Vimalakirti*, Pennsylvania State University Press, 1976, pp. 61-62

11. "Bloody Sacrifice", in *India Today*, July, 15, 1985, p. 77.

Bibliography

A. Pali Texts and Translations

Aṅguttara Nikāya, Eds. R. Morris and E. Hardy, 5 Vols., London: PTS, 1885-1900. Trs. F.L. Woodward and E.M. Hare, *The Book of the Gradual Sayings,* 5 Vols., London: PTS., 1932-1936.

Dhammapada, Ed. S. Sumangala Thero, London: PTS, 1914.

Dīgha Nikāya, Eds. T.W. Rhys Davids and J.E. Carpenter, 3 Vols., London: PTS, 1890-1911. Trs. T.W. and C.A.F. Rhys Davids, *Dialogues of the Buddha*, SBB., Vols. 2,3 and 4, London: O.U.P., 1899-1921.

Itivuttaka, Ed. E. Windisch, London: PTS., 1889.

Jātaka, Ed. V. Fausboll, 6 Vols. and index, London PTS., 1895-1907.

Kathāvatthu, Ed. A.C. Taylor, 2 Vols., London: PTS., 1894-1897. Trs. Shwe Zan Aung and C.A.F. Rhys Davids, *Points of Controversy*, London: PTS., 1960.

Kathāvatthuppakaraṇa Aṭṭhakathā, Commentary to *Kathāvatthu*. Printed in *Journal of the Pali Text Society*, 1889, pp. 1-199.

Majjhima Nikāya, Eds. V. Trenkner and R. Chalmers, 3 Vols., London: PTS., 1948-1951, Tr. I.B. Horner, *Middle Length Sayings*, 3 Vols., London: PTS., 1954-1959. *Majjhima Nikāya* in *Sūtra Piṭaka*, Ed. Kirielle Gnanawimala Thero, Ratnapura: Sastrodaya Press, 1960. *Majjhima Nikāya*, Ed. P.V. Bapat, Pali Publications: Bihar Government, 1958.

Manorathapūraṇī, Commentary to *Aṅguttara Nikāya*, Eds. M. Walleser and H. Kopp, 5 Vols., London: PTS., 1924-1956.

Milindapañha, Ed. V. Trenkner, London: PTS., 1928.

Nettippakaraṇa, Ed. E. Hardy, London: PTS., 1902.

Niddesa, I., *Mahāniddesa*, Eds. L. de la V. Poussin and E.J. Thomas, 2 Vols., II. *Cullaniddesa*, Ed. W. Stede, London: PTS., 1916-1918.

Papañcasūdanī, Commentary to *Majjhima Nikāya*, Eds. J.H. Woods, D. Kosambi and I.B. Horner, 5 Vols., London: PTS., 1922-1938.

Paramatthadīpanī, Commentary to *Khuddaka Nikāya*, Part III, Ed. E. Hardy, London: PTS., 1894.

Paramatthajotikā, II. Commentary to *Sutta Nipāta*, Ed. H. Smith, 3 Vols. in II, London: PTS., 1916-1918.

Saṃyutta Nikāya, Ed. L. Feer, 6 Vols., London: PTS., 1884-1904. Trs. C.A.F. Rhys Davids and F.L. Woodward, *The Book of the Kindred Sayings*, 5 Vols., London: PTS., 1917-1930.

Sāratthappakāsinī, Commentary to *Saṃyutta Nikāya*, Ed. F.L. Woodward, 3 Vols., London: PTS., 1929-1937.

Sumaṅgalavilāsinī, Commentary to *Dīgha Nikāya*, Eds. T.W. Rhys Davids, J.E. Carpenter and W. Stede, 3 Vols., London: PTS., 1886-1932.

Suttanipāta, Eds. D. Anderson and H. Smith, London: PTS., 1948. Tr. V. Fausboll, SBE., Vol. 10, Part 2, Oxford, 1881.

Thera- and *Therīgathā*, Eds. H. Oldenberg and R. Pischel, London: PTS., 1883. Tr. C.A.F. Rhys Davids, *Psalms of the Early Buddhists*, 2 Vols., London: PTS., 1903-1913.

Udāna, Ed. P. Steinthal, London: PTS., 1904.

Visuddhimagga by Buddhaghosa, Ed. C.A.F. Rhys Davids, 2 Vols., London: PTS., 1920-1921. Tr. Bhikkhu Nyanamoli, *The Path of Purification*, A. Semage, Colombo, 1964.

B. MONOGRAPHS

Altizer, Thomas J.J., *The Gospel of Christian Atheism*, London: Collins, 1967.

Altizer, Thomas J.J. and Hamilton, William, *Radical Theology and the Death of God*, Harmondsworth: Pelican Books, 1968.

Anscombe, G.E.M. and Geach, P.T., *Three Philosophers*, Oxford: Basil Blackwell, 1963.

Ayer, A.J., *The Concept of a Person*, London: Macmillan, 1963.

Ayer, A.J., *The Problem of Knowledge*, London: Macmillan, 1958.

Baillie, John, *The Sense of the Presence of God*, London: O.U.P., 1962.

Baillie, John, *Our Knowledge of God*, London: O.U.P., 1949.

Bambrough, Renford, *Reason, Truth and God*, London: Methuen, 1969.

Barth, Karl, *Church Dogmatics: The Doctrine of the Word of God*, Vol. 1, Part 1. Tr. G.T. Thomson, Edinburgh: T & T Clark, 1936.

Barth, Karl, *Church Dogmatics: The Doctrine of the Word of God*, Vol. II, Part 1. Eds G.W. Bromiley and T.F. Torrance, Trs. T.H.L. Parker, W.B. Johnston, Harold Knight and J.C.M. Haire, Edinburgh: T & T Clark, 1964.

Barth, Karl, *Church Dogmatics: The Doctrine of Creation*, Vol. III, Part 1. Eds. G.W. Bromiley and T.F. Torrance. Trs. J.W. Edwards, O. Bussey and Harold Knight, Edinburgh: T & T Clark, 1958.

Barth, Karl, *Church Dogmatics: The Doctrine of Creation*, Vol. III, Part 2. Eds. G.W. Bromiley and T.F. Torrance. Trs. Harold Knight, G.W. Bromiley, J.K.S. Reid and R.H. Fuller, Edinburgh: T & T Clark, 1960.

Barth, Karl, *Church Dogmatics: The Doctrine of Creation*, Vol. III, Part 3. Eds. G.W. Bromiley and T.F. Torrance. Trs. G.W. Bromiley, R.J. Ehrlich, Edinburgh: T & T Clark, 1961.

Bonhoeffer, D., *Ethics*, Ed. Eberherd Bethge, London: SCM Press, 1955.

Brunner, Emil, *The Divine Imperative: A Study in Christian Ethics*, Tr. Olive Wyon, London: Lutterworth Press, 1939.

Brunner, Emil, *The Christian Doctrine of God: Dogmatics*, Tr. Olive Wyon, London: Lutterworth Press, 1962.

Bultmann, R. *Existence and Faith*, Tr. Schubert M. Ogden, London: Hodder & Stoughton, 1961.

Buri, Fritz, *Theology of Existence*, Trs. H.H. Oliver and G. Onder, Greenwood S.C.: The Attic Press, 1965.

Campbell, C.A. , *On Selfhood and Godhood*, London: Allen & Unwin, 1957.

Casteneda, Carlos, *The Teachings of Don Juan: A Yaqui Way of Knowledge*, Harmondsworth: Penguin Books, 1970.

Cerminara, Gina, *Many Mansions*, New York: William Sloan Associates, 1960.

Chardin, Teilhard de, *The Phenomenon of Man*, London: Collins, 1961.

Chardin, Teilhard de, *The Future of Man*, Tr. Norman Denny, London: Collins 1964.

Chardin, Teilhard de, *Le Milieu Divin*, London: Collins, 1961.

Chardin, Teilhard de, *Letters from a Traveller*, London: Collins, 1962.

Cobb, John B., *A Christian Natural Theology*, London: Lutterworth Press, 1966.

Cohen, Sydney, *Drugs of Hallucination*, London: Paladin Books, 1970.

Cuenot, Claude, *Science and Faith in Teilhard de Chardin*, London: Garnstone Press, 1967.

Downing, F. Gerald, *Has Christianity a Revelation?* London: SCM Press, 1964.

Ducasse, C.J., *A Philosophical Scrunity of Religion*, New York: The Ronald Press, 1953.

Dutt, Nalinaksha, *Aspects of Mahayana Buddhism and its Relation to Hinayana*, London: Luzac & Co., 1930.

Eckhart, Meister, *Meister Eckhart*, Tr. R.B. Blakney, New York: Harper & Row, 1941.

Evans-Pritchard, E.E., *Neur Religion*, Oxford: Clarendon Press, 1967.

Evans-Pritchard, E.E., *Witchcraft, Oracles and Magic Among the Azande*, Oxford: Clarendon Press, 1968.

Evans-Pritchard, E.E., *Essays in Social Anthropology*, London: Faber & Faber, 1962.

Farmer, H.H., *Toward Belief in God*, London: SCM Press, 1942.

Flew, Antony, *God and Philosophy*, London: Hutchinson, 1966.

Geach, Peter, *God and the Soul*, London: Kegan Paul, 1969.

Gore, C., *Belief in God*, Harmondsworth: Penguin Books, 1939.

Hartshorne, Charles, *A Natural Theology for Our Time*, Illinois: Open Court, 1967.

Hawkins, D.J.B., *The Essentials of Theism*, London: Sheed and Ward, 1949.

Hick, John, *Philosophy of Religion*, New Jersey, Prentice Hall, 1963.

Hume, David, *Dialogues Concerning Natural Religion*, Ed. Henry D. Aiken, New York: Hafner Publishing Co., 1962.

James, William, *The Pluralistic Universe*, New York: Longmans, 1909.

Jayatilleke, K.N., *Early Buddhist Theory of Knowledge*, London: Allen & Unwin, 1963.

Johansson, E.A. Rune, *The Psychology of Nirvana*, London: Allen & Unwin, 1969.

John of the Cross, St., *The Complete Works of Saint John of the Cross*, Ed. E. Allison Peers, London: Burns Oates & Washbourne, 1934.

Keith, A.B., *Buddhist Philosophy In India and Ceylon*, Oxford: University Press, 1923.

Kluckhohn, Clyde, *Navaho Witchcraft*, Boston: Beacon Press, 1967.

Koestler, Arthur, *The Invisible Writing*, New York: Macmillan, 1954.
Koestler, Arthur, *Drinkers of Infinity*, London: Hutchinson, 1968.
Leary, Timothy, *The Politics of Ecstasy*, London: Paladin Books, 1970.
Lehmann, Paul, *Ethics in a Christian Context*, New York: Harper & Row, 1963.
Lewis, H.D., *Philosopgy of Religion*, London: O.U.P., 1965.
Louria, Donald B., *The Drug Scene*, London: Corgi Books, 1970.
Macquarrie, John, *Studies in Christian Existentialism*, London: SCM Press, 1965.
Malalasekera, G.P. and Jayatilleke, K.N., *Buddhism and the Race Question*, Paris, UNESCO, 1958.
McTaggart, J.E., *Some Dogmas of Religion*, London: Edward Arnold, 1906.
Maritain, Jacques, *Redeeming the Time*, Tr. Harry Loris Binsse, London: Geoffrey Bles, 1946.
Maritain, Jacques, *Existence and the Existent*, Tr. Lewis Galantiere and Gerald B. Phelan, New York: Vintage Books, 1966.
Maritain, Jacques, *The Range of Reason*, London: Geoffrey Bles, 1953.
Maritain, Jacques, *Approaches to God*, London: Allen & Unwin, 1955.
Martin, C.B., *Religious Belief*, New York: Cornell University Press, 1962.
Mill, J.S., *Theism*, Ed. Richard Taylor, New York: The Liberal Arts Press, 1957.
Mill, J.S., *An Examination of Sir William Hamilton's Philosophy*, London: Longmans, 1872.
Mutwa, Credo, *My People: Writings of a Zulu Witchdoctor*, Harmondsworth: Penguin Books, 1971.
Niebuhr, Reinhold, *The Self and the Dramas of History*, London: Faber & Faber, 1956.
Niebuhr, Richard H., *The Meaning of Revelation*, New York: Macmillan Paperback, 1967.
Otto, Rudolf, *The Idea of the Holy*, Tr. J.W. Harvey, London: O.U.P., 1957.
Otto Rudolf, *Mysticism East and West*, Trs. B.L. Bracey and R.C. Payne, London: Macmillan, 1932.
Owen, H.P., *The Moral Argument for Christian Theism*, London: Allen & Unwin, 1965.
Paul van Buren, M., *The Secular Meaning of the Gospel*, London: SCM Press, 1963.
Paul van Buren, M., *Theological Explorations*, London: SCM Press, 1968.
Plantinga, Alvin, *God and Other Minds*, New York: Cornell University Press, 1967.
Rahner, Karl, *Theological Investigations: God, Christ, Mary and Grace*, Vol. I, Tr. Cornelius Ernst, London: Darton, Longman and Todd, 1965.
Rahner, Karl, *Theological Investigations: Later Writings*, Vol. 5, Tr. Karl H. Kruger, London: Darton, Longman and Todd, 1966.
Richmond, James, *Theology and Metaphysics*, London: SCM Press, 1970.
Robinson, J.A.T., *Honest to God*, London: SCM Press, 1963.
Robinson, J.A.T., *Honest to God and the Debate*, London: SCM Press, 1963.
Robinson, J.A.T., *Exploration into God*, London: SCM Press, 1967.
Rodney, Jonathan, *Explorations of a Hypnotist*, London: Elek Books, 1959.
Ryle, Gilbert, *The Concept of Mind*, Harmondsworth: Penguin Books, 1963.
Smart, Ninian, *Philosophers and Religious Truth*, London: SCM Press, 1969.
Smart, Ninian, *Reasons and Faiths*, London: Kegan Paul, 1958.
Smart, Ninian, *The Yogi and the Devotee*, London: Allen & Unwin, 1968.

Smith, Wilfred Cantwell, *Questions of Religious Truth*, London: Victor Gollancz, 1967.

Sorley, W.R., *Moral Value and the Idea of God*, Cambridge: University Press, 1921.

Stace, W.T., *Mysticism and Philosophy*, London: Macmillan, 1961.

Stevenson, Ian, *Twenty Cases Suggestive of Reincarnation*, New York: American Society for Psychical Research, 1966.

Strawson, P.F.S., *Individuals*, London: Methuen, 1965.

Taylor, A.E., *Does God Exist?* London: Macmillan, 1947.

Teresa, St., *The Complete Works of St. Teresa of Jesus*, Ed. Allison Peers, London: Sheed and Ward, 1957.

Teresa, St., *Interior Castle*, London: Thomas Baker, 1930.

The Report on the 1922 Commission on Doctrine in the Church of England, London: S.P.C.K., 1938.

Tillich, Paul, *Christianity and the Encounter of the World Religions*, New York: Columbia University Press, 1963.

Tillich, Paul, *Systematic Theology*, Vol. I, London: Nisbet, 1955.

Tillich, Paul, *Systematic Theology*, Vol. III, London: Nisbet, 1964.

Underhill, Evelyn, *Mysticism, London: Methuen, 1962.*

Waismann, F., How I See Philosophy, Ed. R. Harre, London: Macmillan, 1968.

Wisdom, John, *Paradox and Discovery*, Oxford: Basil Blackwell, 1965.

Wisdom, John, *Philosophy and Psycho-analysis*, Oxford: Basil Blackwell, 1953.

Wittgenstein, Ludwig, *Notebooks 1914-16*, Ed. C.H. Von Wright and G.E.M. Anscombe. Tr. G.E.M. Anscombe, Oxford: Basil Blackwell, 1961.

Worsley, Peter, *The Trumpet Shall Sound: A Study of Cargo Cults in Melanesia*, London: Paladin Books, 1970.

C. ANTHOLOGIES

Abernathy, George L. and Thomas A. Langford, Eds. *Philosophy of Religion*, New York: Macmillan, 1962.

Alston, W.P., Ed., *Religious Belief and Philosophical Thought*, New York: Harcourt Brace & World, 1963.

Altizer, Thomas J.J., Ed., *Toward a New Christianity: Readings in the Death of God Theology*, New York: Harcourt Brace & World, 1967.

Ayer, A.J., Ed., *The Humanist Outlook*, London: Pamberton, 1968.

Feaver, Clayton and Horosz, William, *Religion in Philosophical and Cultural Perspective*, Princeton: Van Nostrand, 1967.

Flew, Antony and MacIntyre, Alasdair, Eds., *New Essays in Philosophical Theology*, London: SCM Press, 1963.

Henry, Carl F.H., Ed., *Revelation and the Bible*, London: The Tyndale Press, 1959.

Hick, John, Ed., *The Existence of God*, New York: Macmillan, 1964.

Hick, John, Ed., *Faith and the Philosophers*, London: Macmillan, 1964.

Hick, John, and McGill, Arthur, Eds., *The Many Faced Argument*, London: Macmillan, 1968.

Hook, Sidney, Ed., *Religious Experience and Truth*, London: Oliver and Boyd, 1962.

Lessa, William A. and Vogt, Evon Z., Eds., *A Reader in Comparative Religion: An Anthropological Approach*, New York: Harper & Row, 1965.

Lewis, H.D., Ed., *Clarity is not Enough*, London: Allen & Unwin, 1963.

Marwick, Max, Ed., *Witchcraft and Sorcery: Penguin Modern Sociology Readings*, Harmondsworth: Penguin Books, 1970.

Metzner, Ralph, Ed., *The Ecstatic Adventure*, New York: Macmillan, 1968.

Mitchell, Basil, Ed., *Faith and Logic*, London: Allen & Unwin, 1958.

Mourant, J., Ed., *Readings in the Philosophy of Religion*, New York: Thomas Y. Crowell Co., 1954.

Pike, Nelson, Ed., *God and Evil*, New Jersey: Prentice Hall, 1964.

Ramsey, Ian, Ed., *Prospect for Metaphysics*, London: Allen & Unwin, 1961.

Ramsey, Ian T., Ed., *Christian Ethics and Contemporary Philosophy*, London: SCM Press, 1966.

Talk of God, Royal Institute of Philosophy Lectures, Vol. II, 1967-1968, London: Macmillan, 1969.

The Institutions of Primitive Society, Oxford: Basil Blackwell, 1967.

Upaniṣads. The Principal Upaniṣads, Ed., S. Radhakrishnan, London: Allen & Unwin, 1953.

D. ARTICLES

Aiken, Henry David, 'God and Evil: A Study of Some Relations between Faith and Morals' in *Ethics*, Vol. LXVIII, January 1958, pp. 77-97.

Broad, C.D., 'Review' of A.E. Taylor's *The Faith of a Moralist* in *Mind*, Vol. 40, pp. 364-375.

Brown, Patterson, 'Religious Morality' in *Mind*, Vol. 72, April 1963, pp. 235-244.

Brown, Patterson, 'God and The Good' in *Religious Studies*, Vol. 2, 1966-67, pp. 269-276.

Campbell, Keith, 'Patterson Brown on God and Evil' in *Mind*, Vol. 74, 1965, pp. 582-584.

Hick, John, 'Theology and Verification' in *Theology Today*, Vol. 17, 1960, pp. 12-31.

Ling, Trevor, 'Buddhist Mysticism' in *Religious Studies*, Vol. I, 1965-66, pp. 163-175.

Leuba, James H., 'A Study of the Psychology of Religious Phenomena' in *The American Journal of Psychology*, Vol. II, April 1896, No. 3, pp. 309-385.

Leuba, James H., 'The Contents of Religious Consciousness' in *Monist*, Vol. XI, 536, July 1901, pp. 536-573.

Mackie, J.L., 'Evil and Omnipotence' in *Mind*, Vol. LXIV, No. 254, 1955, pp. 200-212.

Nielsen, Kai, 'On Fixing the Reference Range of God' in *Religious Studies*, Vol. 2, 1966-67, pp. 13-36.

Pahnke, Walter N. and Richards, William A., 'Implications of LSD and Experimental Mysticism' in *Journal of Religion and Health*, No. 5, 1966, pp. 175-208.

Phillips, D.Z., 'From World to God' in *The Proceedings of the Aristotelian Society:* Supplementary Vol. XLI, 1967, pp. 133-162.

Pike, Nelson, 'Divine Omniscience and Voluntary Action' in *Philosophical Review*, Vol. 74, January 1965, pp. 27-46.

Schrader, F.O., 'On the Problem of Nirvana' in *Journal of the Pali Test Society*, 1904-1905, pp. 157-170.

Slotkin, J.S., 'Menomini Peyotism: A Study in Individual Variation in a Primary Group with a Homogeneous Culture' in *Transactions of the American Philosophical Society*, New Series, Vol. 42, 1952, pp. 565-700.

Smart, Ninian, 'Religion as a Discipline' in *Universities Quarterly*, Vol. 17, 1963, pp. 48-53.

Smith, Huston, 'Do Drugs Have a Religious Import?' in *Journal of Philosophy*, Vol. LXI, No. 17, 1964, pp. 517-530.

Stocks, J.L., 'The Validity of the Belief in a Personal God' in *The Proceedings of the Aristotelian Society:* Supplementary Vol. VI, 1926, pp. 69-83.

Werblowsky, Zwi R.J., 'On the Mystical Rejection of Mystical Illuminations' in *Religious Studies*, Vol. I, 1965-66, pp. 177-184.

Wisdom, John, 'God and Evil' in *Mind*, Vol. XLIV, No. 173, 1935, pp. 1-20.

Wittgenstein, Ludwig, 'A Lecture on Ethics' in *The Philosophical Review*, Vol. LXXIV, January 1965, pp. 3-26.

Index

Absolute, 191, 139, 194, 253.
Absoute Truth, 156ff.
AIKEN, H.D., 42.
ALTIZER, THOMAS J.J., 106ff.
Analogy, 1, 16, 23, 140, 158, 171, 202, 203, 204, 205, 206, 237, 241.
Annihilationist (Extinction) view, 153, 155ff.
A priori reasoning, 39, 49, 51, 103, 113, 193, 253.
AQUINAS, St. THOMAS, 24, 28, 52.
Attitudinal or Perspectival theories, 209ff., 219.
AUGUSTINE, St., 35, 132.
Authority, the Buddhist criticism of, 245ff.
AYER, A.J., 279.
Azande theology, 220ff., 225.
Azande witchcraft, 225ff.

BAILLIE, JOHN, 62, 115.
BAMBOROUGH, RANFORD, 216ff.
BARTH, KARL, 1, 2, 5, 6, 23, 31, 47, 49, 50, 55, 81, 116, 236, 237ff, 244.
Being, 95, 191, 192, 193.
Benevolence, 41-56, 147.
BERTOCCI, PETER, 208, 216.
Bhagavadgītā, 154.
Bhakti, 180, 181.
BONHOEFFER, DIETRICH, 76.
BRAITHWAITE, R.B., 83ff., 214.
BROAD, C.D., 162.
BRUNNER, EMIL, 54, 67, 87.
BUDDHAGHOSA, 9, 12, 20, 26, 35, 36, 37, 86, 153, 156, 167, 170, 254.
BULTMANN, RUDOLF, 25, 38, 148, 242ff.
BURI, FRITZ, 43.

CAMPBELL, C.A., 11, 12.
CAMPBELL, KEITH, 72.
CARDOZO, A. REBECCA, 232.
CASTANEDA, CARLOS, 119, 137.
Causal Continuity, 9, 10.
Causation, 26, 34, 39.
CHARDIN, TEILHARD de, 93, 94ff, 100ff, 105, 110.
CLARK, GORDON, H., 257.
CLARK, WALTER, 120.
COBB, JOHN, B., 19, 93ff., 100. 110, 112.
COHEN, SYDNEY, 125, 133.
Conscience, 6, 77ff.
Context theory, 129ff.
Contingency, 25ff., 33ff., 39, 187, 226.
Conventional truth, 156ff.